D1479317

A Golden Journey

Luther S. Cressman.
(Photo from Pennsylvania State University yearbook,
junior class of 1916–17.)

A Golden Journey

MEMOIRS OF AN ARCHAEOLOGIST

Luther S. Cressman

University of Utah Press
Salt Lake City

Library of Congress Cataloging-in-Publication Data

Cressman, Luther Sheeleigh, 1897–
    A golden journey: memoirs of an archaeologist / by Luther S.
Cressman; foreword by Jane Howard.
        p.   cm.
    ISBN 0-87480-293-8
    1. Cressman, Luther Sheeleigh, 1897–   2. Archaeologists-
-United States—Biography.   3. Indianists—United States—Biography.
I. Title.
CC115.C74A3 1988
930.1'092'4—dc19
                                                        87-30286
                                                        CIP

To the memory of my
MOTHER AND FATHER
who gave me life

and
To the memory of
CECILIA
who fulfilled it:

My ragges of heart can like, wish, and adore,
But after one such love, can love no more.
(John Donne, *The Broken Heart*)

And to our daughter
GEM
who keeps the flame aglow

Contents

Foreword

"You're welcome to stop by here on one condition," Professor Luther Cressman told me when I phoned him at his house in Eugene, Oregon, one hot July afternoon in 1979. He had been expecting the call; I had written from New York to say that I would soon be heading west and hoping for the honor of meeting him.

"The condition," he said, "is that we don't talk about Margaret." "Swell," I thought in my phone booth a few miles away. My main purpose in crossing the continent was to question Cressman about his first wife, Margaret Mead, whose biography I had just begun to research. Fifty-six years earlier, after a courtship no one could call whirlwind, he had become the first of the legendary anthropologist's three husbands. Their marriage ended in 1928, after Mead had discovered her destiny in Samoa and Cressman his in England. Mead's account of this period in her autobiography, *Blackberry Winter*, had struck me as suspiciously one-sided, and from Cressman, now an octogenarian, I was eager to hear the only other firsthand version.

But if he declared his first marriage off limits as a topic, then so be it: I would listen to whatever else he might have to say, which turned out to be plenty. As generations of Cressman's students and friends have learned, he talks spellbindingly on any number of subjects. As much a man of letters as an eminent archaeologist, Cressman in his time has been a priest, a soldier, a sociologist, an administrator, a classical scholar, always an adventurer, always on some level a Pennsylvania farm boy, and, above all, a humanist. Charity and his sense of wonder never fail him. A chance encounter in the laundromat this morning can elate him as much as the Rembrandt self-portraits do in the Frick Museum in New York, or the crocuses in his garden, or the wearers of the 9,000-year-old sandals he discovered during a 1938 excavation in eastern Oregon that changed the course of western prehistory.

In due course, happily for me, Cressman changed his mind and did talk about Mead, shedding invaluable light on the complexities of her character. He recalled being her adolescent suitor, her longtime fiancé, her "student husband" (a Mead term Cressman found so condescending he said it "really graveled me"), and finally her parents' ex-son-in-law. His next wife, a remarkable Scotswoman named Dorothy Cecilia Loch, could scarcely have been more different from her predecessor. The American West at first seemed an improbable setting for their passionate adventure together, but as Cressman's astonishing career unfolded there, they grew as attached to the region as to each other.

A Golden Journey puts into perspective both the author's loves and all his multidisciplinary enthusiasms, sweeping beyond his own time and over much of human history. Let us rejoice that Luther Cressman has found the courage and the energy to give us this wise, eloquent, and shamelessly romantic memoir; and let us also, as he approaches his tenth decade, salute him.

Jane Howard

Preface

My memoir is exactly what one reader calls it: "'. . . a literary work"; and I am pleased he felt it "quite impressive" as such. Like all memoirs mine is sui generis. It is not history, but the historian may find it useful; it is not social science, wherein the units of study are classes of data composed of like designated subjects, but there is much enlightening information for the social scientist; nor is it natural science, but the worker there may certainly find food for thought in it. I have not tried to write *about* my life, for that would make it history subject to the canons of biographical history, but I have made the desperate effort, often emotionally exhausting, to *really relive* mentally those experiences to share, if possible, the original of my concern. I am proud in my doing this to claim the designation, humanist. My book is a humanistic contribution written by a trained social scientist—a Ph.D. in sociology from Columbia University in New York City, 1925—whose earliest collegiate training was in the classics and humanities, with later studies at home and abroad in ecclesiastical thought, along with social history of western Europe and the United States.

Jane Howard in her felicitous, deeply moving Foreword, has alerted the reader to my life's challenges. I in turn attempt to share with my readers my experiences as I met the challenges. When I finally settled into the rhythm of my writing I found that I was doing for my life what I have done for my aboriginal friends: uncovering their past, reconstructing their lifeways, and always trying to empathize with them, actually to live with them in my imagination. Now, however, the writer (the excavator) was also the actual person whose life was the subject of study. Unlike the fiction writer, I could not reorder the dimensions of my plot or the behavior of the "characters" to solve my plot, for I was the character and the plot or problems were all "givens." I responded to the "givens."

As I relived these experiences of my long life, eighty-nine years, I was able to reflect upon them in two very important aspects, both essential for an understanding of my Journey. First, it was necessary to "fix" each event in its definitive context of space and time, and second, by utilizing a kind of "time-lapse" technique in my thinking processes I could see each experience in perspective and its place in the total pattern. Thus, an event seemingly trivial after a lapse of forty years would assume its career-menacing character and justify its discussion.

Fortunately, not all events or all periods in an individual's life are of equal importance, and few will agree on the relative merits in importance of the events involved in shaping a future life. I see the extraordinary importance of childhood and family background and relations in the formation of personality and so give much attention there. My wife Cecilia's background, so very different from any known to most readers today, commands much attention.

My "sojourn in the desert" in the museums of western Europe was crucial to my whole professional life, for it was there that I had to make my decision concerning my vocation, priest or teacher. The challenge I faced was to be met successfully by bringing all my critical thinking to bear on an understanding of the main lines of intellectual thought in shaping the values of Western culture and the church's place in it. I try to share them as I came to my decision. Aware that some of what I had written needed critical scrutiny by a specialist, I wrote my concerns to Professor Jan Van Baal, retired professor of anthropology of the University of Utrecht, with whom I had shared many hours of discussion on these matters while he was a visiting professor in our department. He replied in a letter dated October 22, 1984:

> ". . . your Italian experiences, . . . helped you to liberate yourself from the impact of ecclesiastic doctrine. What is important is not of course, whether young Luther's interpretation of European history is scientifically correct, but what this interpretation did to him. And your description of that process is as fascinating as convincing. That is all that counts in this context."

In the final pages of my book I outline very briefly the formal events leading to my undertaking this awesome task in my eighty-second year. The real compelling force underlying and actuating my effort was Cecilia's charge, so full of confidence and almost her last words, as I supported her dear, wasted body raised from her pillow. She had said she wanted to "talk," both of us knowing well how this "talk" would be our last. "You have important things to say and do and write and you must keep on and do them."

May you find, Cecilia, my book a worthy execution of your charge.

> ". . . the communication of the dead is tongued with fire beyond the language of the living."
>
> (T. S. Eliot, "Little Gidding," *Four Quartets*)

Acknowledgments

The persons over the years, both living and deceased, who have made contributions to my understanding of the processes of which I have been writing are so numerous that I cannot make any honest effort to recognize and thank all of them. I must, therefore, select a few who in the course of my writing have been most helpful and if, by chance, I overlook anyone I beg that person's forbearance. I shall limit my comments to brief pertinent remarks.

Constance (Connie) Bordwell has been my editor from the beginning when she took over my manuscript, a floundering effort to write in a new mode. A long-time family friend, she firmly refused remuneration and by her discipline and skillful help—she read every page, sometimes more than one effort by me before I released copy to my typist—gradually led me into producing whatever literary quality my memoir may have. Retired professor in the English Department of the University of Oregon, editor, writer, Lieutenant Commander, U.S. Navy (retired), I thank you.

Dr. Jan Van Baal in Doorn, the Netherlands, retired professor of anthropology at the University of Utrecht, student of European history and wise in the ways of religious experience has shared his critical knowledge and wisdom by correspondence and, with his wife Hilda, the hospitality of his family home at Doorn, where we had much good talk.

I am particularly indebted to my always reliable friend and colleague, David (Dave) L. Cole, in the field and on the campus of the last forty years for his invaluable assistance in leading me, convalescing from eye surgery, through the final reading of the edited copy. With meticulous care and helpful good humor, he made this final exacting task a pleasant and rewarding experience.

Keith Richard, archivist at the University of Oregon, generously searched university records for information helping me to write accurately on specific references to University of Oregon history. He was also helpful in filling in background information corroborating my positions.

Brief communications with Attorney Orlando John Hollis, Eugene, Oregon, retired dean of the University of Oregon Law School, who became acting president of the University of Oregon immediately following President D. M. Erb's death, confirmed the accuracy of my recollection and reporting of the budgetary situation he found on assuming office. I gratefully acknowledge his assistance.

Gem Nelson, my daughter, provided two important periods of three weeks each, when—although I was supposed to be resting—with the use of her faithful old manual Royal typewriter I was enabled to complete two important sections of my manuscript. She understood my necessity with the statement, "If you need anything, Pappy (her name for me), just let me know."

Fred and Barbara Roll of Carmel, California, shared their family hospitality and the superb facility of their guesthouse with its writer's equipment in two productive visits.

Barbara J. Winnick, my young friend in Eugene, has helped directly with my manuscript and indirectly but importantly by relieving me of household chores, sometimes cooking dinners to permit me to write and insure that I did not skimp in my care for "little brother the body." She has been the reassuring liaison between me and Gem in Pennsylvania. Her help in the crescendo of effort to finish my manuscript by the deadline has been critical to our success.

Dr. Rhoda Metraux, Dr. Nancy Lutkehaus, Drs. Louise Rosenblatt and Sidney Ratner, Professor Franklin and Martha U. West, Professor and Mrs. Vernon R. Dorjahn, Professor Theodore and Mary Stern, Edward and Elaine Kemp, Phyllis and "Scotty" Steeves have all been helpful in a great variety of ways, and I am most grateful to them.

I extend my heartfelt thanks to Mrs. Mary L. Armes, my expert typist, for expeditiously completing, sometimes from difficult copy, each body of manuscript I submitted. She has typed the complete work.

I have done this writing without subvention of any kind and I have not utilized any of the facilities of the university. All work has been done in my study at my home, where I provided the facilities and all the material for my writing from my own resources. It had to be my book completely. Perhaps the production should be classified as "sweatshop," one stage below "cottage industry." But it's done!

To the staff of the University of Utah Press I extend my warmest thanks. My experience has been a happy renewal of the earlier association by which my *Prehistory of the Far West*, what my students and staff called "The Chief's (Chief-of-party) M.O." (magnum opus), was produced.

I am particularly indebted to my editor, Peggy Lee, and to Dr. David Catron, director of the Press, for his interest and commitment by which he has put the publication of my manuscript on the "fast lane" even though the writer is perhaps a little breathless. I find the position customary and a most satisfactory place to be.

I have come here to heal myself, if you like to put it that way.
I return link by link along the iron chain of memory.
I have had to come so far away from it in order to understand it all.
(Lawrence Durrell, *Justine*)

A Golden Journey

In the Beginning

In my beginning is my end. . . .

(T. S. Eliot, "East Coker," *Four Quartets*)

My world was a stable, secure world, and the family into which I was born was a microcosm of it. The house, built atop a slight but dominating eminence, enjoying views of the surrounding countryside to the hills of varying distance, became my home until destroyed by fire in 1917. A sturdy building of bricks and oak timbers, it was built in 1774 to last, on land granted by William Penn to the Pugh family,[1] a member of which many years later would become the first president of Pennsylvania State College. The bricks for the eighteen-inch thick walls, once ballast in a ship sailing from Holland to Philadelphia, had been hauled by Conestoga wagons the forty miles to the building site in northern Chester County. A massive white oak tree, well over two-hundred years old—no one knew how much—stood a sturdy comrade on the south side. House and tree were a highly visible landmark throughout the countryside. My two older brothers, George and Charlie, were born in rented houses, but before my birth, October 24, 1897, my parents had purchased this grand old home. After me, three brothers, Wallace, Morris, and Fred, were born within the safety of its walls. Here, too, three times in my early years, I saw "the old henchman of God" come to ease my elders from their pain. This ambient security into which I was so happily born exerted a profound influence on my whole life.

My home was in the country, a half mile from the crossroads village, Pughtown, named for a Colonel Pugh, and six miles from the nearest town, Pottstown. My father, George S. Cressman, had graduated from the University of Pennsylvania Medical School in 1889—I have heard he was first in his class—where, as he once proudly told

Cressman house from north side, with me sitting on porch.

House and white oak tree in winter; view from south.

me, he had listened to lectures by the famous Sir William Osler, among others. Dad was not quite twenty-one when his class graduated, too young to receive his diploma with his classmates, so gladly acceded to the request of a friend who had been ordered to report to his Navy ship to take his place in line and accept his diploma for him. Dad's friend, after a long and distinguished career, retired November 30, 1928, as surgeon general, U.S. Navy. Many years after that graduation ceremony, Dad collected, not for himself, however, on the promissory note he held against his former classmate. The small kindness he performed that night was to have unforeseen consequences far distant in space and time for persons not then even in existence.

My father's older brother, Mark, a Lutheran minister, was pastor of a country church, St. Matthews, at Ludwig's Corner, some five miles south of Pughtown. He urged Dad to come to this area and start a practice because the country people were without medical services. At the same time Dad also had an opportunity to start a practice in a growing urban center in the rapidly developing New Jersey coastal area and with the support of an important Philadelphia family, no mean consideration. But he characteristically chose the country challenge, and was to serve those people for more than fifty years.

As I tarry along these early stages of my Journey, I plead your indulgence, for I believe the foundation or rootstock of what we become in later life is laid down in our very early years. And, too, this landscape of a secure boyhood in a loving family, poor in money but wealthy almost beyond limit in love, cherishing significant values, in beautiful, quiet country in a world at peace—at least for our part—is in such marked contrast to what I so often see today that I find great pleasure in gazing back upon it.

Neither my mother, Florence, nor Dad (Florie and George or "Doc" to their intimates), who provided the basic models for my life, can be described as individuals apart from their family. All their activities were in some way or other contributions to the family's well-being. There was constant feedback between them and each member of the family and with each other. Although its perimeter, so to speak, was never firmly fixed, our family was an integrated unit. Each individual developed within this recognized system of interrelationships, responsibilities, and interdependence. The "Cressman family" was a well-recognized unit in the life of the countryside, a

Dad's mother and father on porch of Barren Hill home. Date unknown.

Mother, probably at time of her marriage.

Dad, probably at time of his marriage, September 7, 1892.

family that produced individual persons but not "loners." It is within this system of interpersonal relationships that I see Mother and Dad as persons as I try to bring them to life, especially to recall those characteristics I firmly believe profoundly shaped my personality.

My father, born January 1, 1869, cannot be adequately characterized in a few short observations, but certain things reveal him as the remarkable person he was. A man of great compassion, he had a sense of duty and service even above that then expected of a medical doctor. He sometimes drove Mother nearly to distraction because he was so reluctant to give her his patients' bills to send out. He once replied to her urgings, "Well, Florie, when these people are sick is the time they can least afford to pay."

I never knew him to refuse to visit a patient either because of lack of payment for his services or conditions of the roads. I cannot remember how many times I drove with him in a sleigh with an ax, shovel, and wire cutters to help us across fields when drifted snow made the roads impassable. One winter a terrible blizzard had lasted for several days with no signs of abating. High winds drove the snow almost horizontally. All normal travel was at a standstill. On the afternoon of the third day, Dad was pacing the floor and watching the storm.

Finally he said to Mother, "Florie, Bill Miller has pneumonia. I haven't seen him for two days, and if I don't see him, there is a good chance he may die. I'll saddle a horse and make it that way."

"Oh George," she begged him, "don't go out in this blizzard. It's terrible. Can't you wait until tomorrow?"

"The man's sick, Florie. I'll be all right. I'll stay all night; they'll find a couch for me and put the horse up in the barn. Don't worry."

He pulled on his long overcoat, hat with earflaps, and gloves. Then mounting a restless but tough buckskin, he pulled him around into the wind and driving snow; and with heads down, they moved steadily off into it. Of course, Dad made it and so did his patient.

Mother told me an anecdote recounting a similar experience. It is worth repeating, for it shows so vividly Dad's commitment to his profession and his deep sense of compassion. During a blizzard, a call came for him to come see a woman who had pneumonia. Mother dreaded his going out in that storm and protested.

" . . . and you will not get paid for it anyhow."

"Florie, it does not matter if I ever get paid or not if I can save that woman for her children." He went, and she lived.

Dad's professional fees were not calculated to provide an affluent standard of living: an office call with medicine provided, $.50; house call with medicine provided, $1.50; confinement, total cost, $15.00. After World War I, he reluctantly raised his fees $.25, $.50, and $10.00, respectively. The fees were the same for day or night service. Many people, however, could not afford to pay, but he never refused to answer a call, even when the patient's family owed him a substantial sum of money and there was little likelihood they would pay any of it. Many times his patients paid with vegetables, fruit, chickens, service of some kind on the farm, or too often not at all. Barter was for many the only way they could pay.

He had various invitations to establish a practice elsewhere but always declined; his heart was with the country and its people. They had become his people.

We boys, when out of school, liked to ride with Dad on his rounds, and he always liked to have us, except, of course, when he was treating a patient with an infectious disease. One late afternoon following a heavy snowstorm, George, Charlie, and I were in the sleigh with him as he drove across a farmer's field—the roads were badly drifted—under a lowering sky. One runner struck an obstruction hidden by the deep snow, throwing the sleigh on its side and all of us out. As the frightened horse plunged, dragging Dad holding fast to the reins, he shouted, "Get on the fence, boys!" We probably never obeyed a command as quickly before.

Telling Mother about it after our return, Dad laughed and said, "Quick as a flash, there they all were sitting like three crows in a row on the fence before I could even get Bill stopped."

One of my greatest pleasures was to ride about the country in the horse and buggy and talk with him, hear him sing, and be filled with admiration and pleasure as he pointed out to me wild flowers on the roadside, a rabbit hiding under a root, a rare pink dogwood in bloom on the edge of a woodlot, and many other exciting sights.

One cold but sunny day after a heavy snowfall I was with him in the sleigh. Pointing to some animal tracks, he said, "A fox crossed the road there, Lutie."

"How can you tell? I thought they were dog tracks."

"A fox has hair on the bottom of its pads, while a dog doesn't. This animal had hair on its pads, as the snow shows."

Dad taught us about the natural world by helping us participate progressively in its rounds. He trained us in the proper use of guns as we joined him in the hunting of small game animals. Fishing joined hunting in our quest for food, recreation, and as a teaching-learning experience. When we demonstrated expected competence we could go alone to use the lore he had helped us make our own. We thus became familiar with the rounds of the seasons and the life characteristics of each. Our work and play planted in us, certainly in me, the seeds of the awareness of the unity of life, of the interdependence of man and nature.

My father loved music and had a near-perfect ear for key; and, had he ever boasted, he could well have done so of his beautiful, deep bass voice. He shared it with others by participating in the Christmas cantatas at the Pughtown church when his practice permitted. He played the organ and the cornet; thus, with Mother's musical interests, music was at home in our house, where we had both a piano and an organ. One of my warmest memories of those very early years is of Dad carrying me piggyback up the steep stairs to my bedroom over the kitchen and then sitting beside me singing me to sleep.

Dad was a natural teacher. He did not present us with generalizations or ideas but would have a story or perhaps at bedtime, a song, often a folk song carrying the ancient wisdom of experience to make his point. He never left us in doubt about the message: Compassion for living things, the equality of persons, the undesirability of revenge or retaliation, the importance of reading and education, the value of cooperative enterprise like the games we played in which each was expected to do his best but not to the disadvantage of another. Above all there was the requirement of integrity.

Mother once said, "When Lute wants anything, he goes to his Dad." I don't think he ever favored me above the others—I always felt Charlie was his favorite—but there was an extraordinarily close relationship between us. For the model he provided, I am eternally grateful.

Dad died September 26, 1946, three months before his seventy-eighth birthday. He had been in declining health for several years

Dad holding me cuddled on his shoulder, probably early spring 1898.

from Parkinson's disease, for which there was then no treatment. He knew his road well and traveled it with no complaint.[2]

I last saw him not long before his death. I had been to Philadelphia on some mission and came out on my last day to spend a few hours with the family. Someone would drive me to Paoli on the main line of the Pennsylvania Railroad to catch my night train for Chicago. When I went in to say good-bye to Dad, he was sitting in his swivel chair at his rolltop desk and turned to me — he could not stand alone. I took his shaking hand and bent to kiss him good-bye. He didn't try to speak, for his trembling lips were too tightly compressed to keep back tears. But we understood each other. Putting on a much braver face than I felt, I gave him a smart salute, "Be seein' you, Dad," turned, and walked quickly to the waiting car.[3]

Mother survived Dad by twelve years.

Mother, Florence Righter, was born April 10, 1869, four months and ten days after Dad and only a few miles distant from his birthplace, Barren Hill. She writes:

> My sister and I were born at Mount Joy—Spring Mill—a historic old mansion occupied by the Righter family for more than a century. My father's father, John Righter, married Elizabeth Legaux, daughter of Pierre [Peter] Legaux, a French scientist, who came to America in 1786, and settled at Mount Joy. . . . They raised a large family of children. My father was one of twins.
>
> The old homestead where I was born was a lovely old mansion, three and a half stories high, overlooking a curve in the Schuylkill River and the wooded hills opposite. . . .
>
> When I was about two years old, or thereabouts, my father bought a home in Whitemarsh township, about two miles from Mount Joy. It was a farmhouse, and had about 16 acres. My father farmed on a small scale, but he had money at interest, and was not dependent on what he raised. [That source of income was later to be lost when he loaned money to fair-weather friends with insufficient security.][4]

Mount Joy in Pierre Legaux's lifetime was a gracious center for intellectual, aesthetic, and social life. *The Philadelphia Inquirer*, October 15, 1889, records:

> Standing in the spacious hall on the second floor is the first piano made in Pennsylvania, which was built by Conrad Doll, of Lancaster. It is still in good condition and will respond to the most classical performer.

The Evening Bulletin-Philadelphia, January 11, 1929, recalls:

> In this substantial old fourteen-room Colonial dwelling house were entertained the aristocracy of early national history. Here came the Marquis de Lafayette to visit his "dear friend, Peter"—here came General Washington for friendly chats with Peter Legaux, many, many times on his frequent after war pilgrimages to Valley Forge—here was attracted Benjamin Franklin for refreshment in the hospi-

table old home, called then Mount Joy—came Girard, Jefferson, many lights of Colonial times, attracted by the many-sided brilliance of Peter Legaux.

Although Mother never knew her Grandmother Legaux, who died two years before her birth, she often visited Mount Joy for extended periods as a child. The traditions of its gracious past were a part of her heritage, and she proudly shared them with me in my boyhood.

Before Mother could read, her mother's unmarried twin sister, Priscilla, used to read to the small listener cuddled on her lap. Mother continued her fondness for reading and found pleasure and learning in the books of the period: the Louisa May Alcott books, Dickens, stories of the "Scottish Chiefs," the old standby *Black Beauty*, and *Ramona*, among others. She loved poetry, was familiar with the early American poets, and had memorized much from that source. A book of poetry was a highly prized Christmas gift.

She started music lessons in her seventh year along with her sister with only a melodeon for practicing. After a few years their mother bought them a piano. She loved music, and even while in high school at Conshohocken had pupils. After three months at West Chester Teachers College she knew that music, not teaching, was the profession she wanted. She enrolled in the Philadelphia Musical Academy and developed her skill in both the piano and organ.

While at the academy, she played the organ at the Barren Hill Lutheran church and was soon in charge of the choir and other musical activities. The George Cressman she had known as a boy at elementary school was now in medical school. Since he commuted daily, he could sing bass in her choir. The early friendship drew the choirmaster and her bass singer into a deeper friendship and their marriage on September 7, 1892, two years after Dad graduated from the Medical School.

There was always music in our home, but only my eldest brother, George, carried on the family's interest in music, and he on the violin. Mother expressed her love of music by teaching private pupils and helping the country churches, where she trained choirs and served as organist. Her last fifteen years, until she had to resign because of Dad's deteriorating health, found her happy and busy as the organist at St. Matthews Lutheran Church, where more than fifty years earlier her brother-in-law, later my Uncle Mark, had been the pastor who persuaded Dad to come to that rural area and start his practice.

Mother was in general more practical than Dad. He was concerned with his patients and the overall supervision of the farm; she had the responsibility for the day-to-day household management, family care and planning. Dad's work took him away from home for most of the day, whereas Mother's tended to keep her there. This separation of responsibilities indicates only that different demands both in kind and immediacy were made of them. Mother's voice even now comes back so clearly as she spoke to me or a brother: "When you see something to be done, don't just stand there, do it."

Neither Mother nor Dad had been reared in the kind of life they faced after settling near Pughtown. Both had professional educations, were at home in the urban atmosphere of Philadelphia, and were without a farming background. Dad told me that when they began to have a family they saw that they would need, at least in part, to take up the self-supportive ways of life of the farming community because his cash income would never be adequate to support a family. They, therefore, bought the house in which I was born and about forty acres of land on which to raise the necessary feed for the stock: horses for Dad to drive in his practice and provide energy to work the farm; cows for milk; chickens, ducks, geese, turkeys, even guinea hens for eggs and meat; pigs for pork. They raised vegetables and fruits for the family; everything except a few staples was raised on the farm. The barter system by which Dad's patients exchanged vegetables and other products for his services was a way of life. We could use what his patients raised, and they had little cash income. Mother, like the farmers' wives, was responsible for canning and drying fruits and vegetables for the winter in addition to the customary daily household work. Other seasonal activities, such as harvesting and butchering in the fall, brought additional household chores. All this the young music teacher and mother had to face up to. How well she succeeded!

Mother could not help but be very lonely in this utterly new environment, alone in the house for most of the day as Dad's enlarging practice demanded more and more of his time. The birth of their first child, George, August 8, 1893, alleviated at least some of the feeling of loneliness; it also added to her responsibilities. Shortly after George's birth, Mother's Aunt Priscilla, who used to read to her small

Three Cressman brothers, left to right, Luther, George, Charles; the "first crop," as Dad, country-wise, always called us.

niece on her lap, came to make her home with the family. She and Mother were very close, and she gave Mother much-needed support. "She was a second mother to me," Mother once wrote. We called her "Auntie," and there was a very warm relationship between us. I was nine years old at the time of her death. With Auntie's coming, our family had taken the first step toward becoming an expanded or enlarged family, a trait it would never lose.

Auntie, like those who would join or follow her, found certain responsibilities in the family that not only relieved Mother but also gave significance and worth to her own life. Every Thursday afternoon Auntie churned the butter. Fascinated, I watched as she took the unshaped yellow masses from the churn, kneaded them to expel the whey, then made the butter into small pats or shaped pieces of different sizes that she impressed with a wooden stamp bearing the design of a sheaf of wheat or other harvest symbol. On occasion she even let me turn the churn, and I felt terribly important as we chatted together.

Mother's father came to join our family following the death of his wife, September 11, 1901. He, too, had his chores, but outside the house. Grandpop wore knee-high leather boots; and I see him in a black, short but warm coat, bucket in hand, slightly stooped under a slouched hat, making his way in the gathering gloom to the chicken house. Grandpop died the same year as Auntie, his sister-in-law.

These two were very important persons who fitted into the system of responsibilities and rights that applied to every member of our family. Their presence also widened the contacts to which we boys had to adjust, a good training in socialization at a very early age. I think because we were fond of our grandparents and had daily contact with them we learned to have warmth and affection for older people.

Shortly after the deaths of Auntie and Grandpop in 1906, a very sweet cousin of Dad's joined our family and brought light and happiness until her death a few years later.

Sometime before 1912 Mr. Harkness, totally deaf, came to board and make his home with us. He remained with us until his death in the mid-1930s. Conversation with him was limited and was carried on in writing. Reading constantly, he spent most of his time in his room with his stacks of books. We, of course, always treated him as a member of the family.

On the death of Dad's sister, her six-year-old daughter, Sara, was taken into our household. Years later she became a registered nurse and after some years of hospital experience took a position with a physician in Pottstown, where she retired shortly before her death only a few years ago.

After spending two weeks with his children, Hildegarde and Karl, as boarders with us, a widowed German professor at the University of Pennsylvania asked Mother and Dad to keep them while he returned to Germany for a visit. When he returned, about 1910, he left Penn for St. John's at Annapolis, asking Mother to keep the children for a time until he established himself in his new situation—I think he had remarried. Mother agreed, and they continued to live with us as though they were our brother and sister. Hildegarde graduated with me from Penn State in 1918 majoring in chemistry. Karl, being younger, graduated some years later from St. John's at Annapolis. Both, now deceased, always called our home their home.

Although it may be true that the intellectual life of the individual was limited in that world of dirt roads—mud and ice in winter and dust in summer—no telephones, the kerosene lamp, the horse and buggy or horseback for transport, complete dependence upon human or animal sources of energy, yet, in spite of all this, it produced men and women who knew how to live together in understanding, compassion, and neighborliness.

Every Memorial Day saw a small group—each year the numbers less—of veterans of our Civil War and the Grand Army of the Republic gathered at the Pughtown Baptist church for the memorial service, the decoration of the graves of their dead comrades with new flags and fresh flowers. The ending crash of the volleys of memorial gunfire emphasized that this way of life had produced men and women who, when the occasion demanded, had visions and commitments that took them far beyond the limited horizons of their familiar hills and valleys.

Mother and Dad, each twenty-three years old, started their married life among these people and settled easily into the general pattern although both came from markedly different backgrounds. Dad and Mother were the only professionally trained people in the whole area. It never occurred to them, however, to use this advantage to their own profit or as a pretense for a class distinction; rather, they felt obliged to use their training and endowments quite unobtrusively to enrich the lives of the people among whom they had cast their own.

Here their partnership in marriage developed until Dad's death fifty-four years later. They successfully raised a family of six sons.[5] Their personalities were complementary, a shared core of basic values with each having distinctive traits that meshed with those of the other to produce and enrich through the years meaningful husband-wife and parent-child relationships.

Compassion, kindness, understanding, integrity formed the bedrock of the character of the family Mother and Dad established and nourished; it was in this atmosphere my early values were formed.

Like our family, most in our area were enlarged but not to the same extent. It was customary for the elders on the death of a spouse for the survivor to join a family of one of the children. A child on the death of parents would probably be taken into the home of a close relative of the parents. The eldest son, certainly on the large farms, after marriage brought his wife to live with his parents, and he joined his father in the operation of the farm. Younger sons might work on neighboring farms but continue to live at home until marriage. Migration to the industrial cities was still in the future.

Families were interdependent. They interchanged labor as well as services of a more personal kind, as in sickness or disaster. During the influenza pandemic of 1918, Mother risked her own health to go to some of Dad's patients whose whole families were disabled and help them with household activities as well as nursing.

Not all families participated equally in this kind of sharing; some were just less generous than others. The tightfisted owner of the feedstore in Pughtown, apparently rather affluent for the time in his brick house with a wrought iron fence, never offered any more than the law required. It must have been the summer of 1910, when I worked in the general store next to the feedstore and had to serve its customers too, that I was instructed in the manner of selling. Sam (the owner's first name) kept a polished two-by-two-inch stick by the piles of feed, and when a peck or a half bushel of oats was ordered, I was told to heap up the feed in the container and then take the stick and push it across the top of the measure to give an amount equal to that level—no more, no less. Most of the people I knew sniffed a little at Sam's precision; they were customarily used to "one for good measure." Others could, of course, be found like Sam.

Regardless of the family's size, affluence, or social position, one controlling theme directed all its activities: a human's life had to move in accordance with the rhythms of nature. Man and nature were interdependent. Whatever the lifeways in the industrialized cities, in our rural environment the companionship with the sun had not yet been challenged by the tyranny of the clock and machine.

> But now ask the beasts, and they shall teach thee;
> And the fowls of the air, and they shall teach thee;
> Or speak to the earth, and it shall teach thee;
> And the fishes of the sea shall declare unto thee.
>
> (Job 12:7-8)

Men worked primarily in the production-through-harvesting sequence in the fields and barns; women had, in addition to the normal housekeeping duties, clusters of special ones related to production and seasonal cycles. The duties of the sexes were complementary, mutually supportive, and equally important in the maintenance of family life. Sometimes in an emergency, women did "men's work," but it was not regarded otherwise as "the thing to do."

Our recreational activities, like our work, were geared to nature's rhythms.[6] Spring invited us, boys and girls, to the woods to search for the first wild flowers: hepatica, arbutus, blood root and others. Summer found us boys, when not working, playing and swimming in French Creek or nearby Beaver Run. Occasional mixed groups, my mother and friends joining the boys, required bathing suits or trunks. Bathing costumes of the ladies were black cotton stockings and canvas shoes, full bloomers from waist to knee, a skirt of the same length, a blouse with a sailor collar, and topped off by a hat. On one such occasion at our French Creek swimming hole I watched in disbelief and with some trepidation as my teenage future sister-in-law defiantly dropped and stepped out of her skirt and stood exposed in her bloomers. When another followed and the lightning didn't strike, my childish belief in the blind acceptance of the commonly held unquestioned attitude of the validity of custom as a guide to behavior received a severe blow.

Of course, we enjoyed fishing, baseball, and sometimes other games. In winter French Creek provided skating for mixed groups of boys and girls during the day and after dark. At night we spaced lighted kerosene lanterns along the middle of the ice and kept a large fire burning under a huge pin oak on the bank for warmth and rest when tired. Crack-the-whip was a favorite game in which I, as the smallest, was usually the "lash" and frequently cleaned up yards of the ice and not on my skates.

We usually went sledding when there was a good sledding crust—hard enough to bear the sled runners and not icy to permit steering—on the hill on the road by our house, where boys and girls gathered with us after dark. When we tired, most would come into the house and Mother, expecting us, would have freshly baked cookies, sometimes doughnuts, served with cider and hot cocoa. We never bought our recreation, for there was none to buy; we ourselves were responsible for what we might do and, in cooperation with nature, did very well.

Christmas festivities with gifts usually homemade, except for such rarities as oranges and English walnuts, drew substantially upon our

Fishing in French Creek, quite unsuccessfully judging from my expression, with the customary pole, a birch or willow sapling, cut from nature.

companionship with nature since the surrounding country provided the raw materials for us to gather. Fun and pleasure, not work, were part of our preparations. Mr. Blaney, an impoverished patient of Dad's, always offered his gift of cedar tree from his woodlot for the occasion. With good luck there was snow on the ground, and we went with our sleds to cut the tree and fetch it home. The nearby woods supplied mountain laurel and crow's-foot, a ground vine we found by scratching through the snow and underlying dry leaves where we knew it grew.

The nights preceding Christmas offered festivities for all, sometimes with neighbors dropping in to chat or help. One year Mother conceived the idea of a large bell to hang from the middle of the living room ceiling. It was magnificent! It measured at least fifteen inches from top to bottom, the diameter at the bottom perhaps fifteen inches and at the top, ten. Circles of heavy wire provided the top and bottom foundations, which were connected by slightly looped strands of intertwined laurel and crow's-foot. Each pair of strands was separated in turn by a string or strings of popcorn alternating in red and white rows. A large, red, decorative ball as a clapper completed

My grandson, Rick Nelson, fishing in Point Pleasant Park, Pennsylvania, with "state of the art" equipment with the same results I had in French Creek.

the bell. With the bell hanging from the center of the ceiling in the living room and festoons of greens stretching from the top of it to the room's four corners, the decorations were truly an impressive sight. Many visitors came to admire the bell. Mother kept and used it over the years, and one year the young daughter of a neighbor's family borrowed the bell to grace her wedding by being married under it.

Summer brought its abundance of foods, and the rural housewife like Mother was faced with the very difficult problem of preserving those perishable foods that could not be canned or dried. Refrigeration was a rarity except for those few families fortunate enough to have an icehouse. Dad and Mother were among those few. Ours, the customary kind, was a large, circular, stone-lined excavation, perhaps twenty-five feet deep and as many in diameter. Spaced beams, set firmly across the top, supported loose boards on which carriages could be rolled when not in use. A square, gabled building with one side having two large, hinged doors covered the pit. The two elements thus combined into the customary icehouse – carriage shed.

We filled the icehouse when the ice on French Creek, about a quarter of a mile from our home, was ten to twelve inches thick and deep snow lay on the ground. Then the ice, sawed and cut into blocks, could be hauled in a large bobsled pulled by a pair of horses to the icehouse and dumped into the pit. As the team went back for another load, we boys leveled the ice before it returned.

Once the icehouse was filled, we went to a neighbor's sawmill, filled burlap sacks with sawdust for insulation, and covered the ice with it. We always had a plentiful supply of ice in the summer unless we had been profligate in our use. In addition to using the ice for food preservation in an icebox, we used it often to make ice cream. The memories of turning the crank, the gradual firming of the ice cream, then Auntie drawing out the paddle, scraping it to pass to the young assistants to clean with spoon and tongue! "Oh, Auntie, don't clean it so clean!" Those families lacking an icehouse, but wanting ice, had to haul it six miles from Pottstown, an hour's drive over dirt roads.

Filling the icehouse was always fun; it somehow had a festive air about it. The snow was cleaned from the place chosen for cutting and a hole cut through the ice, and then blocks of a size easy to handle were sawed free. The sawyer used a large-toothed saw at least six feet long with a handle at one end that projected on each side since both hands were used to move it. He cut toward himself with long up-and-down strokes of the saw held in the vertical position. Others took the detached blocks, floated them to the loading end of the work area where a sloping surface had been cut through the top edge of the ice, and skillfully pulled them up the slope and out. To move the sawed block and get it out of the water, the worker used a long pole pike. After that we used the usual ice tongs. Occasionally a worker would slip and go into the water, an occurrence I heard of but never saw. The only immediate danger in such an accident was that the unfortunate fellow would go under the ice. His fellow workers usually pulled him out quickly, joshing him for his clumsiness to cover their own sense of alarm, and hurried him home to change into dry clothes. The work was not hard and the men could engage in "men's talk" and exchange gossip while they worked since there was no machinery to drown out their voices. They thus were brought up to date with the real and imagined life of the community.

In the loosely structured society of rural Pennsylvania life during my early years at the turn of the century, the family was the most significant social unit influencing the development of the individual. Its ambience was the wellspring from which emerged those influences impinging on and influencing the growing child at every turn. Every individual belonged to a family in either a natural or foster relationship, but any connection with a church, when it existed, was sporadic and the influence problematical.

The elementary school, at which attendance was compulsory through age fourteen, was supposed to teach the "three Rs," spelling, some grammar, United States history, an introduction to American literature, civics, and arithmetic and algebra. (Oh, yes, penmanship.) As a freshman in high school I had to take the first-year algebra course but found it to be a terrible bore because I had had most of it in my little country school. I suppose the chief contribution the school made to personality development was the training in cooperative living through sharing a common room, organizing our own recreational programs, and the pressure of the teacher on each of us to perform well. The teacher was not expected to teach us codes of behavior beyond the necessity for honesty in our studies (no cheating) and the virtue of hard work to perform well. What happened during the day in the life of a pupil could be made meaningful when explored with him by his parents at the day's end. This sharing of experience and its discussion was a part of our family life, but it was not the custom elsewhere since the lack of educational background in most families prevented it.

A young person accustomed to the rich cultural diversity of today's world cannot easily visualize a world without radio, telephone, television, books, magazines, newspapers everywhere, no Boy or Girl Scouts or any kind of similar organization, no motor vehicles, and many other things. Yet, that is just the kind of world in which my early years were passed. In the absence of these amenities the importance of the ambience of a family greatly surpassed that of today.

Parents, by the very nature of the life-style, were extraordinarily important in providing ideals, role models, for the child to emulate. Intellectual interests exhibited by the parents in politics, literature, religion, education, and contacts with the outside world, its people and thought, provided knowledge of countenanced behavior quite different from that of our quiet countryside insulated by the lack of communication facilities. All these, by their presence or absence in varying degrees, made up the significant world of the growing child.

Because Mother and Dad had intellectual interests far beyond those common to the community, our family was unique in the countryside. Interest in music and its enjoyment, literature, religion as behavior and not dogma, were part of our conversation and experience. Education as an enrichment of life and professional preparation were taken for granted, and we all accepted, as a matter of fact, that we would go on to college and have to work to provide the financial means to do so. I can't think of a single boy or girl of my generation from another family in our area whose education went beyond the country grade school (ungraded) experience.

Fortunate for us boys, our family's propitious cultural resources did not exempt us from having farm duties as a normal obligation as a member of the family, and not for wages. In summer we hired out to neighbors usually for day work in harvesting. Our parents used our home work to build in us a sense of responsibility and discipline. But they went beyond that by providing projects if we would agree to the terms. One year I had a flock of white Wyandotte chickens to take care of, including the cleaning of the chicken house. Dad furnished the feed, but after that I was in charge. I collected the eggs, sold them, and the money was mine. Another year while I was in high school I raised, under the same conditions, eight or ten pigs, finally delivering them to the slaughterhouse in Pottstown. My income from that project seemed magnificent by the standards of the time.

These projects were fundamental parts of our education intended to encourage us to develop a sense of responsibility, discipline, and the recognition that our reward depended to a large extent on the manner in which we carried out our work. We learned to make decisions, accept responsibility, and realize that the work was not something for its own sake but was preparation for some future end or reward. I think we were lucky boys as I look back!

September 1903 called me to follow my older brothers, George and Charlie, to school about two months before my sixth birthday. My memory is completely blank about that "first day" experience, supposed to be so significant as a "rite of passage." Was it so traumatic that I have blocked it completely from my consciousness? I am inclined to think that nothing of any emotional significance happened. Actually, school was on the whole not such a sharp break with my preschool experience. Everybody in the school knew everybody else. All age groups were together both in the schoolroom and on the

The Pughtown school to which all six Cressman boys went for their pre-high school education. I am third from right, standing in the middle row, and Wallace, the first of the "second crop," is seated in front of me.

playground. To some extent, certainly for us beginners, school was more a slight shift in experience than a new one. The shift would have greater significance as we acquired skill in reading and learned from older pupils. All recitations took place with the class sitting on the seats projected from the front row of desks, and I could listen along with others to the recitations in subjects like history or any other that caught my interest.

One vivid memory, however, of a significant experience of those early school days is deeply incised into my consciousness, and what I learned that day has been an inseparable part of my personality. It was a beautiful, autumn morning of my first year and I was walking with George and Charlie very reluctantly toward school. Just as we were going down the short grade past our neighbor Schuyler Wiley's place, a hundred yards or so from our home where the road crossed a millrace and then over the lovely arched stone bridge over French Creek, school finally seemed the last place in the world I wanted to be. I really started "dragging my feet." I annoyed my brothers no end. They didn't want to be late, since tardiness usually invited some punishment; and, furthermore, our parents strongly disapproved of our being late. Their younger brother's contrariness would not have been an excuse acceptable to the teacher. The three of us had reached an impasse without forward progress toward school, when Charlie Wiley, Schuyler's brother, happened to be passing in his horse and wagon. He saw there was a problem, stopped his horse and, sensing it has something to do with me, said, "What's the matter, Lute? Don't you want to go to school? Clyde [his son about my age] is at his grandmother's [our next-door neighbor in the opposite direction], you go and play with him."

Without waiting to reply I took off as fast as my small legs would carry me to play with Clyde, letting my brothers go to their silly school. By the time I reached home I was rather out of breath, and the voice of conscience had wakened. And its song was loud and insistent. I stopped, however, at the house to speak to Mother—a bit of covering my flanks—and tried to be quite casual as I said, "Hello."

"What are you doing home, Lute? You are supposed to be in school. Has anything happened?"

"I don't want to go to school. I want to play with Clyde."

"Your father is out hunting but should be in very soon, and then you can see what he says."

I knew then I had made a very bad mistake and dared not go to play with Clyde; but I didn't want to go to school either. For some reason, I drifted down to the wagon shed over the icehouse and climbed into the buggy Dad would take when he returned and started to visit his patients. A very abashed boy, somewhat crumpled, at least in spirit, sat in the buggy and soon heard his dad's footsteps approach. He came to the buggy, and seeing me, said, "What are you doing here? Is anything the matter, Lutie? Why aren't you in school? You know you are supposed to be there."

"I didn't want to go to school; I wanted to play with Clyde." I was feeling terribly guilty, nearly in tears, but telling the truth.

"You are supposed to be in school, Lutie," he said in that firm and kindly voice I knew so well. "I am going out past the school in a few minutes and will take you. Just wait here."

So I waited and Dad took me along without scolding, for he had sensed that I had learned my lesson. He let me out at the schoolhouse and I ran to the door. As I opened it to enter I looked back and saw a very wise and kind Dad waiting to make sure I would be on the other side of the door when it closed.

That experience taught me a lesson I have never forgotten: that one has obligations, duties if you will, that override any personal desires with which they may conflict from time to time. Without conceptualizing my problem and moralizing—I wouldn't have understood it anyhow—my parents that morning seventy-eight years ago taught me in a quiet but terribly important way that I had to make choices, hard ones, where obligations and duty would demand my loyalty over more pleasant, apparently more inviting alternatives. I never tried to cut school again, and I know I learned to make hard choices.

The method my understanding parents used to help me with my problem is worth the noting. They, as usual, handled it almost instinctively in a positive, creative manner. I think the only reason I was "dragging my feet" was that I didn't want on such a nice day to be cooped up in a room where I had to keep quiet, when there was all that playing waiting to be done—as Christopher Robin said to Pooh Bear and Eeyore, "They are not going to let me do nothing any more." Mother, without scolding, let me know that she disapproved, not because of a personal reason but because I was not doing what "I was supposed to do," and then turned my case over to Dad.

She knew how close he and I were, and what he said to me would count very heavily. Had Dad really punished me I probably would have projected my hostility onto the school for being responsible for his hurting me mentally—we never had corporal punishment. Mother and Dad had used quite independently the expression, "You are supposed to. . . ." If both, especially Dad, knew that "going to school" would be good for me, to help me grow, then there must be something to it. So when Dad dropped me off at the school I well knew that it had his blessing, and that gave me a sense of eagerness to find out more about those things we talked about at home. Out of this apparently childish experience came a sense of direction that would be found in education, on the pathways of which I would walk eagerly, to find myself eventually embarked on my Golden Journey.

My first day of school may not have loomed importantly in my experience, but the very fact of "going to school" did; it reordered my life. Now I would follow a new schedule: my activities began to be channeled in an orderly manner toward acquiring an education to lead eventually to a lifelong profession. Also, my associates now, but not necessarily by choice, were usually my schoolmates.

My "going to school" was significant in a very special way, too, as an influence shaping my personality: my daytime activities were now to a great extent associated with those of my two brothers, George, four years older, and Charlie, two years older. Although I was not the youngest in my series of brothers, the new association put me mentally in the position of the youngest sibling. I felt that I had to keep up with them, that they had no right to dominate me. This attitude meant, too, that I had to achieve in classwork. To be told that I could not do something because I was too young became a challenge, and I had to try to prove I could. I am confident that this relationship to my older brothers was the source of my strong sense of contrasuggestibility that was a part of my adult years.

During the first two years of high school, however, and especially college, where adjustment was difficult, I found the presence of my experienced brothers a great source of help. We three older brothers graduated from college before entering military service in World War I, whereas my younger three *entered* college after the war and had to face a quite different world from that into which we graduated.

The expansion of our family's contact with the urban world, Philadelphia, to add significantly to the world of growing boys, came unexpectedly. It was, I think, at the end of the summer preceding my arrival that Auntie, always practical, suggested to Mother and Dad the idea of taking boarders: "We have visitors coming and going all summer, and, while it is nice to have them, at the end of the summer we are tired from the extra work and there is the added expense for the extra food. But, if we take boarders, at the end of the summer we shall have some money to show for our work, be able to buy a few things we can't afford now and even start a nest egg for the boys' education." Auntie's argument, especially the last part, was persuasive, and it was decided to take boarders.

They would start the next summer and placed ads toward spring in the Philadelphia papers. Replies and inquiries came quickly. Auntie's suggestion had now started the Cressman family on a new road, which in one form or another would last until Mr. Harkness's death in the mid-1930s. Our summer guests brought enrichment to the ambience of our family and so to the lives of all of us, but especially to us growing boys.

The Goedels were either the first or second family to come. The Reverend Dr. Goedel and his wife were German citizens and he was the superintendent of the Mary J. Drexel Home in Philadelphia, a Lutheran institution for training deaconesses. The original Goedel family consisted of the parents and four children, but a fifth, a boy, joined the others some two or three years after their first summer. Dr. Goedel commuted back and forth frequently, but the family usually stayed for perhaps a month. Mrs. Goedel was an accomplished musician, and she and Mother enjoyed many an evening playing duets on the piano, providing entertainment for others as well. The Goedels became like members of the family: the children of the two families played together; both families belonged to the Lutheran church; and Mother and Dad were at home in that urban cultural setting. The Goedels brought not only contemporary ideas and values of the educational and religious culture of a part of Philadelphia life but also of their distant native Germany, to which they returned eight years after our first acquaintance for Dr. Goedel to accept the pastorate of a large church in Berlin.

Quite another type was Miss "Hab" (Habliston) for her laughter, vivacity, and fun-loving participation in life. A Philadelphia school teacher, a bit tall, slightly built and unmarried, probably in her late thirties, she came for several summers before 1904—my brother Morris, born June 6, 1904, received his middle name from Miss Hab and fittingly possessed her same sense of laughter. A complete extrovert, she fitted smoothly and with gaiety into the lives of all of us as she rode with Dad about the country to visit his patients, mixed with her fellow boarders, or played with us boys. She did a lot of that. Because she felt the end of her stay had to be appropriately observed, the last full day of her vacation found Miss Hab, wearing her summer sailor hat, with us three boys solemnly in tow, proceeding down the hill through our apple orchard to French Creek. We stopped on the bank under maple and oak trees where we boys over the years had made a "dam" by piling up a line of stones picked from the bottom to deepen the water and make it more sandy for our feet. Our "dam" slowed the rate of flow of the water.

Choosing a spot on the bank, each boy gathered a pile of throwing stones and stood by it. We had to wait for orders from Miss Hab.

"Everybody ready?"

"Ready," came the reply.

With that word she took off her hat and deftly skimmed it upside down out on the water. We had to wait. When the current picked up

Mr. Ebelhare, our summer boarder from Philadelphia, with the "first crop" and Wallace of the "second crop." I remember my cap as an important security device.

the hat she called, "Open fire!" As always on a range, the first few stones were off target, but then they zeroed in on the hat and down it went. Miss Hab and we looked at each other, suddenly very sober. Another summer with its fun was over.

"Good throwing, boys; we'll do it again next year. Come along now."

As we trekked up the hill through the apple trees we were rather quiet, for I think we had a sense of having participated in a ceremony, exciting, to be sure, but with a significance we didn't quite understand. I thought what fun it would be to be one of her pupils.

The Ebelhares came for several summers before 1907—my brother Fred, who received his middle name from the Ebelhares, was born August 5, 1906. He, if I remember correctly, was an engineer in charge of construction on the turrets of the great battleships built at the Cramps Shipyard in Philadelphia. They had no children, and Mr. Ebelhare and I, then about eight or nine years old, became pals. One summer they brought me a bicycle, a bit used, just the right size, and I learned to ride the hard way on dirt roads with many spills, but I learned.

He was fond of water sports, and a second summer brought a kayak (we called it a canoe), very light, made of canvas over a lattice-work of inch-wide slats, and treacherous for the unskilled or unwary paddler. The kayak was really a one-man type, although two could get into it; but because of its sensitive balance, two paddlers simply doubled its tendency to overturn unless they were really skilled and synchronized their movements. Mr. Ebelhare and I that summer spent many happy hours on French Creek with the kayak while he, the expert, taught me, the novice, the skills to handle the thing. Joyful in the friendship of an older person, a sense of security in his company as he taught me new skills, and a memory of happy days with no recall of any disturbing unhappiness—these were golden days for a young boy. They left the kayak with us, and I had many blissful days in its company.

School and family life meshed to enrich our educational experiences. Mother helped us at night with our homework and was thus closely associated with our progress. Dad involved himself with our school experience in various ways. He kept in touch by asking us often at supper around our large table—I sat on a wooden settee next to Dad—"How did school go today? What did you study today?" Interested in our play activities—we made up our own—he "coached our baseball games from a distance" as we talked over our ball games. When our ball (the conventional hard ball) needed a new cover he took it to a harness maker, Mr. Pennypacker, a patient who always gave us a good job: a horsehide cover.

Many times I went with Dad when he called at the shaded, one-story Pennypacker house on a thickly wooded hillside above Birch Run and the little village of Birchrunville. I was always haunted by a sense of mystery which seemed to enshroud that place, especially on an overcast afternoon when the darkness seemed impatient to take over. Perhaps the story Dad told me, elaborating on it more than once, had something to do with my feeling. Only rarely did I see anyone, but occasionally the stout Mr. Pennypacker would appear—rather like a monstrous gnome in his apron, a piece of harness in his hand—at the door of his shop (a part of the house) for a brief chat with Dad on his way out.

I heard the story of Mr. Pennypacker, the Union soldier instead of the harness maker, on my first drive there. When Dad got into the buggy and turned the horse back toward the main road, I asked, "Was Mr. Pennypacker always a harness maker?"

"Mr. Pennypacker," said Dad, "before he became a harness maker was a Union soldier in the Civil War. At the battle of Gettysburg in Pennsylvania about a hundred miles from here, he was badly wounded by a Minié ball, a bullet almost as large as the front joint of my thumb. He had to be discharged from the army."

"Was Gettysburg a very important battle?"

"It was one of the great battles; a terrible lot of soldiers were killed and wounded on both sides, but after that the Union side began to win the war." He went on sadly, "It would last almost another year and so many men would die."

"Dad, does Mr. Pennypacker talk with you about the war?"

"Only now and then. You see, he has rheumatism, and when the weather gets cold and damp his pains become worse. He told me when I first came how he had been wounded and that the Minié ball was still in his body and he blamed the worsening rheumatism on that Minié ball."

I thought about the gnome-like man with the slug still in his stout body affecting his health. In our history class we had studied about the Battle of Gettysburg, but it lacked reality. And here I could see with my own eyes a former soldier who fought and was wounded at "Gettysburg," and something of the actuality of that historic event and what it meant in human terms took root in me whenever I looked at this kind man who covered our "beat-up" baseballs. He had been there! What textbook could compete with this evidence?

Vivid neighborhood reminders of our colonial history, often discussed at home, stimulated my interest and enriched my knowledge well beyond my school studies. Workmen, some years before my birth, quarrying rock at St. Peters, a small village three or four miles from our home, exposed the entrance to a cave concealed by a huge rockslide. With a kerosene lantern they made their way cautiously into the cave and were shocked, almost frightened by what they saw: the skeleton of a human being lying there and the metal parts of a Revolutionary War musket and bayonet by his side. A reflection of the lantern's light caught their attention. It was a bottle containing some paper, apparently folded. Opening it, they gently removed the paper, finding two notes. One was to whoever might find the bottle, explaining that the writer, a member of an American patrol, had been wounded or separated in some manner from his comrades and had taken refuge in the cave, but his entering movement must have caused the rockslide to close the cave and prevent his escape. He asked the finder to send the other note, a letter, to his fiancée in Virginia; it would tell her what happened to him and so not to wait for his return. That poignant story was a frequent subject of our conversations. We wondered what happened to the girl in Virginia who waited in vain for her lover to return. Did she ever marry? What did she think when he didn't return, while the letter so thoughtfully written lay for a hundred years with its message in the cave? We wondered not about a serial number and a fiancée but about the tragedy coming to a young man and woman engaged to be married when the rockslide crashed down.

Valley Forge, almost sacred in American history, was but thirteen miles from our home. Dad highlighted our conventional history texts by recounting the stories his grandfather had told him as a small boy of how the snow on the road was red from the bloody feet of Washington's soldiers on their bitter march to Valley Forge because instead of shoes many had only rags around their feet.

As I rode with Dad past Warwick Furnace he showed me the swamp where workmen buried cannons cast for, but not delivered to the Colonial troops when British forces were about fifteen miles distant in the southern part of the county. In Dad's time an occasional cannon was exposed, missed in the retrieval, now stark evidence of those dangerous, early days. Our neighbor, George Wiley, while digging a posthole, brought up a solid cannonball, and I held that in my hand the day of the finding. Workmen, about a hundred yards from our house on our property, were clearing brush and earth off our stony batter to expose rock for quarrying and crushing for road metal. Suddenly one called, "Look at this," as he held up a much-rusted Revolutionary War bayonet. The finder kept it but brought it to us in the kitchen to see. The small Luther held that relic in his very own hands, something held once by much larger, stronger hands. Again our questions rose: "Who left that bayonet there? Why?" This bayonet related to a human being; cannons and cannonballs rarely do.

Mother, too, enriched our intellectual life with oral history of the same period, but from another source: the Legaux family. She introduced us to the world of France, where her great-grandfather was reported to have been associated with the Court as an *avocat* and a person well informed in natural history. Legaux, a refugee from the French Revolution, and a group of comrades engaged in an abortive attempt to rescue the king, but had to sail in their ship from the planned staging point, Abbeville, at the mouth of the Somme River, to the New World. Legaux eventually came to Mount Joy. This record was not just another story but the experience of a very special person, an ancestor; and the fact that he numbered Franklin, Washington, Lafayette, and other greats among his friends added to its impressiveness.

The capstone for this arch of my boyhood experience of good fortune was put into place one morning as, quite bored, I followed the cultivator along the rows of corn in one of Dad's fields on a hilltop, looking carefully to remove dirt or a stone pushed on any small plant by the machine. A small white object contrasted sharply with brown earth to catch my attention. I picked it up, a white "flint" (quartz) arrowhead. This was more exciting than uncovering corn. I looked closely around hoping to find another, but a round object, small and flat, caught my attention instead because its shape was unique among the small stones where it lay. Picking it up, I cleaned it by rubbing it first on my trouser leg and then, with tongue and saliva to soften the resistant earth, a final rubbing on my trouser leg. (Many years later I learned I had that morning used a standard operating procedure for all archaeologists.) Corn salvage waited while I tried to improve my cleaning efforts. Then! I, yes, I had found an English shilling bearing the royal profile of King George III and the date 1776!

History, fascinating history, lived for me outside the textbooks in lives of specific persons, known and unknown, the very stuff of history. It lived in the stories that people told of times and persons long since gone; it lived in the earth that preserved the nonperishable remains of the people who used the objects left for the lucky, alert, and thoughtful to discover and wonder over. We tried in our family conversation to establish empathy with these people, really to associate with them as though with friends of our open, rural community. Who dropped that English shilling close to the arrowhead? Were they related in some way? Was there an Indian guide with a British patrol passing through who had to react quickly to some danger? Or was it just some local farmer with a hole in his trouser pocket? Soldier, Indian, farmer, hunter, name forever unknown! I was absorbing history, oral, written, and, yes, archaeological, like the dry earth the gentle rain. This I do now know: these experiences were significant influences in shaping this young lad's professional future.

Racial prejudice was alien to our family's values. Among Dad's patients was a small number of black families, and he treated them exactly like the rest. Bertha Miller, a young daughter of one family, frequently helped Mother during the summer boarder season, as did girls of white families. I used to bring Bertha to work and drive her home at the end of the day. She was treated as a member of the family, a person in her own right.

I can't remember any evidence of racial prejudice in our community. Blacks and whites went to the same churches, sitting side by side, and the same practice was true in the schools. I never knew segregation. Remember: the Emancipation Proclamation freeing the slaves was by 1900 only thirty-nine years old and Appomattox, with the war's end, only thirty-seven. Our community with its Quaker background had made its contribution to the Civil War as the poignant, Memorial Day services recalled. And before the war, a branch of the "underground railroad" moving escaping slaves to the sanctuary of Canada passed through it. The Hawley house, built by Colonel Pugh, for whom Pughtown was named, and in Quaker hands until bought by my parents, had been a "station" on that escape route. Over the huge brick oven in the cellar hung a large kettle in which a small black child had been hidden, successfully eluding her pursuers.

Our family had strong and cherished values, but not prejudices. How fortunate I was to grow up to be heir to that deficiency!

An experience one long-ago afternoon highlights the importance of my family as a teacher of values even before I went to school.

"Lutie, did you do something to Sport?" Sport was Dad's old hunting dog—bred by him by crossing foxhound and beagle breeds—standing half asleep by the walk leading to the kitchen porch from under the big oak tree, where I had grown bored "doing nothing." I saw Dad and Mother standing on the porch, Dad in his shirt sleeves, cuffs rolled up above his wrists as always, talking quietly, but missing nothing that happened that drowsy afternoon. Walking toward the porch as nonchalantly as possible for a four-year-old, I passed Sport and he gave a "yip" and flinched. It was then Dad spoke to me.

"Yes," I replied as I continued toward the porch.

"What did you do?"

"I stuck him with a pin."

"Why did you do that?"

"I wanted to see what he would do."

"Don't you know he might bite you?"

End of conversation. Today after eighty years this experience is vividly a part of me. Outstanding was the fact that even then I had a sense of curiosity, inquisitiveness, wanting to know, a search for answers that would be a lifelong part of me. Equally if not more important was Dad's method of treating me for what was really a stupid act with possibly a painful result for me. Dad said nothing to urge me not "to ask questions" and so put the cherished stamp of his approval on that trait of my developing character, but not necessarily on the act itself. He put the responsibility for my action squarely on me, and it was implicit that I should use the knowledge at my disposal as the basis for my decision. That decision was mine to make. If Sport bit me, he should not be punished, for his action would be the expected response and also my punishment. (I think he should have at least nipped me, but he was a dear old family friend who helped take care of the children.) Dad, with those few words, told me something, something that would be like seeds planted to grow to fruition, like a spark waiting for a breeze to glow to brightness that would evolve through my whole life: the importance of asking questions, seeking answers, AND accepting the responsibility for what my efforts to find the answers might bring.

The growth and fruition of whatever innate seed of curiosity I had, like the "Elephant's Child," were greatly nourished by my contacts with our boarders through the new ideas and relations they brought. Then, too, my experience in close mental association with the Colonial men and women whose fate we wondered about but never knew fanned to glowing that spark of "wanting to know." Dad's corrective comments were all supportive of these desires and clear on my obligation to accept responsibility.

Little significant change had occurred in the slowly moving lifeways of our rural society between the end of the Civil War and the early 1900s. Horse, mule, and man still provided the energy to run the few available machines, with water furnishing the power source for grist- and sawmills. Frequently a windmill was used to drive a pump to raise water for nonhousehold purposes; manually operated pumps raised the well water for drinking and household uses. All transport was by horse or mule and wagon, horseback, or on foot over dirt roads dusty in summer, icy in winter, and muddy in spring. Kerosene lamps "lightened our darkness," and wood or coal furnished the energy for heating our homes. All sanitary facilities were outside, the year around, except in the case of illness. Schools had probably changed little except to add the events of the Civil War, I am afraid rather reflecting the northern point of view, to our study of American history. I think the only difference of any significance between the lifeways of the persons whose fate we worried about around our kitchen table and ours was the cast of actors.

Saturday, September 21, 1901, was a warm, dreamlike, Indian summer day. The harvests were in save for the corn standing in its orderly rows of shocks waiting to be husked. The farmers' wisdom, "Six weeks after the first breeze blows over the oats stubble will be the first frost," had been validated. The maple leaves showing their first tint of yellow and the lonely, haunting cries of the first southward-flying wild geese were sure promises of autumn. Bathed in the pale-blue haze of Indian summer, the earth and all its creatures were resting after the furious fruition of the summer.

Season of mists and mellow fruitfulness!
Close bosom-friend of the maturing sun; . . .

(John Keats, *Ode to Autumn*)

Dad and Auntie stood talking in the sun on the front porch. I, barefoot in the warm dust across the road from the house, was playing rather aimlessly when I saw a man on a bicycle coming toward our place from the direction of Pughtown. Not recognizing him and impressed by the shiny visor on his cap, I eased myself a little further away from the stranger. Resting his bicycle against the picket fence, he went up on the porch and spoke to Dad. I could not hear what was said—I was told later what had happened—but after they exchanged a few words in low voices, Dad went to bring Mother from the house. The stranger, a Western Union messenger from Pottstown, six miles distant, handed her a telegram telling of her mother's sudden death from a heart attack. Answers to queries about funeral arrangements and my parents' presence had to be quickly decided and written for the messenger, who then faced the long return ride over hilly, dusty roads to file the reply. The little group on the porch watched him leave, then turned and walked slowly, arm in arm, into the house with their grief.

These quiet ways we knew so well were not to last; change was waiting out in the urban world, and when it arrived, slowly at first but with ever-quickening pace, we would find ourselves face-to-face with challenges never dreamed of. I would now be a part of history and very much aware of it; my challenges would not be windmills and my "sword and buckler" would be the solid values taught by my family in my early years and enriched by Nature's lessons and internalized in my personality.

The outriders of the approaching storm of change were not long in appearing: a group of men driving a pair of horses and a heavy wagon hauled long, peeled logs, dropping them at regular intervals on the side of the road from Pughtown, past our place, and to Nantmeal village. Another group followed shortly digging holes by hand tools and setting the poles. "We're putting in the telephone," they replied to the questions from us curious young onlookers. They then strung by hand two wires, attaching one on each side of the pole near the top to a glass insulator. The year? About 1903.

One afternoon a worker appeared to run wires into the large room in our house we called "The Office" since Dad used it for that purpose. He fastened a large box to the wall, patiently answering my questions as I stood close by. Finally satisfied, he said, "We'll give it a try; now listen." He turned the crank on the side and the bells near the top startled me by their sudden ringing. He looked at me and smiled. Then he rang four times and I could hear faintly a voice coming from the receiver. It was Mrs. Prizer who lived a mile away, off the Nantmeal road! He called to me, "Now you talk to Mrs. Prizer." Almost too excited to get words out, I stammered something and heard her reply. How could this be? I had spoken on the phone and heard the answer. I wouldn't have to run to, "Please take this note back to Mrs. Prizer, Lutie," anymore. The first telephone! And the messenger boy would never again have to ride those twelve miles to deliver a message. I had participated, even though only an observer, in the installation of the first telephone in our area!

The advantages of the telephone in ending isolation were so obvious that sufficient subscribers were soon found to extend the lines widely, but not every family could afford the novelty.

The winter of 1905–6 was made horrible for our family by diphtheria infecting three brothers, one after the other, and finally my exhausted Mother who had nursed us all through those desperate weeks. Immediately after the first illness, Charlie's, was diagnosed, Dad put us on a preventive inoculation schedule. Mother presided over the infectious room, hers and Dad's large, bright bedroom looking out under the great oak tree.

Dad checked our throats daily for the dreaded white spots. How well I remember one Sunday afternoon lineup! Dad looked at my throat, then said, "Come along, Lutie, upstairs." Opening the door, he said, "Step into the box. Here's another, Florie."

Before starting his visits that afternoon, Dad, as was his practice for Mother, listed the places he would stop and the order and who had the telephone in case she wished to give him a message.

Supposed to get into bed but not wanting to, I, after exhausting most of my delaying tactics, stood before a large mirror trying to see the telltale white spots on my throat. The next thing I knew, Dad and Mother were standing by my bed. I had fainted, and Mother, after somehow getting me into bed, phoned the Seymours, where Dad planned to stop. Fortunately, he had not arrived. "Please tell him Lute has fainted and to come home as fast as he can." Dad arrived shortly after the phone call, heard the message, quickly cared for his patient, then got into the buggy and drove, as he said, "poor old Dolly the fastest she has ever gone." Dad and Mother had brought me back to consciousness. The antitoxin had affected my heart. Had it not been for the available phone that Sunday to get the message to Dad some four miles away, there is a good chance I would not have made my Golden Journey or have memoirs to write. How different from that Saturday afternoon, September 21, 1901, and the Western Union messenger boy on his bicycle!

The automobile and the mobile gasoline engine followed the telephone into our rural area after about five years. Schuyler Wiley, our next-door neighbor on the north, usually the first to get something new, especially as a prestige item, bought the first Model T. Dad and Mother, after seeing how much the automobile would help in his practice, managed somehow to collect enough money to buy the second car, I thing a 1910 or 1911 Model T. It proved all they had hoped for, but there were still places to which Dad had to drive the good old horse and buggy. The car was strictly for Dad's use in his practice — a piece of professional equipment. We continued to drive the horse and carriage to high school in Pottstown and to meet other needs. The car made Dad's work easier and, with the telephone, he was able to extend his services to more people over a wider area.

The single-cylinder gasoline engine, mounted on a truck drawn by a pair of horses from farm to farm to power machinery, both expedited the process and reduced the manual labor in threshing the grain in the barn after the harvest and in sawing wood for winter fuel when the logs were brought to the barn or some other available place. The circular saw of the period was a frightfully dangerous piece of equipment, and I vividly remember that two men, Ed Baver and Schuyler Wiley, had lost parts of arms below the elbow in sawing accidents.

The treadmill, which used horse power, was now displaced except in the most isolated areas. Usually one man, in our case, John Miller, one of Dad's patients, invested in an engine and then, in addition to using it for his own work, rented it out as a business enterprise to other farmers with himself as operator. The gasoline engine did not enable the farmer to increase his acreage, only to do certain work faster and more efficiently than with the horse. The tractor was long into the future. I see our treadmill standing forlorn, abandoned on the barn floor, reduced to a dangerous plaything for us children.

CHANGE, change, with its rate of forward movement always more rapid, would now characterize the economic, social, political, and other aspects of the world we would know. Communication — the automobile, telephone, improved roads — and mechanical energy produced by the internal combustion engine interacted to change our lifeways, not as simple additive factors, $1 + 1 + 1 = 3$, but in the geometric order of $1 \times 2 \times 4 = 8$. Our quiet, rural isolation now belonged to history.

September 1910 marked my personal entrance into this new world when I became a freshman at Pottstown High School. Socially and personally secure enough in my boyhood country life, I was terribly insecure socially and psychologically in my new environment. My main task was going to be to find my security in a way compatible with my earlier background. I soon found that academically I could compete with the best in some cases: algebra, for example, in which I was ahead since I had covered most of the freshman course in our one-room school. But I did not know how to dance, nor was I familiar with the movies as well as other day-to-day cultural activities that made up the world of the town students. I was obviously going to have to make up my deficiencies; and it would not be easy.

Charlie's presence as a secure person during my first two years provided a valuable support. Our daily routine—doing our chores at the barn early in the morning, dressing for school, eating breakfast, and starting the six-mile drive at seven o'clock to Pottstown for eight-thirty classes—was a recognition of the value of the education we wanted.

Our going to high school was really a family enterprise: Mother was up to get the hot, substantial breakfasts we had to have on those winter drives and Dad always harnessed the horse, hitched it to the wagon, and brought it to the house for us. They always saw us off, and in cold weather would place a hot brick or flatiron on the floor under the blankets. We left our horse and the grain for its noon meal at the livery stable, where an attendant unhitched and kept it in a stall until our return after school closed at three-thirty. Our livery stable was attached to the Shuler House hotel, the precursor of the motel with parking lot. The fee was only ten cents per day, but ten cents was the hourly wage of the period. When we came for the horse, the attendant brought it out harnessed and we helped hitch it to the wagon.

Arriving home, we were responsible for stabling the horse and, later, we had our chores at the barn and brought in the wood and coal for the house. After a good substantial dinner (called supper)—I seem to remember always having to dry dishes—there was home-work, with Mother frequently giving us much-needed help with mathematics and grammar. Sometimes there were card or other games or busying one's self with some plaything, such as a steam engine that used an alcohol flame to heat the water. In winter, out-door sports called us, but were permitted only after our homework was completed. This was the time, too, for our reading associated with our studies in literature, both English and American. High school was not some kind of an adjunct to our real life; it was an inte-grated part of it.

I think this sort of daily routine was very instrumental in melding together the values of my early years with those that the new world constantly held before me. So many of the mental images evoked now by perhaps a piece of music, a poem, or even a painting are those I have seen, heard, or felt as a small boy, happy in that lovely country it was my good fortune to know.

I went to high school because it was the thing to do in our family; the choice of a profession would come later. I can only remember that I had some ill-defined sense of expecting to be a teacher. Our parents never tried to direct us into any particular profession; the choice was ours and they would support our decision. Visitors or sometimes a patient making an office call, when talking with Mother, would ask what the boys were going to do when they grew up. "Will they become doctors like their father?" Mother explained that the choice would be up to each one, but I well remember hearing her say, "Sometimes we think Luther may become a minister like his Uncle Mark." I still wonder how much influence that idea so casually and, I am sure, unintentionally planted in my mind had on my later decision. Who knows? But it is quite possible.

A tall, gaunt, intense Mr. Shook taught history with all the commitment of a convert to a faith necessary to achieve salvation; it was the PEOPLE who made the history. History lived—I recalled the stout harness maker with the "Minié ball" in his body from Gettysburg and his exacerbated rheumatism—and he honored my interest by inviting me occasionally to take short walks in the country with him after school and stimulated it further with his comradely conversation. History of a different kind offered itself to me in my Latin studies, written history, poetry created from myth, fable, and legend. And the recorded history of a great empire was mine to share as we read Cicero and participated in the debates in the Roman Senate, where Cato, the Elder, thundered the ending to his every speech—no matter the subject, from the lethal threat of Carthage to the potholes in the streets of Rome smashing the chariot wheels—with the menacing Credo, "CARTHAGE MUST BE DESTROYED!" And so it eventually was.

Literature took me into the lives of different peoples, different lifeways and places as we read Scott, Dickens, Thackery, George Eliot, and others. Three years of French and German opened up new worlds. For some reason, I took no science in high school, but I had an excellent start in a humanistic phase of education.

My last two years following Charlie's graduation permitted me to assume my own responsibility for my actions and their directions. I stepped beyond the purely classroom activities both to participate in the noncurricular to establish my position with my classmates in that area and to take part in other activities as the occasion permitted. The necessity of having to drive the six miles home after classes severely limited the occasions.

To share extracurricular activities with classmates, I went out for track, running the 880-yard race. Although I never took first place, I certainly scored points. I never had any training; I just came and ran—usually after school—and went home immediately after the meet was over. Dad once came to see me run in some kind of an intramural event at the horseracing track at the Pottstown fairgrounds. I think I came in third in a bunched finish—that 880 is a brutal race—and Dad made me lie down on the wooden seat of the bleachers while he massaged my leg muscles. It was the only training I ever had, but I was showing my peers that I could compete with them outside the classroom as well as in.

I stayed in town one night to see a much-advertised play at the Opera House, "Damaged Goods," a homily against premarital sexual activity because of the danger of contracting venereal disease. It was a very daring play to discuss publicly such an indelicate subject. The audience, mostly mixed, was not large. The play obviously made an impression on me.

I cannot remember ever seeing a moving picture during those years. At home we had the hand-held stereoscope, by which we viewed simultaneously two glass slides, about 4 x 4 inches, to produce a three-dimensional image. The slides were standard sets of scenery, travel, and similar subjects. The "magic lantern," the common projector, was used at public gatherings, church affairs, and community meetings to illustrate a lecture.

There were, of course, class and school dances, but I drew back from them because I didn't know how to dance. Then one day a very nice classmate, Elsie Smith, whose family had a summer cottage on French Creek not far from our home, told me I should come to a class dance to be held in a few weeks.

"But I can't dance," I explained.

"That's no problem," she said, "I'll teach you."

So we went, and that kind and brave girl took me in hand at one side of the floor saying, "Don't pay any attention to them," as couples danced by so effortlessly. I was almost shaking with fear at my awkwardness. "I'll show you what to do; come on." That thoughtful girl did teach me, and since I had a good sense of rhythm, we joined the others on the floor well before the last dance. Then came the experience that tended to discourage those nighttime activities: the long, six-mile-drive home alone with the horse and buggy. I remember well that night's drive, under a full moon and clouds playing tag together, with a good wind whipping skiffs of light, new-fallen snow across the road.

Completion of high school found the basic patterns of my personality, my identity, passing out of a formative into an early maturation stage, one required for honing years in time and wide-ranging and deep intellectual and emotional challenges. These patterns, derived basically from my early boyhood, were family instilled: integrity; duty (you are supposed to); compassion and understanding; the necessity to find out (curiosity); the obligation to make decisions on the basis of evidence and the necessity to assume responsibility for my decisions; the equality of persons; the value of cooperative enterprise. These patterns, sharpened in my high-school years, were integrating themselves into a mosaic, the basic structure of my personality. They would be the tools, the instruments, or even the weapons with which I would face my challenges on the Journey ahead. Always at the very center of the mosaic was the value INTEGRITY, and everything else to have validity had to relate to that element. No single pattern could be fully isolated from the total design and retain significance; each was related to the others.

To shape my life, my parents did not provide me with a series of dogmatic norms, commandments from another time and alien lifeway; they gave me a mosaic pattern as a dynamic system by which I could and, yes, would have to face each new challenge on its own terms by reference to my integrated value system. The mosaic itself carried the imperative for my future behavior. The method put the necessity for choice and responsibility for my action exactly where it belonged: on myself. It was a guidepost on an often lonely and solitary Journey. It is worth noting that all my deliberate efforts to establish my identity were based on individual performance. My identity did not derive from membership in some group or other status-giving situation; it reflected only my own self.

Following graduation from high school in June 1914, I worked at various jobs to earn money toward college in the fall. On August 5 my brother Charlie and I were working on a small township road gang quite close to our house. We came home for lunch, which Mother had ready for us in the big kitchen, the center of much of our family life. Sunshine broke through the great oak tree outside the house and lay in scattered patches. I sat at the end of a long table facing the door open to the breeze. As Charlie and I were eating lunch in this peaceful setting, Mr. Harkness, who made his home with us, came through the open door carrying the mail, which had just arrived by rural delivery. As he walked into the kitchen, looking down at the open newspaper in his hands, he uttered three words in a high raspy voice: "WAR! WAR! WAR!" Charlie and I finished our lunch and went back to our picks and shovels unaware of what those fateful words meant for our future and that of millions of others throughout the world.

History as metaphor is two scenarios, one within the other, both rolling forward but not synchronously. The outer film records the great Human Epic, the movements, the swirling current and the quiet pools and the torrents tossing about the fates of peoples; the inner film plays out the life history of each Luther, Charlie, Mary, and Martha as it moves toward its inevitable end through the complex personal and interpersonal relationship of each of us. The outer film unrolls without regard for the actors on the inner; the inner is never completely free from the influence of the outer and is sometimes almost dominated by it, but never completely as long as the individual controls his own mind. Each individual's life is a two-way adjustment: first, to personal problems as an aspect of daily life, and second, to them as they are swept up in the unrolling scenario of the Human Epic.

I looked forward to going to college with some anxiety since it would be the first break in the smooth continuity of life I knew with our family in our friendly old house. War news appeared in the daily papers, often not very reassuring, but it seemed far, far away. Two distinguished statesmen, however, playing significant parts in that outer scenario saw clearly into the future: Viscount Grey, foreign secretary in the British Cabinet, and General Jan Smuts in Capetown, South Africa.

Viscount Grey, in London, August 3, 1914, stood with an aide somberly watching from the windows of his room in the Foreign Office as the lamplighters turned on the lights in St. James Park. Thoughtfully he commented, "The lamps are going out all over Europe; we shall not see them lit again in our lifetime." (War was declared 11:00 P.M., August 4, 1914.)

General Smuts, speaking on the other side of the world, made the very prescient observation: "Mankind has struck its tents and is on the march."

September 1914 I registered as a freshman at Pennsylvania State College, choosing a major in the classics and a minor in English poetry. I planned, although rather uncertainly, to prepare myself for teaching. My scenario, though now running fairly separately, would find its independence of movement progressively intruded upon by its ever more rapidly unfolding companion.

Penn State's student body in the fall semester of 1914 totalled 3,375 full-time students, of which 669 (my class) were freshmen.[7] The curriculum was heavily weighted toward the sciences, especially agriculture and engineering, whereas the College of Liberal Arts was of minor importance. The total faculty in the college was sixty: six full, eleven associate, thirteen assistant professors, and thirty instructors. Five teaching fellows and two of some unidentified category completed the list. Its small size, however, did not prevent it from offering excellent instruction in limited areas. Dr. C. O. Harris, associate professor of Greek, and Dr. Fred Louis Pattee, professor of English language and literature, stand out as distinguished in my entire educational career. I look back after all the years on my four with Dr. Harris in the study of Hellenic civilization as the most seminally significant of my entire life.

Isolated geographically and culturally, the college depended on a symbiotic relationship with the small town, State College; neither could exist without the other. At the foot of Mt. Nittany, honored in college folklore and legend, was Lemont, a small village boasting the nearest railroad station, but it was three miles from the college. Automobile traffic was almost nonexistent. When students arrived en masse, a few autos were rounded up along with horse-drawn vehicles to provide transport, but a lot of plain walking was necessary. Roy Diem, a classmate, and I went each Sunday to teach Sunday School at Lemont as a part of the Y.M.C.A.'s student service program.

Weather permitting, we walked across the fields, and our friendship grew with the opportunity provided us for much good talking during this time together.

Legend has it that when the dynamic revivalist, Billy Sunday, included Penn State in his program of celebrated revival meetings shortly before my time, eager students took a farm wagon to Lemont to provide transportation to State College. With ropes instead of harness attached to appropriate places and two students to handle the wagon tongue for steering, the exuberant students grasped the ropes, and with plenty of manpower pulled the delighted Billy toward the college, singing lustily as they went the revivalist's favorite song, "The brewer's big horses won't run over me! I'm a temperance engyne don't you see. . . ." It's a safe bet that the habits of many of the singing "horses" gave little support to the sentiments of the rollicking song. But what a lark to break the tedium of that isolation!

To mitigate the rigor of our cultural isolation, the college occasionally brought an orchestra or traveling dramatic company from New York to the campus. Townspeople, of course, shared these occasions. I am sure that some of the impetus to the development of student and faculty participation in collegiate cultural activities of, as I remember, a reasonably high order derived from our being forced to rely on and develop our own resources.

By 1914 the outrageous hazing of freshmen had slackened considerably, but some sophomores bound to tradition treated us first-year students as a conquered wartime population. Small green "dinks" worn at all times on the crowns of our heads stigmatized the men; co-eds wore small green ribbons. No freshman might date a girl, town or gown, without the risk of a head shave, publicly administered, as a minimum punishment for daring to break the sacred tradition. Walking on the grass was prohibited along with other activities, the normal parts of decent living. Hazing, although it had quite the opposite effect probably on most, was rationalized as necessary to socialize the ignorant freshman into becoming a responsible member of that fiction, the Penn State Student Body. Actually, too often it provided a social validation of outrageous, barbaric behavior by groups of sophomore "bully boys," which, if carried out in other situations, would have subjected the perpetrators to suits for civil damages.

The freshman restrictions and the ever-present threat of hazing added to the fact that I was, as were many of my classmates, away from home for the first time, which produced a horrible sense of aloneness that first semester. I was helped greatly by the presence of my brothers, George and Charlie, both juniors, who gave me good advice, support and, I remember, sometimes protection. Adjustment to the new life was far from easy, and I became desperately home-sick—so homesick that had I been able to think up some acceptable excuse I would have dropped out. But I didn't. Christmas vacation eventually came, and our family was reunited at that happy time. I regained in those joyous days together a personal confidence and new perspective so that at vacation's end I was ready and even anxious to return to my studies. I always loved my home, but I was never really homesick again. Sharing those happy days with the family at that crit-ical time in my life revived in me the old commitment of "You are supposed to!" and all it meant. I returned to my work knowing that while I was going away from the family I was not really parting from it. My action made explicit what I had recognized implicitly: that I was in the process of carrying out the imperatives of my mosaic of pat-terns leading toward my adult personality.

A second important challenge faced me my first year: the ques-tion of change of a major field of study. I was finding first-year Greek very difficult and demanding, a situation probably compounded by my sense of aloneness. There were only two students in our Greek class; my classmate was Edna Glenn, a scholarship student from State College. The hazing traditions prevented any contact between us out-side of the classroom, so we were unable to share our experiences. My closest friend, Roy Diem, slightly older than I, was preparing for a teaching career, majoring in education and psychology; and from our conversations I had concluded, I am sure, that his program was the easier. If Roy could prepare adequately for teaching by his course of study, why not I? If we shared the same courses I would have a friend with whom I could discuss our work. "Why not change your major?" the siren asked so persuasively.

I rather hesitantly approached Dr. Harris, a man of compassion, understanding and, I am sure, well aware of the problems of adjust-ment I was facing. He didn't try to argue the relative values of the two fields; he talked sympathetically and pointed out how the first year of Greek was difficult, requiring very hard work, but a necessary preparation to enter upon our study of the lifeways of the ancient Greek peoples. He suggested further that, before I made a final decision, I choose some persons from public and private life whom I admired, whose lives I might want to emulate, and discover what their educational backgrounds had been. He put the responsibility for the decision on myself. A little reflection cleared up my motivation, and I made my decision: continue with Greek.

These two freshman-year experiences, seemingly inconsequential in themselves, were actually of extreme significance in my on-going effort to establish my identity. The Christmas experience of a maturing relationship with my family assured me that the values learned in my boyhood from that source were valid, adaptable, and dependable. There was nothing to revolt against; I had only to fulfill. My decision to continue with the classics required me to face up to and accept the more difficult challenge, an act affecting all my future life.

Academically I had had a successful year with straight A grades. Promotion to the rank of sergeant in the cadet regiment for the next year, the highest rank available to a sophomore, brought highly appreciated recognition. At the year's end I was self-confident and assured with the knowledge that for my life ahead I would have to develop and rely on my own inner strength to meet the challenges I would surely face. A very self-confident and perhaps sometimes rash young lad would learn on his adventurous Journey

> Whom God deigns not to overthrow hath need of triple mail.
>
> (Ezra Pound, *Ballad for Gloom*)

How wise my decision to stay with the classics! Someone has written, "Literature is life and life is literature," and so it was with my four years of Greek, four years of companionship with Dr. Harris, with whom I walked along the lifeways of the ancient Hellenes.[8] The idea that Greek was a dead language, that it could be of no use in today's world, was daily exposed for the absurdity it is as we moved happily with our ancient friends, revealed to us by their literature. The Homeric poems with their fascinating tales of Bronze Age folk extolled not only acts of martial valor and comradeship in arms but also all the wide-ranging feelings men, women, and their children can experience. Dr. Harris did not introduce us to the Homeric world by approaching the epic as a subject for literary criticism; it was the story of Bronze Age people often presented comparatively with related problems in today's world.

As an eager, curious young lad from a favored family background, but having limited educational and social experience, truly with Homer I passed on my Golden Journey into a new and shining world.

> Then felt I like some watcher of the skies
>   When a new planet swims into his ken;
> Or like stout Cortez, when with eagle eyes
>   He stared at the broad Pacific—and all his men
> Looked at each other with a wild surmise—
>   Silent, upon a peak in Darien.
>
> (John Keats, *On First Looking into Chapman's Homer*)

Heinrich Schliemann had excavated Troy and Mycenae; Sir Arthur Evans was excavating the Minoan civilization on Crete as we studied. Schliemann and Evans from their respective areas uncovered the mute evidence of the lives of the Bronze Age folk and supported and fleshed out the record from legend and literature. Although we did not call it such—neither the word nor concept was then available—today's archaeological verbalization would say that we were studying the lifeways of a great culture area, the Eastern Mediterranean Bronze Age Culture area. Although there were the expected variations, many basic values were equally shared; and there were sufficient similarities in the variant forms for recognition of a common basic type. When some four to five years later as a seminary student studying the Old Testament I found myself, to my advantage, approaching early Hebraic history and legend as the record of the life of a people who were a part, peripheral in a way but still a part, of this Bronze Age Culture area, this knowledge helped me approach the study of the Bible objectively as the collection of literary sources it is.

Homer's subjects faced problems common to the human condition. Homer recorded the problems and the manner of meeting them often in grisly and painful detail; he was a historian, not a moralist. Later, however, in the hands and minds of the dramatists of the enlightened Periclean Age (fifth century B.C.), situations recorded by Homer became the subjects of some of the greatest dramas of Western culture, enriching my mind and those of countless others. My study of Greek literature through my four college years provided me with my most significant intellectual experience and imbued me with the essentiality of the humanistic approach for any reasonable understanding of the human condition.

A challenging class taught by the pastor of the Lutheran church in the town gave me an exciting new concept of what religion could be about. Young, educated, and articulate, he easily established empathy with us college students composing his class.[9] Our teacher did not talk about dogma—he, of course, could if necessary—but shared with us ideas of values, of behavior, decency, integrity, personal responsibility, matters and ideas in which we were all interested as individuals. He *even quoted poetry* in elaborating his ideas. I responded eagerly to my new discovery. What a contrast to the narrow dogmatism and provincial concepts of the Baptist community of Pughtown to which I had been exposed! I began to visualize religion not only as something to be experienced but also as a subject to be studied as I was then doing with poetry, history, and even science. I found no incompatibility between my Greek studies and what I was beginning to understand about religion. I was entering upon what was to be a long, syncretic experience, one leading to a personality free from the threat of scars inherent in the ignorance from which I had been released.

As I progressed through my second year and beyond, I, of course—even in the uncertainty of the time—had to give some thought to my future profession. I am sure the remark I heard Mother make more than once, "We think Luther may become a minister like his Uncle Mark," was beginning to find a root in my consciousness as I explored and increased my new understanding of religion. The soil was being prepared, but no root had been set.

The war clouds of Europe in that year of 1915–16 moved more menacingly into our experience. To further prepare myself for future service, not if but when it would come, I enrolled in the summer of 1916 in the Plattsburg Barracks, New York, Citizens Military Training Camp for four weeks under the War Department with regular army officers as instructors. This was a no-nonsense, rigorous camp, with rugged training and the last week in field maneuvers with full packs. I had been appointed a sergeant, and on the rifle range won my sharpshooter's medal, missing expert by one point. This experience of achievement among men mostly older and more experienced in which I demonstrated qualities of leadership and performance provided another sturdy support to my developing sense of self-confidence. On my return to the academic life in September, I was given a commission as a first lieutenant in the cadet regiment; this meant I would have instructional duties.

By that autumn of 1916 there was no need to ponder seriously a future after graduation two years ahead, for by now we all knew the rapidly unrolling outer scenario would take care of that then, if not before, because duty in some branch of the services awaited us. The war in Europe had settled into the trench stalemate with its horrible suffering and bloody losses. The Battle of the Somme purchased a few miles of blood-soaked wasteland at the cost of more than 400,000 British casualties and slightly less for the Germans. The poems of the young British soldiers, many of them university students, came to us with their message of commitment to a cause we knew we shared:

> Now, God be thanked who has matched us with His hour,
> And caught our youth, and wakened us from sleeping,
> With hand made sure, clear eye, and sharpened power
> To turn, as swimmers into cleanness leaping,
> Glad from a world grown old and cold and weary. . . .
>
> (Rupert Brooke, Peace)

And again Brooke wrote:

> If I should die, think only this of me:
>   That there's some corner of a foreign field
>   That is for ever England. . . .
>
> (The Soldier)

He found that "corner of a foreign field" on the ill-starred Gallipoli expedition.

Alan Seeger, a young American poet living in Paris, joined the French army and sent this message:

> I have a rendezvous with Death
> At some disputed barricade. . . .
> . . . .
> At midnight in some flaming town,
> When spring trips north again this year,
> And I to my pledged word am true,
> I shall not fail that rendezvous.
>
> (I Have a Rendezvous with Death)

He kept it on a night patrol in a burst of enemy machine gun fire in No-Man's-Land.

Winifred M. Letts wrote of the Oxford men:

> I saw the spires of Oxford
> As I was passing by. . . .
> . . . .
> My heart was with the Oxford men
>   Who went abroad to die.
>
> *(The Spires of Oxford)*

And John McCrae called urgently to remind us of our obligations:

> In Flanders fields the poppies blow
> Between the crosses, row on row.
> . . . .
> Take up our quarrel with the foe:
> To you from falling hands we throw
>   The torch; be yours to hold it high.
>   If ye break faith with us who die
> We shall not sleep, though poppies grow
>   In Flanders fields.
>
> *(In Flanders Fields)*

As we listened to the calls sent us from these poets, campus life seemed to have less and less reality. How could we not grasp the torch?

A messenger came on the stage at the Military Hop, the annual formal dance of the cadet officers held in the winter of 1916–17, and stopped the music. Startled, we stopped dancing. Absolute silence awaited the obviously important announcement: "The State Department today returned his passport to the German ambassador with instructions to leave the country within forty-eight hours with his staff and close the embassy." There was brief hand clapping as we looked at one another knowing full well what it meant. The messenger signaled to the orchestra to start the music, and we picked up the dance. But after this it could not be the same on the campus, and the unease increased. Students, one after another, withdrew to join up as ambulance drivers or to enlist in the French or British armies. The Lafayette Escadrille of the French air force was a unit of American volunteers. Then one day a classmate, a close personal friend, Robert Finney, fluent in French, told me he was leaving that day to drive an ambulance with the French army.

In March 1917, feeling I, too, had to "do something," I wrote my
parents asking their permission to enlist in a specialized naval unit. I
owed my parents this courtesy. With my military training my idea of
enlisting in the navy was almost idiotic, but it shows something of the
mental state at the time. After about two weeks I received a reply
from Mother telling me in almost a matter-of-fact manner that our
wonderful old home had been burned to the ground with practically
all the family's belongings. She asked, that since colleges were granting full credit for the year's work if a student in good standing withdrew for either agricultural work or to go into the armed service,
would I please withdraw and come home and run the farm for the
summer and postpone the consideration of my enlistment. To hear
that the old house in which I had grown up had been destroyed was
shattering. Sensitive to my parents' loss, economic and emotional, I
was almost overwhelmed. Farm labor I knew was almost nonexistent.
I wired I would be home as soon as I could make out the necessary
papers. Arriving home Saturday I moved in with my parents and
others cooped up temporarily in the vacant church parsonage; and
Monday I started being a farmer, doing the barn work and loading,
hauling, and spreading (by pitchfork) manure for fertilizer on the
field I would soon be plowing.

My oldest brother, George, who would be enlisting soon, was
teaching in the Doylestown, Pennsylvania, high school. He had been
invited by the students to give the commencement address. For some
now long-forgotten reason, he had invited me down for a day or two
at the time. The mother of one of his bright young students asked
him to dinner before the address. He explained that he would like to
accept but that his brother Luther would be with him. "Bring him,
too." George accepted and I accompanied him. We arrived to meet
our hostess, Mrs. Emily Mead, and George's student. Her name was
Margaret Mead. "Fatal interview!"

Fifty-five years later, Margaret wrote in *Blackberry Winter* about
that night and the Luther she met. I wrote her on reading her story in
the complimentary copy of her book she had kindly sent me that I
thought the Luther she described sounded like a very nice and
accomplished lad, but I scarcely recognized him. Thanks, Margaret.

> Luther was four years older than I and a senior in college.
> He was studying Latin and Greek, and he gave me books of
> poetry with dedications in verse that he himself wrote.[10] He

was tall and slender and well built. He could drive a car and shoot a gun with great skill and he took beautiful photographs. He danced magnificently. He had an engaging grin and a wry sense of humor, yet he took life seriously and, like my mother, was willing to see life whole.[11]

I returned to my farming and to Penn State for my last year in September 1917.

Two interests dominated my intellectual life this last year of college: military training in the R.O.T.C. — I was the student officer-in-charge — in preparation for entering the service upon graduation and the fulfillment of the promise held out to me that first year by Dr. Harris as we lived and identified with the actors in the series of remarkable plays presented by the great Periclean Age dramatists. They were about the relation of man to man and of man to his divinities — ubiquitous and timeless problems. These plays, weaponlike, pierced deep into my consciousness, especially Sophocles' remarkable tragedy of the lovely Antigone, the young woman who chose to carry out her sacred duties to perform at least ceremonial burial over her brothers killed in the assault against the city ruled by the king who held her prisoner. She could have bought her life by accepting the king's offer to leave her brothers to the scavengers and their souls to endless wanderings. Antigone, in contrast to her sister, Ismene, chose to perform the last rites over her brothers and so joined them in death at the king's hands. Antigone is a timeless heroine. Where is Ismene?

During the autumn, Mother and Dad found a large farmhouse for rent close to Pughtown and settled there, perhaps a quarter of a mile west along the road to an intersection called Daisy Point. Since they now had plenty of room, they wanted all the available family together for the Christmas holidays, a last time before we would all be scattered by the approaching storm. Charlie was already in the Field Artillery Officers' School, George would go shortly after Christmas, and I in June. Wallace, they knew, would join his brothers on his eighteenth birthday, September 6, 1918. He did, too, but via the marines. Only Charlie would be absent. To counterbalance the heavily male contingent of brothers, Mother asked George's "bright young student" and her classmate friend, Esther, the sheriff's daughter, to share in our good times. Esther, a thorough extrovert, was full of fun and laughter and willing to try almost anything in the way of fun on the snow or ice, quite the perfect foil for the rather intellectual Margaret. We did have a good time with indoor games and sledding and skating, for the snow was deep and the ice was hard and smooth. We joined others on French Creek, and Margaret and I skated together, hands crossed, most of one afternoon as I told her the whole tragic story of Antigone, whose agony I had just experienced.

The last night of the year, Margaret and I, bundled up against the cold, set out on a walk toward Daisy Point, our only light the reflection of the stars from the deep snow. Arm in arm, we walked slowly on the snow-covered road, attuned to the brooding silence of that winter night. After about a half mile we turned back. We had said little, but our bodies by some subtle means exchanged messages as we walked arm in arm, our shoes crunching the dry snow in the bitter cold. We were nearly home, and the wordless messages brought us to a stop and turned us facing each other. I embraced Margaret, and as she joined me, I said tenderly, "I love you, Margaret."

Softly, she replied, "I love you, too, Luther." She lifted her veil worn against the cold, and we sealed our pledges with a kiss.

In silence, almost in a state of wonder at what had happened to us, we returned home. We told no one of our engagement.

To my academic interests was now added our engagement, but Margaret and I knew that marriage, itself uncertain in the troubled times, would have to await a time in the unknown future. It did, however, give us a goal toward which our interests would inevitably find direction.

Just before graduation, the headmaster of the Bellefonte Academy, a boys' "prep school" about ten miles from State College, asked me to take over the duties of a teacher of German and Latin who had been drafted. I accepted with alacrity; it filled the gap in time between graduation and departure for the R.O.T.C. camp. My decision had fortunate consequences for my future career far beyond my dreams, though at the time I was completely unaware of my good luck.

Mother and Dad came to my wartime graduation in late April; it was the last time I would see them until I had completed the R.O.T.C. camp—and perhaps not then.

In our correspondence, Margaret and I continued to explore the ideas we had discussed during her Christmas visit, among them that of possible careers. We had talked of teaching, and I had mentioned how the idea of the ministry as a profession has appeared to me in a new light after my experiences in the Lutheran Bible class taught by the young pastor. Margaret, quite sympathetic to the idea, suggested that she thought I might find the ritual and liturgy of the Episcopal church more appealing than those of the Lutheran. At the time, my knowledge of doctrine was minimal. While teaching at Bellefonte and then in camp, I followed her suggestion. As she had sensed, I responded with warmth to the Episcopalian ritual and liturgy.

Early in June 1918, as student C.O., I took the R.O.T.C. detachment from Penn State to the camp at Plattsburg Barracks, New York, where we took the oath of allegiance and became officer candidates.

Training at the 1916 Plattsburg camp had been based on the traditional experience of mobile warfare, the war of movement. By 1918 reality had displaced tradition, and methods of trench warfare determined our training. In 1916 at Plattsburg, using the famous Springfield rifle, we had fired at targets at five and six hundred yards; in 1918 we learned rapid fire with English Enfield rifles at two hundred yards at grouped enemies mounting an assault. Individual combat training in 1918 took much of our time. For bayonet training we confronted bloodless, inanimate dummies motionless on stakes, but the training commands left no doubt that each of us faced a personal enemy. Commands full of hate and distressing detail drove us on.

"Grunt when you shove your bayonet into his guts, twist it."

"Sometimes suction in the wound prevents pulling out the bayonet; put your foot on him and jerk your rifle; if that won't work pull the trigger, then you'll have it out."

"Swing up your rifle butt and get him in the groin; that will stop him."

"If you are too close to thrust your bayonet drop the butt and shove the bayonet into his throat."

Our training always held before us the idea of personal confrontation with an impersonal being called an "enemy." One dared not think that the target of the bayonet thrust was perhaps a husband, father, brother, son, lover—an ordinary human being like oneself. The word "enemy" blinded us to this awareness and presented the object as something that would kill us unless we killed it first.

The sensitive and imaginative among us could not help but find conflict between the utter brutality of the behavior for which we were being trained and the moral values on which our lives were based. We had to accept the work we had to do and try somehow to do our best to mitigate the severity of the injury to our personalities; solutions for the sensitive would be long in coming, but forever denied some, as our postwar hospital population pathetically demonstrated. Acutely aware of my own conflict of values, I attended the Sunday morning services at the Episcopal chapel and, as the days passed, gave much thought to my own difficulty. I knew, however, that in spite of my conflict I would continue doing what I saw to be my duty. But the haunting question of "Why did one, I, have to kill?" would not go away.

Monday afternoon of the last week of camp, on our return to barracks after instruction, an orderly told me to report to the Orderly Room for a short interview with the company commander. Making sure my pocket flaps were buttoned, the dust off my shoes, and my hair combed, I knocked on the door.

"Come in."

"Candidate Cressman reporting, sir."

"At ease," said the C.O. — incidently the best I ever had. Then coming around his desk, he leaned back against it.

"I am recommending you for a commission, Cressman, but because you are not twenty-one you will not receive it. You will return to civilian life. In that case I am interested in your plans."

"I expect to enlist, sir."

"I thought you would, but I want to suggest you not do that now. There is a good chance the draft age will be lowered and then you will receive your commission. You have too much training to enter the service as a private. That's what you would have to do if you enlisted. Wait a few weeks to see what happens and then decide."

"Thank you. I shall think it over, sir."

"Here is something else, Cressman: I am appointing you company commander for the last three days of camp. Report here at 0800 hours Thursday morning." Then extending his hand, not as my C.O. but as my friend, he said, "Congratulations, lad, and good luck."

"Thank you, sir." I did an about-face and went through the door held open by the orderly and returned to my bunk, scarcely able to contain my pride and gratitude, bittersweet to be sure, but through no fault of mine, at this ending to my R.O.T.C. service.

Three or four weeks after my return from Plattsburg, a press release announced that the Field Artillery Central Officers' Training School at Camp Taylor, Kentucky, was soliciting civilian applications and outlined the method of applying. Since I had heard nothing further on the Plattsburg recommendation for a commission, I decided to apply. Applicants underwent a stiff scrutiny before acceptance or rejection, decided by the school in order to be free of political influence. I was accepted and instructed to report to Camp Taylor on August 22, 1918. There I would take the oath of allegiance and enlist for "the duration" as a commissioned officer if successful or, if not, as an enlisted man by way of the replacement depot for overseas service.

Dad drove me to Phoenixville, three miles further than to Pottstown, to take the train. He had a patient in the vicinity whom he could see after my departure. My train would take me to Philadelphia, where I would change to another, eventually to arrive at Louisville, Kentucky.

Dad and I were facing a different kind of "good-bye" from all others we had known. We had to wait some time for the train's arrival. We talked for a few minutes. Then constraint fell upon us as it always does when tension is almost unbearable. We walked back and forth, almost avoiding each other, making such banal remarks as, "The train must be late."

When the train finally arrived, all pretense of nonchalance collapsed in the reality of parting. We turned to each other and smiled.

"Good-bye, Dad."

"Good-bye, Lute."

Then, compressing our lips tightly, we shook hands. When we separated, I discovered that all the while Dad had been hiding some bills in his hand. These he pushed into mine. Neither of us said a word. I climbed aboard. The value of the bills? I have no idea — perhaps five dollars, perhaps more — but at that moment the love they expressed was beyond measure.

As she had promised, Margaret met the train at Philadelphia. Following lunch at her mother's club, we went to the station. Promising to write each other, we kissed good-bye. I boarded the train and found my seat in the coach. As the train began to move, my last sight was of Margaret's back as she walked up the exit ramp to the street, not looking back.

My granddaughter, Pat, up on Fedor, a Hanoverian dressage horse (owned by Betty Hague), at Elk River Club, Banner Elk, North Carolina, July 1987. She is wearing my spurs from my second lieutenant days in 1918.

Lt. L. S. Cressman, 1918.

On my arrival late the next day at Camp Taylor, I took the oath of the soldier for "the duration" and was assigned with my newly arrived companions to an "observation battery" for a two-week period of screening training. After successfully completing that test, we became the Seventh Training Battery, graduation date, December 4, 1918. Here, too, it was my good fortune to have an unusually fine commanding officer, First Lieutenant W. M. Robinson.

After two weeks in the training battery, I became acutely aware of the contrast between this training and that from which I had just come at Plattsburg. There, it was personal confrontation with an enemy; here, we found ourselves parts of a great machine organized for destruction. The object to be destroyed was always spoken of as the "target." Of course the "target" might be enemy troops, but the gunners did not see them and psychologically, on me at least, the effect was quite different; the whole training process in the artillery became a quite impersonal activity. We were learning to fire three-inch guns at unseen targets, directing our fire by the use of probability tables and information on atmospheric conditions, nature of the target, and so on supplied by tables or other sources such as the engineers. The gunners "laid their guns" on the "target" by setting certain instruments on the pieces in response to commands from the executive officer.

Each gun crew, as well as the battery of four guns, was a closely knit, disciplined, and cooperative unit, with each member trained to perform a specific task but capable of taking over in an emergency for a disabled crew member. Eighty-five percent of the instructional time at the school, eleven weeks, was allotted to developing skills in the use of guns, involving, of course, much besides firing them; in contrast, only fourteen hours were devoted to pistol drill (for personal combat) and guard duty combined. The twelfth week, the battery was in the field being tested in the practical application of what we had learned about the handling of guns in the previous weeks.

Our lives were swiftly swept on by the rapidly unrolling outer scenario, but in my infantry camp the inner one dominated. Here, each one of us had to adapt to the swirling currents of history, the outer scenario, some more aware than others of the significance of the problems. I became acutely aware of the necessity to adapt and still maintain my personal integrity.

In the short period of two months I had moved from a way of life devoted to training for personal combat and all its brutality to one organized to develop a high level of discipline and skills designed for handling three-inch guns to destroy impersonal "targets," but never, with good luck, for engaging in personal combat. The end purpose of the training was the same—though opposite sides of the same coin—the destruction of our country's enemies. Our success in the school was determined by our proficiency in the required skills measured by regular, school-type examinations. It was truly a "school." Each experience made a sharp and complementary impact on my personality: an image of the total nature of war. Juggernaut, "Lord of the world," WAR rolled on its relentless, diabolical course, feeding its insatiable appetite with the lives of a whole generation of the young men of the Western world, men who would have been their nations' leaders in the years they never lived to see.

I was young as, of course, were many others. My family background with its humanizing influence and my rich, humanistic college studies had sensitized me to the intellectual and moral demands with which I had now come face-to-face. A limited amount of reading material, sent mostly I think by Margaret, helped me explore my problem, one I discovered was not mine alone, but shared with many thoughtful people everywhere.

Our rigorous study and training schedule—forty-five hours per week plus two hours supervised study each night except Wednesday and weekends—offered little opportunity for establishing close relationships. I was simply one in an organization, 14,000 strong, all dedicated to the same end. Within that mass of men, each person's life was essentially solitary. I could share my moral concerns only with the authors of books in my search for some resolution to this conflict of moral values, both for the individual and society. I remembered Tennyson's lines, which had made a deep impression on me:

> For I dipped into the future, far as human eye could see,
> Saw the Vision of the world, and all the wonder that would
> be;
>
> . . . .
>
> Till the wardrum throbbed no longer, and the battle flags
> were furled
> In the Parliament of man, the Federation of the world.
>
> There the common sense of most shall hold a fretful realm
> in awe,

And the kindly earth shall slumber, lapped in universal law.
(Alfred Lord Tennyson, *Locksley Hall*)

Obviously, others had addressed these concerns well before me.

My immediate problem was, of course, to carry out to the best of my ability the duty I had assumed when I took the oath of a soldier. But I became increasingly aware that after the war I must commit myself to the ideal of eliminating war, the great moral cancer of modern civilization. I was also aware that to make any contribution I would have to work within a significant institution. The idea that the Christian ministry could be the vehicle, an idea given life by that exciting young Lutheran pastor in his Bible class at Penn State and implied by Mother's statement about my perhaps becoming a minister like my Uncle Mark, certainly influenced my decision. While training to be an artillery officer I made that decision, one to influence my whole life. After the war I would study for the ministry, the priesthood of the Episcopal church.

The rhythm of our training continued day after day, undisturbed even by the influenza pandemic that sent four of our five commissioned officer instructors at the same time to the hospital—temporary replacements were assigned—and what must have been nearly half of our battery strength, some to return to duty while others had served their last tour. *All* beds had to be carried out each morning and brought in before noon mess call by those of us lucky enough not to be infected. I belonged to that group. Our class sections were simply smaller. Those who recovered sufficiently to be assigned to duty gradually rejoined the battery. In an effort to control the disease, *all personnel* were confined to camp for six to eight weeks and to the battery street for four weeks except for marching out to instructional areas.

One afternoon's experience, November 4, not concerned with the flu, is worth mentioning; it was not my good day. We faced an hour of driving instruction with guns and caissons. I was assigned to the wheel horses, a pair of huge black brutes, to drive a gun and limber through a thicket of scrub oak and other obstacles on land evidently farmed long ago. Major McBride, chief of driving instruction, was in charge. He was a "regular," a rather slight man wearing an old campaign hat, the brim of which had lost most of its stiffness. He sat his horse as though they had always been together. We were "standing to horse," waiting for the command to mount.

"Prepare to mount!" came the command.

At that, each man was supposed to grasp the pommel with his left hand, put his left foot in the stirrup, and with his right hand grasp the cantle.

"Mount!"

Everybody but Candidate Cressman rose into his saddle. He was still trying heroically to get his left foot into that frightfully high stirrup. His struggle was not unnoticed, for the detail did not move out. At the third attempt Candidate Cressman, by jumping, got his foot in the stirrup and joyfully, if late, joined his fellows.

I had heard a sickening sound on my left leg as I made that successful effort to mount. As we moved out, I looked: I had ripped the inner seam of my left breeches leg from knee to crotch, producing a horrible gap. The character of this disaster becomes apparent when one realizes that we had only two pairs of breeches and had to have one clean pair ready at all times for inspection. As I recall, I "made do" by a generous use of safety pins and being careful how I stood in formation for a couple of days until I could get to the camp tailor.

During that drive—we had a general route to follow with special instructions as we went along—our gun had to make a sharp turn through some sparse brush with the major sitting his horse very close to our turning point, a fence post around which we were supposed to go. For some reason—I don't know whose fault it was, perhaps mine on the wheel pair—as we turned I looked back to see if we were clearing the post and to my dismay saw that we were not in spite of my best efforts. The hub of the right wheel of the gun caught that post and knocked it over as though it was just what we intended. We kept going, and I saw the major watching. The only rebuke was his "Lucky it was rotten, lucky it was rotten."

We drove to the open field to turn the matériel over to the next detail, and as we came out of the brush we could hear a strange noise, a cacophony of sounds. Our relief brought us the news that the armistice had been signed and that the strange noise was celebration at the replacement depot.

We marched to our next class. The next morning we knew that we had heard a false news report. Classes went right on.

During the middle of the night of November 10–11, I was awakened by the lights of our barracks suddenly turned on, loud voices, and the sound of feet.

"Wake up, wake up, the armistice has been signed! Come on, get up!"

"For God's sake, turn out those lights and be quiet; we want to sleep," was the reply after having had one "wolf" cry.

The lights went out and we to sleep. Reveille sounded at the same unearthly hour in the morning, and all classes went on as usual although the report of the signing this time was true.

Orders soon came to discharge all those who wished to be and to continue the school for those who desired to remain to finish the course, but to be commissioned in the Field Artillery Reserve Corps. For them the school would continue as planned. I chose to finish the course.

We spent the last week in the field at West Point on the artillery range. How well I remember that first time our battery fired! I was on the battery commander's detail manning a telephone and transmitting firing data to the executive officer (a candidate), who gave the commands to fire. Our detail was on a slight rise some little distance behind the battery, our target a couple of miles or more distant, announced as an abandoned shack, seen faintly against the background of forest. Two or three ranging shots were fired close enough on target for the command to fire a salvo. Four guns crashed in unison. As the smoke and dust cleared, the target was no longer to be seen. We had learned well the skill of the destroyer.

Graduation, December 4, was a very low-key affair. We were all packing that morning to get in to Louisville to catch trains to our various homes. Our barracks, our home for four months, was a shambles. A sergeant came in and ordered the familiar "Everybody outside, on the double, as you are." I had one legging laced up and the other only halfway, but out I went and into formation. The best of our younger officers was standing with papers held by an orderly. Each envelope held an honorable discharge, a commission as a second lieutenant in the Field Artillery Reserve Corps—a few, because of legal requirements setting age limits for the different grades of officers, received commissions appropriate to their ages—and, as I recall, travel authorization papers. As each name was called, the candidate presented himself on the double to the officer, saluted, and announced,

"Candidate so-and-so, sir."

A handshake, transfer of the envelope.

"Congratulations."

"Thank you, sir."

A salute, an about-face, and back to one's place on the double. I was fearful of what might happen to me with my loose legging cord as I double-timed up to receive my envelope. The officer watched me, and as I made it without disaster, gave me a warm smile. I had completed the task I came for and had a sense of pride. How glad I am now that the end came as it did and that I never had to use my skills as a destroyer and killer of men.

I took the train out of Louisville to arrive at Pottstown early the next evening. Arriving there I phoned home and Dad answered.

"Hi, Dad, this is Lute; I am in Pottstown; can someone come for me?"

"I'll be right over as soon as I look after a patient."

"That will be fine; I'll start to walk."

It was dark by then, and after I had walked about a mile, on the top of a hill, I heard and saw faintly in the dark a horse and carriage coming.

"Is that you, Lute?" came that voice I knew so well.

"Yes, it is."

"Climb in and I'll turn around and we'll head for home."

"How glad I am to see you, Dad."

And life had come full circle from that day at Phoenixville when Dad and I had said our painful "good-bye."

I was home, but where were my brothers at the war's end? The signing of the armistice found them in widely scattered places and in different circumstances.

Charlie, in France after three months in the School of Fire there and three more in the Tractor School, training for the new mechanized artillery, was outfitting for the Front; but his division was ordered home for demobilization instead. After a few days with Mother and Dad, he returned to his position at the General Electric Company at Schenectady, New York, leaving his military gear with Mother to store in their big house. She brushed everything as she hung it out on a clothesline for airing before putting it in storage.

George, in the Ordnance Officers' Training School, on November 11, 1918, and his group were retrieving dud grenades from the range, a truly potentially lethal activity. He took his discharge as soon as possible and returned to his teaching position.

Wallace's outfit, at the Marine Corps Base at Parris Island, South Carolina, was scheduled to ship out for France as replacements for the marine divisions when it finished rifle-range training, a matter of three or four days. The armistice changed the orders and set the outfit instead to Santo Domingo in the Dominican Republic, a far cry from the France for which the men had enlisted. After several months and with some combat experience, he was given his discharge to attend Penn State College in the fall of 1919, where I had enrolled him.

The spring of 1919, to everyone's surprise and delight, brought a large patch of ground under the line on which Charlie's military clothing had hung to air aflame with poppies from seeds he unknowingly carried home in his gear from Flanders' fields.

Dear poppies, may I accept with gratitude on behalf of all your gift of flaming beauty secretly sent to us, to us who did not break faith with you "who died in Flanders' fields"? Your loveliness signaled the end of the war and commanded life, love, and creativity. *Allons*!

One morning two or three weeks after I arrived home, I was luxuriating in peacetime life—no commands, no whistles, no pounding of army boots on the barracks floor as we turned out "on the double," only gentleness again in association with women and children, loved ones, the normal world of peace—when Mother called me to accept a long-distance phone call.

"This is Jimmy Hughes, headmaster of the Bellefonte Academy. The position you helped out with last spring will be vacant, and I would like you to take it again, starting in January 1919, for the rest of the school year and under the same conditions if you are free."

"Thank you, Mr. Hughes. I am happy to accept." I saw my immediate need for work satisfied.

I started, with that acceptance, on a short but significant segment of my Journey. I was painfully aware that I had to plan for the program of studies necessary to prepare me for the profession I had chosen while in camp, but I was completely in the dark concerning the steps I would have to take. At Camp Taylor, I had arranged with the help of a personable young lad, representing the Episcopal church in its service office, for the rector of a church in Louisville to give me on a few Saturday afternoons, when the influenza quarantine permitted and I could get leave, sufficient instruction to prepare me for confirmation. When the rector felt I was ready, he arranged a meeting with the bishop, who confirmed me.

When I arrived at Bellefonte that January 1919, this experience represented my total preparation for my future theological studies. I did, however, have a fine humanistic education, and in my military service I had learned much about the qualities of leadership and their exercise together with an understanding of human relations under conditions more demanding than any academic milieu.

My faculty duties at the academy included proctoring, so I lived in the dormitory and took my meals in the Commons with the students. Of all the academy faculty I remember only Miss Hill, and English teacher, slightly past middle age, with whom I frequently shared the same table at meals. A communicant of the local Episcopal church, she spent her summers as a sewing volunteer in a small convent of English Sisters in a low-income neighborhood on the Lower West Side of New York City, probably making ecclesiastical vestments for the convent's projects. We shared common interests both from past experience and current hopes, and our long conversations were always helpful.

As soon as possible I contacted the young, educated, intellectually stimulating rector of the local parish. He and I became warm friends; my counselor, he really took me under his wing. Through church services and personal, if informal, instruction he helped me grow in my knowledge of the Episcopal tradition, its liturgy and ritual, and explained the course of study I faced through the various steps leading to ordination. To my pleasure he offered to arrange for my admission application to the General Theological Seminary in New York City. He did, and I was accepted as a regular student to start in September 1919, the Michaelmas Term, with some financial assistance assured. Thanks to my rector, I was now really on my way.

I had not the least idea of what the General Theological Seminary was like or of its location in the city. I found on my arrival that it occupied an entire city block, Chelsea Square, on the Lower West Side of New York City between Ninth Avenue, with its elevated line, and Tenth Avenue and 20th and 21st Streets, both residential. The seminary was a highly visible landmark in what was to me a depressing area of tenements, cheap apartments, and business buildings.

The seminary gave me my first but limited experience of living in a large urban center. I took a taxi from the Pennsylvania Station to the seminary entrance at 175 Ninth Avenue. Pulling open the heavy door, I walked into a hallway at right angles to the entrance with the registrar's office on my left. Ahead I looked through a pointed, arched doorway across the seminary close within a long U-shaped row of buildings joined by a high, spiked iron fence. Almost in disbelief, I stared across this refuge of quiet and peace insulated by the closed entrance door from the bedlam that was Ninth Avenue, for the buttress of seminary buildings deadened the cacophony of both motor and locomotive transport that served the piers and businesses on Tenth Avenue. For a moment, surprised and amazed, I looked across this refuge isolated from the city's surging life and realized that this close, its buildings, and its life would be my physical and spiritual home for the next three years. Here I was because, a year before, while learning to be an artillery officer, I had made my decision to enter the priesthood of the Episcopal church. The idea and my commitment to it provided me with the direction and continuity between these two strikingly different lifeways.

Entering the registrar's office, I introduced myself and was warmly welcomed. Registration was a simple, informal process, quickly completed. My corner room, I was told, was on the third (top) floor, Tenth Avenue side. Two men shared a suite, two bedrooms separated by a large study-sitting room. My roommate would be Hollis Smith, an overseas veteran, expected in the next day. Professor Pomeroy, who taught church history, and his King Charles spaniel were to be my neighbors across the hall in a corner suite. Someone was called to bring a hand truck to help me move my footlocker and bag to my room and answer any questions I might wish to ask about facilities. The registrar then handed me my room key. I was a student at the General Theological Seminary!

It was shortly before noon that sunny day when I unlocked the door and walked into our large, light study. The windows faced west across Tenth Avenue and the Hudson River toward New Jersey. I just stood and looked. Down below on cobbled Tenth Avenue people were coming and going, children playing, and a pair of traffic-wise mongrel dogs were scavenging the gutters as trucks rumbled to and from the piers to deliver and pick up loads to and from foreign ports. I could hardly believe it when I saw a small steam engine, preceded by a flagman on horseback, pull a few freight cars on the dockside track.

Above the roofs of the piers and warehouses rose a forest of masts of docked liners and freighters. The superstructure of a liner towering above the piers flew the blue peter from her mainmast to tell all who could see of her imminent departure. Smoke drifted lazily from her huge funnels. Fascinated, I stood absorbing this scene of teeming life. A hoarse whistle shattered my securing silence, the great liner's au revoir. Smoke began to rise purposefully from her funnels and the blue peter moved, ever so slowly, as the little tugs huffed and puffed, churning the water to nudge and push her easily and surely into the channel.

These first few minutes of my first day I watched almost in wonder as I saw, and saw with more than my eyes, the vital processes of a great city at work and how that city was a gateway to an international world. But—*it was all outside the close!*

I knew no one at the seminary or in the whole of New York City. Both this situation and my recognition of how little I knew and had to acquire to participate meaningfully in the learning experience at the seminary insured that this first year I would have to focus my whole attention on my studies. I came to the seminary, as to all my undertakings, determined to achieve the highest standard of performance within my capabilities. To do this I had to accept, certainly at first, the life and beliefs of which the seminary was guardian and transmitter. My attitude was not one of blind acceptance, but I had to know the values well before I could subject them to skeptical scrutiny.

I was happy that first year; I was moving into a whole new world of experience: ritual, liturgies, creeds, history, Hebrew as a new language, and the recognition of the church as a great cultural institution of Western civilization. I began to make friends with other students and had the opportunity to evaluate the potentials, as I saw them, of various faculty members. Most of my life, physically and intellectually, went on within that seminary close. All the while, my horizon expanded to expose new pathways to beckoning landscapes both fair and challenging. As I moved, my life was enriched by my two faithful companions, the *Book of Common Prayer* and the *King James Translation of the Holy Bible*, together my vade mecum of the faith.

The General Theological Seminary of the Episcopal church was founded in 1817 "for the better education of the candidates for holy orders in this Church," to be under the "superintendence and control" of the General Convention and "to have the united support of the whole Church of these United States." General has tried to present "the Anglican tradition in its full depth and diversity. To be general must mean to embrace and incorporate all those triads of which Anglicans are so fond: Scripture, Tradition, and Reason; Catholic, Evangelical, and Liberal; High, Low, and Broad; Present, Past and Future; Doctrine, Discipline, and Worship; Academic, Spiritual, and Practical."[12] In its long history, General has reflected in its character great outside movements: the Oxford Movement of the 1830s and 1840s was the source of its catholic ideals; the development of science toward the end of the last century provided the basis for the "liberal intellectual tradition in theology."[13]

My first year at General, 1919–20, enveloped me in a new kind of world, a world of order in the seminary close, completely alien to that of my last two years of college with military service a certainty and the final period of military duty where far distant fortunes on the battlefield decided the future. In a religious organization where conformity is usually the rule, General's tradition of tolerance of attitudes and beliefs and respect for the individual's integrity was a remarkable achievement. This extraordinary atmosphere of intellectual freedom and integrity was never talked about, it was just there, a part of General, accepted without question like the air we breathed. Often we questioned an individual's judgment, intelligence, or competence, but never his integrity. My sense of integrity, cultivated by my parents, found a comfortable and reinforcing home at General and would be the final judge or censor of my behavior both as a student and later as a priest.

A systematic lifeway accepted without question or reflection ordered our activity as seminarians. The different doctrinal and liturgical commitments responded to a common ordering force: the repetitive rhythm of the daily offices of the *Book of Common Prayer*, Monday through Friday, throughout the academic year. Faculty and students jointly shared in the chapel the same experiences: the early morning service—thought of as the Holy Communion or the Mass according to the doctrinal preference of the individual—the exultant Morning Prayer to start the period of classes, and at six o'clock the triumphant Evening Prayer (Evensong) with its benison at day's end. No sermons, no exegesis of any kind except on special, infrequent occasions interrupted the cadence of these rituals. Some persons crossed themselves at appropriate times, others never; but these external forms were ephemeral, idiosyncratic, for each accepted the *basic elements of the faith* embodied in the offices in the *Book of Common Prayer* and repeatedly made visible and audible by the rituals and liturgies of our daily services. The historic liturgies with their beauty of language and accompanying rituals drew us as a body into the continuity of the great Western Catholic tradition to strengthen the sense of order. The chapel, even now, provides my image of the seminary.

Secular life, too, within the close generally moved to a common rhythm. The seminary had its own kitchen, trained dietitian, and cooks. All meals were taken in common at scheduled times in the beautiful refectory in Hoffman Hall, designed on the pattern of Magdalen College, Oxford University. At one end, on a low platform extending completely across the hall, was the High Table where the Fellows and unmarried faculty sat — I, too, my last year as a Fellow. At the opposite end was the raised minstrels' balcony or loft. Students sat at small tables for six or more and served in rotation as waiters. Regularly scheduled hours each week found various faculty families "at home."

All students wore caps and gowns to lectures; and the amount of wear-and-tear of a gown revealed the wearer's class. Faculty wore caps, gowns, and hoods to lecture, except dear, elderly Father Jenks. He always appeared in his cassock to read his lectures on St. Thomas Aquinas, sometimes with hesitant difficulty, for his aged typescript had faded badly in places. His intonation of the Mass was the most beautiful I ever heard, and he did it with reverent perfection.

These religious and secular patterns of seminary life separated us sharply from the swirling currents of life outside the close. The intellectual atmosphere did not encourage curiosity or turn a mind, eager to range, loose for discovery. One, yes, only one explicit instance of instruction questioning values stands out in my mind starkly against the flat landscape of acceptance. It occurred in Dr. Dickinson (Dicky) S. Miller's class in apologetics, a small class he met in his study. Dicky always used the Socratic method of teaching.

One afternoon as soon as we were comfortable and informally seated, he suddenly jolted us with the question, "Why is sacrifice good? Sacrifice is always held to be an admirable value. Is it, Mr. Stone?" We were off that afternoon to an exciting and disturbing session.

I am not attempting in any way to denigrate the high quality of the professional education provided by General, quite the contrary. Its faculty, like those of other institutions, was of unequal ability and vision; some members were distinguished in their fields, others certainly not. General was a professional school founded for the better education of students preparing for ordination to the priesthood. The basic functions of the priest are to celebrate the sacraments and "be the shepherd of His flock." There are two classes of priests, the regular and the secular. The former consists of those who enter a monastic order and spend their lives according to the rules (regular) of the institution; the latter are the parish priests, who in addition to celebrating the sacraments are responsible for the spiritual welfare of their parishioners. The celebration of the sacraments is the common function binding both together. To provide educated priests for this purpose, General offered studies in church history, philosophy, theology, textual criticism and its results for an understanding and intelligent interpretation of the sacred writings from Hebraic and Christian sources. The individual's response, as in any learning situation, determined the outcome of the process.

But I must say in all candor that I think the seminary faulted us in our pastoral training. To be sure, there was a course in "pastoral theology" taught by a parish priest who visited the seminary to give his lectures. He never initiated or invited discussion. At best the course was innocuous. The only detail I can recall is how he repeatedly used an English walnut separated into halves as a teaching aid. I still see him pull a small, brown paper bag from his coat pocket — he never wore a cap and gown — extract the nut, hold half of it up for us to see clearly, and with a triumphant smile say, "Gentlemen, this is a representation of the human brain." The purpose of the analogy now mercifully escapes me. We, the students, had nothing but contempt for the course.

Administrative duties in addition to his sacerdotal make heavy demands on a rector's attention. A parish is a self-supporting division with its own church within a diocese. The rector with his official lay organization, the vestry, is responsible for the day-to-day administration: budgetary and all other matters involved in the life of the parish. There are also both official and unofficial relations to the diocesan authority, the bishop, that from time to time require the rector's attention. This whole area of our future obligations was neglected.

Although it is true that most graduates went to their appointments as assistants, that is, curates, not everyone did, and all of us should have had significant introduction to that mundane but necessary area of responsibility.

That most sensitive and important of all relations, the priest and the parishioner, in which the priest must be somehow more than counselor, calls on all his reserves to help a parishioner face that ultimate problem, death, or its agonizing, slow but certain approach; this is when the young priest must meet an almost overwhelming challenge to his faith and mind, and this was never addressed. During my fourth year at the seminary, I would have to face that challenge and *on my own*. It would prove to be a shattering experience.

I think it fair to say that the ambience of the close turned the direction of our thinking backward in time and subject matter. It need not have been that way. General, Union Theological Seminary, and the Graduate School of Columbia University had a triadic arrangement by which qualified students at one might take courses, tuition-free, toward an advanced degree at any of the others. The administration at General never, to the best of my knowledge, commended this remarkable opportunity to us.

Father Pomeroy, my informal counselor, called it to my attention and urged me to take advantage of it. I responded enthusiastically to his suggestion, for I saw the opportunity to take my place again in the world of change in which my whole preseminary life had developed and which had left an indelible impression on my personality. So, at the end of my first year at General, I decided to break out of the seminary's refugium atmosphere. I registered in September 1920 at the Graduate School of Columbia University in the Department of Sociology. I chose that field because I thought it would be supportive of my seminary studies. Columbia would become a source of enrichment, an addition to, not a substitute for study for the priesthood.

The same month I registered in Columbia's Graduate School, Margaret, with eager expectation, registered as a sophomore in Barnard College, the undergraduate women's college of Columbia University. Her first year at DePauw University at Greencastle, Indiana, had been extraordinarily unhappy socially and completely lacking in intellectual stimulation. We now had for the first time since our

engagement, three years earlier, the opportunity for close companionship. Together, as we could, we took advantage of the unique
opportunities offered by the resurgent postwar life of New York City
in the theaters, museums, and lecture halls. The theater questioned
many of the "certainties" our generation believed World War I had
deservedly destroyed but were still mouthed by the unconvinced.
Columbia was a mecca for distinguished lecturers from home and
abroad who brought to us word of exciting new discoveries and ideas,
some delayed in transmission from Europe by the war, others the
product of postwar experience. I made friends with Margaret's and
my new associates at Columbia and found myself in a world where
the *future* was much on our minds. My lonely personal existence in
New York City was now behind me.

As part of our training, the seminary expected each of us to establish a connection with a parish for in-service training, perhaps a substitute for pastoral theology. It was not an adequate substitute. Father
Sparks, the rector of St. Clement's Church at 420 West 46th Street,
New York City, and a Fellow of the seminary, had invited me to join
him at St. Clement's. I gladly accepted his invitation. I started with
service in the Sunday School and advanced to greater participation as
I gained experience.

At St. Clement's between Ninth and Tenth Avenues, close to the
notorious Hell's Kitchen district, I made my first real acquaintance
with tenement-house existence. Unbroken lines of brick buildings,
four or five stories high, stretched along each side of the street. Each
building unit was served by a single interior stairway against the wall.
A floor consisted of two "railroad apartments" separated by a hallway. An apartment was a series of rooms continuous from front to
rear, separated by horizontal, partial partitions extending to a narrow
aisle at the hallway side; windows at front and rear were the only
sources of daylight. Each apartment housed one or more families.
Usually a single toilet off the hallway provided the sole sanitary facilities for the tenants on that floor, but in some cases, even in 1920, the
only provision for an entire building would be one at ground level in
the small, enclosed yard or space in the rear. A naked, 25-watt bulb,
continually lighted, hung from its wire over the stairs to wage a losing
battle with the darkness. Father Pomeroy warned me before I entered
pastoral work in these tenements: "When you meet someone on the

stairs always stop with your back to the wall and make him pass in front of you." In all my work there, I am proud to say that I was never molested in any way.

My decision to enroll at Columbia proved to be far more significant in influencing my Journey than the mere act would imply; one must view it in the context of my life at the time. It meant that during the next five years, especially the last two, I would be caught up in the impact on each other of values and ideas between two worlds: those extolled in the life of the seminary close and those of the new world outside, the fabulous world of the 1920s in New York City.

Now my life in the close merged with that of the city. The dichotomy was forever past. Could I build a compromise between the best of the two worlds by which they would provide mutual support? Would confrontation result in antagonism? Where would my sense of integrity, for that had to be my guide, take me? I would have to find out and face the consequences.

My joint studies at Columbia and General added a new dimension to my education. At General, church history and social ethics stand out in importance, primarily because they dealt with life outside the close and brought the church into relation to it. Columbia provided from sociology and cultural anthropology the tools for social studies: the concepts of social structure, comparative cultures (cross-cultural study), and the relativity of values.

At General, church history developed as the companion of economic, social, and political history together with the study of the conflict of ideas (doctrines and their expressions). We intensively examined the lives of charismatic religious leaders and powerful political figures, both secular and ecclesiastical, and their roles in church development. The accepted methods of study of social history were applied to a particular institution, the church.

Social ethics treated social problems as the reactions of groups of human beings to odious living conditions in which society held them. The rise of the labor movement, social insurance in various forms, public welfare, and movements for population limitation were studied in the context of the human condition. The ethical teaching of Christianity set the values that these movements strove to activate through their leaders and mass support. Sir Charles Stewart Loch and the Charity Organization Society, G. D. H. and Margaret Cole, the

Webbs (Sidney and Beatrice) of the Fabian Society, all in England, were associated with movements to change or ameliorate social conditions. Margaret Sanger, R.N., in the United States and Dr. Marie Stopes in England were valiant leaders in the advocacy of birth control. Here was the active contemporary world, and our social ethics class made it ours.

My seminary years became a period of growth in knowledge and understanding of the church, the nature of human society, and their interrelationship. My instructors, Father Pomeroy in church history and Father Hunt in social ethics, supported me warmly in my program of studies. I found no basic confrontation between the aims and content of my theological and social science studies, only mutual support. Information from anthropology, sociology, psychology, and biology, much of it very recent addition to our knowledge, helped me to comprehend the observable, mensurable world of which the church is a part. I saw the church in that world as something more than doctrine, dogmas, and creeds, indeed as a vital part of human life as the source and strength of those elements which support the human spirit and give that meaning to life which is not to be derived from creature comforts, no matter their nature or amount. I felt the breadth and depth of my educational experience was fitting me for significant and compassionate service as a parish priest.

My regular course of study at General would end in June 1922. I was ready to take my canonical examinations for ordination to the diaconate that spring. Since I came from the diocese of Harrisburg in Pennsylvania, I went to Harrisburg to be examined. I satisfied the examining committee and was ordained a deacon April 15, 1922, in Saint Andrew's Church, Harrisburg.

My duties at St. Clement's were now expanded to assist Father Sparks with the services: reading the lessons for Morning and Evening Prayer and assisting with the Mass. I continued in charge of the Sunday School.

I was extremely gratified when the seminary offered me, shortly before graduation, a fellowship to continue my studies through 1922–23. The completion of an acceptable thesis in that time would qualify me for the S.T.B., Bachelor of Sacred Theology degree, the only academic degree granted by the seminary.

In my senior-year study of church history we explored the impact on the church of the intellectual forces of the Enlightenment of the eighteenth century, the rise of scientific thought of the nineteenth and early twentieth centuries, and the Industrial Revolution with its social, economic, and political consequences. One subject, although not particularly emphasized, excited my imagination: the difference between the responses by Protestantism and Roman Catholicism to the same cause or stimulus, the use of the scientific method in the study of the Scriptures, the creeds and historic doctrines of the church. Both denominations accepted the results derived from the scientific study of the Scriptures, but differed widely when the same methods of study were applied to the creed and doctrines of the church and their derivation.

The Protestant response, in short, was to treat the creed and doctrines as symbols of values, as ideals for behavior, resulting often in some clergy turning to preach mostly a social Christianity, whereas others left the ministry to carry out their ideals of service in various organizations devoted to social amelioration.

Catholic doctrine, conversely, held that divine revelation through chosen human vehicles was the source of its basic doctrines and beliefs: the Virgin Birth, the divinity of Jesus, the Resurrection of the body, and so on. Because these elements of the faith were revealed, they could not be only symbolical, they represented reality. The Catholic church also held that, since it existed before it adopted the Bible in its final form in A.D. 367 as the compendium of Sacred Writ, its doctrinal teaching held priority over the Bible; but nothing could be taught as necessary to salvation that was in conflict with the Bible.

Some priests of the Roman Catholic church as a result of their studies did adopt the Modernist position, yet kept a commitment to their vows and believed they could continue honestly and effectively with their sacerdotal duties. The hierarchy understandably took the position that the affirmation of belief at ordination and its repetitive expression in liturgy and ritual each time one celebrated the Mass were in direct conflict with the Modernist's symbolical interpretation that denied the authenticity of "revelation," the essential base of Catholic doctrine. The Roman Catholic priest as Modernist might not remain in the practicing priesthood; he had either to recant or be excommunicated.

I now, to use a military metaphor, saw the first probing by reconnaissance patrols from my intellectual forces armed by my new studies in the social sciences at Columbia University. The probing would go on spasmodically while the main forces were engaged elsewhere.

The autumn of 1922 and the full year of 1923 were filled with significant experiences. The main part of my seminary studies revolved around the preparation of a thesis. Father Pomeroy, during one of our discussions, very much aware of my interest in social-economic history, suggested that I use John Wesley's *Journal* as a source of information for a modest study of the social conditions in industrial cities in England at the time of the Industrial Revolution, a kind of "Industrial Revolution as seen by John Wesley." This caught my imagination and I followed up with it.

The importance of my study—after fifty years when I read a carbon copy of some stage of the paper I found it very immature—lay in the fact that it took me completely out of the ambience of the close, and that with Father Pomeroy's support. The intellectual tools I used in my analysis of Wesley's methods of crowd manipulation came from my Columbia University studies. My thesis was accepted and I received my S.T.B. degree with honors at the 1923 June commencement.

At the same time, I was doing the research at Columbia and writing my thesis for the Master of Arts degree in sociology. Professor W. F. Ogburn, with whom I had developed a warm relationship, thought I might find a comparative study of the educational programs of labor unions and industrial corporations challenging and rewarding. After some consideration I decided to undertake this study,[14] and received my master's degree from Columbia University at its 1923 June commencement.

The year 1923 also brought me to the goal of my four years of concentrated study, my ordination to the priesthood, the end toward which all my study had been directed. On January 31, 1923, in St. Stephen's Church, Harrisburg, Pennsylvania, James Henry Darlington, Bishop of Harrisburg, placed his hands on my head as I knelt before the altar and said the words ordaining me a priest of the Anglo-Catholic church. The impact of this experience was almost overwhelming when, after my affirmation of beliefs, I felt the bishop's hands on my head and heard his words granting me sacerdotal authority and responsibility. I was now an individual in the long line of men in the great historic Western Catholic tradition charged in that position with the highest responsibility both for my own life and

At the General Theological Seminary, 1923.

those of others. The *Book of Common Prayer* from the "Form and Manner of ORDERING PRIESTS" explains my new role precisely:

> Rubric: *When this Prayer is done, the Bishop with the Priests*
> *present, shall lay their Hands severally upon the Head of every*
> *one that receiveth the Order of Priesthood; the Receivers humbly kneeling, and the Bishop saying,*
> Receive the Holy Ghost for the Office and Work of a Priest in the Church of God, now committed unto thee by the Imposition of our hands. Whose sins thou dost forgive, they are forgiven; and whose sins thou dost retain, they are retained. And be thou a faithful Dispenser of the Word of God, and his holy Sacraments; In the name of the Father, and of the Son, and of the Holy Ghost. Amen.
> Rubric: *Then the Bishop shall deliver to every one of them kneeling,*
> *the Bible into his hand, saying,*
> Take thou authority to preach the Word of God, and to minister the holy Sacraments in the Congregation, where thou shalt be lawfully appointed thereunto.

Next, all candidates repeated the Nicene Creed with its amplified affirmation of beliefs. The experience was then brought to a climactic close by the solemnization of the Mass, or Holy Communion.

Each one of us responded to this experience in his own particular way as past events, present beliefs, and future dreams dictated. I was taken to the top of the highest mountain and my guide was no Satan.

"There is *your vision*, my son, the *vision* the *young men* will see."

Then saw I all the kingdoms of the world merged into a single great kingdom, but not of geography, or wealth, or power, but of people, of people mingling without regard to color or sex or power or age; all shared one dominating trait and this sharing gave to each equal worth. They were the CHILDREN, yes, CHILDREN, all equal in the Kingdom of God. My guide held out to me no reward, only the opportunity for service in a way now peculiarly mine as a priest to give. With his forefinger my guide placed the sign of the cross on my forehead as I knelt in awe and wonder to receive his blessing. I was left, but not abandoned, to descend alone to the plain.

One August day in 1918 I had taken the oath of a soldier in the service of a sovereign, political nation to protect it against all enemies and to obey all lawful commands, and while in that service I had decided to study for the priesthood. This day, January 31, 1923, I had made a solemn affirmation of belief and acceptance of my status and role as a priest in the service of all people, not a single nation, but of the Children of the Kingdom of God. The overwhelming character of my experience culminating in my ordination made me unaware that challenges past would be dwarfed by challenges future.

After my ordination I returned to the seminary and found myself now much more sensitive to my sacerdotal responsibility. My awareness was not an overnight achievement, but a gradual growth as I continued to assist Father Sparks at St. Clement's. He told me that I would say my first Mass, the early service, on Easter Sunday. Before me stretched the long penitential devotions of Lent in which I would have my first experience as a priest to lead. My absorption in my religious duties took precedence over my involvement in my Columbia University studies during this period, and the reconnoitering patrols my mind had earlier sent out I now recalled temporarily to their base.

The Lenten period came to us in the seminary with special significance, for life in the close moved with the rhythms of the Christian year. The chapel became a repetitive source of emphasis with its daily Lenten services. In contrast to the activities of lay people, we had to give full attention to our Lenten responsibilities and not share them with occupational duties even on a minor scale. I was particularly sensitive in the Lenten period, coming so soon after my ordination, to its message of penitence and hope. The repetitive day-to-day services gradually built up a sense almost of spiritual crisis to be relieved by the climactic joy of the Easter experience: the forgiveness of sins, the Resurrection of the body, and life everlasting. What dramatic sequence can surpass, even equal this long vigil of the soul and its victory? Since I am writing about the Anglo-Catholic (Episcopal) communion and my experience, let me quote the Collect for the Ash-Wednesday service which starts the long period of penance and then that for Easter Day. The Ash-Wednesday Collect states:

> Almighty and everlasting God, who hatest nothing that thou hast made, and dost forgive the sins of all those who

are penitent; Create and make in us new and contrite hearts, that we, worthily lamenting our sins and acknowledging our wretchedness, may obtain of thee, the God of all mercy, perfect remission and forgiveness; through Jesus Christ our Lord. Amen.

The rubric then orders: *"This Collect is to be read every day in Lent, after the Collect appointed for the day."*
The triumphant Easter Day Collect reads:

Almighty God, who through thine only begotten-Son Jesus Christ hast overcome death, and opened unto us the gate of everlasting life; we humbly beseech thee that, as by thy special grace preventing us thou dost put into our minds good desires, so by thy continual help we may bring the same to good effect; through Jesus Christ our Lord, who loveth and reigneth with thee and the Holy Ghost ever, one God, world without end. Amen.

I moved devoutly and without reservation through the Lenten sequence with its heightening spiritual tension made now infinitely more impressive by my priestly responsibility and participation. I knelt with my Lord in his passion in Gethsemane, and during the three-hour Good Friday service I suffered with Him as I shared with the congregation His desperate words of sorrow and despair: "Have ye no compassion all ye who pass by?" And finally that ultimate cry of desolation: "My God, my God, why hast thou forsaken me?"

That night, though emotionally drained and physically exhausted, I looked forward expectantly to Easter morning and my privilege and obligation as a priest to offer the sacrifice of the Mass with its reassuring message of the forgiveness of sins, the Resurrection of the body, and life everlasting.

Well before eight o'clock, the hour of the early service, I was in the vestry of St. Clement's to prepare for my first Mass. Indeed, I knew apprehension as I anticipated this transcendent experience. Could I meet this challenge?

Members of the altar guild helped me put on my vestments. As the chasuble, the special, outer eucharistic robe for the priest, was lowered over my head to drape my shoulders and hang in front and back, I whispered a prayer for help.

Father Sparks came and said, "It's time now." As my server he preceded me into the chapel and the chancel, where he moved to the side. Flowers glorified the altar, and candles on each side lighted the cross. Worshippers filled the little chapel.

I stopped before the altar stairs to make my brief supplication. Now my personal identity dropped away. Every word I spoke, every gesture I made would be that of the priest until the last "amen" was said. I was a priest—a priest ordained by unbroken transmission of apostolic authority and robed in eucharistic vestments, satin and gold, and aesthetically fitted to their holy purpose. The beautiful, ancient liturgies and rituals I would now repeat were the same audible and visual symbols performed by priests everywhere the Anglo-Catholic faith is held. My vision from the mountaintop of the Kingdom of the Children of God and service in it swept through my mind. I believed devoutly and was completely absorbed by the significance of my actions as a priest, unlimited in time and space; my personal identity seemed not to exist. The rubrics (italicized here) of the *Book of Common Prayer* of the Episcopal church make very clear that it is not an individual person performing these acts, for they read, *"Then shall the Priest turn . . . ,"* or *"say,"* etc., in all actions immediately concerned with the eucharist.

The service starts with the priest leading the worshippers gently by prayer and admonition into the presence of God, and then the General Confession is made by the *"Priest and all who plan to receive the Holy Communion, humbly kneeling."* The priest then stands and pronounces the absolution.

Worship proceeds with a heightening sense of exaltation as the priest reads the special *Preface* appointed to be read *"upon Easter-day, and seven days after,"* to sharpen and emphasize the unique significance of the Easter observance:

> But Chiefly are we bound to praise thee for the glorious Resurrection of thy Son Jesus Christ, our Lord: for he is the very Paschal Lamb, which was offered for us, and hath taken away the sin of the world; who by his death hath destroyed death, and by his rising to Life again hath restored to us everlasting life. Therefore with Angels and Archangels we laud and magnify thy glorious Name; evermore praising thee, and saying, Holy, Holy, Lord God of hosts, Heaven

and earth are full of thy glory: Glory be to thee, O Lord Most High.

Then the priest, kneeling before the altar offers this beautiful prayer, fittingly called the Prayer of Humble Access:

We do not presume to come to this thy Table, O Merciful Lord, trusting in our own righteousness, but in thy manifold and great mercies. We are not worthy so much as to gather up the crumbs under thy Table. But thou are the same Lord, whose property is always to have mercy: Grant us therefore, gracious Lord, so to eat the flesh of thy dear Son Jesus Christ, and to drink his blood, that our sinful bodies may be made clean by his body, and our souls washed through his most precious blood, and that we may evermore dwell in him, and he in us. Amen.

"Then the Priest, standing before the Table . . . shall break the Bread before the People, and take the Cup in his hands, he shall say the Prayer of Consecration, as followeth," followed by the Oblation and Invocation:

. . . For in the night in which he was betrayed, he took Bread; and when he had given thanks, he brake it, and gave it to his disciples, saying, Take, eat, this is my Body, which is given for you; Do this in remembrance of me. Likewise, after supper, he took the Cup, and when he had given thanks, he gave it to them, saying, Drink ye all of this; for this is my Blood of the New Testament, which is shed for you, and for many, for the remission of sins; Do this, as oft as ye shall drink it, in remembrance of me . . . humbly beseeching thee, that we, and all others who shall be partakers of this Holy Communion, may worthily receive the most precious Body and Blood of thy Son Jesus Christ. . . .

As the "amen" closes the beautiful prayer of Invocation, the priest receives his Holy Communion, followed by any assistants. At a signal from the priest the communicants then present themselves kneeling at the chancel rail. *"And when he* [the priest] *delivereth the Bread, he shall say:"*

The Body of our Lord Jesus Christ, which was given for thee, preserve thy body and soul unto everlasting life. Take and eat this in remembrance that Christ died for thee, and feed on him in thy heart with Thanksgiving.

"And the Minister [the priest who has consecrated the wine] *who delivereth the Cup shall say:"*

The Blood of our Lord Jesus Christ, which was shed for thee, preserve thy body and soul unto everlasting life. Drink this in remembrance that Christ's Blood was shed for thee, and be thankful.

The Lord's Prayer and one of thanksgiving follow in that order and then the triumphant *Gloria in excelsis*, "Glory be to God on high, and on earth peace, good will towards men. . . ." The benediction by the priest then stills the tumult of the soul:

The Peace of God, which passeth all understanding, keep your hearts and minds in the knowledge and love of God, and His Son Jesus Christ our Lord: and the blessing of God Almighty, the Father, the Son, and the Holy Ghost, be amongst you, and remain with you always. Amen.

As the congregation stood, the priest and his assistant filed out.

In the vestry, as members of the altar guild helped me remove my eucharistic vestments, I could only whisper, "Thanks." Still wearing my cassock, I found a chair. I could not talk, nor did I want to; I wished only to return slowly from my state of exaltation. I knew I could never again experience the same ecstasy. After a few minutes of quiet, I rose, changed my cassock and biretta for coat and hat, and walked out to the street, the person, Luther Cressman, student-priest, but certainly not the same one who entered the vestry of St. Clement's a short two hours before.

In peace is ended the long delirious fever of the heart.
(George Santayana, *King's College Chapel*)

After spending a few days of Easter week in the quiet of my family and the peaceful Pennsylvania countryside, I returned refreshed to my life in New York City and picked up again the tempo of my studies temporarily reduced for the Lenten and Easter seasons. At General and Columbia my most pressing work, fortunately in each case, the preparation of theses, was progressing well. In addition to some expansion of my duties at St. Clement's, I accepted an invitation to offer the early Mass once a week at a small Anglican convent of English Sisters in a low-income area not far from the seminary. I found this service one of the most satisfying experiences of my career: an eager, committed young priest offering the sacrifice of the Mass to a small, devout group of worshippers with never a shadow of uncertainty of the nature or purpose of our acts intruding upon us.

After the Mass I was served breakfast in the refectory, alone at the head of a long beautifully polished table, my place marked by a spotless white linen doily. My sole companion was a rather matronly Sister who stood on my left, slightly in front of me to be at my service, her arms folded under her habit. After serving my breakfast she respectfully waited for me to start any conversation, as was only seemly when appointed to serve the young priest. I discovered in one conversation that I was serving in the convent to which Miss Hill, who taught English at the Bellefonte Academy where I taught before coming to the seminary, came each summer to sew for the Sisters.

Margaret's undergraduate years at Barnard were coming to an end in June, and she planned to enter the Graduate School at Columbia to work for her doctorate in anthropology. Since I would have a large segment of the work for my doctorate completed in June 1923, I decided to continue with that program.

Margaret and I had been engaged for nearly six years, and decided that, even though we would still be students, we should plan to marry before beginning the fall semester at Columbia. My service at St. Clement's was terminating, but I had an appointment to a small church in a New Jersey suburb where I would conduct the regular Sunday services, those on major feast days and any special services: baptisms, marriages, and funerals. I could live in New York and commute. A small but reasonable compensation was provided.

Margaret had accepted the offer of part-time secretary to Professor Ogburn, under whom we had both studied. In addition she received a small "fellowship" through the courtesy of Ruth Benedict, her close friend and mentor and assistant to Professor Boas, head of the Department of Anthropology. I congratulated her on her graduation from Barnard with a gift, the *Oxford Book of English Verse*.

Margaret and I had, during our long engagement, discussed at length the personal aspects of marriage as we visualized them: what married love *should* be like, for example, with all the assurance of inexperienced young dreamers. We had ideals both about marriage and the integrity of the participants. We believed, as I still do, that love is the only justification for marriage, and when that foundation no longer exists, dissolution is called for or else the pair prostitutes the marriage bond. We knew that children would have to wait until we completed our graduate studies. Margaret planned to spend the summer with her family and make the arrangements for our marriage. I continued to live at the seminary and carry out my church duties and studies.

My Journey, as I moved along that spring, was really golden. I was, for once in a very long time, "taking things as they were," with my intellectual patrols held at their base. Santayana expresses my mood in a few lines:

> I sought [had found] on earth a garden of delight,
> Or island altar to the Sea and Air,
> Where gentle music were accounted prayer,
> And reason, veiled, performed the happy rite.
> My sad youth worshipped at the piteous height
> Where God vouchsafed the death of man to share;
> His love made mortal sorrow light to bear.
>
> ("Poems," *Sonnet I*)

Late in that halcyon spring, one of our parishioners suffered a tragedy that suddenly shattered the serenity of my life. A young mother giving birth for the first time died in convulsions at the hospital, leaving healthy twins to survive. She and her husband had shared a basement apartment with her family in a building close to St. Clement's, an obviously low-income situation. The father had tried to reach Father Sparks to ask him to come to her spiritual aid, but could not. They then tried to call me, but were again unsuccessful. The young woman died without whatever aid and comfort her church might have given her.

In the afternoon I learned of the tragedy from Father Sparks and was shocked by the news and all its implications. After a short period of reflection I went out to walk to try to put my confused thoughts into some decent order. Had that family had sufficient money to pay for prenatal care and proper food would the tragedy have happened? Perhaps, I thought; but certainly the chances of its happening would have been lessened. My thoughts tumbled on. I felt resentment at the inequalities of life by which needed care for life's basic functions that should be available to all was available only to a favored few with money enough to buy it. As I walked up that avenue enveloped in the sound of rushing traffic, anger at the inequalities and injustices people were exposed to seethed in me. What did the church have to say about this? Our social ethics class showed that the church was not unaware of it, yet as far as our seminary training went it might not have even existed. How could I, feeling as I did, have repeated with any honesty the prayers of consolation the prayer book provided? How could I, when perhaps this death and all it portended need not have happened?

I suddenly felt a sense of relief move over me that I had not been found by the family when needed, for I did not have to meet the challenge. This feeling was short-lived. My sense of integrity pulled me up sharply: Do you think you have nothing significant to say in such a situation? What of your vision from the mountaintop? What of your words at Mass on Easter day? Are you faithless to your vows at the first test? I felt

self-contempt, bitterer to drink than blood.

(Shelley, *Prometheus Unbound*)

That night I went, as I well knew I had to, to call on the bereaved family and give whatever consolation I could. As I walked down the half-dozen steps from the pavement to the apartment's entrance, I could only hope that in some way I could help the grieving people within. As the door was opened to my knock I saw in a very dimly lit room the indistinct forms of a few family friends talking in subdued tones. As I spoke quietly in greeting, I glanced through an open door leading into the brightly lighted kitchen and saw stacks of used dishes on a table. Friends had brought food to be served with coffee or tea, but apparently did not stay and wash the dishes. In a flash I saw what I could do to help, what I had to do.

I went into the kitchen, took off my coat, saying, "Please give me an apron, for I am going to wash dishes, something I am very good at from my boyhood training." Looking surprised but grateful, the two or three women present didn't argue, and one found a long apron and tied it on me. In my clerical collar and vest, wearing my nice long apron, I washed and dried dishes and occasionally chatted until the last caller had left. I was happy, if tired, but I had found something to do immediately helpful to the family. Three nights running before the funeral, I returned to wash dishes and offer companionship to my friends in the kitchen. I could not offer prayers; nor was I moved to.

What I did was purely an act of compassion. My motivation, at least its expression, came not from my religious training at the seminary but from the ideals of compassionate behavior transmitted to me by my mother and father as they served the people of their countryside. I was also, I think, performing a self-imposed penance for what I considered near treason to my vows.

Later, Father Sparks told me the family had told him how much my kindness had meant to them and how grateful they were. The response of the people affected gave me reassurance that my decision to serve in a lowly but useful manner was correct. I felt that I had won back at least some measure of my self-respect.

After the requiem Mass I rode with Father Sparks in a covered horse-drawn carriage, front and rear seats facing and capable of carrying four passengers, for the long drive to and from the cemetery in the Bronx. My memory of that drive is mostly of silence between us. I was too deeply involved with acutely disturbing thoughts for conversation. I returned to the seminary with my mind occupied by what in a rather ill-formed way was a portentous problem: where did I stand with reference to my vows? I knew much self-analysis and loneliness would be my lot ahead as I sought to find answers to the question, answers that would be long in coming, difficult to find, and possibly painful to accept. The search would be my close companion on the next stretch of my Journey, and I alone would have to find the answers and accept the consequences.

An experience of seemingly slight importance but of significant meaning to me occurred that summer at St. Clement's. One Sunday's Evensong at eight o'clock—I talked with my small congregation more than sermonized and believed in the Lord's saying, "Ye shall know the truth and the truth shall make you free"—I quietly urged my listeners, in order to be informed, to try to read more than one source of news, since one source might well be biased. In the vestry following the service, Father Sparks said to me quite curtly, "Don't preach any more of that New Republic stuff here." I did not reply.

During the summer I took up again my exploration into the subject of Modernism. Continued reflection after my earlier shocking experience at St. Clement's along with the implications of some of my Columbia University studies and others at the seminary began to raise strange misgivings in my mind. Yet, as I continued performing that beautiful ritual of the Mass, I always was rewarded with a feeling, a sense of emotional assurance, of security. Strange misgivings and from the same experience a sense of assurance and security—what was the nature of this disturbing partnership in my mind? I sensed feeling a certain kinship with the Modernists about whom I had been studying. Perhaps if I could explain the Modernist's enigma I would be well on the way to a solution of my own. I looked forward eagerly to the continuation of my Columbia studies and marriage with Margaret as we worked for our doctoral degrees.

My life now, as I saw it, would enter a distinctly new phase, organized in a threefold pattern: my religious responsibilities, my academic studies, and marriage. My challenge was, with Margaret, to mesh these three portions into a significant design, a mosaic. The design would inevitably change from time to time as the relative importance of any of the three components might change, but the challenge and the hope would be to maintain the integrity of the mosaic's pattern. The vista ahead was exciting, and I accepted it eagerly.

Margaret and I took our marriage vows September 3, 1923, in Trinity Church, the tiny, rural Episcopal church just outside the village of Buckingham, Pennsylvania, where Margaret was a communicant. Father Pomeroy, my very close friend from the seminary faculty, celebrated a nuptial Mass at eight o'clock in the morning and the rector solemnized our marriage at eleven by that beautiful liturgy used wherever the Anglican service is held: " . . . and thereto I plight thee my troth." We held no mental reservations.

A luncheon-reception for our families and a few special guests followed on the spacious lawn of the Meads' nearby home. About mid-afternoon we departed in the Meads' black Studebaker touring car kindly loaned us for our honeymoon.[15]

We drove slowly, arriving on the fourth day at the summer cottage of Ruth and Stanley Benedict on the shore of Lake Winnepesaukee, New Hampshire. Stanley, a biochemist, was on the faculty of the Cornell University Medical School in New York City. After a pleasant two or three days we drove south toward our destination, Hyannis, a quiet village on Cape Cod, but lingered in Boston for two nights, one of which Louise Bogan and a friend brightened with their company and good talk. We arrived the next afternoon in early autumn sunshine at the little cottage loaned us for the occasion by Margaret's maternal uncle.

I, and I am sure Margaret, too, looked forward eagerly to our marriage, expecting it to provide that wholeness, when added to the intellectual aspect of our lives, we had longed for but until then had not known. We came to each other at marriage as virgins.

Although quite sophisticated intellectually and verbally, we were both physically and emotionally immature. I, four years Margaret's senior and with much wider experience, was the more mature. During these early days of our honeymoon we both, I think, had a sense, an awareness we could not quite conceal that something expected, hoped for, was lacking. How were we failing? We surely didn't want to fail. Margaret writes:

> It was pleasant [on our honeymoon at Cape Cod] to sit and talk over breakfast with a sense of great leisure we had not known before and were seldom to again, as we were both plunging into lives that combined study and a great deal of hard work. Our enjoyment of these long lazy hours did not mean that even after an engagement of five years there were not moments of strangeness and disappointment to overcome.[16]

Margaret's firm announcement as we were settling into our lovely honeymoon cottage that afternoon did little to enhance the full enjoyment of those "long lazy hours."

"We are going to use separate bedrooms; I have a seminar paper, a book report, to prepare for right after our return and I have to do some skull-splitting thinking."

She, of course, wanted to do very well on her first seminar appearance. The book she had to review was one of those stupid publications spawned by the Army Intelligence Tests and written by a psychologist who wanted to be in the swim of things. I read it subsequently, only to find it required little effort to see the fallacies of the author's arguments. Margaret, as she so often did, was dramatizing a situation and, I think, seeking to avoid an experience and a possible emotional commitment she preferred not to have.

We used separate bedrooms. My only memories of the remaining days are of driving to lunch with a relative of Margaret's at Falmouth and the beauty of the rocky coast as the surf broke in the warm sunshine and, on an overcast day, of a drive to Provincetown at the cape's tip. Memories of walks on beaches and drives have been completely blotted out of my consciousness. Santayana's poem, *Cape Cod*, has always been a favorite of mine, partly, I am sure now, because it so vividly recalls my own state of mind and spirit during those days.

Cape Cod

The low sandy beach and the thin scrub pine,
The wide reach of bay and the long sky line, –
    O, I am far from home!

The salt, salt smell of the thick sea air,
And the smooth round stones that the ebbtides wear, –
    When will the good ship come?

The wretched stumps all charred and burned,
And the deep soft rut where the cartwheel turned, –
    Why is the world so old?

The lapping wave, and the broad gray sky
Where the cawing crows and the slow gulls fly, –
    Where are the dead untold?

The thin slant willows by the flooded bog,
The huge stranded hulk and the floating log, –
    Sorrow with life began!

And among the dark pines, and along the flat shore,
O the wind, and the wind, for evermore!
    What will become of man?

I am afraid we were both rather relieved when our days on the cape came to an end. We cleaned the cottage and stashed our bags in the car. I seated Margaret beside me, gave the cottage a final security check, and with a last look toward those symbolic, tossing waves climbed under the steering wheel. I leaned toward Margaret. We kissed and smiled—so wistfully. I started the motor, wheeled the car out on the road, and headed toward New York City. Late in the day we arrived at our little apartment at 419 West 119th Street, eager to start our schedules of "study and a great deal of hard work."

The next day Richard, Margaret's brother, retrieved the Mead family's Studebaker.

New York City of the 1920s was the vortex of new ideas derived from discoveries in science, reaction to and reflection on the lessons of the war, and an awareness that a new phase of life for the Western world had come on stage with the Russian Revolution and the world's response in fear and hope. New ideas vigorously challenged the old; and the old, under critical scrutiny, we often rejected as outdated. There was excitement in the air as theaters, journals, and new types of schools and other institutions responded to the challenge. This was the ambience of the fabled city, available to enrich and certainly challenge our lives. We, the young, accepted the challenge, and gladly.

Columbia University dominated the Morningside Heights district of the city, a middle- to upper-class neighborhood. The president, Nicholas Murray ("Miraculous" to the irreverent among us) Butler, always wished to make the area the Athens of the New World with Columbia its Acropolis. Columbia University, certainly as represented by its administration, the "Establishment," stood magnificently apart from, undisturbed by the turmoil of the city's intellectual ferment to which some of its own faculty brilliantly contributed.[17] The response of students to the intellectual excitement of the city, the flint on steel, depended almost entirely on the individual student and whatever sympathetic comrades gathered about the central one. This situation certainly encouraged individual initiative usually to eventuate in support of the new against the "outmoded old."

As president of the graduate students' sociology club, I unexpectedly met the "Establishment" as opponent. To my amazement I discovered that university regulations required me, as the club's president, to secure prior approval from the administration before inviting a nonuniversity person to appear on the campus as our guest speaker. Most of us were veterans of World War I, some from combat, others with several years of teaching or other significant experience; yet I had to ask the university's permission to invite the stimulating young Lewis Mumford and W. I. Thomas, a distinguished social psychologist, both brilliant lights on the contemporary scene, to address our club on campus. The situation was intolerable. With the support of the sociologists and other student groups, I decided to challenge the administration's regulation.

Our club had as an adviser a sympathetic young political science faculty member holding, as was frequently the case, a joint appointment at Barnard College and Columbia (his name but not the memory eludes me). We decided to avoid confrontation, if possible, for defeat almost certainly lay in that approach. We and Dean Fackenthal, who administered the regulation, had a number of meetings, but with little success. Each time I thought we had a solution the dean, like a slippery eel, escaped from our grasp. Finally, I submitted a proposal: a club would submit a list of proposed speakers to the dean's office; and unless the club was informed of the administration's objection by a certain date before the extension of the invitation to the speaker, it would be understood that none existed. Apparently the dean found the suggestion acceptable, for we never heard anything more about "permission." We had changed the procedure by putting the burden of proof on the administration, which, rather than accept it, dropped the requirement or let it die. The result was the same.

Our little apartment, with living room, bedroom, bath, and shallow alcove about the size of a wardrobe for a kitchenette with the sink and two-burner gas plate, faced onto an enclosed court. Small though it was it had an importance in our personal and educational life utterly unrelated to its physical size. As Margaret and I grew in our new relationship with each other, our friends came in to talk freely about the things that graduate students everywhere talk about. Our closest friends came from anthropology, psychology, and the humanities. We had, or course, other friends besides the close ones so often in our apartment. I was the only sociology representative, and I brought in addition to that field my interest in and association with religion. Here, in pairs or threes and fours, sometimes with more crowded in, we discussed and argued about our interests, ideas, visiting lecturers, theaters, museums, public policy, anything challenging in the swirling postwar world. At different times, Lewis Mumford and W. I. Thomas, when I was president of the sociology club, graced our apartment as dinner guests.

As I relive these days, I like to recall a statement by the distinguished anthropologist, Robert Redfield, from his Charter Day lecture, "The Genius of the University," at the University of Oregon in 1956. It describes the Columbia University experience, at least for some of us graduate students who had the good fortune to be part of the fellowship of our little group:

> When Paul Henry Newman spoke so eloquently of the idea of a university, the one he came to found in Dublin was not really in existence. So he could see it as it should be, "a place to which a thousand schools make contributions; in which the intellect may safely range and speculate, sure to

find its equal in some antagonistic activity, and its judge in the tribunal of truth." And he continued: "It is a place where inquiry is pushed forward, and discoveries verified and perfected, and rashness rendered innocuous, and error exposed, by the collision of mind with mind, and knowledge with knowledge."

The university itself did not produce our informal association of questing young students; but I am convinced that the nature of our experience was possible only at Columbia in the ambience of the city of the 1920s and the seminal haven of our little apartment. We cast in our lot with the postwar world; we accepted its challenges, believing that we held in our own hands much of the responsibility for our futures. At least we had the opportunity for choice; and if we had choice, we had freedom; and without freedom, there is no responsibility.

We, with our roots set in the prewar world, grew into adulthood during World War I, hardly swayed by the gentle winds of change beginning to appear before that storm. The violent shock of the war shook but did not destroy us. In the postwar period we still had a badly shaken but viable root system. The tree we were flourished in the shifting winds of the new years. Products of change but mindful of our past, we met the challenge of the new on our own terms.

We were participants in a critical time of change in human history, observers and critics of the process by our training, and to a certain extent we tried with our own lives to influence the direction of its course. In contrast to the present's seemingly inevitable movement into fractionation of knowledge and dehumanization of life and values, we in those few years participated in a different effort, one toward unifying knowledge from related fields into more meaningful systems and its direction toward the improvement of the human condition, a humanistic goal.

"New knowledge" in Robert Oppenheimer's imaginative expression "transcended the old"; the rapidly occurring and often exciting discoveries of science were used to correct, expand, and make meaningful the old. The information on mutation, the gene, and their roles in biological change, when combined with the new understanding of the roles of the environment with reference to survival of the organism or species, explained how natural selection worked and gave support to Darwin's theory. Out of this combination of ideas came the concept of ecology, the interdependence of plant and animal communities adapted to a specialized atmospheric and terrestrial environment.

Anthropology, psychology, and sociology were merging into a body of knowledge shattering the old idea of instinct or other biological traits as prime movers in the behavior of the individual. Here was the beginning of the behavioral sciences concept, though I think the first use of the expression waited in the future.

It was inevitable, I believe, in the humanizing trend of thought that anthropology should gain a place of leading importance, for its field is the total human condition. Further, it studied all peoples because it held that all lifeways were capable of contributing to the understanding of human behavior. Long-standing theories of eugenics and biological traits as the determining factors in human achievement came under vigorous and often devastating attack.

There was a wave of new communication: books, radio, and lectures to popularize the new knowledge. We were all eager to get any knowledge we could that would help us to understand "Why," as an anthropologist wrote, "we behave like human beings." Paul Henry De Kruif popularized the new discoveries in chemistry and biochemistry affecting human health and disease. James Harvey Robinson wrote the "new history," in which ideas and ordinary human beings instead of only dynasties and upper classes were the worthwhile subjects for the historian's study. Popularization of knowledge by responsible and capable writers furthered the humanization of knowledge. Machines and instruments, very new and scarce in our laboratories, we welcomed to use in our work to expedite our projects, but they were always instruments. The dehumanization of the human being and the loss of the sense of community were in the future.

I am not arguing that our small group was unique or that we represented the whole of Columbia University; I am trying to convey the sense, the feeling of the vitality of a few nuclear years in the small group, to which Margaret and I were central, in a period and lifeway I am sure can never be repeated. It is interesting that the members of the group all devoted their lives to education, even the shy Léonie Adams sharing her poetry with students. Among the close but less intimate friends were Dorothy Swaine Thomas in sociology and Otto Klineberg in psychology, both of whom gained well-deserved recognition. Louise Bogan, from outside academia, needs no introduction to those who know poetry. The really close friends, Margaret, Melville Herskovits, Louise Rosenblatt, Ruth Benedict, Margaret's teacher and confidante, and I have made contributions to enrich the lives of students and others. The future will weigh and evaluate the significance of our efforts, but for us to whom the little apartment at 419 West 119th Street offered sanctuary in the 1920s

> Bliss was it in that dawn to be alive,
> But to be young was very heaven!
>
> (W. Wordsworth, *The Prelude*, book 11)

From time's perspective, three men at Columbia stand out as extraordinarily effective teachers, their influence becoming a part of me. What I write will also serve perhaps as a mirror to reflect my own intellectual growth. My remembrance of these men I give in the order of their ages and not to indicate in any sense my evaluation of their relative influence.

Franklin H. Giddings (b. 1855, Sherman, Conn., d. 1931), head of the Department of Sociology, was in his sixty-ninth and seventieth years when I had the good fortune to be one of his students. I recall an impressive figure with a good head of hair and a full, well-trimmed, salt-and-pepper beard. He had dignity and gave the impression of enjoying an inner security. The small doctoral seminar and his large lecture course on the development of human society provided my formal instructional contacts.

In the seminar he was always excited and pleased when we tangled on some controversial subject, trying to come to some conclusion by the clash of antagonistic arguments—I think he sometimes skillfully directed the course of argument to that end. He always stood to lecture to his class of perhaps more than two hundred students, complimenting us by that gesture of respect and in turn showing that he considered both his students and the subject matter important. By contrast, I sat in the same room, also filled, for a semester, perhaps a year, to listen to the distinguished authority on business cycles, Dr. Wesley Mitchell, who, as far as we knew, completely lacked legs, for he always sat sometimes as though rather bored by the whole thing. The economic behavior he described seemed never to be related to human beings in society, yet the effects of what he talked about were universal. He was much younger than Professor Giddings, who conversely caught us up in the sweep of social history as he communicated with and involved us in the movements. I remember vividly after sixty years a lecture dynamically unrolling through time the sweep of social history in the Middle East. Social history was people.

A generous man, he was interested in his students' progress. When I started work on my doctoral dissertation, "The Social Composition of the Rural Population of the United States," a statistical-demographic study, I wished to change my adviser to Professor W. F. Ogburn in whose field the subject lay, and I went to Professor Giddings as head of the department to make my request. After listening sympathetically to my reasons he agreed that my request was quite proper, but rightly insisted that I should ask my adviser and secure his permission, for me to make the change without it would cause intradepartmental friction. I asked my adviser, and he curtly refused my request. I am sure Giddings knew quite well that I would work informally with Ogburn and maintain formally correct relations with my adviser. If he did, he was quite correct.

Student folklore about professors may not record history, but it clearly provides information about a personality and his character. One story comes to mind. The Russian novelist Maxim Gorky came to New York on a lecture tour. Under ordinary circumstances there would have been no lack of invitations from the socially arrived and the aspiring for the Gorkys to be their guests. The circumstances turned out to be not normal, for the lady accompanying the novelist was his mistress. Mores acceptable in czarist Russia were not in New York. Hotels were no more accommodating than were families. Then the Giddings stepped in and asked the Gorkys to be their guests in their New York apartment. Whether the story was true or not we never knew, but we were sure it could have been, and we warmed to them.

He maintained contact with students past and present through the Franklin H. Giddings Club, membership in which was by invitation. At a meeting of the club, a no-host dinner near the end of my last year, he showed his integrity and unselfishness. Rising to speak, he told how the president of the University of Chicago had come to him a short time before. The president wanted to add to his Sociology Department the best young man in the country in the field of statistical sociology; and he had come for advice, knowing that Giddings was knowledgeable about the younger men. "I thought for a moment, hesitating, then I said, the man you want is in my department: Professor Ogburn. I hate to lose him but I have to recommend him. My friends, Professor Ogburn who is sitting just to my left, I am sorry to say for Columbia but happy for Chicago, will be joining the University of Chicago faculty this fall. We all wish him well."

Giddings was a social philosopher. He carried on the traditions and methods of the turn of the century and the early twenties, but—and this is important—he was alert to the new. In this way he empathized with his young students of the post-World War I generation. He did not throw aside the past, but brought it into the world of the new. Let him tell it as I, too, remember:

> I have endeavored to bring discussion and exposition to date. The nearly completed first quarter of the Twentieth Century has not been marked by the discoveries comparable to those that lifted the second half of the Nineteenth Century above all other years in the history of knowledge; but it has been a time of rectification in science. Logic has abandoned absolutes for variables and pigeon hole classifications for frequency distributions. Physics and chemistry have begun to build from electrons. Biology has become experimental and Mendelian. Psychology has become experimental and objective. It has discriminated between reflex and conditioning; between original nature and habit. Anthropology has discovered elements of religion older than ghosts, and found more variates of primitive social organization than Morgan and McLennan knew. These corrections of fundamental notions and inductions that are data of sociology have made the revision of sociology obligatory. I offer here an individual contribution to that formidable undertaking.[18]

Franz Boas (b. 1858, Minden, Germany, d. 1942), sixty-six to sixty-seven years old when I studied under him, was an extraordinary teacher; he entered the room and went directly to the small table he used for his forearms or hands; he never had a note or any paper. Sitting to position his head so that the right side was turned slightly toward his class to lessen the effect of the sight of the horrible postoperational scar on his drooping left cheek, he began his lecture speaking slightly from the right side of his mouth to insure clarity of enunciation. His lecture proceeded with all the economy and directness of a mathematical equation.

He studied at the universities of Heidelberg, Bonn, and Kiel in that order, with his first specialization in physics, theoretical rather than experimental, and mathematics. This interest changed first to physical and later cultural geography, where, as well as in anthropology, his intellectual approach always reflected the rigorous standards of his earliest interests.

A. L. Kroeber writes:

> In physique, Boas was dynamic and wiry. Below rather than above medium stature, he was well proportioned in every limb in age as well as youth, powerful for his weight, and seemingly immune to fatigue. He never made a flaccid motion nor an over-hasty one. . . . His eyes were coal black and piercing: they were what one saw first and never forgot. His mouth and nose were generous but firm. His black hair, beginning rather far back even in younger years, reared in a bold crest. The whole face and head had in them something aquiline, resolute, decisive and poised. . . .
>
> Hunger or thirst, heat or cold, danger or exposure, exertion or luxury, he took in the same stride. Discomfort he disdained to recognize; often perhaps he hardly felt it, so strong were the drives of his energy. His manner was spartan, his goals unspartan in their breadth.[19]

Boas's doctoral dissertation (1881) at Kiel was "Contributions to the Understanding of the Color of Water." He had followed from Bonn his major professor, Theobald Fischer, a geographer who was shifting his interest from physical toward cultural geography. During the year of Boas's doctorate, Professor Fischer published a long paper on the role of the date palm in North African and Western Asiatic life and later surmised that perhaps sharing his ideas with the young Boas during the writing directed his thoughts toward ethnology.

Early anthropological study was well advanced both in Europe (much under the name of anthropogeography) and America although still in an ill-defined form when Boas was a student. Information on non-European peoples increased in volume as the colonial system brought more and more previously unknown populations to the attention of government officials, missionaries, scientific travelers, and others. These contacts and the diverse lifeways reported in various books and articles written by these observers were to become a rich source of information and a powerful stimulus to students of the human condition.

By 1860 the fact that man had been living at the time of the great mammals of the Ice Age had been demonstrated. The knowledge of the high antiquity of man and the great diversity of his lifeways became a part of the great intellectual revolution of the Victorian Period. Efforts to explain the diversity of lifeways, both as then known and in changes through time, drew mainly upon two explanations at first, a biological and then an environmental one. Adolf Bastian and Friedrich Ratzel, both Germans and contemporaries of Boas, represented, respectively, these approaches, although not of course to the extent of denying other accessory factors.

Boas, with his interest in cultural geography, wanted to travel to broaden his knowledge and arranged a trip to Greenland, an area on which he had written a geography paper. The German government maintained a meteorological station at the head of Cumberland Sound as its contribution to international polar exploration, and here he would have a base for his study in 1883–84. Ruth Benedict writes:

> He embarked on his first trip to the Eskimo specifically to study reaction of the human mind to the natural environment. As a student in Germany in the '70s and '80s, he believed himself a thorough-going materialist in his philosophy, and he imagined that his subject of study among the Eskimo would be to show how their natural environment had determined their sense reactions. A year among the Eskimo taught him how much more complex the problem actually was and this discovery meant to him that materialism, as he had embraced it, was inadequate. He learned that the facts of experience could not be explained merely by reference to laws of physical or material substances; they depended even more largely upon man-made conventions, products of the human mind. These cultural inventions could fly in the face of objective reality, they could be rational or irrational. They had their own *rationale*, however, and he believed this could be discovered only by tracing them in detail in specific cultures. . . .[20]

Boas the geographer returned from Baffin Land Boas the ethnologist by way of St. Johns, Newfoundland, to New York City, where he wrote articles for both German and American publications and made important social and scientific contacts. His experience that winter, 1884–85, although he probably did not realize it at the time, was to have an important influence on his future.

On his return to Berlin he was given an appointment as an assistant in the Museum für Völkerkunde, founded and presided over by Bastian. He also received an appointment as *privatdozent* in geography at the University of Berlin, where his association with Rudolf Virchow, perhaps the most important of those years, developed. Virchow, a great pathologist, was the dominant spirit in the Berlin Society for Anthropology, Ethnology, and Prehistory.

The same year after his return to Berlin he characteristically took advantage of an "exhibition" in Berlin of a group of Bella Coola Indians from the northern coast of British Columbia to study their language and customs, a field study right at home. This experience developed his interest in the Pacific Northwest and led to the long period of study of the area and its people with which his name is dominantly associated. He persuaded Bastian to finance contingently a field trip to the Pacific Northwest coast. On his way he attended the summer meeting of the American Association for the Advancement of Science at Buffalo, New York, where his friendship with F. W. Putnam, then general secretary of the A.A.A.S., began, an association to be long-lasting and significant.

Stopping in New York on his return, he was offered, and accepted, an assistant editorship of *Science*. His American contacts were expanding. He continued his field studies of the Indians of British Columbia at the invitation of the British Association for the Advancement of Science, and became acquainted with E. B. Tylor, the leading British anthropologist and chairman of the B.A.A.S. Committee on the Northwestern Tribes of Canada, thus extending his personal association to a third national sphere. He was now internationally known personally and as a contributor of articles in scientific journals.

President G. Stanley Hall of Clark University, in Worcester, Massachusetts, a newly founded progressive institution modeled on the German pattern, invited Boas to join the faculty and he accepted, starting in 1888. Clark was poorly endowed financially, and the new appointee started at the lowest rank, docent, the same he had held at the University of Berlin but had never exercised. In the summer of 1888 he started his studies of the Indians of British Columbia for the B.A.A.S., a program he continued in for seven years. The first doctoral degree in anthropology in the United States was given under him in 1892 to A. F. Chamberlain, the year of his resignation to accept a more remunerative and promising position as "Chief Assistant under Putnam of the Department of Anthropology at the Chicago Exposition — the World's Columbian.''[21]

One wonders why he left the exciting, exuberant, intellectual life of Berlin for what must have been by contrast, except for the vision of Hall, a *terra deserta*. It is possible that he saw that the Clark appointment offered the opportunity to be nearer the area of his fieldwork as well as the facilities to deepen his control of the anthropological field. He certainly had little financial inducement, for Clark had none to offer.

Kroeber, exploring the question of Boas's motivation, writes:

> . . . He said later [after 1888] that though his boyhood was filled with hopes for the future unification of Germany, he also grew up in the family tradition as an enthusiastic republican and ardent individualist, to whom American democracy seemed ideal. He sensed the German conventions that tended to restrict a young scientist to a routine University career without wider fields of activity. . . .
>
> He added, nearly thirty years after, that he found in the United States an opportunity for activity that would not easily have been open to him in Germany; and that if he were young once more, he believed he would again seek a field in which he could expand freely. At the same time he had come to realize that American individualism, so congenial to youth, is fully attainable only in a young country, and that in an older and denser population self-control is a need in the interest of society, which tends to be imperfectly recognized in a young and still expanding country.[22]

Boas became curator of anthropology in the new Field Museum following the departure of Putnam to Harvard, who later moved to the American Museum of Natural History in New York in 1894. Exactly what happened at the Field is not clear, but some disagreement developed between the scientific staff and the administration; and when the crunch came, Boas was left to face the higher powers alone and lost both the decision and his position. After a short and difficult period financially, Putnam offered him a position at the American Museum as curator of ethnology and somatology, probably sometime in 1895. Columbia appointed him lecturer in physical anthropology in 1896, and in 1899, professor of anthropology. The American Museum in 1901 made him curator to replace Putnam, who left to "assume a directorship at California in addition to Harvard." Kroeber writes at the time of Boas's first appointment to Columbia in 1896, "In less than ten years since coming to the United States he had not only hit his essential professional stride but identified himself with all the widespread domains of anthropology which he, and he alone, was to control thereafter. This was at the age of thirty-seven."[23]

He continued at the museum and directed the research, publication, and exhibition programs for the next ten years, probably its golden period, during which the Jesup Expedition, a full anthropological program of research into the life of the peoples of the Pacific Northwest coast was planned and carried out. After coming into conflict at the museum with a "new, very ambitious director," Boas either resigned or was dismissed but retained as part of his agreement the "editorship and control of certain funds of the Jesup Expedition." His separation from the American Museum was probably a good thing, for now he could devote all his attention to his professorship.

His first two courses at Columbia were Statistical Theory and American Languages, courses that he retained, although others came and went, for the forty years he was to teach at Columbia. Kroeber describes his first class:

> His first class, which met Tuesday evenings at his home around the cleared family dining table, consisted of an archaeologist from the Museum, a teaching assistant of English, and an adventurous nondescript who soon after rolled himself out of anthropology as suddenly as he had rolled in, and who required some quarts of beer in a can from the nearest saloon to overcome the tension of a two hours' session with Chinook or Eskimo.[24]

In my final year I thought I should know something about physical anthropology and so registered for Boas's course, anthropometry. The course moved along fine for about three lectures, and then one morning before starting his lecture he suddenly asked, "How many of you have had calculus?" About half the hands, but not mine, in a quite large class were raised. His face showed no surprise, but he said, "I shall teach you some." With that precise but hopeful statement he went to the blackboard—one ran the whole length of the side wall from the entrance to the end where another continued across the narrow end, a lot of blackboard—picked up a piece of chalk, and started to write functions at the upper end of the long board, coming down the first section, then to the next. He continued until that board was full and then as methodically filled the end one. We were in a state of shock as he returned to his table and sat down. "Now we shall go on." And on some went. Since I had never had calculus and it was necessary for the rest of the course, which dealt mostly with the growth of children, I did not return. Many years later I would teach myself what I wanted but failed to get there.

Boas, as a result of his experience among the Eskimo, changed his theory of the relation of man to his environment and introduced an entirely new method and conceptual framework for the study of social behavior. The purpose and unity of all ethnological study, he maintained, was the understanding of the "relation between the objective world and man's subjective world as it had taken form in different cultures."[25] The kind of study he envisaged was the investigation of the mental life of man as it expressed itself in all aspects of culture, conceived as a study on a par with "investigations of the natural world." The study of mental life meant to him the study of human behavior under tribal social conditions. His experience among the Eskimo had taught him how essential it was to understand their ideas, not his, of how they interpreted experience and the expected behavior based upon them. The investigator had to live with, share the day-to-day experiences of his people; and this is "fieldwork," the basis of inductive study. "If it is our serious purpose to understand the thought of a people, the whole analysis of experience must be based on their thoughts not ours."[26]

He pointed out that institutionalized forms of behavior grouped conceptually in similar categories might in actuality be quite dissimilar in different cultures, for in each their meaning depended on their relationship to other aspects of the culture and the understanding of them held by the particular social group. " 'The first aim of ethnological inquiry must be critical analysis of the characteristics of each people. This is the only way of attaining a satisfactory understanding of the cultures found in wider areas,' and this study would enable us 'to view our own civilization objectively.' "[27]

Professor Boas brought to his Columbia graduate classes the same rigorous standards of scholarship to which he had been accustomed in the German universities. His lectures were always well organized with no excess baggage. He had the idea that the purpose of the university was to teach and carry out research; and institutional regulations which in his opinion interfered with that purpose did not demand compliance. When Ruth Benedict started her doctoral program she wanted to receive credit for courses she had taken at the New School for Social Research under A. A. Goldenweiser and other anthropologists who had been in New York. The New School was not accredited; it was new and outside the pattern of the conventional university, and Columbia refused to accept the work even though it was given by recognized authorities. Boas took up her case and fought it through to a successful conclusion. When Queen Marie of Rumania was invited to the campus to be given an honorary degree, even though her country was one of the most violently anti-Semitic countries in Europe, President Butler announced that classes might be dismissed for the period to permit faculty and students to attend the ceremony on the steps of the Low Library. Boas did not dismiss his class—I was in it—saying we had work to do, the regular lecture, and he considered that more important.

His lectures, always topical, revealed in the course of delivery his basic philosophy of the nature of anthropology and the proper methods of its study and application to problems. Of course he didn't point this out, but it was implicit in his procedure and method of presentation of data. His lectures were not meant to be essentially informational; they dealt with theory and the use of appropriate data, illustrations, to explicate the theory by application. His purpose was to train the mind, free it and make it the superb intellectual instrument it could be, and turn it loose. This he did for the capable and willing.

My study under Boas was probably the most intellectually provocative and important of these years at Columbia both because of its intrinsic value following on my previous experience and because at the time I was facing exceedingly difficult personal problems. The intellectual world to which he introduced me gave me the essential means to analyze my personal problems and make reasonably rational decisions with which I have been able to live responsibly.

When I first sketched these words about Boas I tried to think of some single word to characterize him adequately. It was impossible. These traits, however, I offer instead: intellectual integrity, intellectual courage, discipline. There was a charisma about the man, setting him apart from all others. Kroeber, who knew him so intimately, wrote:

> It has long been notoriously difficult to convey the essence of Boas' contribution in anthropology to non-anthropologists. He made no summating discovery; he had no one slant, no designable and therefore closed idea-system. His ideas were multiple, at once in flux and in balance like the world of phenomena which he dealt with. Hence no label fits him. The best he could find, in groping to make his anthropological attitudes clear to others, was the epithet "dynamic"; which is true enough in a sense but also colorlessly inadequate. It was the man that was dynamic, and his ideas; not any ideology or methodology that he invented.
>
> He was of the Titans—a self disciplined Titan; a Prometheus rather than an Apollo or Hermes. In many ways the epithet of greatness describes him better than that of genius.[28]

What a privilege to have studied under him!

William Fielding Ogburn (b. 1886, Butler, Georgia; d. 1973), the third in my triumvirate of creative teachers, was born in a small town in rural Georgia some fifty miles south and west of Atlanta, a sharp contrast with the birthplaces and total environment of the other two men. Over six feet tall, he moved with the slow grace of an athlete, deliberate and unhurried. Tall, handsome, smooth shaven, and fair, he walked into his classroom, put a few 3 x 5 cards on a little table, then looked up at us with a warm smile of welcome and immediately established empathy with the class—"We're all in this together" type of thing. He was eleven years older than I, and I always felt, perhaps in part because of that, a closeness in our relationship I did not even hope for with the others. I always felt secure with him, rather like the young recruit in his first combat under the care and guidance of his veteran sergeant.

He was reported in his younger days to have been fond of boxing, though his head bore none of the expected stigmata of the activity. He loved tennis; and being tall, ambidextrous with his long arms, he was a formidable opponent. He retired from the University of Chicago, a Distinguished Professor, in 1951 and showed his good sense by moving to Florida. The Old Henchman made a surprise and totally unexpected call on him in the midst of a tennis set; he, like Boas, was blessed with the favor of "whatever Gods there be." Boas answered the call in the midst of a luncheon he was hosting for the staff at Columbia Faculty Club in honor of his friend, the French anthropologist, Rivet. The Old Henchman chose different but characteristically appropriate settings to make his calls.

Ogburn received his master's degree from Columbia in 1909, taught at Princeton in 1911, and received his doctorate in sociology under Giddings at Columbia in 1912. Those years at Columbia saw the changes Giddings was introducing into the field and the development of cultural anthropology. I am sure he had courses under Boas. The fall of 1912 found him teaching at Reed College, the new liberal arts college founded the year before in Portland, Oregon, a place where all the new discoveries in the arts and sciences found a warm welcome. In 1917 he moved to the University of Washington in Seattle. During the year 1918, he served with the War Labor Relations Board as a troubleshooter to investigate and recommend appropriate action in labor disputes, mostly in the lumber industry, that threatened the war program. In this work and at Washington, he was associated with Carleton Parker, a brilliant young labor economist, who when he died, I think from the flu, was reassured by the promise that "Will Ogburn could carry on your unfinished work." These two men brought insight and compassion to the understanding of labor troubles, especially in dealing with members of the I.W.W. in the logging industry as decent human beings often subjected to the harshest of conditions in the woods and facing extremely antagonistic social attitudes. Among the average citizens in the area the accepted attitude was "the only good I.W.W. is a dead one." His experience in this work brought to his teaching a record of enlightening, firsthand knowledge.

Columbia University invited him, and he joined the staff in the autumn of 1919. In 1927 he moved to the University of Chicago, from which he retired in 1951. Sometime during these years, before 1920, he visited the Indians of the American Southwest to see at firsthand the agricultural Pueblo peoples and their neighbors, the pastoral Navajo. He made vivid his teaching at appropriate places by using the firsthand knowledge he gained from this study.

My formal study under Ogburn was in his class, Psychological Factors in Social Problems; it might equally well have been called Social Change, the name of a book he had just published. This class met weekly at 4 to 6 P.M. Monday throughout the year. His course, rather like Boas's, concentrated on methodological principles of problem definition and analysis using informational data to illustrate and verify his propositions. He brought to these studies all the resources of the new contributions from psychology, psychopathology, and statistics with heavy emphasis on probability theory and variability. He also called on the contributions of anthropology and brought all these sources of information to aid in the scrutiny of race problems, class differences, labor-industry relations, the family, and many other facets of our social life. He gave immediacy to the problems by drawing upon his personal experience. Theory was always submitted to the scrutiny of facts. What are the facts? If you don't know, find out, and build your theory from them; never impress your theory on your array of facts. This might have been Boas talking or, in a slightly less pointed way, Giddings. Such was the advice the teaching of these three men gave us as they held up to us the ideals of scholarship and helped us into the world of ideas, old and new, which became our instruments in our quest.

Boas wrote, "We [in anthropology] must also inquire whether society as a whole undergoes autonomous changes, biological, linguistic, and cultural in which the individual plays a passive role"[29] but never investigated the problem. Ogburn took us into this field by sharing with us his research on the nearly simultaneous appearance of the same invention or discovery quite independently in cultures without physical or other contact when they have the same cultural bases. This process he called the "inevitability of invention." Modern technological competition among industrial nations is constantly offering evidence of the validity of Ogburn's proposition.

Another concept, I believe first formulated by Ogburn, useful in the study of social change, is cultural lag. This occurs when two elements of a culture, an independent and a dependent variable, are adjusted to each other; then the independent changes, but the dependent "lags" behind and maladjustments in the social structure occur. Since the independent variable is often an element of the material culture and the other of the nonmaterial, such as values, the change in the values appropriate to the change in the independent element lags behind and social problems result. Of course, all these things involve people, but the concepts show how the changes are structured and provide for a method of analysis. Both these concepts are of extreme value for the social or political planner.

My association with Ogburn ripened into a warm and lifelong friendship. He suggested the subject for my master's thesis. When my adviser refused my request to change to Ogburn for my dissertation and I reported the outcome, his comment was, "My God, Luther, has it come to this?" He served, however, informally as my adviser. When I was discussing a possible doctoral research thesis project, his advice was, "Don't try to do your magnum opus now; there are lots of years ahead. Get a good small research problem, get it done, and get your union ticket [Ph.D.] and get out." It was he who recommended me as the best man for the field they wanted to develop at the University of Oregon: "A person to direct advanced research in the social sciences and develop the field of cultural anthropology." I didn't let you down, old friend.

These three extraordinary men, High Priests of Learning, to use René Dubos's felicitous phrase, each having a distinct and strong personality, complemented one another in their educational impact upon me; they shared, too, certain significant values. They were interested in people, the understanding of the individual, for it is the individual who behaves; each was interested in the development of the potential of the promising student; implicit in all their teaching were the concepts of freedom of inquiry and the right of dissent as basic to all learning. I drew from their examples the values and methods I would use professionally for the rest of my life. It is significant that I studied under these three men at the same time when, because of my previous experience, I was ready and when future personal problems were coming into sharper focus. What these men gave me would be a critical help in their resolution. My years under them gave me a richness of experience not often offered a student even in a great university, and I offer these words in brief testimony.

Margaret started her graduate studies in the fall of 1923, the same year I had received my master of arts degree, but in June. She planned to complete her work in two years, an extremely heavy schedule even if one had no outside work or commitments. The completion of her schedule as planned would enable us to finish our programs at the same time, June 1925. In her first year she also had to finish her master's thesis in psychology, a project of psychological testing she had started the summer before. This project, in addition to her full program of anthropological studies and her part-time secretarial work for Ogburn, saddled her with an extraordinarily heavy load. The fact that she was entering into a new network of personal and intellectual relations added a further burden, but one in which she was psychologically at ease and quite happy.

Late in the summer of 1924, Margaret attended the meetings of the British Association for the Advancement of Science at Toronto, at that time an extremely small group where close association was inevitable. Here, for the first time, a realization came to her, one that would influence her whole later career: that each anthropologist has his or her own group of "people" and is recognized as the authority on that "people." She returned convinced that she, too, would have to have "her people." The idea flowered; she knew that she did not want "her people" among the American Indians, where everybody else seemed to be well established. The idea of finding "her people" became a driving force.

My schedule of work was equally heavy, but of a different nature; it lacked the pressure-cooker atmosphere of Margaret's. In addition, I think that I had a different method of meeting problems. When I undertook a project—for example, training at officers' school, studying to be a priest at the seminary, or graduate study at Columbia—I concentrated on each program with the intent to fulfill my objectives to the best of my ability. Other considerations and future plans were laid aside until the job was done. What I would do after completing my training, I would decide at that time. Margaret, however, was always looking, planning far ahead, and her immediate commitment became subordinate to her future goals. My pattern in this respect, deep-seated apparently from my boyhood, served me well all my life. It was pragmatic because I could concentrate on the immediate task, do it on its own terms to the fullest depth required and not in relation to some possible future events. I believe this personality difference between Margaret and me was far more important in shaping our relationship and value systems than is apparent from a casual glance.

I still had my pastoral duties at a small mission church in Brooklyn on Sundays and other days as an occasional marriage, funeral, catechetical class, or other special event called me. The work carried considerable responsibility, was gratifying, and I enjoyed it, especially the Sunday Masses. The compensation was small but, with Margaret's income, sufficient to support us. Margaret in *Blackberry Winter* mentions that I had a small graduate fellowship,[30] but that had been for my last year at the seminary, 1922–23. In my first year of doctoral study, I was offered one of two fellowships available in the Sociology Department at Columbia. I would have had to give up my pastoral work to accept it. I thanked the department and refused the offer.

Well into my first year, a fellow student, C. Luther Fry, asked me to help him prepare for his doctoral written examinations. He explained he could not pay me cash, but he offered something of value instead. The Institute of Social and Religious Research, of which Fry was a staff member, wanted a study made of the social structure of the rural population of the United States that lived outside of incorporated areas, using duplicate census cards in its possession as the sample. They had no money for the study, but—and this was important—if Columbia would approve the project as a suitable thesis research subject and accept it as my dissertation, the institute would publish the report and have a galley proof ready at the time of my examination. Since no one at Columbia then could receive the doctoral degree without having the thesis either in published form or in galley proof as evidence that it was in the process of publication, Fry was offering me the answer to the graduate student's prayer. With Ogburn's advice fresh in my mind, I hastily accepted Fry's offer. With my help he passed his exams, and my research went through without a hitch, to be published by George H. Doran Company.[31]

In *Blackberry Winter*, Margaret, for some reason unknown to both of us, wrote, "It was a hectic spring, Luther had to finish his thesis, *which dealt with the disappearing rural church*" (emphasis added).[32] I had sent her at her request "to avoid making errors of fact" in her autobiography a complete bibliography and vita. She was never able to explain her error, one, needless to say, she deeply regretted as do I.

One evening early in the spring semester of 1925, a representative of the Department of Government (an umbrella name for several departments) at the College of the City of New York surprised me at our apartment. He explained that Professor Drachsler, who taught sociology and anthropology, was ill and a replacement was needed for a few days. The Department at Columbia had recommended me and would I help out. Since my thesis research was done, I eagerly accepted the offer since I could afford the time. After it was clear I could handle the work, I was informed that Dr. Drachsler was terminally ill and the college wished me to stay until the end of the year. Of course, I accepted. I knew the experience was good for me, and I found teaching stimulating and challenging.

Margaret, during the winter, had succeeded in persuading Professor Boas to support her desire to go to Polynesia for her year of fieldwork. Boas always felt a personal as well as a professional responsibility for his students in the field. Instead of acceding to her request to go to the remote Tuamotu group in the Marquesa Islands, he suggested that she go to American Samoa, a much less remote area, where a boat touched every three weeks unless prevented by storms. The U.S. Navy administered the Government of Samoa — in other words, governed the islands. Margaret agreed to Professor Boas's plan; although American Samoa did not offer the degree of unacculturation she wished, the native culture was sufficiently intact for her to do her study, and she started the necessary planning.

While I was home with my family for a few days that spring, I told Dad about Margaret's plan to go to Samoa, that it was a safe place and administered by the U.S. Navy. He looked at me reflectively for a moment, as though dredging up some memory from the distant past, then said, "I wonder if this would help Margaret." He reminded me about the graduation night of the University of Pennsylvania Medical School when, too young to receive his own diploma, he had stood in for a friend who was entering the Navy and had been ordered to his ship just before the graduation exercises. This friend was now surgeon-general of the U. S. Navy, Rear Admiral Stitts. Dad offered to write him if I thought it would help and collect on that promissory note he had held for so long. I could only say, "We have it made, Dad." He said he would write, and in a few days came the reply: "Dear George: I shall instruct all Navy personnel under my command in Samoa to do everything possible to facilitate the success of your daughter-in-law's project. . . ."

In addition he provided Margaret with a letter of introduction that was invaluable. Margaret wrote in *Blackberry Winter*:

> Without the letter from the Surgeon General, I do not know whether I would have been able to work as I wished. But that letter opened the doors of the Medical Depart-

ment. The chief nurse assigned a young Samoan nurse, G. F. Pepe, who had been in the United States and spoke excellent English, to work with me an hour a day.[33]

I regret that Dad did not live long enough to read that gracious acknowledgment; he would have been so pleased.

The subject of juvenile maladjustment and delinquency as a function of adolescent growth held in the early 1920s an important position in all discussion of public policy related to it. There were two scientific theories: one held that, since adolescence was a universal phenomenon of human growth, the stresses and their various forms of deviant behavior would be universally expressed as a function of the common factor, the adolescent growth stage; the other was that the stage might very well be expressed in a variety of ways in different cultures as a result of dissimilar value systems. To get pertinent evidence on the problem would require a study in which adolescents from a culture different from ours were the subjects. If, on the one hand, the cultures were different and the adolescent behavioral patterns were the same, the evidence would favor the theory of biological determinism. If, on the other hand, the behaviors were different, then the reasonable conclusion was that the culture influenced the behavior. This question had a strong popular appeal and caught Margaret's interest. It was particularly suited to a young woman, who would work with adolescent girls in studying the problem. It was something no male could possibly do. Here was a perfectly good problem for Margaret to study. She formulated it as a hypothesis to be verified in her application for a research grant. Of course, neither she nor Boas knew what the result of such a study would be; she would go to verify a hypothesis.

With Professor Boas's support she applied to the National Research Council for a fellowship and, on April 30, 1925, received the exciting word of the success of her application. On May 8 she passed her doctoral exams, as, of course, I knew she would. I returned to our apartment to find her the center of a small group of her closest friends in a state of benign shock—the usual postexam syndrome. I walked over, kissed her and presented her with my present, Amy Lowell's recently published two-volume *Life of John Keats*. There was little change in the pressure of work, just a change of focus, as she prepared for her Samoa field trip.

My examinations, written and oral, lacked any significant unpleasantness. For the written exam, my adviser, Professor Tenney, gave me three sealed envelopes numbered I, II, III, each devoted to a certain portion of the field. I was permitted to take these to any place I chose, but each set of questions had to be completed in one day. I asked if I might outline my answers in appropriate detail to avoid much time-consuming writing and reading. Permission was given. I took all the questions and a good supply of blue books down to the seminary library, where I would be undisturbed. Arriving at eight o'clock in the morning when it opened, I worked there all day until it closed at ten and returned to our apartment with the whole exam completed. I was told, quite informally, in a few days that I had passed.

I was scheduled to take my orals using the galley proof of my thesis in its defense. It was customary to provide on the last galley a vita showing the staff members under whom the candidate had studied. I had registered for a course in advanced statistics under Smith, the junior member of the faculty, for my last year. After three or four sessions, it was clear that the course would be excessively time-consuming because we had only hand-operated calculating machines. Also, my return in the course would not justify the time consumed when related to the time required to finish my thesis. I therefore dropped the course to concentrate on the more important area. That was the only course I had ever registered for under Smith. I did not include his name in the list of faculty under whom I had studied because I didn't think the experience under him warranted it. At least that was the ostensible reason, but perhaps my unconscious would have reported it differently.

The day of my oral exam I was in the large departmental office trying to be as relaxed as possible, leaning back against a desk waiting to be called before my committee, when Smith came in, picked up his set of galleys, obviously the first time he had seen them, and said, "Where's your vita, Cressman?"

"On the last galley."

He read the vita. As I saw his face flush—he was that kind—I said to myself, "Oh, oh, Cressman, be very careful!"

In the exam everything went along fine until Smith's turn to question. He tried to give me a bad time, but I took care of myself. With a kind of glee he came to his critical question, but I fielded this successfully by calling on a method from anthropology. That was a mistake, too, for Smith took a very dim view of anthropology and all its methods. Then I almost crawled under the table when the enthusiastic young representative from the law faculty on the committee interrupted: "That will hold you, Smith!" I could happily have dispensed with that friend at the moment, because Smith closed his questioning with, "I don't think you have made your point, Cressman."

Fortunately, the committee thought otherwise, and I was called back into the room to receive their congratulations. In the hall outside, Ogburn came to me to congratulate me personally saying, "Don't pay any attention to what Smith said." In June 1925, along with more than one hundred others, I received my Ph.D. degree from Columbia University. Another "rite" was passed, and in the act I had gained a bit more insight into some unpleasant aspects of "higher learning."

Now that Margaret was assured of her fellowship to go to Samoa, we were faced with the prospect of complete separation for nearly a year, certainly not a state to which we looked forward with any pleasure, but one we recognized as built into the life-style we adopted. I could have remained at CCNY; teaching, together with the church, would have supported me adequately. But I was more interested in gaining further knowledge of juvenile court procedures and studies in population problems, especially the developing movement for population limitation through birth control. England was much further advanced than the United States in these movements, and I thought, if I could get there, I would have an excellent opportunity for additional studies in those fields of interest. The General Theological Seminary had at its disposal the John Alsop King Travelling Fellowship for one year in the sum of $1,000, which permitted the holder to travel abroad and secure the benefits to be derived from that source in addition to the chance to investigate a specific problem or problems. I called on Father Hunt at the seminary under whom I had had a very valuable course in social ethics in which we discussed the problems and the people most intimately concerned with them in this country and abroad. He was sympathetic and instructed me to make out a brief application with my plan of study. I did and was granted the fellowship. So, while Margaret would be in Samoa I would be in Europe on my new study. We planned our reunion in Marseilles in the late spring or early summer of 1926. I would resign my appointment at the little church in Brooklyn and my position at CCNY. Characteristically, I did not worry about any plans after my fellowship; my year in Europe had to be taken on its own terms. After Marseilles, Margaret and I would team up again.

As we moved through our exciting last year of graduate study, 1924–25, it was clear that unfolding social and political events showed the mentality of our postwar society unready to incorporate our belief and hope for the better future for which so many had given their lives. The power centers and probably most ordinary people found it uncongenial to treat with understanding the idea that our postwar world had entered a new phase of social, economic, and political development. The intellectual excitement, the outreach for new ideas so characteristic of the ambience of the great city of New York was to be found in only a few places raising new volcanic cones above the level of the quiet, ancient, intellectual sea. Revolutions, changing the whole social fabric of the Old World, warmly applauded at first, were soon regarded with fear and abhorrence as the "old order [changed] giving place to new." Proposed plans for social reforms that seemed to challenge the wisdom of either of the two dominant political parties were labeled "socialistic," "radical," or, more derogatorily, "communist." Our Congress officially turned our country's back to the Old World, not realizing that it was really the New being born, and validated its decision by refusing to join the League of Nations, thus continuing into mistakenly assumed "splendid isolation."

Vigilante groups in some areas took the law into their own hands, vowing to "keep out the reds." Labor leaders, the organizations they promoted, and union members were all denied their constitutional rights of assemblage and organization, especially in the forests of the Pacific Northwest and the coal mines and industrial areas of Pennsylvania, West Virginia, and elsewhere. I remember the Pennsylvania State Constabulary, mounted, wearing black uniforms called "Black Cossacks" by the miners and other workers because they were used to break strikes and prevent labor movements as tools of the "operators," who held financial and political power over the local police and civil officials.

The attorney general of the United States, A. Mitchell Palmer, directed the notorious "red hunts." There appeared for the first time the syndrome of a suspect's death by suicide: "The suspect being interrogated in a department office on the 11th floor suddenly jumped from the window before he could be restrained to avoid further questioning. He was killed." Verdict? Suicide. Who believed it? Very few of us indeed, certainly not we younger ones. The syndrome has spread internationally since that time. The Ku Klux Klan multiplied in members and rode — rode even to control high political office and persons in some states. It was the period of the notorious Sacco-Vanzetti trial, which I along with many responsible men and women from various stations in life honestly believed was a monstrous miscarriage of justice, convinced that the two men caught in the anti-red hysteria were railroaded to their deaths for their "radical" union activities.

Disillusioned by the enthusiastic support given by the American Legion to the new repressive forces, I had resigned my membership because I saw the developing program as a betrayal of the Legion's original purpose.

Racism grew to alarming proportions and in intensity. The professed intellectual roots used to justify the attitude were grounded in the misuse of the Darwinian hypothesis of organic evolution, specifically the premise, the survival of the fittest. The premise, simply stated, is that when a number of species compete in a given environment for food and space, the species which most effectively adapts to that environment survives over the others and, in so doing, shows that it is the *fittest in that particular environment*. Darwin was applying his theory only to the organic level of life. Others took the premise as having a universal application to social as well as organic life. By this misuse it was easy to extend the premise to explain social conditions. It seemed reasonable to many to conclude that occupation of different statuses by different groups — classes, races, even individuals — was a true reflection of their relative capacity to achieve the levels possible for those groups. The theory was welcomed to justify a class society based on hereditary status and the status quo, from the blacks who had been in slavery to the whites to the highest classes who "spoke only to God."

Racists found a rich field for plowing in our immigration history. The earliest white immigrant population to our country, except for the American Southwest, came from northern and western Europe, which continued to be the main source until well into the second half of the nineteenth century. In the early part of this second half, Chinese coolies were brought into California to work the mines, build the railroads, and do other heavy labor for very low wages. They brought, too, a different language, religion, and cultural habits. No effort was made to assimilate these people—quite the contrary.

The year 1885–86 saw a significant change in the pattern of European immigration; the majority of immigrants that year for the first time came from eastern Europe and the Mediterranean area. These men and women provided the labor supply for the industrial development of the North after the Civil War and its expansion westward to the Pacific. Developing industrial sources in our country needing cheap labor promoted the migration. These people built our cities and the subways and surface transportation systems that made them livable; they dug the coal for our industries and brought out the mineral resources from the earth. Railroad sidings in far western desolate places bear the names of men or the towns once their original homes. I remember one such siding in a desolate, volcanic, flood-gutted landscape in southeastern Washington: Odessa. We stimulated this immigration by all the means our industrial system and supportive government could devise.

This new population, diverse as it was, differed visibly in many respects from our "old"; in addition, the people brought new languages, religious affiliations, different legal systems, and many customs. Ethnic groups tended to form enclaves for mutual support and in so doing inevitably maintained their separateness. They produced a laboring class of unskilled but specialized labor, such as miners, steelworkers, and others. Because of the association of these new immigrants with the laboring levels of our population as distinguished from the managerial level from the "old," class differences inevitably developed and were rationalized by recourse to the misuse of Darwin's premise. The whole demographic character of our population was changing and causing conflict in moral and social values.

Questions began to be raised, and not by rabble-rousers at first, about the danger to our society from the infusion of these inferior (read "different") people. The Aryan myth was born and cultivated: that a single family in the distant past in that land of fable, the

"High Pamirs," in the western ranges of the high Himalayas was the origin of the speakers of the Indo-Iranian (European) languages and thus, too, of the fair-skinned white race.[34] Race and language were held to be inseparable, with language treated as a racial trait like skin color. Our "old" populations considered themselves to belong to this "racial" group. The aristocracy of wealth in our population, the people who held power in politics and business, could in most cases trace their past to the northern and western European group, and they validated their theory of superiority by appeal to the premise that survival proves superiority. Two names will suffice to illustrate the type of men who promoted the theory of white (Nordic, Aryan) superiority. Madison Grant, a zoologist on the staff of the American Museum of Natural History, wrote to bemoan *The Passing of the Great Race*. Lothrop Stoddard, an outstanding journalist, wrote very persuasively for the uncritical reader among other books, *The Rising Tide of Color*, of course with reference to the Asiatic peoples and their threat to the white race. I remember well a group of us students discussing Stoddard's book; one said wistfully, "If only Ogburn could write like Stoddard and Stoddard like Ogburn."

A side product of World War I, completely unforeseen at the time, provided much improperly used, highly volatile fuel for the fires of discrimination. Psychologists had constructed batteries of tests to select a reservoir of manpower from which candidates could be chosen for further training for commissioned and noncommissioned officers. After the war, analysis of the results of these tests showed differences between black and white performances and among different ethnic groups. This was to be expected, for the tests were culture bound (that is, performance depended on the social environment of the tested), even those prepared for non-English speakers. Racists of one sort or another seized upon these test results as demonstrating the proof of their prejudices. All this hullabaloo has long since been laid to rest, but in the early twenties it sparked a veritable grass fire. The propagandist use of these test results was a powerful weapon, when added to the underlying atmosphere of discrimination rampant in our society, to bring about the Immigration Reform Act of 1924, by which the Congress with its quota system redirected the flow of European immigration from east-central Europe and the Mediterranean area back to the "Nordic" northern and western European nations. Our country had for the first time decided to direct the demographic character of its future population, but not on scientifically defensible assumptions.

The new repression, a social miasma, moved across our land. Those of us who had dared to dream dreams of a new world found ourselves staring wide-eyed into a darkening sky of chaos. Uncertainty and dismay replaced our postwar euphoria to challenge our fondest hopes. Sensitive as I was to the effects of social conditions on men and women and their children, I responded strongly to the new repression. What now of my priestly vision from the mount of the people of the world as the Children of God? Despair for the first time threatened to gain a foothold in my life, to destroy my hope and confidence in the future. I was now faced with a new threat to my spiritual and intellectual integrity and would eventually have to meet it head on. In the meantime, I had to handle it as best I could in the milieu of my life as a married graduate student and my own personal religious problems.

During my first two years at Columbia, as I carried on simultaneously my pastoral duties and a full graduate program, I became increasingly aware of the marked differences in intellectual content and attitudes between them; the former largely the performance of special duties for which I had been trained, whereas the university experience was the exploration of new fields of knowledge and the methods by which relevant hypotheses could be verified, the difference between static and dynamic experiences. My life threatened to fall into a dualism in contrast to the basic holistic attitude established by my rural boyhood and pre-World War I undergraduate years in college.

My first hesitant efforts to break out of the static intellectual atmosphere of the close by taking courses at Columbia University in sociology was, although I am sure I did not recognize the fact conceptually at the time, a first questioning of the apparent dualism into which my life at General was drifting. It was not lost on me that I had called on my early Columbia studies to provide both the method and substantive information for an understanding of the work of John Wesley in my thesis research at the seminary.

More important than that, however, was the intellectual ferment produced by my introduction in church history at the seminary to the movements, Modernism and Liberalism. Here, within Western Chris-

tianity, the use of the scientific method in the study of the scriptures
and other sacred documents and doctrines produced strikingly different results in the Catholic and the Protestant denominations. The
core of Catholic faith is the Mass, constantly repeated. Modern scientific studies held that the doctrines made audible and visible in the
Mass were but symbols of great universal truths defining the human
condition. The long-established doctrine of the church was that the
events so beautifully depicted in the Mass were divinely revealed realities and thus not subject to scientific study, only acceptance.

For the priest a very important element in the celebration of the
Mass is the ecstatic sense of participation in the sequence of events, as
one especially ordained for that sacred service, in an unbroken line of
succession from its apostolic source. Modernists, who had come to
accept the symbolic nature of their actions in celebrating the Mass,
felt, in spite of their acceptance, the ecstasy they had always known.
How could this contradiction between belief and action be rationalized? The solution was really an escape; the position taken, "It is true
because it works," was not subject to verification by any valid test.
Furthermore, there was no observable difference between the behavior of two priests celebrating the Mass, one of whom was an orthodox
believer and the other a Modernist. The parishioners as worshippers
could only believe that both priests shared the same significance of
their actions. The Modernist priest celebrating the Mass as though it
represented revealed truth as his parishioner thought, when he
believed the whole ceremony was only symbolical, was creating for
himself an anguishing problem of intellectual integrity. As I pursued
this problem further, the aspect of intellectual integrity began to cast
an always longer shadow, especially after the bitter experience of self-
recrimination that afternoon when I was needed to give spiritual
assistance to the young woman dying in childbirth and I found myself
secretly glad that I could not be found. The problem of Modernism
now acquired a new, a very personal aspect, one I knew would harass
me until I settled it to my own satisfaction.

I tried to discuss my problem, the question of intellectual integrity, with chosen seminary faculty members, who reassuringly told me
what I already well knew: that the interpretation of the scriptures had
changed greatly through time. When I raised the question of the
priest who apparently sacrificed his intellectual integrity by pretend-
ing to a faith he intellectually rejected, they only shrugged their

shoulders, apparently either never having faced the question or else preferring to evade the rather awful implications involved in it. I knew when I left the seminary to enter Columbia that I carried a heavy burden, one I would have to bear alone — and alone, eventually, to ease it from my shoulders in freedom, for I found myself intellectually in sympathy with the Modernists.

By my final year at Columbia, with my additional experience, I began to take up again my Modernist problem, now very much mine. I began to make a careful analysis in context of all variables involved as I would any other problem of social behavior. Most of the work I did alone, although I did talk it over from time to time with Margaret. I began to reduce my thoughts to written form. Gradually the roles of ritual and liturgy began to loom large in my analysis. Margaret, in reply to a question I raised, referred me to a study by two psychologists at Barnard College under whom she had studied; in their work I began to find my answer in the role of ritual. I would work three more years on that paper — perhaps the most significant one I ever wrote — before I had it ready for publication.[35] By the time I finished my work at Columbia I had not yet answered the question of my role as a priest, but I had at least made good progress toward an understanding of the kinds of decisions I would have to make to that end in the years ahead.

The last two years at Columbia would bring about a fundamental reorientation in my intellectual life, a change germane to the basic personality traits of my rural boyhood and the distinctive experience of my study of Greek life of the Periclean Age, when the field of speculative thought was being developed. During these earlier years I had been learning to ask those fateful questions, what, and how, and why, and how to go about the search for answers. Graduation from Penn State and entering the military service had suddenly changed all that. In the officers' training school for five months of concentrated study there was a single clear objective that had been determined for us: to gain the competence required in certain skills to function as a commissioned officer. The necessity of the skills and the methods by which they were transmitted were "givens," not questioned, nor was anyone expected to do so. My decision, while in the service, to enter the priesthood after the war had been a sincere personal questioning of our cultural values, not of the methods of training artillery officers.

The seminary was a professional graduate school and, in a way, its function was analogous to that of the officers' school, but the objective was to train its students to be priests. Here, too, the validity of the methods and objectives were accepted as "givens." There was nothing about the seminary's program to encourage intellectual initiative; answers to all questions had been achieved and were available to the inquisitive. My first tentative effort to question the adequacy of the intellectual life of the seminary was to take my first courses in sociology at Columbia University. My full-time enrollment at Columbia took me suddenly into a new world of the mind; here the basic objective was not to teach us "what to think" but "how to think." I found myself back with the intellectual values of my boyhood, the holistic view of life, and the speculative thought of the great Athenians. Under Boas I learned the necessity and methods of cross-cultural analysis and how essential it is in attempting to understand human behavior fully, to study it in its cultural context. Giddings saw society in its dynamic aspects of change with an insistence of the recognition of the new. Ogburn insisted that we ask, "What are the facts? If that is true, what of it?" and "Quantify if possible."

At Columbia I was in a truly new world, one in which all values were subject to critical analysis. The new value became the defensible idea. The objective was the trained, the disciplined mind with the ability to function in a rapidly and sometimes frighteningly changing society. Politics, religion, sex, industrial production were NOT GIVENS for special space and time, but an aspect of a wider world in a process of change and each to be accounted for at any point in space and time by cultural-historical study. This was a reorientation of my intellectual life, and my future would be a product of it.

My, yes, our married life, like my academic experience and my deepening awareness of my religious problems, was a learning process, but distinct from them; marriage is a unique experience, a relationship between two individuals and their relation as a pair to society, and the growth of the union must be a reciprocal process, neither under the control of nor the responsibility of either partner alone. Successful marriage, consonant with its unequaled richness of living, requires the most difficult adjustment two personalities will ever have to make to each other and as a family unit in the society of which they are a distinctive pair. This adjustment process is a life-long responsibility, for both the social milieu of the family and the individuals concerned change, each a natural condition of the fact of growth. Love can never be taken for granted.

> For freedom, we know, is a thing we have to conquer afresh for ourselves, every day, like love; and we are always losing freedom, just as we are always losing love, because, after each victory, we think we can settle down and enjoy it without further struggle. . . . The battle of freedom is never done, and the field is never quiet.[36]

Margaret and I, young, idealistic, naive, and avant garde, entered marriage in 1923 under conditions that would make heavy demands upon us. Full-time academic schedules and extracurricular duties left little time and energy to devote to our new, extremely important process: learning to live together in marriage. Too often it was probably taken for granted that the very inner dynamic of marriage itself would insure success, and I say this without animus: by Margaret more than by me. When we returned from our honeymoon on Cape Cod we were, even in that very special time, aware of tensions arising from the competing demands for time and attention made by the desire for high academic performance and the winning of love. That Margaret had chosen academic performance was a storm flag of warning we both recognized for the voyage ahead.

We brought to our marriage certain basic values certainly rather unusual for the time, even perhaps at any time in our culture. I never have had any sense of jealousy—envy perhaps, but not jealousy. Neither, I think, did Margaret. We believed that the integrity of the individual in the achievement of life's goals should be respected and assisted by mutual support. Neither of us had any sense of "possession" over the other. We both believed that love was the only defensible basis for marriage, that love would be the energizing force in maturing our marriage in which the fullest development of each of us could be realized. The melding factors of our marriage were not custom or convention but the respect each felt for the integrity of the personality of the other, mediated by the ideals we shared. Margaret, in *Blackberry Winter*, wrote: "I had what I thought I wanted—a marriage that contrasted sharply with my mother's, a marriage in which there seemed to be no obstacles to being myself."[37]

We had, I believe, in spite of the positive if exacting aspects of our marriage, different values and expectations of the significance of sex in life in general and in marriage in particular, although it was only after marriage that these differences began to become explicit. I had then, as I still do, a holistic view of sex in relation to total activity, a view probably derived from my boyhood in the country, although not then made explicit. Spring, the renewal of life, was always a joyous experience and a significant, expected part of the sequences of nature. I came to think of sex as the joyous, repetitive, creative source of life in its widest aspects, that part of life the human mind felt compelled to use for its expression of beauty in literature, art, architecture, and music. Sex as love was not a separable segment of life, but a pervasive influence growing and enriching the individual's life. Marriage is society's validation, even blessing, on the intimate association of two individuals for reproduction and the full range of sexual experience between them, the ultimate means of communication. The sexual experience between spouses or lovers—I don't mean to separate these categories—can be successful only when all masks are discarded. Masks daily used in relationships must be stripped away. Bodies have an uncanny sense of perception and understanding.

On reading *Blackberry Winter*, I wrote Margaret, chiding her in a friendly way about calling me her "student-husband." I asked how in 1925 a student marriage was different from any other, pointing out that at our marriage in Buckingham we took our pledges with the same understanding: to enter upon an intimate relationship transcending any temporary status, one to be terminated only with the loss of love. February 27, 1978, she replied in a letter:

> I'm sorry you don't like my saying, "student-husband," but I have always thought of our marriage as the very best kind of student marriage, in which first as an engaged couple, and then as graduate students, we were free to study. After all the year you had the church in E. New York, I never functioned as the minister's wife which I had originally planned to be—and the next year (after Europe you were leaving the church and starting some new career). So it is my student years and yours that fitted together so well. I am sorry you don't like it.

But Margaret, you never spoke of yourself as "Luther's student-wife."

Margaret's explanation in 1978, as she saw it after fifty years, was certainly not appropriate to us in 1923–27. Her letter of explanation in view of temporal and contextual differences seems to me, perhaps wrongly, to make our marriage, a marriage of students, into primarily a convenience arrangement for the satisfaction of our sexual needs, dating, and other affairs normally attended in pairs. In other words, to her our marriage released time, normally used in search for partners, for academic pursuits. Today when students want that kind of an arrangement they do not bother with marriage, and society approves their action. If Margaret was ahead of her time in 1923–27 in holding this point of view, it was a well-kept secret, not one of Margaret's best-known traits. Margaret is wrong; it never applied to us. When Margaret and I took our vows before the altar in Trinity Episcopal Church I did not believe, and I don't think she did, that they were to cover only the student period of our lives. We both understood that vows are ideals of achievement that happily may be realized or may not because of personal culpability or forces beyond the individuals' control. For me to accept Margaret's statement in her letter, which amplifies her use of the expression in *Blackberry Winter*, as applicable to our situation at our marriage rather than a later rationalization, I am required to accept a belief in the young Margaret's dissimulation that I find intolerably repugnant. That we had married and had to have a divorce showed that we both made a personal and social commitment that bears little relation to today's "live-ins."

Readers of these pages and *Blackberry Winter* will find contradictory statements about some of the events affecting our lives. When it is a question of reporting, not interpretation, I insist on claiming authority. Margaret, a historian? NO! A dramatist? OUTSTANDING! Personal and interpersonal relationships fascinated Margaret, not such mundane things as objects of one kind or another unless they related to some aspect of social behavior. Dates, chronology, order, much of the meat of history, held a low nutritious value in her intellectual diet. I have spent most of my professional life in arranging artifacts of all kinds in chronological and spatial orders in the hope of inferring the behavior and life-styles of their users.

In graduate school as in other social groups, attitudes and loyalties tend to combine and in turn differentiate groups. Anthropology was a relative newcomer to the Columbia campus, but the intense sense of loyalty of its few students and devotion to its goals produced individuals who, I am sure, sometimes disparaged related disciplines more out of a sense of loyalty than any deep familiarity with the subject of their disdain. Boas certainly did not suffer fools gladly; and among his Columbia colleagues, with his fierce sense of scientific honesty, he confronted many. I majored in sociology and Margaret in anthropology, so there was a friendly juxtaposition. We were not in opposition to or in competition with each other, nor had we anything to prove to each other. I took all the courses I could under Boas and Ogburn, who crossed the boundaries of various disciplines, courses at the New School for Social Research, and others besides my regular Columbia program courses. There, too, was Margaret's chiding effort to "save" my lost (nonanthropological) soul. It, my soul, was having a very good time. Her damning accusation against "you sociologists" was that sociology was an "armchair" science (?), whereas anthropology was all good, hard science based on fieldwork. There was a kernel of truth in these accusations, but Margaret ignored the changes occurring in sociology. Ogburn was certainly not "armchair." My research in the graduate school was inductive, with some fieldwork, and quantitative. I am not aware that Margaret had read any sociology text per se. She carried the lance high for anthropology and the quality of its products, and rightly so.

Margaret and I never really quarrelled; there seemed to be no need to, much less excuse for it. We certainly had differences of opinion; who wouldn't? I think we felt almost instinctively that a quarrel would settle nothing, only sour the atmosphere. Whatever the cause, I am glad we had that memory. The tensions, indefinite as to cause — perhaps a feeling of not communicating, with not getting through to the other, that left a sense of uncertainty, ill-defined and meaning unclear, as in a state of being mistlike — increased during our second year as the time for our separation approached. To Margaret's other problems were added Edward Sapir's insistent attentions. To keep this in its proper perspective did not ease her concerns.

One summer evening shortly before the end of our New York period, we planned a festive evening with dinner at Pettipa's, a French restaurant and a bit of a speakeasy on West 28th Street, to be followed by taking in Joyce's play, *Exiles*, at a small, Lower East Side playhouse. Everything went as hoped, and then an incident occurred: two characters, a man and a woman, were talking across a round coffee table, the man was speaking, *so intently*, gesturing: "We are exiles, all exiles from happiness."

Of that whole play, why do I remember that alone? Or at all? It must have pierced both of us, for I cannot recall *our* discussing it. Our festive evening out ended on a very somber note as we returned with little talking to our apartment and beds. Had we sensed that night some portent too painful even to talk about? Exiles?

Shortly before her departure for Samoa, we had, courtesy of our relatives, a blessed week for a vacation free from duties. We became borrowers again, this time of Charlie's red Buick roadster that Margaret would have had us take for our honeymoon—I don't blame her, for it was a very nice little car. A relative of hers provided a plain but very comfortable cottage at some point on Narragansett Bay, in a grassy field a couple of hundred yards in from the muddy, tidal shore—not good for bathing. I appreciated the isolation of our little temporary home when I saw on the floor by one side of the bed, apparently to be mine, a lethal-looking carpenter's hatchet placed exactly in the position ready for the occupant to grasp if danger threatened. It was a part of the room's decor for which I fortunately had no use. The weather was kind to us in spite of a shower or two. A nearby restaurant added to the charm with its memorable swordfish steaks and strawberry shortcake.

Despite our imminent parting, or perhaps even because of some dimly sensed apprehension of future pain, this week was for me the most significantly happy of our married life. All competing affairs had been laid aside; and without intrusion, we were "living together in marriage" a kind of second and true honeymoon. I am sure the range, detail, and intensity of my remembrances of that happy week, along with the warm feeling bathing them, is reasonable proof that my memory has not betrayed me.

Even the best must end. Our last day found us reluctantly but duty bound, returning to the Mead home at Holicong, outside of Buckingham, for the final days before Margaret's departure.

Richard, Margaret's brother, drove us into Philadelphia to the Baltimore and Ohio Railway Station, where Margaret would board her train for San Francisco. Darkness was lowering when we arrived. How filthy that station housing the boarding platforms with the coal dust of years and the hissing steam of waiting locomotives! *Gloom* is the only word adequate to describe the atmosphere enveloping our small group, almost inarticulate in the face of imminent separation, a new experience. Feeling my intimacy with Margaret was of a different kind from her family's, I embraced her warmly, said a few endearing words, and kissed her au revoir. With a "Good luck and see you in Marseilles next spring," I stepped well back from the family group, a fitting distance for my swirling feelings.

As I stood watching the family's lingering farewell, I think I appreciated perhaps more than anyone else could have this lovely, not beautiful, young woman, my wife, willful at times, stubborn, sometimes quixotic, never simple, brilliant, goal-oriented and her course laid out, not permitting any interference with her steady progress in that direction, with an absorption in her work to which everything else had to be secondary in the long run. She was hitching her wagon to a star, and I felt grateful I had never stood in her way but had helped in so many phases of the hitching. At the last call she climbed aboard her pullman, turned, and waved to us from the platform. The porter closed the door, and she was gone. We waited on the concrete platform until the last car cleared, then suddenly the yawning emptiness of the station enveloped us, empty, empty. I sent a wish to her hitching star to please be kind to the young one when she brought her wagon to be hitched.

I took Margaret's mother's arm to walk slowly and thoughtfully toward the car—the men were already there, continuing their platform discussion on the desirability of buying new tires for the car—and she said in a voice asking for reassurance, "You will meet her in Marseilles next spring, Luther?"

"That is our present plan and I don't anticipate any change, but sometimes I wonder what we both will be like after such different years apart."

I returned with the Meads to Holicong and after a few days to Pughtown to my parents' home until I should leave in a couple of weeks for New York and Europe.

Perhaps two weeks after Margaret's departure, coming home under the overcast of a late afternoon with Dad after he had visited his patients, I found in a handful of mail my first letter from Margaret following her departure. I took it, turning the rest over to Dad, and walked out the drive toward the garage to savor the pleasure of reading my letter alone. Disappointment surged over me when I saw a very short letter written in San Francisco and mailed just before she sailed for Honolulu. I could hardly believe what I saw. I reread it. She had written:

"I'll not leave you unless I find someone I love more." Two or three short sentences completed her letter.

Shocked, I sat down on the running board of the car against which I had been leaning and looked again at the letter. Cryptic and in context truly enigmatic, what did it mean? It was a strange letter, an au revoir letter to a husband after two years of apparently reasonably happy marriage, albeit with tensions, and facing a year's separation. It was the first real suggestion, not teasing, that she might be even considering such a step. The sentiment she expressed was not new to us. Early in our premarital days I had stressed to Margaret my belief that love was the only valid basis for marriage; and if love ceased, as it well could, or were challenged by a stronger love, the appropriate change should be made unless more compelling considerations intervened. Was she holding up to me, for whatever reason, the ideals I had brought to her in those earlier years, ideals to which she held so eagerly?

I tried to place her letter in the context of the tensions, especially those of a personal nature. She was trying to tell me something, but what? With full knowledge that I may be completely wrong, I offer this suggestion. I was unaware and only learned from Ruth Benedict some six years later that Sapir had been arguing with Margaret over divorcing me and marrying him. She had refused. Perhaps her letter was an affirmation to both of us in terms of what we knew of her position in case I should become privy to Sapir's pressure.

Then, perhaps Margaret was just taking advantage of the opportunity at a crucial moment to nail her colors to the masthead. Who knows? But I *do* know that the uncertainty of her meaning when added to the other tensions we were experiencing gave me an increased sense of anxiety just before I sailed for Europe.

When the ship sailed, I stood forward, leaning my hands on the starboard rail, alone, as I had come from my Pennsylvania home and as I had gone aboard. I looked across Tenth Avenue at the line of buildings, remembering in brilliant detail how, six years ago almost to the week, I had stood in my top-floor room that first day at the seminary and looked in amazement across Tenth Avenue in the opposite direction at the row of masts and funnels, then turned back to my life in the close.

A hoarse whistle signaled our departure, and the tugs nudged us out to the channel, turned us to head downstream, and we were on our way to a world I had seen in my imagination that memorable day six years before. The New York skyline became less a thing of concrete and steel as the haze and our increasing distance softened the lines of the buildings, in turn to drop from our sight. Then through The Narrows into lower New York Bay, where the ship reduced speed slightly to drop the pilot, then increased it to head into the open sea. My Old World was behind me; my New now lay far ahead. I had not moved from my place at the rail, but stood gazing reflectively over the waves thinking how those six years in New York had seen me develop into a different lad from the one who had looked almost in awe from his seminary room window at the masts and funnels. As I gazed at the horizon my thoughts shifted to the year ahead of me. My only certainty was that it would be a year of challenges, but their nature and my responses I could not foresee.

A bell sounded and I went down to my cabin to prepare for lunch and settle in for the voyage.

Our ship had been built before World War I as a steerage-class vessel for the immigrant trade. With the war it was requisitioned for a troop ship and, having survived the North Atlantic horrors of the U-boats, after the war was outfitted as a student-class passenger ship, supplied with the necessities but not the luxuries of ocean travel. The round-trip fare was $90.00.

In the early twenties, interest in Europe encouraged special, cheap, student fares, usually about $90 per round trip, which brought about a great summer overseas invasion by students. Since the rates for passage held all year, travelers like the passengers on our ship took advantage of the favorable conditions for foreign travel during the other months. All multiple-class liners had a small section for student-class passengers, who had a small deck space provided for and restricted to them. Since ours was a single-class ship, we had the run of its space and facilities. Our passenger list was small, and there was much camaraderie. I made two special friends, Rossiter, a wounded Canadian veteran returning for university study, and Betty, a New York girl going to Paris and other cities in the hope of gaining experience as a couturiere. Our crossing took ten days, in part because we stopped at Halifax to pick up freight; and since the weather was generally good, there was plenty of time for reading, talking, games, and one's own affairs.

In 1925–26 a year in Europe on a traveling fellowship provided a unique opportunity for one in my position with serious problems to solve. I was twenty-eight years old, married, without children; my professional training was completed with my Ph.D. degree just granted. These favorable conditions did not reveal my spiritual and intellectual ferment. I had been unable to resolve my spiritual turmoil in relation to the priesthood. I was also really suffering deep disillusionment arising from the apparent renouncement by our society of those social and moral values that my brothers and I, along with thousands of other young men, had enlisted to fight and, if necessary, to die for. Finally, my marital relations were in a swirl of uncertainty. Here on this ship I had no answers, only the problems—and they were strictly personal. I had to solve each by my own efforts, except, of course, my marital problems involving Margaret. I was engulfed by a sense of aloneness in a world that didn't care, nor was there anyone to provide the much-needed support in my efforts.

In this state of mind one evening after dinner, I took a deck chair and blanket and, in the early evening overcast, found a place to be alone back along the starboard rail. Here I could look out over the sea and reflect. Driving scud increased, greatly reducing visibility. Suddenly a totally unexpected sight a short distance to starboard startled me: a Breton fishing boat, under full sail, homeward bound from the summer's fishing on the Grand Banks, absolutely alone in that vast, tossing sea except for our overtaking ship. I thought I had never seen anything quite so alone as that small boat sailing purposefully into the night. As we passed I watched it, fascinated, sailing so confidently.

I felt akin to that small boat, alone in the world of encompassing darkness. Then I reminded myself that the boat had a home port where loved ones waited and reliable charts and a trustworthy compass to guide her, if properly used, to her destination. And, the crew on board supplied each other with mutual support. I thought of the lovely passage from the Evening Prayer, "protect us from all the terrors and dangers of the night," and whispered it for that crew and their boat—and, I am afraid, slipped in a bit of a petition for myself.

That experience was deeply significant for me as the clarity of my recall after more than half a century shows. I began to apply its lessons to myself. I, too, had instruments, reliable ones of the mind, which should guide me if properly used. But to what? That I had to find out, but the same instruments were essential for the discovery and the guiding. I knew what I *had* to do: I had to find my real self by integrating the major facets of my personality, intellectual, religious, and marital, into an interrelated, balanced, functioning whole; then everything either would fall into place or could be placed there. The search, the finding, and the recognition was now my PURPOSE. I, like the crew of that boat, had a purpose and the instruments at my disposal to achieve it. A challenging year lay ahead; and I had a sense, a feeling, but nothing explicit, that I would achieve my purpose.

One night, as a cold wind swept the ship, a small group of us huddled in blankets below the port rail to get out of the wind and talk about whatever it was that young people of that time talked about.

Suddenly someone said, "Did you see that? It looked like lightning ahead."

"There it is again."

"I saw it, too, that time."

At regular intervals of a couple of seconds, the flashing light broke the darkness of the sky ahead. Just then a sailor came past.

"What's that flashing light ahead, sailor?"

"Oh, that? That's the Lizard."

"What's the Lizard?"

"The Lizard light—the lighthouse on the Scilly Isles; them's the farthest west of England. Have a good time, for we dock tomorrow."

And we did at Tillbury if my memory is correct. Rossiter kindly took me in tow and, although I don't remember the kind of conveyance or the route, together we went to a bed-and-breakfast accommodation he had arranged for.

I was "in England now."

My friend, Dorothy Thomas, who had taken her Ph.D. degree at the London School of Economics, had given me a letter of introduction to her close friend in London, Dorothy C. Loch, and written her personally about me. Miss Loch, having been secretary of the British Sociological Society, was thoroughly knowledgeable in the subjects of my interest, knew the persons I should meet, and would help to arrange meetings. Dorothy said warmly, "And she is a delightful person in her own right. I am sure you will like her." Of course, I had the letter with me to present as soon as possible.

My stay in England was to be short, only long enough to have a tailor provide me with some clothing, since all I had was the rather threadbare pieces I was wearing. I had available a small amount of money, savings, and the first payment of $250 for the first three months of my fellowship. Rossiter took me to a tailor on High Holborn, who assured me he could fit me with a three-piece suit and an overcoat, all wool, and a three-piece dinner suit for approximately $100. At the end of ten days I was appropriately dressed with good clothes for what seemed quite a modest sum. I still have the overcoat, which has raglan sleeves and is in good condition; it should be in style again any time now.

I planned to go to Paris as soon as I was outfitted; France was the only country where I could live for any length of time on my income. When I entered France in October 1925, the franc was worth nineteen to the dollar. I learned when I went on an extended trip out of France always to buy a round-trip ticket so that when my money began to be alarmingly low I could take a train and return to Paris.

I sent my letter of introduction to Miss Loch on my second day, after establishing my address at the American Express office. She replied promptly, asking Rossiter and me to meet her and her sister Freda at Previtali's in Soho for dinner. To assure us of their proper identity, they would wear narrow green ribbons like decorations on their left lapels. The evening went as planned, and I found that Dorothy Thomas was quite right when she said that Miss Loch "was a charming person in her own right," a quality I found she shared with her sister Freda. We talked about my plans in general among other subjects, and Miss Loch and I arranged to meet for tea the next day at the Plane Tree across from the British Museum to discuss my plans more in detail and how she could help me.

At our next meeting I told her I was married so there could be no misunderstanding of my intentions. I discovered from her discreet listening that she had been well informed by Dorothy Thomas. We understood quite well that our relationship would be that of friends. She also introduced me to the British Museum, the National Gallery, and the Tate. Dorothy—we had agreed to call each other by our first names—was working part-time more or less as a private secretary to Norman Wild, a friend and associate of Victor Branford for whom she had worked when he was president of the British Sociological Society. Because of her mother's ill health, Dorothy could work only part-

time. Wild had organized an institute to try to bring together capital
and labor cooperative enterprise in postwar England. Part of her work
was to attend the dinner meetings and record the discussions in short-
hand for subsequent transcription. Often she failed to get any dinner, she told me. In this work she met many of the industrial and
labor leaders in England through their attendance at these
conference-dinners, and the only people to treat her as a person in her
own right were the labor representatives. We talked about my plans
and what I would want to do when I returned to England so some
planning could be done to expedite my work at that time.

We also discussed my own intellectual situation and the personal
problems I faced. The war was still very fresh in England with its terrible toll of lives, and Dorothy had relatives and close friends among
the lost. She, a participant not just an observer, shared along with
others the postwar disillusionment, a feeling that led some to suicide.
We found our experiences were closely akin—how closely I did not
know until later when I returned to England—and we found it was
mutually helpful to share our thoughts. Dorothy was an extremely
perceptive person and knew how to listen. In those conversations,
maybe a half-dozen times in those ten days, she clearly sensed my
aloneness and desperate need for support. We promised to write, and
she would be prepared to help me with my work on my return
whenever it should be. And with that we said au revoir.

I believe it was a Saturday afternoon near the end of my stay, in
my strolling about to see what I could of London in that short time,
that I paused at the intersection of Oxford and Regent streets and, in
the well-dressed crowds in the autumn sunshine, was startled to see a
familiar couple across the street who stood out from the others in their
casual manner of walking and dress. I crossed the street to find a
couple, Scudder and Velma Mekeel, I had married some months
before in a small chapel at the Cathedral of St. John the Divine in
New York City. They were now students at the University of
Strasbourg and had been in London for a few days, and as surprised
and pleased to see me as I them. A brief discussion of my plans followed. They were returning to France in two or three days and suggested that we go together so they could help me on the trip and to
my hotel. What a piece of good fortune! I admit that with my limited
facility with the French language I had looked forward to this step
with some anxiety. We arranged to go, I think, the next Tuesday.

Paris! October 1925. And what difference that we arrived after dark? But my heart sank, and my face must have showed my disappointment, when the concierge of the small hotel to which I had written said that they had never received my letter asking for a room and that they had none available. He must have seen my face, for when Scud spoke briefly to him he picked up the phone, exchanged a few quick remarks, and said to me, "Yes, the hotel up this street has a room and will be glad to have your friend."

He looked at me and smiled as he saw my evident relief. Perhaps a mental flashback brought a memory from those dark days in 1918, its roots deep in the camaraderie of the battlefield: he less stout then in his horizon-blue uniform and pals from the States in their olive drab. Now, in a small way to him but so very meaningful to me, he was happily returning a favor. His kind act and his smile infused a warmth into my arrival that was to color my year's experience. After more than half a century the image of that night's experience is sharp and clear in my mind.

We thanked him and went to find the hotel. After seeing me settled in, the Mekeels went on to their hotel, promising to return in the morning to help me find accommodations more in keeping with my modest means.

Paris! No bad dreams that night! Before going to bed I had peeked discreetly between the draperies to see what was outside. I saw a courtyard enclosed on the opposite side by a wing parallel to mine. I woke to sunlight calling me to get up as it found slits between the draperies. A phone call to the concierge brought a croissant and chocolate to my room for breakfast and to start my French acculturation.

The Mekeels arrived early, and together we found the small hotel recommended by the concierge of the one where I had spent the night. It was on a narrow street, Rue St. Germain des Prés, which led without intersections up to the Place Saint Germain (with the church of the same name) and the famous Café des Deux Maggots. Up three flights of stairs to the top floor and there was my little room. A single bed, a bureau, and a small table were the furnishings. The ceiling on one side sloped to the wall, and its casement window provided me an almost breathless view of what seemed to be all the chimney pots of Paris—the sight that impecunious artists, poets, and dreamers always saw in the books I read. And now I had joined their ranks! This little room with its view would be my home for the next three months. Hot and cold running water came to a basin in the room, but I would have to arrange with the concierge for a bath. Across the landing was a very primitive, at least by my standards, toilet facility, the crouching kind fairly widely in use in France at the time. With my steamer trunk, suitcase and briefcase, I settled in. Luncheon with the Mekeels gave them the chance to advise me about language instruction, such ordinary activities as getting around the city, and other practical matters. After lunch we parted, they to return to Strasbourg and I to try to realize the significance of what now lay before me.

I was now completely on my own, my problems and I; the opportunity and the obligation were now mine to find their solutions in the days and experiences ahead.

To further settle in I went to the Bankers Trust Company to verify my account established in New York as a depository for my fellowship stipends. I could not write checks against the account, but had to withdraw the amount needed in cash or travelers checks. This provision was a good discipline on my spending habits, for I had at any time I left Paris a certain amount and had to live within it. I then went to the American Express office to establish my address and a place to receive and handle my mail. Next I bought a map of Paris and a pocket French-English dictionary. I had found a satisfactory restaurant when lunching with the Mekeels, and this would serve as a base until I had the opportunity to look around. I had to go out of my hotel for breakfast, but that created no problem since the Café des Deux Maggots was but a short distance up the street from my hotel. Croissants and chocolate or coffee were always available there, and it provided a view of certain aspects of Parisian life. Thursday I spent in orienting myself with my map and feet, and Friday I went to L'Alliance Francaise, a French school maintained to teach foreigners some facility with the language. I arranged to enter a class starting the next Monday. I felt I had made a fairly good start.

I took a very important step during the weekend when, eager with anticipation, I walked through the imposing entrance to the Louvre, Le Musée de Louvre, with its treasure of Western art. But my degree of anticipation in no way prepared me for the actuality of what I found. I can compare its effect on me to that of a much later experience when I unexpectedly came upon an Alpine meadow in the Oregon High Cascade Mountains so ablaze with a diversity and richness of loveliness that I had the sense only of the riches of the whole with no clear impression of a single flower. I left the Louvre that afternoon looking ahead eagerly to the excitement and gratification of coming to know the component parts of the treasure.

My early weeks in France were inevitably somewhat disorganized as I tried to find my way through the vast array of new and exciting opportunities afforded me. I haunted the museums, visited cathedrals and churches and, from outside and in, gazed down their long perspective of ecclesiastical and secular history.

Two experiences in the Louvre stand out with the clarity of "yesterday's occurrence": first, the day I saw and made the Venus de Milo part of my life; the other, when I stood enraptured before the Winged Victory of Samothrace.

I devoted one afternoon specifically and exclusively to my first meeting with the Venus. Expectantly I entered the long, narrow exhibition hall where at the far end, jewel-like, stood that white marble creation, alone against purple velvet hangings in back and on two sides. I moved slowly, hesitant to approach that ideal figure, encapsulating in my imagination the best of my classical studies. This was not just a piece of marble sculpture, solitary and isolated; it was the visual representation of all the best of my understanding of the Greek way of life explored so happily ten short years before — but what a significant period in terms of experience. "Know thyself" and "nothing in excess" were the two Greek ideals the Venus brought sharply to my mind. I was the lone admirer of that magnificent figure that October afternoon, and I lingered until my eyes and mind could absorb no more. The vision is still a part of me.

A later morning, I stood almost breathless below, slightly in front of, and to the side of the Winged Victory of Samothrace, the famed Nike, and feasted my eyes on that seemingly airborne figure. How could marble be so ethereal? Here was all the verve, sense of balance, pride in achievement, exaltation in the victory of those who had stood valiantly against the intrusion of an alien culture of the east into that of Greece, Greece exultant in victory.

During these exciting days the thought of where I stood relative to my priestly profession constantly intruded, a Rubicon eventually demanding a decision. As I visited cathedrals and churches I experienced them only as ecclesiastical and architectural expressions, and I did not attend services. I felt no pressing urge to. Late in October I decided to put myself to a test.

On November 1, All Saints' Day, Catholicism calls upon the full panoply of worship to pray for the souls of the saints departed, known and unknown. At the seminary I had saturated myself with and been tremendously moved by the history and the unique beauty of the Cathedral of Chartres, only an hour by train from Paris. I decided to participate as an observer in that festal service of worship. I asked Betty, my shipboard friend, staying at the hostel maintained for American women students by the American Association of University Women, to accompany me on my venture, for I felt the need of companionship. We were going simply as friends; Betty was aware of my marriage. Within this arrangement I carried my personal spiritual problem, but it was essentially secret, my own, compelling and inescapable. How would I experience this holy day, bringing my problem into focus in the beauty of this storied cathedral? I had to find out.

We found space at a kneeling bench—I don't recall any seats—well back in the nave's north side, from which we could, by a little twisting, see the south and west windows. The warm, afternoon sunlight glorified the exquisite windows in that music-filled cathedral as the procession moved slowly down the main aisle. The crucifer, with the choirsters following in their white surplices, led the procession; their flickering tapers cast dancing shadows as they passed down that column-bordered aisle, their voices rising and falling. The habited nuns and monks assigned to the cathedral chapter followed; the vested clergy, the bishop, appropriately last, closed the long procession. The dramatic impact of this scene, presenting for me the most appealing aspects of Western Catholicism, was staggering. Yet, "something" in my mind held back, pulling, tugging me as though back from a brink, and that "something" kept repeating Santayana's lines from his poem, *King's College Chapel*:

> The College gathers, and the courtly prayer
>   Is answered still by hymn and organ-groan;
> The beauty and the mystery are there,
>   The Virgin and Saint Nicholas are gone.

I came away fearing that I, too, as he, was an "exile" from the "spirit's realm, celestial sure/ Goal of all hope and vision of the best."

Betty and I shared the secular day as a beautiful experience, walking about Chartres in the environs of the cathedral, sensing its protective mood as we gazed up from the "Street of the Massacre" toward it towering above the dwellings clustered about its close. We returned happily to Paris, but, I, shaken inwardly by my personal experience and its troubling portent.

I kept busy at L'Alliance Francaise with classes and various efforts to improve my facility with the French language and, of course, trying to see all the treasures about me. Betty secured from time to time at the hostel complimentary tickets to chamber-music concerts and shared them with me. I thus became acquainted with music of Chopin and Debussy. Occasional theater provided experience in hearing properly spoken French as well as enjoying the play itself. I saw a French presentation of Shaw's *Saint Joan*, and the Maid seemed very much at home on the French stage. Having been enthralled by the incomparable Pavlova in New York, I had to enjoy again her poetry of movement when she danced in Paris. Complimentary tickets also took us to the opera for a performance of *Thais*.

These complimentary tickets were a boon, for I had to keep within my allowance. I quickly learned to handle money like a native, that is, in the French context. When one translated the inflated French currency into U.S. dollars, everything seemed very cheap. But disaster quickly ambushed anyone following that path. I remember very well going to lunch at some low-priced restaurant—my usual style—with a friend, a Dartmouth student I had met at L'Alliance. Our lunch, a quite modest one, cost us five francs each. The franc at that time was worth about four or five cents. To the French workingman, who lived by French currency, five francs was a reasonable price for lunch. My friend and I considered the weighty question of "Would we have dessert?" That would cost fifty centimes, a half-franc more. In U.S. currency it would have been a negligible two or three cents, but to us these fifty centimes equaled ten percent of the total cost of our lunch. We went without.

In November I went to spend a few days in Strasbourg with my friends, Velma and Scudder Mekeel, who were studying at the university there. I found all streets with both French and German names, evidence of the post-1918 takeover by the French after almost fifty years of German sovereignty. I attended with Scud a French class for adults provided, I believe, by the municipality in its efforts to meet the problem created by the ruling language having changed from

German to French. The instructor warmly greeted the visitor from the "land of George Washington" in English, as difficult for me to understand as my French would have been for him. He was very proud of his effort.

A short walk one morning took me by a butcher shop, where an unexpected sight—horrible to me—caught my eye. Outside on the pavement against a building were stacked the carcasses of three huge, wild boars, eviscerated, but still with their bristly hides and heads on and their huge jaws wide open, products of the hunt. I suddenly felt terribly far from home. When I took the tram for the railway station, I asked the motorman in French if the car went to the station. I was rewarded with a blank stare. A second effort was no more successful. Then, remembering, I asked in German if it "went to the *Bahnhof.*" "*Der Bahnhof? Ach, ja, ja.*" And with that I started back to Paris.

After my return to Paris the welter of new experiences began to fall into a kind of order. I began to see order in various forms in time and space in the art, architecture, even in the different behavior of populations in various places, such as Paris and Strasbourg.

The Louvre offered me the artistic treasures of different times and places in the Western world, Euro-Hellenic Culture. The great cathedrals: Notre Dame; Chartres, the unique, with its incomparable windows and two towers built two hundred years apart with the earlier one pure Romanesque and the other full-blown Gothic; Amiens, the Gothic ideal of glass supported by a framework of stone; Rheims with its exquisite rose windows, where the ancient kings and queens of France were crowned. Each of these I had come to know to some extent and saw in them variants of ecclesiastical, theological, architectural, and sociopolitical values. Before autumn's end I knew what lay before me: I had to take advantage of all these riches available to me. The museums and cities of Europe provided in unique fashion the material for a significant comparative and developmental study of the major values of Western culture. I now had the opportunity, yes, obligation to integrate my classical, theological, anthropological, and sociological studies—all humanistic—into a total experience. Knowing what I had to do, I started orderly planning.

I decided first to go to Grenoble, a provincial town in southeastern France, with its well-known university, where Louise Rosenblatt, a close member of our group at 419 West 119th Street, was studying preparatory to attending the Sorbonne in Paris to study for her doctorate in comparative literature. I wanted to talk my plans over with her. I stayed in her pension, run by Mademoiselle Richard, a very thin spinster past middle life with a wry sense of humor. She, in company with Louise, prescribed for my tonsillitis: "Put your shoe on the foot of the bed, toe up, and drink black walnut liqueur"— she offered some, black as draftsman's ink and potent—"and when you see two shoes, stop the medicine; when you wake up you will be feeling fine." I didn't have to take the whole dosage. Her unmarried brother had served with the crack Alpine troops, the Chasseurs Alpines.

How different that old French town was from Strasbourg! Louise returned with me to Paris and the hostel of the A.A.U.W.

Letters from Margaret were few and long in the coming, halfway round the world by surface mail. Mail left Samoa by boat every three weeks unless storms forced the boat to bypass the islands on its scheduled trip. She was desperately busy, involved in her first field trip; therefore, much of her writing was not to friends or me, but of a professional nature to her department, especially Professor Boas and Ruth Benedict. She reported on her work, sought advice, and, of course, their support.

Dorothy Loch and I corresponded as we had agreed to do. Our letters were timely as to the events and experiences discussed and appropriate to my situation. They were impersonal as far as any personal relations were concerned. Dorothy, having sensed in those few days in London my spiritual loneliness, tried to provide supporting interest in what I was doing from day to day. Whenever she found a poem she thought I would like or find helpful, she would copy it and send it along without comment as an enclosure in a letter. I had written her about my new plan, that I would like to spend January in London and then make an orderly tour of the Continent after working out the details in London. I told her of the people and activities I wanted to see in London so she could, if possible, help arrange the necessary contacts. I also wanted to see again the London museums and galleries, in a way the real start of my tour. She wrote back promptly with the address of a bed-and-breakfast lodging where she had made reservations for me—it was, I discovered, where Professor Bronislaw Malinowski stayed when in London—and the promise to start making the contacts for me. I wrote that I would stay the night of my arrival at the Russel Square Hotel.

It was just after New Year's Day, 1926, that I crossed the channel late in the afternoon, three hours from Dieppe to Newhaven, a crossing straight out of a night in *Macbeth*. Wind and rain whipped the channel into a fury. I saw a freighter plow its bow into the waves and have the water cover it, and, as the bow heaved up, two cascades of water poured off the deck. Our neatly bearded French captain paced the deserted deck, stopping occasionally, feed wide apart, visored cap pulled tight, pipe held tight in his teeth. He wore a pea coat with a fur collar and, with hands pushed deep into its pockets, he scanned the sea and clouds like Dad's old beagle hound used to, sniffing for a good scent.

The rain threatened to soak my bag, so I took it to the large cabin below deck. Most passengers were returning from an international football game — I believe between Scotland and France — and the cabin was crowded with miserable, seasick men and women. The stench of vomit made the place unbearable. I dropped my bag at the foot of the stairs and dashed back up on deck, for I felt it was better to be wet than sick; I knew if I lingered below for even a minute I would join the rest.

My return to the deck was rewarded by an unexpected example of Gallic gallantry. I saw there was another passenger on deck, a very attractive young woman wearing a long, heavy overcoat, a tam with her hair escaping out from under it and over her ears, her cheeks very red in that foul weather, but looking as though she was bred to it. She was going to be sick right there on deck. A sailor, seeing her plight, hurried with a basin, not a bucket, and standing there in his sailor hat with its red pom-pon, gallantly held the basin for the charming but sick passenger. They stood facing each other, he holding the basin steady in both hands, she steadying herself by some stanchion. The gastric reflexes took over, but the sailor never moved. Then the whole thing struck them both as so hilarious that they broke out in laughter even though the visceral spasms were not over.

When we entered the quiet Newhaven harbor I retrieved my bag, a bit wet, and boarded the boat train for London. At the hotel I found my heavy overcoat was wet clear through, but under it I was dry. That night I slept well and the next day took a cab to the lodgings Dorothy had reserved for me. I found a note of welcome she had sent with instructions of how and when to contact her and word that she had started the necessary steps for my meetings.

I was in England again, to start another and perhaps the most significant stage of my Journey.

How fortunate I was to have had the introduction to Dorothy Loch! Her service as secretary to the Fabian Labour Research Committee and later the British Sociological Society together with her own family background had made her familiar with the ways of the British bureaucracy as well as the customs of the English class society. To start making my contacts she introduced me to the appropriate person at the English Speaking Union, an organization whose function it was to assist visitors like myself to get done expeditiously what they had come for from overseas. I very quickly had appointments scheduled with Dr. Marie Stopes, the leader of the birth-control movement in England, for a visit to an internationally known juvenile court I especially wanted to see and an interview at the Union with the commander of the London Women Police.

After these appointments were made I turned my attention to the museums as a start for my organized study. Here again, Dorothy, through her familiarity with the cultural riches of London, facilitated my work. I was deeply committed to my study ahead on the Continent. To organize it, at least intellectually, I bought a copy of Mather's *A History of Italian Painting*, an authoritative source book especially suited to my needs. He writes:

> This book has grown out of lectures which were delivered at the Cleveland Art Museum in 1919–20. There I had ideal hearers, beginners who wanted to learn and were willing to follow a serious discussion. . . . I have had as much in mind the intelligent traveller in Europe and the private student. Throughout I have had before me the kind of introduction to Italian painting that would have been helpful to me thirty years ago in those days of bewildered enthusiasm when I was making my *Grand Tour*.[38]

Professor Mather's book became my vade mecum to guide me in my "bewildered enthusiasm" through my Journey in the days ahead. It is before me as I write. It shows, as all good books should, the signs of wear; and the marginal notes with those on end pages, rather faded after fifty years, attest to the use to which I put it. At various museums, especially outside of Italy, I expanded the information in Mather by using local sources. With Mather as my guide I studied the offerings of the National Gallery and the Tate in London, and the first intelligible forms of order began to appear.

To improve my knowledge of the birth-control movement abroad before leaving New York, I had had conferences with Dr. R. L. Dickinson, who was conducting studies for the Committee on Maternal Health of the New York Academy of Medicine, and with Margaret Sanger, R. N., the activist leader of the birth-control movement in the United States but working in New York City. She had been jailed more than once for providing birth-control information, especially to working-class women who visited her New York City clinic, in violation of New York State statutes. She advised me to talk with Dr. Marie Stopes, her English counterpart but not subject to the kind of opposition faced in our country. Dr. Stopes was not a doctor of medicine, but had a Ph.D. degree, I believe in earth sciences.

Dr. Stopes graciously invited me to tea at her home in Surrey(?), where we enjoyed two or three hours of pleasant conversation as she filled in the gaps in my knowledge of the English movement. She had a small, flat museum case about two by two and a half feet in size in which she displayed prominently a collection of hideous devices, of metal and other materials, that women had used at different times and places to prevent conception. How any desperate user of these devices could avoid hemorrhaging and blood poisoning was beyond my understanding. But her exhibit taught an important lesson: that among women there has been the drive to limit conception by whatever means desperation made necessary and that the birth-control movement was the contemporary expression of this deep-seated, long-acknowledged need which women were bound to try to satisfy. I accepted with pleasure her invitation to a public lecture in London on birth control where she was the main speaker. I noticed that the large audience was mostly women, apparently working-class housewives. What a difference from the intellectual climate of New York or any American city at the time, where such a meeting would have been raided by the police and arrests made. That was January 1926!

Judge Clarke Hall's juvenile court sat at an address in Shoreditch, a slum area. I came up from the Underground into bright sunlight to a surprisingly wide street with rows of depressing tenements three or four stories high. Try as I would, I could not see an entrance seemingly appropriate to a public building housing an important function of the government. I felt completely lost until reassured by the familiar sight of two constables on patrol. There was a tall, impressive sergeant with a younger companion. I hurried to them for help and the younger moved out of earshot for me to speak alone to his superior officer. I told him that I had an appointment to attend a meeting of Clarke Hall's court but could not find the address given me.

"I don't think the court is sitting this afternoon, sir."

"But, Sergeant, I was given this appointment by the English Speaking Union."

"Just a moment, sir, I'll ask my colleague."

He moved up and asked his "colleague," who confirmed that the court was sitting.

"You are quite right, sir, the court is sitting this afternoon; you see that entrance" — pointing to the spot — "just past that building with the poster on it? The court is one flight up that stairs, on the right."

"Thank you, Sergeant."

Following the sergeant's directions I found a door marked with the invitation to "Enter." I went inside and was met by a receptionist who said that they were expecting me. After a few words of welcome she led me into a spacious, well-lighted room dominated by a large, bare, rectangular table in the center with a number of straight-backed chairs on each side and a somewhat more comfortable looking armchair at the head. Straight-backed chairs lined the walls on each side of the room, and the receptionist invited me to take my seat on one and explained the court would be in session shortly.

In a few minutes the door at the end of the room opened and a surprisingly small group of principals entered and walked to the table, where Clarke Hall took his seat at the head. A social worker sat at the right side of the table, and across from and facing her were two small culprits, boys, well dressed (undoubtedly for the occasion), about ten years of age (perhaps a little older), looking rather defiant but also a bit on the apprehensive side. Immediately back of them in civilian clothes stood a rather slight, neatly dressed constable in charge of the boys. Apparently the offense in question was a theft. All the investigation by the constable and the social worker had obviously been done, the whole case discussed, and the decision arrived at before this confrontation. There was no question of innocence or guilt to be decided here, no details of the proceedings, all of which had been done in informal but organized discussions preparatory to this meeting. The purpose of the court was to avoid the trauma associated with the adult type of trial to a child. It represented the new concept of the 1920s that the problem of juvenile delinquency should be treated in a manner appropriate to that age group. Only a few courts in the United States had been pioneering enough to use the new method; among these I recall but two, that of Judge Ben Lindsey in Denver and the other of Judge Hoffman in Cincinnati, where the psychologist who worked with the judge was my close personal friend.

The proceedings I visited in Clarke Hall's court were obviously the closing events of the case, with the youngsters being made to realize that it was not all fun and games. I can recall in detail only these remarks as the judge closed the meeting. The judge said, "I wish to congratulate you, Constable Brown, on the efficient manner in which you have handled this difficult case." And the constable replied, "I would just like to say, sir, that I only did my duty."

With that the court adjourned; it had officially closed its participation in this part of the boys' behavior problem.

Another afternoon, the commander of the London Women Police graciously found time to talk with me at the English Speaking Union for more than our expected two hours about the problems of juvenile delinquency, especially among girls, as well as problems specifically related to women. Commandant Allen, a very attractive, matter-of-fact woman, showed a sense of understanding and even sympathy for her sisters falling afoul the law for offenses under her jurisdiction. In January 1926 prostitution was, if not legalized, tacitly recognized as a social condition permitted to exist so long as the participants did not create social disorder by otherwise disapproved behavior. In other words, keep the situation under control within the social order. She explained that the prostitutes had, to a certain degree, their own social order; as long as they maintained it, there were no problems requiring police action. I vividly remember her telling me with a wry sense of humor how the Burlington Arcade—a small street coming into Picadilly—was the recognized territorial boundary between two groups working Picadilly. This fiction was clearly recognized by the women, who might stand and have a friendly gossip with one another across the invisible boundary line, but let one cross it for professional or other purposes and "the fight was on," usually requiring police intervention to establish order.

Through Dorothy I met men associated with the London School of Economics and was invited to attend Malinowski's famous anthropology seminar. I also secured a reader's card for the British Museum Library and thus had access to library sources. Dorothy also arranged for me to meet at tea or lunch with men and women engaged in research in fields of my interests as well as with artists and journalists. She and I lunched and had tea and dinner together as often as we could at modest-priced restaurants, especially Previtali's in Soho where we first met, and we talked and talked. I had the pleasure of meeting her family at tea at their home, 46 Harcourt Terrace. We visited museums and churches, finding a special favorite, the small St. Patrick's in Soho, which became a kind of spiritual sanctuary. The world was so much with us and we had so many kinds of shared experiences to talk about that we often felt the need to experience together the quiet peace of that little church. My personal problems and her experiences, together with my plans for months ahead and future professional and personal expectations and hopes, gave us much to talk about. Our association had developed in its own right into a deep, meaningful friendship, mutually supportive and empathetic, never feeling the need for validation by any physical experience.

Inexorably that month, uniquely rich in experience, came to an end. I was to leave by night boat from Harwich for the Hook of Holland. Dorothy and I had dinner together at the Plane Tree, a favorite restaurant across from the British Museum. It was a wretched night with a cold mist turning the street lights into blurs. We walked to the underground entrance where I would take a train to Harwich. At the street level we said our good-byes with a sense of desolation, neighbor to the enveloping mist, for we feared that we would not see each other again. I picked up my bag and briefcase and with a last brave smile we parted, and I descended the stairs to the platform. At Harwich I boarded the boat for the night crossing of the North Sea to Holland, very pleased to see that London's fog did not extend to us. It was a clear night with a nearly full moon. I stood on the forward deck as our boat moved but, seeming to follow the moon's beam, a bright path on the sea's surface, into the North Sea. Shortly, a rather unpleasant corkscrew-like roll which our boat had acquired suggested

that my berth would be a more desirable spot. Following the suggestion I was soon sound asleep, to wake up in the morning finding our
boat tied up at the dock, the Hook of Holland. Eagerly I took some
kind of conveyance, I don't remember which — train, tram, or
bus — to Amsterdam. Amsterdam! The city of Rembrandt, sturdy
Dutch houses, canals and museums, and such a rich history! My
Wandeljahre had really begun, and what a starting point. I was now
again on my own, very much alone, as so often in the climactic
decision-making phases of my life.

In London I planned my journey after Amsterdam to take me
systematically through some of the major cities of northern Europe
with outstanding art museums and/or significant urban architectural
features, to return then to Paris.[39] My finances by then would be
exhausted. Hopefully, my quarterly fellowship stipend would arrive
in time for me to reach Rome for at least a part of Holy Week, but
certainly for Good Friday and Easter Sunday. I believed the experiences of those two days in this center of Catholic Christianity would
have a significant bearing on my spiritual problems. After Rome and
Naples, both cities to be centers for shorter trips, I would go up
through the hill towns of Orvieto, Assisi, and Siena to Florence, that
repository of the Renaissance, a fitting aesthetic and intellectual
climax to my journey. After Florence I planned to return to Paris for a
short stay until time to go to Marseilles to meet Margaret. I looked
forward to our enjoying together, as carefree tourists, the Provence
and Loire country of France before our return to New York. By that
time I would have gained a reasonable perspective in my personal
problems; have come to a decision concerning my commitment to the
priesthood; and, hopefully, Margaret and I, as we renewed our relationship after the year's separation, would be working out the tensions in our marriage.

My early classical training, excellent grounding in both secular
and religious history of western Europe, and the scholarly discipline
and understanding of social processes provided by anthropology,
together with my devotion to a clearly defined program, were the
emotional and intellectual means preventing my Journey from continuing in a state of "bewildered enthusiasm." Instead, it became a
totally enriching experience, orderly, disciplined, and significant. I
was seeing everything in a total cultural context. Christianity was the
wellspring for the development of the plastic and graphic arts, going
back to the Hellenic culture, transmitted via Byzantine Christianity,

for Judaism most rigorously forbade both (Thou shalt not make unto thee any graven image, or any likeness of anything that is in the heaven above, or that is in the earth beneath, or that is in the water under the earth. Exodus 20:4). Among, if not *the* earliest paintings are those for the reredos, a background (often a series of three panels, a central one with a wing on either side) to beautify the altar, the most sacred spot in the edifice. Most of these paintings, very plain at first, were in two-dimensional form and portrayed the artist's concept of some biblical scene, usually something centered on the birth of the Christ child. As these works expanded into frescoes, they must have had a powerful influence on the faithful, for they were, outside the spoken word, the sole means then of communication. As the church developed through the centuries in Italy, its influence and oversight penetrated into every cranny of the individual's life on earth, and it provided the only mediator for the sinner in life in the afterworld. The church, administered from the Holy See in Rome, was a dominating force in the political and social life of the feudal city-state society.

I have often thought the political act of Emperor Constantine I in A.D. 313 designating Christianity an officially recognized religion of the Roman Empire was a catastrophe for the church instead of the benefit conventionally ascribed to it. It is true, Christians would no longer be "lions' food," a change no doubt very comforting to the individual Christian; but there was no longer the winnowing process, the necessity to make a decision fraught with great danger, even to one's life, to join a despised sect. It was so respectable now to be a Christian! And what did it cost the church? In my opinion, its very soul! For now it not only "rendered unto Caesar that which is Caesar's," but it soon shared duties and privileges with Caesar. The bishops did not know—or perhaps did they?—and looked forward with some yearning for the time. But the truth is:

> If once you have paid him the Danegeld[40]
> You never get rid of the Dane.
>
> (Kipling, *Danegeld*)

A vision of political power shared is a Fata Morgana for the soul.

By the time I returned to Paris, my position with regard to the priesthood was clear, I neither could nor would "pay the Danegeld."

The only liege to whom I owed or could owe service and loyalty was the value *integrity* and its fellows: compassion, love, and understanding. I had sworn my fealty there in my boyhood, and have endeavored all my life to be faithful to my vow. I have never paid Danegeld to any person or organization; integrity is still my liege lord.

I cannot say exactly at what point I came to my decision. I had lived through the pomp and pageantry of Easter in Rome, but I could not see "The Virgin and Saint Nicholas." I did see the Vatican, the capital of a political-ecclesiastical papal state. My day at Chartres kept returning in vivid memory. In Rome I saw the temples of that imperial power; and at Paestum, south of Naples, I looked with awe upon the exquisitely designed Greek temples to Poseidon, my first visual experience of something I knew so well from my classical studies. Finally, at Assisi early one rainy morning on my northward journey to Paris, I entered with a deep sense of humility the Basilica, the center of the Franciscan Order founded by St. Francis long before on the simple but strict discipline: chastity, poverty, and obedience.

The contrast between the humble St. Francis, who preached so gently to the birds, for all creatures belonged to God, and this monumental building was emotionally shocking. I found a stairs leading to the crypt and descended slowly to a landing from which I could see below without intruding. At one end was an altar with lighted tapers and flowers, and before it a small group accompanied a young couple taking the sacrament of Holy Matrimony. The liturgy, the vows, and the charges to the couple are the same the world over wherever the Roman Catholic faith is held. Why this episode made so deep an impression on my mind I have never understood. I think perhaps I felt some sense of the monstrous incongruity in the contrast between the structure and the event; the vivid details of my mental image suggest as much. Was this experience deep in the Basilica at Assisi the decisive event in building my awareness of the hard course before me? I think not; my developing awareness is best described by Shelley's metaphor:

> The sun awakened avalanche! whose mass,
> Thrice sifted by the storm had gathered there
> Flake after flake, in heaven-defying minds
> As thought by thought is piled, till some great truth

Is loosened, and the nations echo round,
Shaken to their roots, as do the mountains now.

(*Prometheus Unbound*, act 2, scene 3)

What now of my vision from the mountain after my ordination, that world of the Children of the Kingdom of God? The vision had not changed, only the manner of the seeing and the response I would have to make. I now knew that Revelation yielded to Discovery in the understanding of and empathizing with the Children, each as a unique individual in his or her own right, regardless of sex, age, or color of skin. Discovery was a product of the mind; Revelation, an act of faith. Discovery required the training of disciplined minds. My decision was not a matter of little consequence (again to follow Shelley's metaphor) with a few rocks loosened and rolling down the slope; the mountain was shaken to its base. I knew I could no longer serve in the Anglo-Catholic priesthood, nor could I be a titular priest. Intellectually I was a Modernist, but for me to accept the Modernist rationalization that a belief was "true because it worked" would have been my first installment of Danegeld to dishonesty, hypocrisy, and self-delusion, a payment I refused to make; rather, their implacable adversary, I chose to fight these ubiquitous and timeless enemies of humankind.

My decision was in no sense a repudiation of either religion (for I believe it to be a basic need of humankind when properly defined) or the essence of the Christian expression in particular; it was specifically directed at my spiritual and moral problem: the conflict I found between what I believed to be the legitimate demands of the priesthood and my personal values. It was not easy to accept that my whole life would be changed, but that would be both the cost and the reward.

Neither was my action a betrayal of my decision in the Artillery Officers' School; only the method of working toward my goal, as I saw it then, would change.

How I would do this I did not know at the time and, characteristically, I felt no concern about that aspect. I knew my problem had to be solved on its own terms, not as something subordinate to some future long-range plan. My future action would evolve from my decision. My teaching experience at the College of the City of New York in the spring of 1925 had been exciting and stimulating, and I had reason to believe the students found it so. My *Wandeljahre* had given me a richness of experience and depth of perspective to fructify my academic and seminary training, and it had provided me with a deep humanistic insight that could serve me well in university teaching and research, if my course should go that way, where minds are developed. And I enjoyed the rewarding knowledge that I had served well my liege lord, integrity.

My disturbing sense of awareness that I might be unable to accept what I believed to be the intellectual imperatives of the priesthood was, I am sure, part of the generalized feeling of despair that I felt, along with so many of my postwar generation, over the reversal of course our social and political life was apparently taking. To suggest a separation between my despair about life and my questioning my vocation is simply a device to explain differences in nuances and development. My exposure to the intellectual challenge of Modernism in the seminary had a catalytic effect, and whatever the end might be it would affect my intellectual outlook, my world view, and my role in it. I came to my intellectual-spiritual Rubicon in 1926 with excellent equipment and training in its use to throw my bridge across the river and go to face whatever the other side could offer. I stepped off my bridge, not a neophyte, but a well-trained explorer eager to come to terms with the intellectual landscape lying ahead.

As I moved through these three months unique in my experience, Western cultural history in art, architecture, behavior patterns, until then known to me only from books and museums, became objective and in context. It was also of the greatest importance that I saw these expressions of the human mind and hand developmentally; I observed their life cycles.

At Paestum, Louise Rosenblatt and I strolled about the Greek temples to Poseidon, savored their architectural beauty, and reflected on their mythic-poetic conception of the relation of man to the sea and his efforts to placate its hostility by the generous use of sacrificial offerings. The memory of my last night at sea coming to Europe slipped into my mind, the repetitive flashing of the Lizard light at Land's End bringing our ship and all others within its bearing into port. The hard, mental work of many thoughtful men, explorers and scientists over many years, not revelation, had produced that navigational aid.

At Rome I stood in the Coliseum and tried to recreate the sight of a festive afternoon when that huge stadium was filled with fervent, yelling men and women, probably both the drunk and the sober, cheering as hungry lions were turned loose on a huddled band of Christian men and women, adults and children whose sole wrong-doing was their commitment to a new teacher out of Galilee and their steadfast refusal to deny their belief in the truth of His teaching. I saw it as a much earlier stage in the life cycle, represented by the splendor of the worship that All Saints' Day, 1925, at Chartres, which nearly overwhelmed me. Their message along with many others was convincingly clear: that change in our lifeways from as far back as the record goes has been beneficial for the human condition and that the dynamic forces have been the IDEA and the COMMITTED INDIVIDUAL.

The development of Catholic Christianity for centuries was the dominating force in Mediterranean and western European history; actually, it was that history which illustrates forcefully the roles of the idea, the individual, and the institution in the process of change. An individual could espouse this new religion of hope only at great risk, for its refusal to recognize the emperor's divinity made it a treasonable activity. Its message of hope was not for this world's goods but for future blessedness; its appeal was to the poor, the slaves, the despised. And it was a simple message preached by Jesus and carried on by His disciples. For mutual support and safety the converts usually gathered at night in basements or other safe places. Communication between various groups was limited largely to word of mouth and letters occasionally carried by messenger from one to another. The growth in converts to the new religion brought about an organization into congregations in various cities, and these in turn had to have their relation to one another defined. Each congregation was at first autonomous, with a number of elders (presbyters, priests) in charge of interpreting the faith as they understood it in the absence of a written source and, too, the training of younger men to succeed them. The whole situation was fraught with the tendency for separatism and diversity.

As the church grew in numbers and acceptance, it developed an organization modeled exactly on the Roman pattern of civil government. Each city had a bishop presiding over the priests (congregations) in that place; in each province the chief city boasted an archbishop or metropolitan who exercised authority over the churches in the province; above the archbishops were the patriarchs, usually bishops of the most important churches. By the sixth century there was a patriarch of Rome, but others of much longer standing were at Constantinople, Antioch, Jerusalem, and Alexandria. The bishop of Rome was soon called instead of "patriarch," *Il Papa*, the pope. This has been the basic organization of the Roman Catholic church; it provided for the recruitment of its clergy (officers) and all aspects of its relation both internal and external. The Roman poet Horace wrote a poem containing the line: "Greece taken captive, took captive Rome" (*Graecia capta, cepit Roman*). This insightful observation might be used as a model to describe the church's fate by reading, "Rome taken captive, took captive the church."

Some fifty years into the development of Christianity a significant step was taken when the first council, the Council at Jerusalem, was convened. The most important action taken was to free the new church from its formal connections with the Hebrew religion by declaring that a convert need no longer be first a convert to Judaism. The council also was the first step in setting the pattern for the development of interpretation of the faith at this highest level of administration.

The bishops, following the pattern, took a step of the greatest significance for the future of the Christian faith by calling a council at Nicea in A.D. 325 to consider and deal with the pressing problem of lack of agreement on exactly what the necessary basic articles of faith of the Christian should be. The diversity of ideas had increased as was to be expected, for the eastern Mediterranean world had always been a hothouse source, as it were, of religious expressions. The council reported its findings in a statement clearly and authoritatively setting forth what it conceived to be the essential articles of faith although not all council members agreed with the statement. The council adjourned without agreement, but Bishop Athanasius (A.D. 293–373). patriarch of Alexandria, addressed (at a later date) a letter to all bishops directing that the statement of the council be accepted as the official doctrinal statement of the church. It became the Nicene Creed, and it thus accepted and enshrined the essential articles of the Christian faith to become the basic orthodox body of the Catholic faith, Eastern, Roman, and Anglican. I repeated in 1923 that creed of affirmation of faith along with my fellow deacons as an essential part of our ordination to the priesthood. Since this faith was believed to have been "revealed," its acceptance and enshrinement by the church circumscribed it against change except by further "revelation," a most unlikely prospect.

I was a spectator on Easter Sunday, 1926, at the magnificent pageantry of the Papal Mass at St. Peter's in Rome. My mind flashed back to Easter Sunday three short years before when I said my first Mass in the little chapel of St. Clement's Church, close by Hell's Kitchen. Every detail of that ecstatic experience, unique in my whole life, became again a part of me. The creed I recited that morning, the words of the Mass, "This is my body . . . ," "This is my blood . . . ," the gestures and even some of the vestments, the stole, the alb, and the chasuble, all these the celebrant at St. Peter's and I shared in our common purpose except the language. His was Latin; mine, English. We two priests shared the essential elements of our faith enshrined in the Mass through the centuries, only the trappings differed. How explain this stability and change in the same phenomenon? A simple anthropological analysis of the problem showed that aspects of worship and administration, although related to the basic beliefs (the creed), were never considered an essential part of it and might be changed or added to as cultural-historical factors became a part of the ongoing life of the church. The creed, however, provided the future reference for determination of orthodoxy and heresy among its members and clergy. The church had institutionalized its body of belief as *a revelation of truth to be accepted, not discovered*, and in doing this it capped the mind of the individual from exploration and made it subservient to the institution itself. Development of knowledge that might conflict with the creed became impossible for anyone within the church. There were but two choices for the individual who pursued that route: conformity or evasion. The church could not and did not permit defiance.

When I left Paris for Rome on that Wednesday before Easter on the night express, the city was enveloped in a cold, penetrating mist. I shared a second-class compartment with seven others expecting to arrive at Rome at eight o'clock Friday morning, Good Friday. On Thursday, our first morning, we suddenly emerged with a most pleasant surprise from a tunnel's darkness into incredibly clear air and warm Mediterranean sunlight, a contrast as difficult to appreciate as the experience was welcome. Until then my experience had been in

the transalpine countries, even to the far northern seas. Now suddenly, I discovered the genial Mediterranean climate at Mentone, the
custom station on the French-Italian border. In the northern countries I found the climate harsh and demanding and the trees the old
familiar pine, oak, elm, and beech. The novelty of the palm, the
olive, fig, and somber Mediterranean cypress had worn thin by the
time I reached the "hill towns" in the western foothills of the
Appenines. Here I was to feel more at home in the environment, and
it was here that my mind had come face-to-face with the necessity for
decision making and an explanation of my rationale.

I had started my *Wandeljahre* in January 1926, intending to study
as far as possible the development of Western cultural history by
examining systematically the major art collections in the museums of
the source countries. My study, a superbly rich postdoctoral year, I
anticipated would provide the basic guidelines for my future personal
and professional life. My anthropological training enabled me to
coordinate my excellent knowledge of ecclesiastical, secular, and art
history, to see them in context and as the complex of social processes
they were. I had done this in my examination of the development of
the concepts of creed, revelation, and authority in the Mediterranean
world and saw clearly how the role of the idea of revelation enshrined
in the creed became an inviolate concept to hold the church everywhere to a static intellectual configuration in an explosively changing
world. But I had not yet brought into sharp focus in my mind how
the social forces that had produced the Renaissance in Italy had even-
tuated in the transalpine countries into the Protestant Reformation
and eventually our modern intellectual world with its value system of
the dignity of the individual, the freedom of choice with the acceptance of responsibility, and the inviolability of the individual conscience. I now tried to focus sharply on an understanding of and a
feeling for the significant forces in the process and their meaning for
my life.

Western European history from the time of the Roman Empire at
its height has been characterized by two great traditions, the
Teutonic-Protestant in the transalpine countries and the Mediter-
ranean-Catholic in the cisalpine south. I had been reading and
reflecting on this matter in the course of this writing and believed
that intellectually I was well aware of the differences between the two
and their significance. I discovered, however, that I had never really

felt this until in the pre-Christmas season of 1983, while immersed in this writing and deeply involved with the tender beauty of the story of the Christ Child and Bethlehem, I watched after dinner with my hostess and her husband the first TV program of the Wagnerian Ring, the Siegfried story of Wotan, incest, murder, and hate. This visual experience carried such an emotional impact that it brought so sharply into focus in my mind the significance of the contact between the two traditions that I returned home with an intellectual understanding of what I call the "Protestant process" enriched and buttressed by my emotional experience.

I shall now try to flesh out the skeleton of the thoughts in those last days of my *Wandeljahre*, to make explicit what was implicit in my experiences, my understanding of them, and the reasons for my decision. My study of Modernism, a transalpine development, had convinced me that it was fundamentally a product of the development of ideas resulting in our cherished values, "the inviolability of the conscience," "the right of freedom of choice," and the "dignity of the individual." More than a thousand years of tumultuous, bloody history separate the "Edict of Milan" officially recognizing the Christian church and the mature Petrarch, man of letters, leader, and perhaps most distinguished of the Italian humanists.

I do not intend to attempt to give even a short synopsis of that turbulent history; but as the anatomist in his laboratory dissects out, "teases," a nerve fiber or blood vessel to follow its course through and around masses of tissue and bone, I try to isolate and follow the intellectual filament through the masses of human history until it glowed brightly in the values of conscience and human dignity and I describe how I identified with the end process. My training insured that I would see the filament in its social, cultural, and environmental contexts.

The Edict of Milan, A.D. 313, set in progress a concatenation of fortuitous historical processes that were to dominate the history of western Europe for the next thousand years. During the century before the collapse of Roman authority, the church had time to develop its administrative organization throughout Italy, even within the distant northern frontier; it closely paralleled the Roman. With the collapse of Roman authority about the mid-fifth century A.D. the church became the only source of order in a world plunging swiftly into the Dark Ages. Many of the northern invaders were at least nominal Christians and respected the churches, which provided islands of sanctuary in an otherwise orderless world. In this world the bishop of Rome, the pope, was well on his way to becoming the secular as well as the spiritual head of whatever government functioned.

The priests, alone literate within the general population, were responsible for the instruction of their communicants, that is, everyone in the parish. I have described how the early mosaic art forms of Byzantine derivation were used in the decoration of the early churches to dignify the altar or sanctuary. A second, very important function was to teach by pictorial illustration stories from the Old and New Testaments, a practice which, from the start, effectively limited the field of opportunity for the potential graphic artist to the subject of ecclesiastical themes. New chapels, churches, and monastic buildings provided for many centuries the only available outlet for the Italian artist.

It's a commonplace of anthropological knowledge that no culture area develops all facets of its potential equally. I think it fair to say that Italian culture for more than a thousand years concentrated its main creative energy in the field of the graphic and plastic arts, culminating in the High Renaissance. It was in this field of Italian art, especially painting, that I isolated, at least to my satisfaction, the filament I was searching for, the nature of the artistic impulse itself and its development in its field of opportunity. I saw a demon—a demonic compulsion of the spirit—driving the creative imagination, whether in the effort to communicate some perceived value graphically, or by sound or words, or even to discover the nature of light and the processes of communication.

The creative drive of the artist, the creative imagination, carries its own inherent imperative of performance: to increase the depth of understanding of the challenges and continually to try to improve the methods and efforts to meet them. It is a war without armistice. When the prophet Isaiah said, "I shall see the travail of my soul and be satisfied," I have always understood him to mean that only when he sensed his soul to be in travail could he be satisfied. When the creative imagination, the artist, is satisfied, his soul no longer in travail, he is done, finished. His soul must be in travail! This was the filament I teased out of the riches as I moved through the museums of Italy that winter and spring of 1926 to see finally the bright flame glowing in the High Renaissance.

During the fourteenth and fifteenth (the famous "quattrocento" of Italian art and painting) centuries, two closely related cultural processes gradually merged because of their essentially common axes of interest: the human being as a living person. Italian humanists were interested in promoting the concept of the dignity of man, the importance of human felicity and human excellence in contrast to the otherworldly attitude of the church. The church viewed life as a miserable period between birth and death, beset mostly with sorrows and suffering in which the poor body that did all the suffering was simply a vehicle to convey the soul from birth to death.

Practically all humanists conformed outwardly to the church, and indeed some were members of the clergy, but the infusion of the pagan, humanistic ideas of the classical literature as they became more readily available initiated a growing skepticism. The rise of powerful families with their entourages provided sources for the ideas to be discussed and even transmitted as was done by the great humanist-poet, Poliziano, the tutor of Lorenzo de' Medici's sons. Although skepticism of the church's teaching might be stimulated among the like-minded friends, there was no obvious anticlericalism. Neither did the Italian universities provide sanctuary for humanist men of letters.

As humanistic ideals gradually infused thinking persons with the sense of the value of the human being, their contemporaries and friends, the painters, were effectively improving their capacity to paint the body to conform to the humanistic ideals. The artists had been free to experiment from the earliest time with one aspect of their religious painting, the *bambino*, which provided the living model for the Infant. Other figures were reconstructed according to convention. The growing enrichment of the artists' concepts required the use of the human form, the body either clothed or with scanty or filmy covering. I believe two aims, not explicitly made clear, as often happens, combined to encourage the artist driven by his demon toward the realization of painting the human body both as an object beautiful in its own right and as an appropriate sanctuary for the being which the humanists, their confreres, wrote about and which they doubtlessly discussed at length with them.

The climax and fulfillment of my orderly study was the sense of awe and reverence that overwhelmed me when I first gazed upon and then tried to comprehend the totality of Michelangelo's *Creation of*

Adam on the ceiling of the Sistine Chapel at the Vatican. Adam—the name, a transliteration from the Hebrew word meaning "from clay," a potter's metaphor—is *already alive*, stretching out, perhaps somewhat reluctantly, his left hand from his arm resting on his left knee to receive God's touch. No, God is not creating Adam, the man; he is doing something far more important as I see the action in context. God could have "breathed into Adam the breath of life," but that was already there as shown by Adam's expectant pose. *The critical item is the touch of God's hand!* Something is flowing from God's finger into the hand of the living Adam. One of the most cherished and basic beliefs of Catholic Christianity is the "apostolic succession," the doctrine that the apostles gave to the bishops by the laying on of hands the power to ordain priests, that is, the gift to them of power to celebrate the sacraments. Every priest in the Catholic tradition, as did I, becomes a member of that unbroken line of succession when the bishop lays his hands on the candidate's head and accompanies the act by the appropriate words and prayers. The right of investiture is critical for the continuation of the priesthood and church and became the basis of a serious conflict in the Middle Ages between the church and the nobles. This was a struggle the church had to win, and did.

The concept of a person, or object, or place imbued with more than natural power that may be shared by contact is widespread in the world and certainly was not unknown to the Italian people of Michelangelo's day. It survives in our rational(?) society in our concept of "luck," "let me touch you," a "lucky penny," and so on. The possessor of the power loses none of it by the sharing with another.

I see in Michelangelo's painting God sharing with HUMANS through our representative Adam HIS very own nature. He raises MAN from the beautifully modeled clay creation to share HIS own divinity. He "gave man speech and speech created thought, which is the measure of the universe"; and when He gave man thought He gave him power to make choices, which he has to have in order to have freedom to evaluate alternatives; and then, and only then, could he and would he be held responsible for his action. He is giving us opportunities and reciprocal responsibilities, separating us from the rest of the animal kingdom and making us moral beings. This fearsome challenge is what I saw in the flame of the filament I was following. Here was the conceptual climax of the Humanist-Renaissance achievement.

Michelangelo, architect, painter, sculptor and poet, probably the .greatest intellect of the High Renaissance, used the ceiling of the Sistine Chapel at the Vatican, the central point of the Catholic church, as a decorative field (offering incidentally the attraction of preservation), to challenge the antihumanistic dogma of the Papacy; and thus with a marvelous sense of irony made the Papacy the carrier of his message, that all humankind, all ages and both sexes and every race, shares equally in those aspects of divinity the Creator shares with all of us, the Children of God. My eager if lonely search through the museums of Italy had come to a felicitous and convincing consummation.

As the Renaissance moved slowly into the transalpine countries it had to adapt to the sociocultural realities of the Teutonic tradition. I remarked earlier how I sensed a contrast between the hard, natural and social environments of the north with those of the genial Italian country. In the cathedral at Orvieto in the spring of 1926, I read in my vade mecum this statement about the frescos painted there by Signorelli about A.D. 1500: "This sturdy, upright art seems hardly Italian. The spirit of it is ruthless, and Northern."[41] I felt assured that I was not standing alone in my assessment of the difference between Italy and the transalpine north. I could not conceive of a Botticelli painting the *Birth of Venus* in Nuremburg or any other northern city. Ruthless is the correct word to characterize the ethos of the Teutonic culture. And in the countries characterized by that culture, those values composing the Italian High Renaissance interacted to produce the Protestant Reformation. Out of these developments I drew values that, combined with those I had won from my Italian study, gave me the fulfillment of my personality—identity, if you will—which was the goal of my anchoritic quest.

To attempt to explain in the briefest terms what seemed to me to have been the most significant idea in the bloody and torturous history of the northern countries leading into the Reformation and beyond, I must change my metaphor from that of electric illumination to that of the stream starting high in the mountains from a small spring to make its way under, through, around, and sometimes over obstacles in its irresistible course to the sea—an aspect of nature with which I am happily familiar.

I saw the source of the stream, the idea that would eventually develop into our concept of the rights of the individual, in the nascent idea of democracy in the value system of the Germanic tribes, according to which they elected their king and at his death divided his property equally among his male heirs along with the right of each to govern his inheritance. Charlemagne's empire, built with the aid of the clergy, both secular and regular, in response to his request, collapsed because of this requirement that broke his empire into three "equal" parts each ruled by an incompetent son. After Charlemagne, all efforts to reestablish his empire at the secular level collapsed, although it was tried even to the nineteenth century. The powerful church he established not only held its ground but also continued to strengthen and expand its powers.

The development of feudalism was a powerful confluent stream leading toward the recognition of the individual. Kings in the fragmented society following the Carolingian collapse had to lean heavily on the nobles for support to govern even in the slightest degree. Powerful nobles with fighting men maintained whatever order existed in their areas. Since the king could not raise an army of his own, he had to rely on the nobles for support. The nobles in turn exacted their pound of flesh by forcing the king to recognize and legitimize their rights, especially by agreeing not to interfere with the administration of justice by the nobles in areas under their control. This right was very important, for the imposition of fines was the major source of "cash income" for a noble. He did the same for abbots and bishops, who held the same power as lay nobles. In A.D. 847 a law was passed "that every free man must have a lord who would be responsible for him and whom he must serve."[42]

Commendatio et beneficiam, the Latin name for this relationship, a "service" and a "reward," was the core of the feudal system. The individual is recognized in a given status and it is a two-way relationship. There was no theory of the value of the individual in his own right apart from some relationship, but the seed from which that plant could grow was being planted. An individual gained significance according to the status he held; and it is to this concept that our expression, "the right to trial by one's peers" is to be traced. Earls' Court, Barons' Court—place-names now are survivals of the feudal law requiring the accused to be tried by a panel of his peers. A key provision of the Magna Carta wrung from King John by the barons at

Runnymede, June 15, 1215, was that no freeman was to be imprisoned or punished except in accordance with the law of the land. The struggle between the nobles and the king swayed back and forth through the years; in England by the end of the fourteenth century the royal prerogatives were limited by the rights of the people, but on the Continent, especially France, the results were quite the opposite. The important element, however, is that in these countries there had developed as a recognized fact the right to petition and oppose higher authority, even the king. The theory was developed in the feudal system that the king held all the land in fief from God and, therefore, was responsible only to Him, his liege lord, and that he ruled by divine right—a theory not accepted by everybody, but it was risky to admit one's doubts. Skeptical pragmatists received support for their position in A.D. 1649 in England when the Parliamentarian Party, Oliver Cromwell's soldiers (derisively called "roundheads" because of their short-cropped haircuts), chopped off King Charles's head and the predicted divine retribution of disasters did not occur. It was a precedent-setting beheading and foreboded ill for royalty.

The ecclesiastical authority at Rome continually tried to expand its power by the extension of the canon law—the *decreta* codified in the twelfth century by Gratian that had come to be the legal code applied in ecclesiastical jurisdictions to a widening range of actions, situations, and conditions—by issuing new *decreta* to meet these new situations. Violation of each was punishable by a fine or worse. The nobles understandably objected to this attempt to expand ecclesiastical judicial power for a very sound, economic reason. Fines, the most frequent punishment, were paid to the vassal who held the fief in which the trial took place and probably were the major source of cash income or its equivalent. Because the bishops' courts had the reputation of being more fair and more lenient than the barons', an accused, if jurisdiction was in doubt or could be questioned, tried to have his hearing in the ecclesiastical court. If he were successful and was convicted, as seems usually to have been the case, the fine went to the church, thus depriving the noble of much-needed income. Neither bishop nor baron was troubled by any concept of justice or law, only raw personal advantage.

The expansionist ecclesiastical program generated the expected reaction from the barons. The opposition by the barons was recognized as legitimate, if ill-advised by the church, but the recognition of legitimacy showed that when a class at least believed the church was wrong it might protest, in other words, become a legitimate opponent of the ecclesiastical authority.

The Crusades, too, oddly enough became a confluent stream to the main current. Many crusaders by the fourteenth century had had their intellectual horizons vastly widened by their experiences against the Muslims, not to mention each other at times. They had seen a world quite contrary to what they had been led by the church to expect, in many cases a civilization vastly more sophisticated than the areas of Europe from which they had come. They had even found that some of their Muslim enemies exhibited a knightly standard of behavior equal to the best of their own. The reflective men among the crusaders could not help but question the nature of the church whose teachings under which they had lived and come to the Holy Land were so much at odds with what they saw for themselves. When they returned home they brought not only stories, like all soldiers, but cloth, jewelry, and games, and "souvenirs" to show where they had been. These men brought back and spread, I think probably without hostile intent but effectively, their own sense of skepticism of the teaching of a church that had failed them when the test came.

Universities in the northern countries contrasted strongly with their counterparts in Italy; they provided a base for the humanists to teach instead of disassociating themselves as did the Italians and, by their actions, contributed an extremely important addition to the volume of the flowing stream. By the fifteenth century the best scholars in Greek and Hebrew were to be found in the northern universities. Theology was a subject for study and analysis by theologians as was mathematics or any other subject. Most humanists were members of the clergy and not usually anticlerical. Erasmus, frequently called the most distinguished of the northern humanists, was an Augustinian canon and ordained to the priesthood April 25, 1492. He had been temporarily released by his prior from the monastic life to pursue his life of letters. In 1514 his prior instructed him to return to the monastic life, but he replied with a plea for freedom, applied to the pope for a dispensation, and continued his secular life while awaiting the pope's reply. On April 9, 1517, Erasmus was in England and there received at the hands of his close friend, Ammonius

Andreas, the papal legate, two dispensations, one allowing him to live in the world and the other dispensing him from wearing the dress of his order.

Johannes Kepler's experience at the University of Tübingen, where he took his bachelor's degree in September 1588, illustrates how the ecclesiastical prohibitions were circumvented at the faculty level, albeit by individuals. Kepler had intended to enter the ministry when he came to Tübingen. There he came under the influence of one of the faculty, Michael Maestlin, a student of and strong supporter of the Copernican theory, which the church denounced as heretical. Kepler's new teacher secretly—secretly, mark you—introduced him to and explored with him the Copernican theory. Instead of entering the ministry, Kepler expanded his studies and in 1594 accepted the position of professor of mathematics at the University of Graz, where he brilliantly developed the Copernican theory. Kepler's contemporary, Galileo, mathematician, astronomer, and physicist, who held a life appointment at the University of Padua, resigned to accept a post in the service of the Grand Duke of Tuscany because of the greater freedom for research. Galileo had been forced by the church to "recant" as heretical his theory of the law of falling bodies, experimentally arrived at. He did not dare to pass on even secretly to an eager student, if he had one, his intellectual discoveries.

The gradually increasing skepticism about the validity of the church's dogma and claims of authority appeared as a threat to the church, which responded by establishing, first in Italy, the notorious Inquisition to root out the heretics. Trials were secret, and the suspect might be tortured to secure a confession. A convicted suspect who persisted in his heresy was handed over to the secular powers to be burned and his property confiscated by the kings. The kings, hard up for cash, were quite understandably interested in maintaining the Inquisition. Even if an accused recanted and professed conversion he could be imprisoned for life or suffer a variety of other distasteful lifetime penances. The Inquisition was a grim, an odious institution feared by the people. In Spain the long, religious wars with the Moors increased the powers of the clergy and the spirit of intolerance. Ferdinand and Isabella, who supported Columbus for his voyage of discovery to the Indies, established the Spanish Inquisition, which became so iniquitous in its proceedings that its name is frequently used for the institution as a whole.

A wide-flung intellectual ferment marked the life of the trans-alpine countries in the later years of the fifteenth and early years of the sixteenth centuries, causing the stream to reach flood levels. The great ocean voyages of the period originated in the transalpine world —I include Portugal because it became a part of Spain only after the accession of Ferdinand and Isabella. Perhaps Spain, because of its centuries of history of resisting and eventually defeating the Moors, deserves to be considered a special case in western European history. Venice and Genoa, both seaports on the Mediterranean Sea, fur-nished expert navigators; but Columbus, from Genoa, and John Cabot, of Venice, had to go to the north to secure the intellectual and financial support for their voyages. Oporto, the seaport of Portugal, provided the home port for Magellan and other Portuguese naviga-tors.

The Cabots secured the backing of Bristol merchants on England's west coast for their voyages, and this relationship of merchant-explorer represents a new social development to be eventually of pro-found significance to the whole world, the colonial system based upon exploration, and subsequent exploitation by the great trading companies. The stories brought back from Africa by Portuguese of strange humans, probably chimpanzees, and the more reliable reports from the New World stirred peoples' imagination and pro-voked questions concerning the nature of what they had been taught. A little loss of confidence can be an ominous threat to a status quo that is already the subject of questions, with the right of protest at least for certain classes fully established.

The church, especially in its feudal position, as both a secular and ecclesiastical power had become arrogant, wealthy, corrupt—at the time of Henry VIII's confiscation of church property in England about one-twentieth of the land of England was under control of the church, and the situation on much of the Continent was probably no better—for many of the clergy were false to their vows of celibacy, poverty, and obedience. The terror of the Inquisition and the repres-sion of intellectual freedom in and out of the universities, an indig-nity for men who knew the value and validity of their new studies, all created an ambience of hostile fear. Transalpine Europe in the latter part of the fifteenth century was an explosion waiting to happen. A charismatic leader was the spark needed for ignition.

Martin Luther, aptly called "a man of Earth and God," certainly not at all a lovable person, stands out historically as the charismatic leader needed. An Augustinian monk, he was infuriated by the immorality of the clergy, and he denied the validity of the doctrine of transubstantiation and challenged the claims of the pope to ecclesiastical and secular power as fraudulent. He left the monastery, married a nun, raised a large number of children, translated the Bible into German, taught at the University of Wittenberg, and carried out a host of other activities. He was accused, but the church that accused him was forced by secular pressure to give him a hearing to defend himself at the Diet of Worms in 1521.

He was found guilty as charged, excommunicated, and, according to some sources, spirited away by friends before the council's assassins lying in wait could get to him. Excommunication at the time was a terrible punishment — it isolated the victim from all human contact but did not imprison him — but Luther had the backing of too many nobles anxious to see papal power curtailed for their own advantage for the ban to interfere with his work. He ended his defense before his jurors with the words, famous in the free world, *"Hier steh' ich. Ich kann nicht anders. So hilft mir Gott"* (Here I stand. I cannot do otherwise. So help me God). With these defiant words his break with the church emphasized the moral value that a person's conscience has to be the final judge of the morality of his acts. The Protestant Reformation was born with this basic and dynamic idea: *"Hier steh' ich. Ich kann nicht anders."*

The stream flowing toward the freedom of the individual conscience had flowed over and broken through the massive ecclesiastical obstruction, and its course ahead would be diverted, obstructed by hostile powers but facilitated by the actions of brave men, both Catholic and Protestant, who chose to protest against despotic authority and obvious ignorance. Out of the intellectual dynamism activated by the Protestant process came the Age of Enlightenment to enrich the intellectual life of western European culture, to lead in turn to our modern concepts of science and humanism, the humanistic-scientific imperative of our time. A sense of realism tells us that the stream still has a long course to follow; only the scenery on the banks has changed.

It was clear to me how the Renaissance in the northern countries had developed into the Protestant Reformation. It was also clear that the artist in Italy and the intellectual searcher in the north had each a demon that drove him on his quest. Many of the intellectual leaders in the north of different persuasions paid with their lives for their courage. They refused to pay the Danegeld. To paraphrase the early Christian epigram, "The blood of the martyrs is the seed of the Church," I would say, "The blood of the protesters is the seed of liberty."

Toward the final days of my *Wandeljahre* as I lingered in the fabled environment of Florence in a reflective mood, I saw Michelangelo's *Creation of Adam* as the Christian adaptation of the Prometheus myth, in which God as Prometheus, the intellectual benefactor of humankind, activates the inert mass of clay made man as He touched and shared His divinity with him. I heard Shelley's words and accepted the challenge to me:

> Gentleness, Virtue, Wisdom, and Endurance,
> These are the seals of that most firm assurance
>   Which bars the pit over Destruction's strength; . . .
> These are the spells by which to reassume
> An empire o'er the disentangled doom.
> To suffer woes which Hope thinks infinite;
>   To defy Power, which seems omnipotent;
> To love, and bear; to hope till Hope creates
> From its own wreck the thing it contemplates
>   Neither to change, nor falter, nor repent; . . .
> This is alone Life, Joy, Empire, and Victory.

(Prometheus Unbound, act 4)

And out of the past of my boyhood I heard the voices of my parents, "You know, Lutie, you are supposed to. . . ." How good it was to hear and sense the continuity of life! *"Hier steh' ich. Ich kann nicht anders."*

I returned to Paris that spring of 1926 secure in the knowledge that the spiritually troubled lad who had come ashore in London the previous autumn had by free inquiry found the object of his quest, his identity. Thanks to my *Wandeljahre* I had been able to bring all my life into a total, organized body of related experience. The self-confidence of my youth had matured into that of the man, and I could and would meet on its own terms any problem the future might bring and accept my responsibility for my decision. I had crossed my Rubicon, fought my battles, and won my objective.

I was eager to return to London for a last visit with Dorothy; I owed her so much for the support she had given me, especially for those months after we parted, I to go to Amsterdam and then wrestle with my problems across much of western Europe. During those months my only correspondence from New York was an occasional letter from Ruth Benedict. My letters from Margaret were few and long in coming. It was one of Ruth's letters, written after the department at Columbia finally got word of Margaret's safety, which gave me the first information that there had been a typhoon. Dorothy's friendly, interested letters during the autumn were really the only outside communication with any frequency.

During my first days in London she had told me how a very close young friend, an associate from her wonderful days at the Fabian Research Council, in his despair had taken his life, persuading his girl friend, also a friend of Dorothy's, to accompany him. Going through her papers after her death I found a bundle of letters to her from friends to whom she had written apparently feeling a desperate sense of guilt that she had not done more to prevent the tragedy by being more insightful and sensitive to his need. The letters all assured Dorothy that she could not have done any more to help the lad, because he no longer could accept help. It was only later in our relationship that I sensed she had seen a parallel between her friend and my state of mind when we first met. She would not fail this time!

Her frequent letters, friendly, not affectionate, for we respected my marriage, were in touch with mine and what I was doing and thinking. She copied poems she thought would interest me, many from Ezra Pound, for she discovered we both liked his work. She introduced me to Yeats, whom for some odd reason I hadn't known. My paper on Modernism went through a typing at her hands. She wrote her letters in longhand, but typed the poems late at night after everyone else was in bed and shared the latent heat from the dining room's coal hearth-fire — her room had no hearth — with a nocturnal visitor, a small mouse she called, for some now forgotten reason, Henry James. For several weeks I followed her delightful reporting of Henry James's exploits in picking up bread crumbs from the carpet and running over her toes as he ranged for tidbits. The two were close friends. Then the stories ended on a tragic note; Mary, the maid, came into the room one morning and discovered that Henry James had had a glutton's feast the night before on the green leaves of a favorite geranium. Mary's anger was such that she "fixed" Henry James, who came no more. The exploits of Henry so charmingly told,

along with her chatty, interested participation in my progress, gave
me support, a sense that what happened to me was important enough
to someone else, to her, to want to share and discuss. Other than Dorothy's support I was alone; and with the kinds of thoughts and
decisions I was facing every day, loneliness can have a very hostile
mien.

I wrote Dorothy from Paris asking if I might come to London so
we could see each other for a last time and, if she would like, set a
date and place to meet. I gave her the date I planned to leave for
Marseilles to meet Margaret. She wrote me to come to Jordans, a small
village in Bucks with Friends' history, where she would be staying at
the hostel for a few days. I should arrive on Sunday morning, her last
day, so we could walk in the springtime country and in the late afternoon return to London, I to my lodgings she had reserved for me.

I arrived as planned after an uneventful Channel crossing at night
from Dieppe to Newhaven, and Dorothy met me warmly at the little
station.

"Have you had breakfast?"

"I am afraid not. I came straight from the boat train."

"I thought so. I told Mrs. George that we should probably want
breakfast. Jacques"—a mutual friend—"came out to walk one
Sunday and I assumed he had breakfast before he left, but unfortunately he hadn't and was too polite to tell me, so that at the end of
the day I had a very hungry and tired Jacques on my hands."

After a short rest following a good breakfast we started our day's
walk, going first to the old, very plain, dignified meeting house. Here
we knelt and sat for a short period of silent meditation and reflection.
This rewarding experience set the tone for our day. The May morning's early mists trailed thin veils to vanish into the sun's increasing
warmth. White hawthorn hedges were breaking surf, and bluebells
shared the grass with other wild flowers. It was a day of rare beauty.
We found a quiet spot at the base of an ancient oak to enjoy our
lunch surrounded by this loveliness. We relived together my lonely
search for my identity. Alas! This day too had to end with our return
to London. There in the next few days we spent as much time
together as we could in the country when Dorothy could get time
from her work and caring for her parents. In the city we managed
brief periods of quiet reflection in our little sanctuary from the
January days, St. Patrick's, Soho.

That Sunday at Jordans, the meeting house meditation, the day-long walking and tarrying in the beauty of the English countryside bursting into spring was the completion of my *Wandeljahre's* search. We did not talk about the ruins of ancient cultures, the contributions of Freud to human happiness or distress, or other topical subjects of the day; we talked about the resurgence of life vivified now in nature and its continuity, about one's personal problems and related them to the message of what we saw so convincingly enveloping us. Without knowing it I was calling up strength from the deep springs of my boyhood in the country and seeing my life and all as a part of a whole, governed by the whole's imperative. It was a day in which, with Dorothy's deep personal insight, I found the last elements of my identity. That day Dorothy and I placed the capstone on the arch I had built.

The night of my return to Paris found us at Waterloo Station. We said our good-byes with heavy hearts, but happy in the knowledge that I had found myself and that she had played so important a part in the search. We promised to continue our friendship on those terms, friendship, for it had become too rich to drop, and to not let it interfere with any other relationship. The whistle blew and there was a last embrace and good-bye before I boarded the boat train to Newhaven for the night crossing to Dieppe.

The smooth crossing was fascinating as I sat in a deck chair under a starlit sky. With the first sign of the sun over the horizon, three Muslims unrolled their prayer rugs on the deck, knelt side by side facing Mecca, and paid their homage to Allah.

Paris, when I arrived, was clean in the early morning sunlight after its washing by a night shower. I directed the taxi driver to my little hotel near the Sorbonne. What a drive! Fortunately, the streets were practically empty. My driver went "like Jehu," tooting his horn at intersections to dash through without slowing down, as I braced myself for a shock and hardly dared look. I had underestimated his skill, for he pulled up triumphantly to a stop at my hotel with car and passenger unscathed. I got out the opened door and handed the driver the proper amount as shown on the meter with a 10 percent tip. Smiling, with a slight shrug of his shoulders, he refused my money but said, *"Regardez l'avis, monsieur."*

I looked at the *avis*, notice, on the meter and read that between midnight and six o'clock the tariff was double. I looked at my watch, and it was three minutes before six. Then the driver held his watch for me to see, and it agreed with mine. We both laughed as I doubled both the fare and the tip.

"*Merci bien, monsieur.*" And he climbed into his cab.

"*Il n'y a pas de quoi,*" I replied and went to my room.

How appropriate that this unique and happy week should end in laughter early on a lovely spring morning in Paris.

The night of my return, some inner compulsion, which I must admit I made no special effort to restrain, moved me to write Dorothy a fervent love letter, my first transgression of any kind of our bond of friendship. It was not a letter asking for anything then or in the future, but an outpouring of my heart for all she had done for me as I sat in my room that night reliving the experiences of the week just past. It was a statement of a feeling I wanted her to know I had, a present assertion of a truth — just that. I mailed it with some hesitation, but the compulsion was stronger.

Dorothy's answer, eagerly awaited, came in a few days, perceptive, understanding, appreciative, to bring me gently but firmly back to earth. Never again did I transgress our bond, but I am glad for just that once.

My last few days in Paris before going to Marseilles to meet Margaret passed *so slowly*. In my eagerness to rejoin her, I had even hoped I could meet her ship, the *Chitral*, a great Peninsula and Orient liner on her maiden voyage from Australia before it docked. Since Port Said was the only possible place and both time and money were insufficient, that dream of a surprise meeting had be abandoned for Marseilles. We would have a few days to ourselves in Marseilles to get reacquainted, as it were, then Louise Rosenblatt would join us after the completion of her year at Grenoble. We three would see some of the storied sites of Provence, cross to Carcassone, then go north to Tours in the Loire country and finally to Paris for a short but exciting time before I returned to New York. We would be carefree tourists. After I left Paris, Margaret planned to attend some scientific meetings, visit several museums, and meet some authorities in her field of anthropology. I had found a large, sunny hotel room for our short stay in Marseilles.

I was at the pier when the *Chitral* tied up, waiting for the gangplank to be lowered. As the passengers started to disembark I ran up the gangplank to greet Margaret. But *no Margaret*! I waited a few minutes, then stood back to watch the passengers. *Still* no Margaret. I returned to the pier and walked along the side of the ship, looking up at the rail high above me and hoping somehow, I don't know how, to see Margaret there. I saw a young woman leaning on the ship's rail too high to recognize her as an individual. Not to waste any chances I waved. Courteously, she waved back. More waves back and forth, then she turned and walked away obviously bored with the whole business. I returned to the foot of the gangplank almost ill with disappointment and fear that something had happened to Margaret. Just then she appeared at the head of the gangplank with a tall, rather handsome young man, who zipped back out of sight when he saw me. Margaret, very crestfallen and completely without enthusiasm, met me as I hurried to her.

She hastily explained, "I'm sorry, but we were talking and didn't know the ship had stopped."

"Just so you are all right; I was almost sick with worry and disappointment."

The luckless nature of our meeting and Margaret's sense of depression and lack of enthusiasm enveloped us both in a smothering cloud of dejection. I took her baggage check, got her trunk, and helped her clear customs; and we took a taxi to our room, flooded with sunshine when we arrived.

Shortly, while sitting across my knees in near silence, *tres triste*, she turned to me, saying, "Do you remember how you said before our marriage . . . ?"

Here it comes, I thought, that San Francisco letter again. "Yes, of course, go on."

"Well, I met someone on board ship I love that way and I want to marry him."

"Tell me, Margaret, what's he like?" I said, trying to conceal my feelings and keep her talking.

She told me of a brilliant, young New Zealand student on his way to Cambridge University on a two-year fellowship awarded for his work on dreams. He was the first person of that caliber she had met since leaving Hawaii on her way to Samoa. She was a young woman anthropologist, the first in his experience, returning from an exciting field trip, who could and would talk eagerly, intelligently, and sympathetically with him about his work, something quite lacking at home. It was a long voyage on a fine ship ideally suited to a summer romance. They had talked and talked and talked and apparently were still talking, "debating" Margaret wrote, when the *Chitral* docked.

I did not behave as a husband whose honor has been challenged, nor was I threatened with the loss of a cherished possession, for neither Margaret nor I were possessions of the other. I was a very much interested party in the problems of a young woman I was married to and in love with. I think my newly won maturity with the resultant self-confidence helped me to respond sympathetically to a very serious problem instead of "getting up a great head" of emotional steam.

"Let's go to lunch," I said. "I think we both need it and will then feel better."

We took a taxi, and I gave the driver the name of the restaurant I wanted to go to. He started to move out of his parking slot, when to my chagrin Margaret suddenly sat up and almost shouted at him, "*Tu vache, tu vache!*"

At some time in my life, before she went to Samoa, she told me if I wanted to berate a French taxi driver I should do just what she had done, for it was a really derogatory expression when so used. I never made an effort to find out, and I had many warm memories of rides in French taxis. The driver turned his head and seemed to be going to stop. I spoke to him in French, "Madam is not well; she has just come from the ship after a long voyage from Australia."

Apparently satisfied, he proceeded to our destination. I gave him a very good tip. I have never understood what could have possessed Margaret to do this, first to suddenly take over responsibility when I was in charge—with her agreement ("You choose the restaurant; you know where to go")—and then her completely shocking outburst at the driver for no discernible reason whatsoever. She was obviously in a state of extreme emotional tension to the extent of being capable of irrational behavior.

For the few days until Louise joined us we moved as a rather depressed young couple. We talked about our past year's work and, of course, the young man, Reo Fortune, who had gone to England, not to return to Paris to see Margaret, certainly not while I was there. Louise shared our problem shortly after joining us, for the unexpected state of mind she found was too obvious not to take her into our confidence. Together we tried our best to enjoy the Roman ruins, the old cities of Nîmes, Arles, and Avignon, where we didn't feel like dancing *"sur le pont"* had it been possible.

We stopped at storied Carcassone where, as Margaret writes in *Blackberry Winter*: "At Carcassone I re-chose Luther."[43] I remained unaware of her act until I read it in *Blackberry Winter*. I remember almost nothing of Carcassone save the lyric beauty of the architecture as I tried in my imagination to repopulate it with knights, their ladies and squires, jousts and tournaments.

Tours was our next stopping place in the Loire country of châteaus. I went to the American Express office to pick up any forwarded mail, and to my surprise and delight found a cable, just arrived, from the College of the City of New York offering me again the same position under the same conditions I had held before sailing for Europe. I cabled my acceptance immediately, for I had been successful and liked the students. Since I had not had the least idea of what I might do when I returned to New York — I knew the church was an impossibility — this piece of good luck was "manna from heaven." After a few days of being tourists we moved on to Paris.

Margaret and I had expected to have time in Paris to ourselves, but we had scarcely arrived when Margaret received a letter from Reo saying he was coming to Paris to see her, his sole reason. According to Margaret he was frightfully jealous on shipboard, and I suppose that made him break the understanding we thought we had. His arrival would be nothing but an irritant, but I knew I had to handle it as best I could.

He wrote that he wanted to see Margaret at a certain date and time without bothering to ask if it would be convenient. There was no address to reach him, so I told Margaret I would go out for the specified time and they could close out their conversation before I returned, when he would have gone. I was on my way out and stopped to tell the concierge at her desk, a young woman with combed-back black hair and dark eyes, that a young man would be coming to call on Miss Mead, when a tall, good-looking young lad stepped up beside me and interrupted my conversation with the concierge without apology.

"Tell Miss Mead that Mr. Fortune is here."

"I am Luther Cressman, Reo, and glad to see you. Margaret is expecting you."

Reo was speechless. The concierge looked at me with a "What goes on here?" expression. I told her in French that Mr. Fortune was a friend from the voyage from Australia and that it was quite all right. Then turning to Reo, speaking in English, I said, "Go on up, Margaret is expecting you in room 12." *"Merci bien,"* I said to the concierge, who gave me a charmingly enigmatic smile as I turned to walk out so as to end this strange contretemps, for she was not unaware that interests were involved, especially when Reo remained speechless. I saw him but once after that and inadvertently when I returned from "absenting myself awhile" so they might go out together. I came down the curving drive toward the hotel entrance and saw them in a close embrace under the light over the door. I quietly reversed course without making waves, took a turn around the block, and came back to find all clear. I went upstairs, but I *never mentioned* that episode to Margaret. I gave a small dinner at the American Association of University Women's hostel for Margaret and some of our friends from New York in Paris for the summer. Louise was one of our guests. I told Margaret to ask Reo, who was alone in Paris, to come if she wished and Louise would look after him. I think he came, but cannot remember.

Reo had apparently expected some confrontation, perhaps violent, with me, since that is the way it always was in the movies of the period when one man wanted to "take" another man's wife. Oddly enough I did not think of the problem in those terms, but rather that the wife had an equal voice with the others in coming to a decision without confrontation. When he found out that I was an unexpectedly decent fellow, he didn't know how to handle *that* situation. He wanted to accompany Margaret on her museums tour, a wish intended to provide the opportunity to move their relations to a more intimate degree than they had known. I understood this, for Margaret had discussed the idea with me.

Margaret and I talked and talked about what she should do. She obviously was convinced that she was very much in love with Reo but she had no idea if the dream would become actuality or remain fantasy. There was but one way, Reo's, to find out. Margaret was facing perhaps the most important decision of her young life and whatever decision she made would affect her life for an unknown number of years. I was in love with Margaret and wanted to help her, and I think my desire was buttressed by my own recent experiences in having successfully met my challenges, although of a different kind. So when Margaret asked me if I could give her the address of a responsible source of birth control to which she might go in England I didn't take it as a piece of preposterous impertinence, since she wanted the information in case she and Reo went together; I thought it was pretty sensible. Of course I gave her the address; Dr. Stopes had supplied me with that information for public use and here was a case for it. Margaret thanked me and later told me she had made use of the information. Margaret's assumption of the responsibility for this aspect of their proposed relation was a 180 degree reversal of the situation between us, and I wonder if it signalled an idea—one I did not pick up then—she had that in case it came into being the new relation between them would reflect this difference. I also looked upon sex as a many-faceted experience to be understood in terms of the cultural-social context in which it is embedded at any given time and place in history. And I had known only too well what the lack of help meant in my problems, and with these attitudes I tried to help her.

Margaret kept urging me to tell her what she should do, a request I steadfastly refused, for through three years of marriage I had learned that Margaret did not welcome advice on behavior from men, and a husband in particular. More important, I believed she should have a choice of actions, decide between them, and accept the responsibility for her decision. I told her that I thought she would never be satisfied until she knew whether her dream was reality or fantasy, and it was my opinion that she should find out. To do that she had to have freedom of choice, and I was offering it to her; if I told her what to do, I removed the freedom and she had neither choice nor responsibility. My opinion, not my "telling her," was that she should attempt to verify her dream. If it proved to be fantasy and she wanted to share my life as my wife, I would love to have her; I intended my love to be a releasing force to help her fulfill her life, not to encase her, even loosely, in a straitjacket of restraints. I told her that, in terms of her own conscience, now she had a choice, she had to make her own decision, and accept the responsibility. I believe, however, as I write these words Margaret would rather have won her freedom of choice than have it thrust upon her by me.

Reo's arrival and the subsequent tensions in Paris took the kernel out of the nut of our planned Parisian days. My new appointment at the College of the City of New York provided me the opportunity to free myself by possibly moving up the date of my departure on the excuse of preparing courses and securing an apartment. Professor Ogburn, in Paris and without information on our emotional problems, offered to lend me the necessary books so I could stay on, but I refused as graciously as I could.

I succeeded in moving up the date of my return with passage on the *George Washington*. Louise came with Margaret to see me off at the Gare St. Lazare for Cherbourg. In the few minutes before the train was whistled, Margaret was in tears.

"Tell me what to do, tell me what to do."

"No, I have offered you a choice and freedom, and you must make your own decision."

The boarding whistle blew, I embraced and kissed Margaret and swung onto the bottom step and called to Louise holding Margaret weeping on her shoulder.

"Take care of her, Louise, take care of her!"

The train pulled out.

After arriving in New York I quickly found a nice apartment at 610 West 115th Street, a large, light, all-purpose living room, small kitchen, bedroom and bath, between Broadway and Riverside Drive in one of the high-rise apartment buildings forming a quadrangle about a concrete court on which our living room faced. It was close to Columbia and had convenient transportation for Margaret to the American Museum of Natural History and me, either by subway or walking, to the College of the City of New York.

When I went ashore in England in the early autumn of 1925 I knew that I had to solve three problems: the brooding sense of despair which threatened me, my relationship to the priesthood to which I had been ordained, and my marriage. The first two involved only myself, but the last, a dual one, could be solved only by our cooperative efforts. Of the three, only my marriage remained unsolved at the end of my *Wandeljahre*. Since I devote most of the remainder of this section to this problem, it is imperative to make clear just what I shall try to do.

I am writing about the *young Margaret*, with whom I had the unique, good fortune to share those exciting years of growth and maturation in the early 1920s as her fiancé and husband. Because of that relationship I think I am more qualified than those who did not know me then to write understandingly of the remarkable young woman and human being she was—a quality I fear some of her admirers tend sometimes to forget. I am not writing about the Margaret of our postdissolution years, for I didn't know that Margaret. I kept no photos, no memorabilia beyond a few books of poetry or belles lettres she had given me. For over fifty years we had no regular communication until the publication of her *Blackberry Winter* brought the exchange of a few letters between us on matters discussed in her book. With the exception of Ruth Benedict I had no contact with any of the close circle of our friends of the Columbia days.

I am writing about Margaret and myself as wife and husband, and to know what she thought about our marriage and its termination beyond my memory I must go to her *Blackberry Winter* as her apparently final, valid statement. As the other person in the relationship I have an obligation to share in presenting the record as I see it. I stated earlier how she and I disagreed about her accuracy in reporting certain readily ascertainable pieces of information, some not important in themselves, but others were quite the contrary. I was simply reporting corrective facts, not engaging in criticism of her; Margaret was a social anthropologist, not a historian, whereas I am a historian and humanist. If my record of our marriage and its dissolution contains historically verifiable statements in conflict with hers, they carry their own validity. Opinions are of a different order of experience, but significant in their own way and deserving of consideration on their terms. When I offer an opinion that differs from hers, I am not attacking her competence or integrity, but simply expressing that I differ and in what manner, in an effort to aid in the understanding of a very complex personality. Disagreement to be sure, but denigration? Of course not!

I met Margaret on her arrival from her summer's tour at the pier and brought her to our new apartment. She was happy to be home, generally enthusiastic about her contacts, but felt there were many other anthropologists she needed to meet and museums with which she needed to become familiar. We settled easily into our routines. Margaret took up her new duties as assistant curator at the American Museum of Natural History and started the analysis of her field material from her Samoa study.[44] I found my teaching exciting and rewarding because I found it easy to establish empathy with my students.[45]

At CCNY each staff member in the Department of Government, which included the disciplines of sociology, political science, and anthropology, had to teach a section of the basic course in American government in addition to his special field, in my case cultural anthropology, sociology, and criminology.

My interest in criminology focused my attention on the New York State Legislature's public hearings on a proposed change in the laws relating to felonies by which it expected to prevent such acts by the prescription of extremely severe punishment, in this case compulsory life imprisonment for the fourth conviction. Professor Raymond Moley of Columbia University was, I believe, the executive secretary of the Baumes Commission (as it was called), and presided at the hearings, one of which I attended. The philosophy of the group advocating this perennial nostrum was either ignorant of history or chose to ignore it, for it was in conflict with the history of crime prevention in English-speaking countries. I rather hesitantly thought I should write an article, hopefully for publication, to expose the fatuity of the proposed change. My attendance at the hearings convinced me that I had to write it. I drew most of my material from the English experience at the end of the eighteenth and beginning of the nineteenth centuries. The proposed bill became law before my article was finished, so I had newspaper reports of the brief experience under the enforcement of the new law to support my argument. In the context of our English heritage in the field of jurisprudence and our values of human rights, I predicted the law would fail to achieve its objectives just as the English laws had failed. I submitted the article to the *American Review of Reviews*, a leading journal of opinion.[46] Imagine my pleasure and surprise to receive in the morning mail in a very short time a letter of acceptance and an apology that they could not pay me more than $100 for which a check was enclosed. Hard-pressed financially, I thought the payment was munificent, especially since I had not anticipated anything.

Later, I prepared an article from some of my unused data and new sources on the futility of capital punishment as a deterrence to homicide. I submitted it to *The Survey*, a journal devoted to social issues. It was accepted and published as the lead article,[47] but *The Survey* did not pay for its volunteered contributions. My experience with these two articles while engaged in full-time teaching was of the greatest importance, for it built up my self-confidence in my professional ability to see and formulate a problem, do the necessary research to come to a reasonable conclusion, and publish in journals of wide distribution and high respect. I found reenforcement of my previous year's experience in my personal life.

Our lives settled easily into daily routines of productive work and association with earlier friends and some new, especially for me with my contacts at CCNY and Columbia. I no longer had contacts with the church or seminary except for casual meetings, such as one day, much later in the year, while walking across the Columbia campus in front of the Low Library I met a classmate from the seminary in his clerical dress. We stopped for a brief chat.

"I hear you have left the church, Luther," Frank said questioningly.

"Yes, Frank, I have."

"I wish to God I could!"

As we parted I thought, "You poor devil, but worse your poor parishioners."

Our lives together, in the familiar academic and social environment we knew so well, moved apparently as smoothly as those of other young married professional couples both working full time. Our new apartment was like the old at 419 West 119th Street: a center for stimulating social life, a sanctuary for a friend in need of a bed for the night or longer, or just some company and talk. There was, however, a certain significant although not very explicit difference: gone was the euphoria of those exciting years of our early postwar period and replaced, certainly for Margaret and me, by a maturity of judgment and certainty of professional goals.

Most of our social life involved our peers, but on occasion there was an invitation to dinner with the family of a former professor. The Pacific Islands then, well before World War II, were a widespread source of romantic fantasy stimulated by steamship lines' travel advertisements. Margaret, wearing the aura of her year in the "romantic Pacific Isles," was rightly the center of attention at a dinner our former professor and friend, Ogburn, and his wife gave for us. Margaret could tell a good story with a dramatic flair and was a good conversationalist. That night she was clearly the star of the show. At the time, a very successful play on Broadway about the Brownings, *The Barretts of Wimpole Street*, always had Robert spoken of as "Mrs. Browning's husband." It was in this context as we walked home in a light-hearted mood that I asked Margaret teasingly, "Am I always going to be referred to as Dr. Mead's husband?"

Under the apparently smoothly flowing surface of our marital relations there was agitation, but not turbulence. Not long after her return from Europe Margaret told me Reo's and her summer plans for intimacy had been frustrating and disappointing: there had been none. In *Blackberry Winter* she ignores completely this subject, so important in our discussions during those last days in Paris.

During the year 1926–27, while trying to develop my academic work and find rapport with Margaret, I had postponed any action relating to my priesthood. Finally, I decided I had to face that anguishing decision and on March 2, 1927, I wrote my bishop:

> My dear Bishop Darlington:
>
> It is with a great deal of distress that I find myself compelled to write this letter. However, I know that your understanding will give it a sympathetic acceptance.
>
> I have had several years experience in pastoral work and about an equal number in teaching. As a result of this experience I am now convinced where my work really lies. As a teacher I am more successful, more satisfied and happy than in pastoral work. These two facts, my greater success in teaching and my greater happiness in that work leaves no doubt in my mind now what work I should do.
>
> Therefore, since I do not care to remain a titular priest, I am asking that my name be removed from the list of the clergy for no reason affecting my morals or character, and that I be returned to the status of a lay communicant.
>
> > With best wishes, I remain,
> > Very respectfully yours,
> > (signed) Luther S. Cressman

He replied March 4, 1927, very understandingly and asked me to meet to discuss my request with him:

> Dear Mr. Cressman:
>
> Your communication of March second, stating that you do not longer "care to remain as titular priest," and "ask-

ing that your name be removed from the list of clergy for no reason affecting your morals or character and that you be returned to the status of a lay communicant," is received.

According to Canon #36 it is required that I defer formal action for three months, and meanwhile lay the matter before the clerical members of the Standing Committee, and wait their action.

You pleased the Examining Chaplains and others who met you at the time of your examinations and Ordination, and I know they will unite with me in feeling sincere regret that you have determined to resume the status of a layman.

I hope you will consider the matter carefully, and as I have been telephoned to be at my sons rectory next Monday night, March seventh, and if you can find it convenient, I wish you would call at 65 East 89th Street, and talk the matter over with me.

We have three or four vacancies in the Diocese now, to one of which I would be glad to appoint you if we could make arrangements; and if you still retain your Holy Orders.

God bless you in whatever you determine upon, and guide you in all your ways, is the prayer of your friend and Bishop.

Very sincerely yours,
(signed) James H. Darlington

Our discussion was warm and friendly, but he understandingly was reluctant for me to carry out my decision. I don't believe he really understood, like most other clerics I talked with, the real nature of my problem. When I saw that there was little chance of convincing him, I tried a different approach and said, "Bishop Darlington, I regret very much to have to tell you this but it is essential. I am afraid our marriage is on a very uncertain course and it may be that my wife will want a divorce to marry another person, and, if so, I shall not stand in her way. You know, Bishop Darlington, that you could not tolerate a divorced priest in your diocese."

He remained silent, and I too, for perhaps a couple of minutes; he was obviously reflecting deeply on our problem. Then he turned to me not as a bishop to his priest but as an older man to a younger and said, "I'll tell you now, Mr. Cressman, what I told a parishioner a few days ago—she was grieving terribly over the loss of her baby in childbirth. I said to her, 'Mrs. James, you must stop grieving for your lost baby. What you must do is start another and think about that.' And so, my young friend, I give you the same advice in your regrettable situation.''

I could hardly believe the reality of this sudden, complete change in status and role, but my respect for Henry Darlington as both bishop and plain human adviser, the man, was greatly increased that night. He then told me what formal steps he would have to take under canon law and that he would be in touch with me. We parted as two friends with his warm words, ''God bless and help you, my young friend.''

I also knew I had to write to Dean Fosbroke at the seminary and explain my decision, a requirement well beyond a simple courtesy. On the same day on which I wrote my bishop I wrote the dean. A part of my letter follows:

> I accepted the church and all I did while I was connected with it was that I might serve it more efficiently and honestly. This change in my attitude is something that no one could have foreseen. I never acted under false pretenses and I certainly am not now. To go on as a priest would be to change all that and be false to those very values for which the church stands. You, I know, though you may regret the necessity of this action, as I do so acutely, will understand what I have done.
>
> I can never adequately express my sense of indebtedness, in a non-material even more than in a material way, to the seminary for the new life it opened up to me. Let me assure you that the fine things it gave to me are a part of me and my efforts shall be to keep them so. If at any time I am financially able to do so I shall repay to the Seminary the money it advanced to me for my fellowships. I shall not cease to urge and teach those fine things which you have given, because I have left the priesthood, and so I want to believe that although the Church may have lost a minister the fundamental things for which she stands will not have lost a loyal protagonist who will serve their cause even though in an alien field.

On December 21, 1927, in St. Stephen's Church, where on January 31, 1923, I was ordained to the priesthood by Bishop

Darlington, he read the canonically required notice in response to my request of March 2, 1927:

> . . . a majority of the Standing Committee . . . declare that such renunciation is accepted, and that said LUTHER SHEELEIGH CRESSMAN, not being amenable for any canonical offense, and his renunciation of the Ministry being not occasioned by foregoing misconduct or irregularity, but voluntary and for causes assigned or known, which do not affect his moral character, is hereby suspended for six months from the Ministry, and if the renunciation be not withdrawn within that period, I will then pronounce sentence of deposition from the Ministry.
>
> (signed) James Henry Darlington
Bishop of Harrisburg

My receipt of this notice, expected as it was, had, nonetheless, a certain shock impact; a stage of my life had come to an end—a stage that in its wonder and even pain could never be repeated. My mind called up my vision from the mountaintop, the unique ecstasy of my first Mass on Easter Day in 1923, the agony of doubt, the moving pageantry of Chartres on All Saints' Day and the religious-political drama acted out at the Vatican on Easter 1926, the sight of the wedding deep in the Basilica at Assisi with the final realization that I could not serve in the priesthood. Santayana's poem echoes so beautifully my experience:

> Slow and reluctant was the long descent,
> With many farewell pious looks behind,
> And dumb misgivings where the path might wind,
> And questionings of nature, as I went.
> The greener branches that above me bent,
> The broadening valleys, quieted my mind,
> To the fair reasons of the Spring inclined
> And to the Summer's tender argument.
> But sometimes, as revolving night descended,
> And in my childish heart the new song ended,
> I lay down, full of longing, on the steep;
> And haunting still the lonely way I wended,
> Into my dreams the ancient sorrow blended,
> And with these holy echoes charmed my sleep.
>
> (*Sonnet II*)

As the year wore on the friendly banter Margaret and I enjoyed over the relative merits of sociology and anthropology continued, but with a more serious character now; we each knew that we were talking about our future in marriage. I remember so distinctly a conversation one Sunday morning after a lazy breakfast when I suggested the possibility of my joining her on her next field party, which we had been discussing. She made it quite clear that it would not work because I lacked whatever it was she wanted in a co-worker. I was a sociologist, not an anthropologist. My contribution would have to be limited to minor elements of material culture, a subject with which she was not concerned in the planned study. The upshot of the discussion was that she had made it clear I was not desired as a field co-worker.

Shortly after this conversation she was promoting a proposal in case our marriage ended to arrange a marriage between Eda Lou Walton and me — and I interrupted her.

"It would never work, we are too negative."

"I didn't know you saw that."

I saw, dear Margaret, a great deal more than you realized.

Margaret planned to go to Europe in the summer of 1927 to broaden her knowledge of Oceanic cultures by visiting museums and conferring with specialists in that area. We used my experience in Europe to help plan her trip. Reo had written that he was passing through Europe to Australia, where he had received a research grant; naturally, they planned to meet.

I saw her off at the pier — I was teaching in the Summer Session at CCNY — and we looked forward to her return to continue our marriage. She wrote me just before her ship docked at Hamburg, where her letter was posted, a letter full of confidence in our future together. A few days later another from her arrived from Berlin, where she had met Reo apparently three days after the posting of the Hamburg letter. It was short, abrupt, and final, no premarital preamble escape hatch as at Marseilles. She wanted a divorce so she and Reo could marry. The letter was a shock, but somehow I carried out my day's lecture schedule. If she finally wanted a divorce I would agree to it, for it was always in the unwritten bond of our marriage.

The day her Berlin letter arrived I had a dinner engagement with Dorothy Thomas, who called at the apartment for me following her afternoon work. She was sitting in a large wing chair, I on the floor facing her. Somewhat tearfully, to her consternation, I told her about the letter; then I broke out laughing.

Dorothy stared at me incredulously and asked, "What's the matter?"

"Don't you hear that?"

"No, what is it?"

"Listen."

A radio was blaring out of a window into the courtyard, of all things, "Love's Old Sweet Song"!

"The cream of the jest," I said. "Let's go to dinner."

A quotation from a long letter I wrote Dorothy Loch in London on July 7, 1927, explains my record of the event, Margaret's request for a divorce, and it differs somewhat from Margaret's, at least in the impression her account in *Blackberry Winter* conveys.[48] Dorothy and I had continued our correspondence as we agreed to when we said "good-bye" and on the same friendly terms as during my year in Europe. Her letters always came to our apartment and were, of course, no secret; Reo's, I suppose, went to Margaret's museum address, for I have no memory of them arriving in the morning's mail at our apartment. My letter begins:

> At last this letter which I dreaded and hoped so hard that I would not have to write has found its place in the scheme of things. I told you in the post-script to my last letter [that would have been a week or ten days before] about Margaret and Ray [for some reason I called Reo "Ray" in that letter] Fortune. [And now] Margaret's divorce request. . . . Margaret sailed quite certain of coming back to continue our life together. Her letters from the boat including the Hamburg [one] wrote of a calm, composed mind and a sureness of the impossibility of the venture. . . . And then she met Ray in Berlin and after about three days decided to marry him. . . . [Inferred from the dates on her letter.] A week before she had been writing me about choosing an apartment together for next year, visiting France together, perhaps next summer and other plans. Then all of a sudden this. . . .

I met Margaret at the pier on her return late in the summer. Not unexpectedly, our meeting was imbued with a sense of melancholy. She was firm; she wanted the divorce. Of course, I kept my bond. Our last week together was not besmirched with quarrels or recriminations. Why Margaret did what she did the way she did it I have never fully understood. I am convinced, however conceived and for all the hurt, it was the best way.

> Shot? So quick so clean an ending?
> Oh that was right, lad, that was brave. . . .
> (A. E. Housman, *A Shropshire Lad*)

The manner of Margaret's action killed forever, as clean as a gunshot, the basis of our marriage.

Margaret, with my approval, agreed to file for divorce in Hermosillo, Sonora, Mexico. Each was represented by counsel, and our only point of disagreement was my refusal to pay half the costs of the proceedings, which she felt I should. The decree became final the next year.[49]

On August 19, 1927, I moved to an apartment on Charles Street in Greenwich Village. I planned to sail shortly for England to spend a hastily planned week with Dorothy in the country at a place of her choosing before starting teaching again at CCNY.

When I moved to the Village, Léonie Adams gave me a copy of her recently published volume of poetry, *Those Not Elect*. She wrote this inscription:

> For L.S.C.
> Bred to a harder thing than triumph . . .
> Be secret and exult
> Because of all things known,
> That is most difficult.
> Léonie Adams
Summer, 1927

Léonie's thoughtful gift is with me as I write.

L'Envoi to Margaret

As I reflect from my vantage point after a half century since the divorce, I am convinced that our marriage was ill-starred from the beginning, although we were happily unaware of the fate awaiting us. The juxtaposed stars were our utterly different early years, so important in shaping personalities. Mine I have described; Margaret recounts hers in *Blackberry Winter*. Margaret's childhood was lived almost exclusively in an academic atmosphere, a conceptual world, in a family with little integration and less community participation. She had none of the close relation to nature that was a part of me. Her ideas of the nonacademic world derived almost entirely from books. Exercise of authority and leadership were early thrust upon her; by the time she was six her family gave her much responsibility for her brother and sisters. Her parents never let her fail to remember that she was to be a leader, to have an outstanding career; in contemporary idiom she was programmed to achieve distinction.

Her play activities were always in the intellectual field, never a part of the group activities related to the rhythms of nature that were characteristic of a rural population: skating, fishing, swimming, small groups of friends on a Sunday, walking the fields and woods in search of spring flowers. Her capacity for fantasy found an outlet in the dramatic activities she organized. She usually wrote the script, chose the cast, and directed the play, with herself in the lead. Her fantasy world provided the outlet for her remarkable imaginative, intellectual capacity. I became involved in her early life, and I must look at it briefly in that respect, as I think I can, with understanding and objectivity.

Margaret recalls in *Blackberry Winter* with obvious pleasure her close association in her early years with the spinster daughter of the rather charming, elderly rector of the little Episcopal church at Buckingham. She gave herself completely to membership in the church and its ritual life — Margaret never did anything by halves. I think it is quite probable that the rector's daughter found in the devoted young Margaret a surrogate for the child she had forgone. If one compares the tensions Margaret describes in her family with the apparent peace and security of the rector's family, she must have found the latter very appealing. I never felt there was any real warmth of maternal affection in the Mead family. I remember more than once Margaret's comment: "Poor Mother, she is so naive." There was mutual respect between Margaret and her mother, and her mother had the utmost confidence in her daughter's future achievements. But that is not the same as a warm, affectionate relationship. I think Margaret found in relations with the rector's daughter the substitute for the warm, affectionate kind lacking at home.

Margaret projected this role-family imaginatively as the ideal to produce her own future happiness with, of course, the addition of a large number of children—I think we settled on six since I was one of six and would be comfortable with that number—to complete a family. This was part of our speculative conversation in our very early days when we saw each other but infrequently and my future was still uncertain, but with the ministry as a possibility. We dreamed together. When Margaret went away from home to college at DePauw, I was in my first year at the seminary. Her dream seemed to be moving toward realization.

The year at DePauw was a turning point in her life; she discovered how cruel the real world of one's peers and others can be. She learned the hard lesson that, if she were going to achieve, it had to be and could only be by her own efforts and not by reliance on membership in some status group. She learned that lesson well; and I could understand, for I, too, had learned it. She came to Barnard College, but the early dream world had crashed. She still dreamed, but instead of her dreams being the source of her aims, now her new world of knowledge became the source of her dreams. She wrote:

> In the autumn of 1920, I came to Barnard, where I found—*and in some measure created*—the kind of life that matched my earlier dreams. In the course of these three undergraduate years . . . and by the end of these years I knew what I could do in life. [Emphasis added.][50]

The intellectual growth and change she just described also applied to her attitude toward the church and my position in it. During her first (sophomore) year at Barnard, my second at the seminary, I was the superintendent of the Sunday School at St. Clement's and asked Margaret to help by teaching a class of youngsters. This she gladly did and met a group of pupils from a social background entirely new to her—I think she taught through her school year. After that, her interest in the church, at least toward my association with it, declined; the only subsequent occasion was one night in the autumn of 1924–25 when the congregation of the small church in Brooklyn graciously held a reception for the new priest and his wife, Margaret and me. It was not a happy or successful event. Although Margaret tried hard to fit into her position, she was ill at ease, a feeling obviously experienced by all. That single experience was another significant portent. Margaret's dream of a future as the wife of an Episcopal minister in a peaceful country parish clearly belonged to the past. We were then both in graduate school, and she dreamed new dreams and saw visions. The solid foundation now, however, was her discovery of anthropology and how her dreams could be realized.

Margaret never really understood or was interested in the acute personal problems of belief I faced in the challenge to my priestly profession by the releasing power of discovery through research I was finding in my graduate studies at Columbia University. My life was in a continuous dynamic intellectual state in which decisions had to be made, inevitably to affect my whole life. Margaret's comments in *Blackberry Winter* on my religious activities clearly reveal her nearly complete lack of involvement.

A trait I know well from those early days at 419 West 119th Street is important, I think, in understanding the Margaret I knew and perhaps the later person too. Melville Herskovits, with his Ph.D. degree in anthropology, older and vastly more experienced than Margaret, was finishing his postdoctoral research on the American Negro, and for several weeks was going through the throes of deciding whether to accept a position at Western Reserve or Northwestern University. He was a welcome and frequent guest who always enlivened our conversations. He used to "rag" Margaret for what he called her unscientific way of coming to conclusions. The arguments, always friendly, were sometimes heated. Mel asserted and gave chapter and verse showing how, when she found untenable a conclusion or description of behavior, etc., her defense was always, "If it isn't, it ought to be," and then chose the "ought to be" position. Margaret's escape was usually, "Well, what's so bad about that?" and the discussion would continue, but on another subject. As I recall those pleasant evenings I think the more-experienced Mel's "ragging" was an effort to help Margaret sharpen her thinking.

One night not long after Margaret's death I was talking long into the morning with a close friend of hers and I mentioned this trait, "If it's not, it should be." The friend was silent for a moment, thinking, and then replied just one word, "Yes."

I was surprised recently in the course of a TV interview by Dr. Bruce Dakowski on the Margaret of our years together to have him mention this trait of Margaret's and ask if I thought it interfered with the accuracy of her scientific observations in the field. I replied, "Of course not knowingly, any more than you or I would permit our biases to distort our observations." Where he got his information I don't know. Her co-workers and those who have seen her field notes insist that she was a meticulous observer in the field. What I have mentioned was a reality in our daily life.

Margaret offers an involved explanation of why and how she decided to terminate our marriage.[51] It is not good history, only rather bad reporting. It is worse when one remembers she had the documents to have avoided errors of fact. I think that she was writing in a terrible hurry, "off the top of her head," and the trait I have described became unwittingly the integrating factors at the time in her thinking and writing. I am not interested in picking over old bones only in trying to explain what happened in our relationship: that the two youngsters who pledged their love that bitterly cold night in a snow-covered world on December 31, 1917, had grown apart in the normal course of maturation. We did not quarrel, we respected each other, and we retained our dignity. Margaret makes clear in one paragraph that quite frankly she decided to make professional qualification the basic requirement in the choice of mate and co-worker; I still believe that the basic requirement for any marriage is love.

Our parting in 1928 was without bitterness but not without hurt, a hurt I submerged deep in my subconscious until I had to dredge up the whole experience in this writing; only then did I realize the depth of the feeling. During the year following our separation we saw each other perhaps a half-dozen times, as far as I can remember, either fortuitously as guests at social affairs or over dinner to discuss our business matters. Margaret's statement that I did not want to discuss my hoped-for marriage with Dorothy Loch is true; I had to wait for Dorothy's answer, not anticipate it. Through the next forty-five years I lunched with her alone at the American Anthropological Association meetings in New York and, later, Margaret had Cecilia (Dorothy) and me as luncheon guests when Cecilia accompanied me to those meetings. Later still we entertained her in our home.

A few years before I retired June 30, 1963, I saw Margaret again at the national meetings. I wanted to talk with her, just a friendly conversation about where our ways were eventually taking us. Happily, I finally found her in a rather empty corridor and greeted her.

Her reply: "Hi, where is room . . . ? I want to hear a paper which is being read there."

"I suppose it's down the hall, but I would like very much to talk with you; if the paper is worth anything, it will be published and you can read it then. Let's talk."

"I come to meetings to hear papers," and strode toward the room.

I shrugged my shoulders, looked after her in wonder as she scurried, her hands full of miscellaneous papers, down the hall to hear another. I never again asked Margaret to talk or meet me. Margaret or someone acting for her arranged our subsequent meetings.

On her last lecture trip to Portland in August 1978, Margaret, terminally ill, stayed with the Wests—Martha Ullman West was Margaret's goddaughter—and I gladly accepted their invitation to be their overnight guest. That evening Martha planned a special dinner for Margaret and me. Margaret, Sara Ullman (Martha's mother and Margaret's close friend), Frank West, Martha, and I made up the dinner party. Martha wanted it to be a festive affair with no thoughts of illness. So it was.

The next day Margaret delivered the lecture she had come to give. She had to use crutches and a wheelchair to and from the car. Martha, who took her to the lecture, told me later that as soon as she started to speak the adrenalin began to flow and the old Margaret was at work. On Margaret's return to the house, I watched her painful struggle as she was assisted inside. After having rested, she said she could see me. I went to her room for a few minutes to say good-bye. In those few minutes we talked about inconsequential things—what nice people the Wests were, what a charming young daughter they had. We knew it was our last talk together.

Rising to leave, I took her poor wasted hand and kissed her good-bye, saying as I held it, "It has been a good life, Margaret."

"Yes, it has," she smiled in reply.

I gently lowered her hand, turned, and left the room to return home.

It was dark, August 20, 1978, when I boarded the Greyhound bus for Eugene, a nonstop run of two hours and fifteen minutes. Rain had started. On that steadily rolling bus, with inside lights dimmed, seeing the rain streaking down the windows and windshield as lights of approaching cars struck the wet glass, a lot of things "came unstuck" from where they had been fixed in my mind a half century before.

While I was sitting alone at breakfast, November 15, 1978, my phone rang; it was Martha West calling to tell me of Margaret's death that morning before I should hear it on the radio. A few minutes later an uncustomarily quiet voice on the radio confirmed Martha's thoughtful message.

Voila!

Some six months after Margaret's death I stayed overnight with a close friend of Margaret's. We talked and talked about that interesting person, trying to understand her complex personality, I bringing my knowledge of the young Margaret, and my friend, hers of the mature person.

At last completely puzzled, I said, "Freda, why after all those years did Margaret in the last years of her life want to see me badly enough to ask her young friends, the Wests of Portland, even during the oil embargo, to drive her down to Eugene for lunch with Cecilia and me, a round trip of 250 miles, not once but twice?"

"Luther," she replied, "Luther, Margaret loved you."

I still shake my head, not in negation but in puzzlement.

Margaret was indeed an extraordinary person. She gave me much during the 1920s, and I in turn gave her gifts that helped shape her life: support during her formative years, freedom to explore, belief in herself and her own values, willingness to make painful decisions and accept responsibility for her actions. I am recalling, reliving my life with her, if you will, as I prefer, the young Margaret of those three traumatic years, 1925–28, the flaming torch she was—not a torch of "smoky pine," but of a pine knot that flamed brightly as the resin caught fire to throw shadows, sometimes surprisingly grotesque, but brilliantly clear images at others. I proudly nourished the flame and helped her to hold it high.

Her ashes were buried—I was not present—in the tiny cemetery pressing close against the little church in Buckingham, where she and I had been married fifty-five years before. Thinking of that simple burial, I wrote Martha West that Margaret had been a citizen of the world and her "handful of gray ashes" should have been scattered from a high-flying plane, half over the Pacific Ocean and the other over the Atlantic. I have wondered many times, dear Margaret, if your desire for burial in this peaceful little cemetery was a symbol of an unconscious longing in all the rush and exciting bustle of your career as a celebrity for something more lasting than the ephemeral fame.

Some inner compulsion told me that I would have to visit Margaret's grave to close the circle, that important segment of my life. One lovely, late October morning in 1979, while visiting my daughter Gem's family some twenty to twenty-five miles north of Buckingham, Gem, who had never met Margaret, drove me at my request to see Margaret's grave and to place a white rose there. In response to my query, Gem replied that she, too, would like one placed there from her. Then I added three more: one from Martha West, who asked me to add one each for Rhoda Metraux and Margaret's daughter, Mary Catherine Bateson.

Gem, knowing my love for that beautiful Pennsylvania country and sensitive to the emotional significance of our mission, avoided the distraction of heavy highway traffic by taking back roads through country especially lovely in vivid autumn colors.

Fifty-six years had passed since my marriage to Margaret in the little Trinity Episcopal Church. In 1979 the country village of 1923 was the built-up intersection of two major highways connecting large metropolitan centers. I was completely lost. My sharp-eyed driver, however, spotted the church as we passed, then came back and pulled into the parking lot.

The lot served the needs of the congregation of the newly built church. We arrived just before noon as well-dressed, young parents from suburbia were picking up equally well-dressed, small children emerging from a church nursery school to be taken home in smart-looking station wagons. Though adjacent to the new church, the small cemetery seemed to snuggle close against the old church with which it had "grown up." A large tree, uprooted from close by the old building by a recent storm, still lay across the corner of the cemetery among overthrown headstones and a smashed monument. The storm's ravages and flowerless graves along with the weather-beaten stained stucco of the little church gave a forlorn aspect to the cemetery.

I went into the parish house to introduce myself to the rector and explain that I was not a casual visitor, but found he was out for the day. The secretary, however, took Gem and me to Margaret's grave, then unmarked except for the little plastic plate left by the morti-

Margaret Mead's headstone in Buckingham, Pennsylvania. Photo by L. S. Cressman.

cian.[52] She explained that the old church was no longer used by the parish, but had been rented to another denomination. The parish congregation now had the "nice new church." She left Gem and me alone at the grave.

We stood in silence for a few moments. Then I asked Gem to stand back and guide me in the placing of the roses. A few more minutes in silence, then we walked to the new church and entered. It had a restrained, simple beauty. Again I sensed the "beauty and the mystery" and felt the same tug of invitation as I had on All Saints' Day in Chartres cathedral more than fifty years before. The peace of the place was like a benediction. I took Gem's hand as she whispered, "How lovely." We walked out into the bright autumn sunshine and to Gem's friendly old car.

We drove two or three miles to Lahaska, the small village where in 1923 I ritualistically spent the night before my marriage to Margaret, but now described aptly by my matter-of-fact, twenty-year-old grand-daughter as a "tourist trap." There we lunched lazily and shopped, not really buying, just enjoying a slow release from the emotional tension of our earlier experience.

Midafternoon shadows were lengthening as we passed the "little church" on our return. We slowed for the traffic signal, and I turned toward the cemetery. My last sight was a shaft of warm sunlight falling aslant Margaret's grave and our gift of white roses. I whispered, "Shalom, Margaret," as I remembered the good life we shared in those exciting formative early years and was thankful for it. And I would not have changed a moment of it, especially our going our separate ways.

"Shalom, dear Margaret, Shalom."

The circle was now closed.[53]

Gestation's Interlude

There are two births; the one when light
　First strikes the new awaken'd sense;
The other when two souls unite,
　And we must count our life from thence:
When you loved me and I loved you
Then both of us were born anew.

Love then to us new souls did give
　And in those souls did plant new powers;
Since when another life we live,
　The breath we breathe is his, not ours;
Love makes those young whom age doth chill,
And whom he finds young keeps young still.

(William Cartwright, *To Chloe Who for His Sake*
Wished Herself Younger)

Late August afternoon, 1927, and the *S.S. Leviathan* docks at Southampton. Quickly through customs and on the boat train to Waterloo Station and murky London atmosphere, a cab to the British Museum to meet Cecilia. (Dorothy Loch and I had chosen to call each other by our middle instead of our first names; Dorothy and Luther became Cecilia and Sheeleigh. It signaled a break with our old lives and the beginning of new ones, but we retained with our families our first-name usage as the ones they had become accustomed to.) As I stepped from the cab and passed through the gates, everything seemed massive and uninviting against my eagerness. To add to the fortresslike character of the place I had to assault stood a huge helmeted constable, his tunic brightened with campaign ribbons of past wars and the top of his helmet towering well over six feet. I put down my bags beside him and looked up into a strong and kindly face.

"I have just arrived from Southampton on the boat train, Constable, coming from the States to meet a young lady who has a desk in the library and I should like to tell her I am here."

201

"Do you have a card, sir?"

"I am afraid not; my 1926 card expired after my return to the States. I am a little early, and all I want is to let her know that I am here. She has taken lodgings for me, but I don't know where, and I have come a long way."

He looked down at me, his face very sympathetic. Somehow a half crown slipped quite unobtrusively from my hand and found a warm and equally unobtrusive welcome in his.

"What is the young lady's name, sir, and do you know her desk number?"

"Her name is Dorothy C. Loch. I don't know her desk number, but you may easily find that out at the desk."

"I'll be only a moment, sir. Just wait here."

In a couple of minutes, back came my huge constable, no longer a formidable obstacle to a lovers' meeting but a coconspirator. He smiled, "The young lady will be right out, sir."

"Thank you very much, indeed, Constable."

We passed a few words, and out of the huge doors of the museum came a very small-appearing Dorothy Cecilia Loch with her attaché case and looking a little flustered. I hurried to meet her.

"This kind constable carried my message to you," I said, and we both warmed to his understanding smile.

In the cab, Cecilia said to the driver, "Number 5 Upper Bedford Place" —my lodgings.

Then settling back, she said, "Now tell me, Sheeleigh, *how* you got that nice constable to come for me. He startled me frightfully when I looked up and saw him. 'Are you Miss Loch?' A surprised and somewhat shaken 'Yes' came from Miss Loch. 'There is a young man who says he is from the States outside who says that you are expecting him.' Oh, such relief! 'Tell him I'll be right out, and thank you, very much.' Now tell me *really*, how *did* you get him, a *constable*, to come for me?"

"Well, I thought he had a *kind* face and appeared rather sympathetic to my need, which I admit I had not played down. When I saw him warming to the needs of young lovers to meet, I simply passed quite casually into his large and receptive hand a half crown."

"Oh, Sheeleigh, do you mean to say that you bribed a constable?"

"Oh, not really. It was just a pre-performance reward."

"You shouldn't have done it" —and moving closer— "but I am glad you did."

A moment of silence in that jouncing cab as the wonderful awareness of what was now happening infused us.

Then, Cecilia said to Sheeleigh, "I took reservations, as you suggested, at a little hotel in the South Downs country in East Sussex, where it is inviting walking, and Freda [Cecilia's favorite sister] works in a nice tearoom called Glass Castle, and, all in all, it is a good place for talking."

"The place, dear?"

"Uckfield, not far in from the channel, and it is very peaceful country."

But, before we go to Uckfield, who was this remarkable young woman I had just met, who would share my life for the next fifty years, and after her death with whom the sharing goes on? I have referred to her briefly in earlier pages. Now I must introduce her more fully, for the rest of our lives were intertwined and all achievements jointly won. If my introduction is colored by wisdom and understanding jointly gained through the years of common effort, then it more nearly approaches the truth, nearer the mark of what it should be. How can one, anyhow, ever comprehend the fullness and the diverse richness of so distinctive a personality? And after her death my quest goes on.

> And what the dead had no speech for, when living,
> They can tell you, being dead: the communication
> Of the dead is tongued with fire beyond the language of the
> living.
>
> (T. S. Eliot, "Little Gidding," *Four Quartets*)

Dorothy Cecilia Loch was born Sunday, June 10, 1888, at Rosebank, Lugwardine, Herefordshire, England. She was the last of seven children, five daughters and two sons. Her oldest sibling, Violet, was eighteen years older, the spread in years reflecting the family separations incident to their father's service in India. Cecilia was the last to bear the Loch family name in a line long distinguished in Scots and English history. Her immediate family was, of course, conservative Victorian; and although she was born into and spent her early years in that kind of social environment, her "years of decision" came with the explosion of the new world of 1914 and World War I.

Cecilia's death, in the early morning darkness, January 25, 1977, ended a long life that had its roots in the finest traditions of the great

Victorian Age and the post-1914 years, which saw those traditions and values winnowed by the winds of a new world where "Mankind has struck its tents and is on the march" (General Jan Smuts, 1914). Cecilia's remarkable personality was, therefore, a selection of the past's best, supported and carried through her life with the best of the new. These roots would support her in a world where permanent values seemed to have ceased to exist.

Family position in highly stratified societies, such as those of Scotland and England into which Cecilia was born, was extremely important in shaping the personality and future of the individual. Thus sons — I emphasize sons — in the Loch family line had opportunities in education, the professions, and public service not open to the less fortunately born. In these services their associates were of the same class or above. The thrust of their education was the inculcation of the sense of responsibility and obligation inherent in their class and the duty to carry it out. "Responsibility accepted and duty well done." Such was the Loch family tradition, and Cecilia was a superb example of its finest expression.

Often I heard Cecilia, talking about her father's life in the Indian Civil Service, tell how an individual might have home furlough due, but at an outbreak of cholera or the occurrence of some other catastrophe all leaves were cancelled and all available British personnel were rushed to the site of the disaster. The wording of the order was "The exigencies of the Service do not permit" or "The exigencies of the Service require that. . . ." One's duty was always to the "Service," whatever the circumstances.

Cecilia was never family conscious, yet she was well aware of her family history. She had worked part-time for two years in the British Museum doing research on the Loch family for her cousin, Colonel Gordon Loch, who wrote the book, *The Family of Loch*. A thoroughly balanced view and a real sense of humor characterized her attitude toward her family. Her uncle, Sir Charles Stewart Loch, had developed the Charity Organization Society, the major social welfare and relief organization in England, into the very effective program it became, an achievement for which he was knighted. Often when the temperature was very low in winter, Cecilia would say, "It's as cold as my uncle's charity." She had a justifiable pride in her family; and in spite of the fact that much of her life before our marriage was spent in England, she always replied to the query, "Are you English?" with a slightly defiant, "Scots."

The Lochs, originally landed proprietors in Peeblesshire, south of Edinburgh, in the latter half of the fifteenth century moved to Edinburgh, where by 1500 a David Loch was made a burgess of the city. The family prospered, gained considerable wealth through commerce and especially by land acquisition. Their position in the city's life brought them into close contact with the royal house, and thus they became supporters of the Stuarts. Records show that Queen Mary commissioned one Patrick Loch as a privateer to "proceed against the enemy [the English]."

In 1613 James Loch, who was made a merchant burgess of Edinburgh and later treasurer of the city, became wealthy in trade with Sweden and the Low Countries. "In 1644 he lent 5400 merks towards the upkeep of the Scots Army in England employed against Cromwell."[1] In 1643 he purchased Drylaw, an extensive estate on the western outskirts of Edinburgh and thus established the family in the landed-gentry class. Thereafter, the line of James Loch was always spoken of as the Lochs of Drylaw; it is to this branch that Cecilia belonged. The acquisition of Drylaw and its later loss were events of the greatest importance for the future of the Lochs of Drylaw.

For nearly a century the lairds of Drylaw played an important role in the history of Edinburgh and Scotland, economically and politically. The extensive land ownership provided the economic base necessary for social and political power.

The fortunes of the family, however, began to decline in 1733, ninety years after the acquisition of Drylaw, when a later James Loch (1698–1759) succeeded to the ownership. James, a recluse, was more interested in his excellent library of travel and scientific books than in the management of the estate and, unfortunately, placed it in the hands of an inept young relative. In addition he placed large sums (estimated to have been £10,000) at the disposal of the exiled Stuarts—in effect, giving it away.

George Loch (1749–88) succeeded as heir on his father's death in 1759, and during his stewardship the family's fortune worsened. He had to serve a minority of eleven years before taking over the management of the estate. He appointed an inept brother-in-law as manager, while he spent most of his minority abroad, largely in Rome satisfying his interest in art. His incompetent manager not only permitted the estate to continue its decline but also added a further encumbrance by building another house. In the meantime, George had let Drylaw to Lady Weymss. In August 1779 he married Mary

Adam, granddaughter of William Adam, the famous architect. A month later Lady Weymss died, and the young couple returned to reside at Drylaw to find the property in a truly desperate state.

They made heroic efforts to turn around the deteriorating course of Drylaw's decline, George even plowing with oxen, certainly a kind of work not expected of a laird. Their efforts were unsuccessful and in 1786 Drylaw was sold to William Ramsay for the sum of £24,000. Thus ended Drylaw, the landed property, and the economic and social base of this branch of the Lochs of Drylaw family.[2]

After the sale of Drylaw the family moved to Edinburgh to a house George had bought just before the sale. They lived there but a very short time and then left Scotland for Surrey, England. Here George died two years later in failing health and of a "broken heart." His widow returned to the Edinburgh house, where she raised the children. In nine years of her married life she had borne her husband seven children, four sons and three daughters. Two of the girls died almost in infancy, and the third at thirteen years of age. The four boys, all of whom reached adulthood, had distinguished careers, but not those customary for the landed gentry.

James, the eldest of the four sons, studied law at Edinburgh, was called to the bar in England at Lincoln's Inn, but abandoned the practice of law to become the very successful administrator of huge estates belonging to the Duke and Duchess of Sutherland in western Scotland and England.

John, the next in age, entered the naval service, eventually becoming a director and chairman of the Honourable East India Company and a member of Parliament.

William joined the Honourable East India Company's Bengal Civil Service and died at the age of thirty-eight after a short and successful career.

Francis Erskine Loch entered the Royal Navy and culminated a highly successful career as rear admiral of the blue.[3]

The careers of these men show vividly that:

> . . . the whole position of the Family underwent a change from a Scottish land-holding Family with their interests centered in Edinburgh, they became, while still retaining their Scottish character and an abiding love of that country, a Family devoted to the Service of the empire.
>
> From that time to the present day, that is to say in the century and a half between 1780 and 1933, there have been

sixty-two male descendants of George Loch and Mary Adam, of whom forty entered the Naval, Military or Air Forces, and six in the Civil Service, of the Crown or the Honourable East India Company. Thirty of them spent the whole or the greater part of their service in India. Many of them reached positions of some distinction. No less than eleven were killed or died in the execution of their duty.

. . . from the time that John Loch became a Director and Chairman of the Honourable East India Company, the Family as a whole devoted itself to service in India: interwoven in their lives are all the threads of a great tapestry of the rise of the Indian Empire.

A long tradition of service to the Crown culminated in the remarkable record of the Loch Family in the European War 1914–1919. Of nineteen men of military age, fourteen were officers of the Regular Army and one the Flying Corps; one was in the Civil Service and was employed on munitions work [Cecilia's brother]; two joined the Army from private avocations. Others, both women and men, undertook war work of different kinds. They served in France, Italy, Gallipoli, the Balkans, Egypt, East Africa, the Cameroons, Mesopotamia, Arabia and the North-West Frontier.

Cecilia, a great-great-granddaughter of the last laird of Drylaw, George Loch, and Mary Adam, was always especially proud of the Loch-Adam tradition in her family.

Young ladies in the social class to which the Loch family belonged were not expected to find an occupation; according to the Victorian custom, they would either enter on a suitable marriage and bear a large number of children or pass a spinsterhood in "indolent apathy." To break out of this restrictive pattern required women of strong personality and courage. Two of Cecilia's cousins—one, two generations earlier, Catherine Grace Loch (1854–1904) and the other, one generation, Ruth Loch (1864–1955)—broke the customary pattern very successfully. The examples of these two women were not lost on Cecilia. Although she knew Grace Loch but slightly, she did know Ruth Loch quite well.

Nursing provided the only professional opportunity for the young Grace Loch to escape the stultifying atmosphere of the conventional family, and so at eighteen she asked her father's permission to enroll as a probationer. He strongly urged her to wait until she was twenty-five to make sure that her interest was well grounded and that she was strong enough for the work. On his deathbed—she was twenty-five—he acceded to her request. She was evidently a remarkable person, for her rise was rapid:

1879 - Accepted as a probationer
1882 - Night superintendent, St. Bartholomew's Hospital
1887 - In charge of men's surgical ward
1887 - Offered services to India Office for nursing service in India
1888 - Posted to Rawalpindi, India, in northern Punjab
1888 - Defied orders and accompanied Black Mt. Expedition
1891 - Received the Royal Red Cross from the sovereign for "distinguished service," the highest civilian decoration
1892 - Decorated at a "parade of all troops at Rawalpindi on 4th of July 1892."

Here was this woman, thirty-eight years old, who only thirteen years after entering the hospital as a probationer, attained the highest civilian honor the sovereign could give a woman and had her decoration presented at a special parade. And her father doubted her commitment! I am quite sure that his objection had been based on his idea that nursing was not an appropriate activity for his daughter. Little did he know! She continued only a few more years in India. Because of failing health she returned to England, where she continued to advise in the development of the nursing service for the troops in India. She died in 1904 only twenty-five years after receiving her father's permission to enter the nursing profession.

Cecilia greatly admired Ruth Loch (1864–1955), daughter of John Charles Loch and Ann Orr. Ruth was born in India and, conforming to custom, sent to England, where she was educated at Notting Hill High School. Sir Harold Nicholson wrote the following appreciation in either *The Scotsman* or *The Times* following her death:

> Miss Ruth Loch, O.B.E., who had died at the age of 91, was in her way a pioneer in feminine enterprise and independence. At the age of 21 she startled her family by refusing to accept the life of indolent apathy then expected of Victorian spinsters; she resolved to earn her own living and entered the General Post Office where she served with gay efficiency until she reached the retiring age. Beginning at the bottom of the ladder, she ended by becoming Controller

of the female staff of the Money Order Department with an office in Queen Victoria Street and a secretary in an adjoining room. In her flat in London and in her little chalet on the rocks near Dinard one would meet a varied assortment of intelligent men and women, Civil Servants and scientists, artists and writers. She believed fervently in the precept that happiness is activity in congenial surroundings; her activity was indeed exuberant and her gaiety such that her surroundings always became congenial. She brought light and laughter into many a murky corner; hers was a useful and therefore a very happy life.

I remember well, when Cecilia and I were talking about the position of women in our society, that she spoke with admiration of her cousin Ruth's achievements and apparent happiness, adding too, "The life of a spinster, as long as it is directed toward some significant goal, certainly is not all bad."

A third person on the distaff side, a first cousin seven years Cecilia's senior, Mary George Loch, called Cousin Maisie, was important in Cecilia's life both as an individual and because of the different family and professional environments that marked her family. Cousin Maisie's father and Cecilia's father were brothers; both also had along with their wives the Anglo-Indian family background; but while they were undergraduates at Oxford their individual lives diverged. Both families lived in London and their association was close.

Cousin Maisie went to Newham College, Cambridge, a definite first for young ladies of the Loch family, taking a Classical Tripos, 2nd Division of Class III. She prepared for work in the Charity Organization Society in which her father was the moving force, but instead of continuing in that work married Robert Mowat, a Fellow and associate tutor of Corpus Christi College, Oxford, who subsequently became professor in the History Department of the University of Bristol. Returning in late 1941 from the United States and Canada, where he had been presenting the Allied position in World War II, he was killed in a plane crash in the fog almost in sight of home. Cousin Maisie, though sixty years of age, was an air raid warden at the time of her husband's death and continued to serve throughout the war in that capacity during the very heavy bombing to which Bristol was subjected. They were a large family and served both on land and sea during the war.

Cecilia's personal contacts, always close and frequent, with her cousin were of course broken, except for correspondence, with our marriage and moving to the States. In 1958, however, Cecilia and I were in England, where I was studying late British prehistoric sites and museum collections. Cousin Maisie invited us to visit her in the family home in Bristol where she still lived, and we happily accepted.

Just outside of Bristol was an Iron Age hill fort, quite different from those I had studied in southwestern England, and I needed to examine it. Cousin Maisie, way ahead of me, was familiar with the fort and aware of my study program; and before I could raise the question of the fort, she informed me of it, saying that she would take Cecilia and me to it.

When Cecilia and I came to breakfast on the morning of our expedition, we found that our seventy-seven–year–old hostess, tall and rather gaunt, had already ridden her bicycle — to the consternation of traffic and the police who knew well her independent ways — to her favorite bakery and returned with three freshly baked Cornish pasties for our lunch.

We took the tram out of Bristol to the terminus, happily at the base of the hill on which the fort had been built so long ago. A road wound around the hill up to the fort, but that was not for our guide. She took us straight up that steep hill, which was strewn with good-sized rocks and strung with barbed wire fences to control the grazing cattle. On the hilltop within the ancient fortifications, we could look across the Bristol Channel toward Swansea in Wales, visible on a clear day. That day our view, unfortunately, was obscured by the heavy haze hanging over the channel. There we sat and chatted while we ate our large, fresh pasties. Then I went about my work while the two cousins had their good talking, a far cry indeed from the setting of teas, restaurants, concerts, and theater of those years in London so long ago when Cecilia and I were completely unaware of each other's existence.

The social and professional environment, ambience if you will, of Cousin Maisie's family was probably in an unobtrusive way influential in shaping Cecilia's personality. The family background was the same: both girls' fathers and mothers born in India to a family in the Honourable East India Company's Civil Service; the brothers sent home to Glenalmond College, Edinburgh, for their preuniversity education; both went to Balliol at Oxford, but then their courses began to diverge.

Charles Stewart Loch, with a strong interest in art, followed a course of studies in the classics and history and entered on a professional career in England. Cecilia's father, Willie Walker Loch, after two years in classical studies, took degrees in law and history and went into the Indian Civil Service, which had been established by the British Government to administer India after Parliament took over the government of India from the Honourable East India Company following the crushing of the Sepoy Mutiny in 1858. The government then established the system of competitive examinations to staff the Indian Civil Service as the means of ensuring a high quality of men for what was to become an elite corps.

The different choices of professions followed by the brothers resulted in totally contrasting family situations: Cousin Maisie's family remained together in England (her only sibling, a brother, entered the military service in the engineers and went to India), whereas Cecilia's family was together only during her father's brief intervals of "furlough" until he retired in 1896 at fifty years of age after twenty-eight years of service. Cecilia was the youngest of seven children, and only she and a brother, who died at the age of twelve, were born in England. She was about six years old when her father returned to India from his last furlough. He retired two years later.

The intervening two years were a very unhappy time for Cecilia, who was left in the care of a maternal aunt, whom she disliked intensely, with a son Cecilia's age with whom she had to spend most of her time in spite of the fact that she found his companionship quite distasteful. All this changed when her father came home, and in the reunited family, their very close relationship developed.

As pointed out earlier, Cousin Maisie's plans for a career in the C.O.S. were thwarted by her marriage into the academic world to which her father had belonged for several years.

The background and postretirement years of Cecilia's family carried her along for nearly twenty years in the late Victorian life-style. To break from that, as her cousins had done, required the same kind of personal qualities. With the war of 1914–18 she made the break.

The independence of mind and self-discipline so characteristic of the mature Cecilia were to begin their development in her eighth year, with her father's retirement. His long absences in India while the earlier children were growing up had made him and them more like relatives than parent and children. Freda, five years Cecilia's senior, was her closest sibling and at thirteen was in some ways closer

Cecilia's father, Willie Walker Loch, I.C.S. Date unknown.

Cecilia's step grandfather, Capt. Telfer-Smollett, owner of Cameron House.

Cameron House, by Loch Lomond, with large greenhouse for vegetables and flowers. Cecilia's room was in the tower under the flag.

to her older brother, Richard, and older sisters than to Cecilia; oddly enough in the end they became extremely close friends. Cecilia's father at fifty found his eager, eight-year-old daughter the family member who presented him with the promise of an unbroken relationship of the father to his child. He became her teacher, and they shared a close friendship and a relationship of mutual understanding until his death in 1928.

He had had an excellent education in the classics, humanities, and some science. At Glenalmond in his final year, he won the prize of the college for scholarship, a large complete volume of the plays of Shakespeare. This was his vade mecum through his whole life; and after his death it came to Cecilia, and now it is the treasured possession, water-stained and worn, of his granddaughter, Gem, our daughter.

Along with teaching the usual subjects, he also inculcated a sense of responsibility and discipline. Cecilia told me the following anecdote, which she had heard from her mother, as illustrative of her father's character.

The government intended to make the Indian Civil Service a responsible governing body free from the abuses that had marked the period of the Honourable East India Company, whose object had been the acquisition of money. Bribery of officials was a way of life in India. It was not to be tolerated by the Crown, at least of its own officials. From April to November 1880 Cecilia's father was assigned to be "Tutor to the Gaekwar of Baroda," apparently to clean up what had become a "very sticky mess" of bribery of British officials by either the Gaekwar or his officers or both. Loch's title sounds rather euphemistic unless he was to instruct his student in the "facts of life" under the new regime.

Baroda was a large state in the northern Bombay presidency. The period, April to November, was the hot season. Cecilia's mother, of course, accompanied her husband to his temporary station. The Gaekwar's lady and her associates went to their cooler summer residence and invited Mrs. Loch to accompany her party. Her husband strictly forbade her to accept, even though she would have been more comfortable. He forbade her to accept any gift, even flowers, for according to the Indian custom such exchanges were always a quid pro quo, and he was there to make clear that such exchanges were not tolerated in the process of government. This rule had to apply without exception.

A sense of responsibility, duty, and discipline—the rule in public life—he nurtured in rather gentler terms in the young Cecilia, and she became a fine example of an adult in which these virtues were internalized.

He read poetry to Cecilia and Freda and always asked his young listeners, "Now, what does that mean?" and they had to explain. He read to them from the great English classics, by which Cecilia became familiar with the best traditions of the culture. Cecilia, when about twelve, became ill. Her illness was diagnosed, fortunately incorrectly, as consumption, and she was ordered to bed, where she spent most of that year. It was a time of reading, and every night her father came to her room and read systematically to her from the great English writers. He also played games, checkers and others, suitable for her situation. She always said that he was "so kind" to her that year and taught her much, breaking in many ways the tedium of her loneliness. I never heard her speak of her mother in connection with that year. Compared with those lonely, unhappy two years she had spent with her aunt as mentor, these with her father were pure happiness.

In those early years, along with the introduction to Shakespeare, the English novelists, and the great traditions of British culture, she became an accomplished pianist, and somewhere during this time gained a certain proficiency in French. Later, when her work required her to read documents in medieval Latin, her father helped her, even teaching her the basics of the language she needed. Again, when as secretary of the British Sociological Society she had to translate a volume of Desmoulin, the French sociologist, her father came to her rescue with much-needed help. Botany they studied in the Edinburgh Botanical Gardens and in their long walks on the moors during the summers the family spent at Cameron House on Loch Lomond, belonging to Cecilia's step-grandfather on her mother's side, Captain Telfer-Smollett.

These summers were periods of unalloyed happiness for Cecilia and later provided cherished reminiscences during our life together. One in particular is worth recounting. It was a customary right, and perhaps in the common law, that once a coffin with a corpse had been carried over a piece of property, the course the trail followed became known as a "coffin trail" and thereafter was available for public use. The villagers had been insisting that there was a "coffin trail" across her grandfather's property and they had the right of use. The captain, however, thought otherwise. He asked Cecilia's father to examine the moor and search for the supposed trail.

"Come along, dear," her father said, and together the pair searched the moor, sometimes together and then separately to cover special parts. She found sheer pleasure in beating her way through the knee-high heather and more than once falling on her face to get up again and help her father. To have him want her company and trust her to give responsible help in a man's work gave Cecilia not only pleasure but also self-confidence. She recounted many reminiscences of the moors; but this one, which I heard more than once, was one of the happiest and most vividly remembered.

This close and happy association with her father gave her an experience she needed badly: an understanding friendship with a man whom she trusted and admired. At Cameron during the summers there were other men of the family and friends for longer or shorter stays. The organist of Hereford cathedral was usually an annual guest. Her grandfather frequently had the two pastors of nearby churches, one the Presbyterian and the other the Church of England, to tea together. Cecilia, present at these teas, observed with her keen perception that her grandfather invited these men of the cloth together because he enjoyed seeing them disagree, and it provided him with entertainment as well as them with hospitality. She remembered coming to breakfast to find her grandfather reading a book of Tobias Smollett's and chuckling as he said, "A gay dog, this relative of yours"—the Smollett and the Loch families were related in some manner, but I cannot remember how, although Cecilia at one time told me.[4]

During the years Cecilia's family lived in Edinburgh (about 1899 to 1912), the winters were occupied with the social life of the Anglo-Indian families and to some extent faculty members and wives of the University of Edinburgh and the officers of the garrison, usually highland regiments. Of course, the associations were not limited to these groups; there were other families of like social and educational background with whom friendships were built up. This was the time when Cecilia, like the other young ladies of the time, learned the graces and manners of social life, those skills and sensitivity to social situations that were to be such a distinguishing characteristic of her life in Eugene, Oregon.

During the winter when she must have been about eighteen, she met Mabel Forbes, of an old Scots family, a few years older, educated and traveled. This acquaintance rapidly developed into a seminal friendship that was soon to give a new direction to Cecilia's life. Mabel Forbes introduced her young friend to The Outlook Tower, the group organized by Patrick Geddes of the University of Edinburgh faculty to study town planning with special reference to their own city. The friendships with Mabel Forbes and the Geddeses flourished and broadened Cecilia's social and intellectual frontiers beyond the boundary of the Anglo-Indian tradition. Mabel invited Cecilia to accompany her on a voyage to the Grand Canaries with a stop in Portugal. Through these friendships Cecilia was moving into a whole new world in which she was happy.

Mabel Forbes, very alert to and interested in the social movements developing rapidly before the 1914–18 war, suggested to Cecilia, then living in London, that she try to secure a position with the Labour Research Department of the Fabian Society. Cecilia followed her friend's advice, but not without family opposition. The Fabian Society was a socialist organization under the leadership of G. B. Shaw and Sidney and Beatrice Webb. The Research Department was a small group of devoted and idealistic young people: a small salaried staff and volunteers from Oxford, Cambridge, and the metropolitan area. The young Professor G. D. H. Cole from Oxford, who would become the recognized authority on labor in England, was the secretary. Margaret Postgate, the daughter of a distinguished Cambridge Latinist, was acting secretary and would later marry Cole. Margaret Postgate's younger brother was a volunteer. The men and women Cecilia would meet were an exciting group, interested far beyond labor in the arts, theater, music, journalism, and so on.

The socialist Fabian Society was, however, anathema to the old Victorian sense of class and political values. Cecilia's family, immediate and more removed, tried to dissuade her from going to work with that "lot of socialists; you don't know what they will do to you," *except her father*. His background in India and public service gave him a more realistic view of the world and of his daughter, too. He said, "Take the position. These men are good people who think rather differently on some matters than we. It will be good for you."

Cecilia took the offered position at a very modest salary, and it was one of the most important decisions in her whole life.

Cecilia, a self-taught secretary, was very fortunate in having her first work experience with this group of young people close to her own age. The individuals in it were united by a common ideal, although they came from varied backgrounds: poverty and wealth; universities and working class; agnostic certainly, and perhaps atheistic, and Quaker; Roman Catholic and Anglo-Catholic and various other Protestant persuasions. Men and women treated each other as equals. When she applied for the position, Cecilia was very apprehensive that she would be rejected by Beatrice Webb, because Sir Charles, Cecilia's uncle of Charity Organization Society fame, was the leader of the movement in social-work improvement diametrically opposed to the Webbs' socialist ideas. Her fears, however, were unfounded. Mrs. Webb treated her like any other member of the group and even indicated to Cecilia that she was well aware of her family.

Her employment at the Research Department brought her into contact with Sir Arthur Acland, a former don at Oxford, who had left the church and gone into politics. He was minister for education in the Asquith cabinet. Sir Arthur introduced Cecilia to Lady Acland and their daughter, Mamie. The friendship with Sir Arthur was short-lived, but that with Lady Acland and Mamie lasted until their deaths. Lady Acland, an invalid confined to bed, had warm and vivid memories of their Oxford days and the great Victorians who had graced Oxford. She took great pleasure in sharing her memories with Cecilia and provided another tie to the fine traditions so well represented in her father.

In those eighteen months in the department she often saw agonizing personal examples of what her father had taught her from his experience in India. She saw how devotion to conscience and duty could compel individuals, *her friends now*, to entirely different lines of action: conscientious objectors going to a prison, and not a pleasant one either, that they knew awaited them; others to substitute work; still others to the armed services. One of these last was a lad, Maitland Hardyman, seven years Cecilia's junior in age, urged by Mabel Forbes to look up a young lady at the department when he would be in London on his return to the front from convalescent leave and have tea with her; she was a nice person to talk to. All took place as Mabel suggested. This lad from the University of Edinburgh, a person of great intellectual promise, had enlisted in 1914 and was wounded three times. On his last leave he wrote his own epitaph: "He died as he lived, fighting for abstract principles in a cause which he did not believe in." In May of 1918 this twenty-three-year-old lad had been promoted to lieutenant-colonel, had received the D.S.O., and was the youngest officer of that rank in the British army. On August 11, 1918, he was "killed in action."

He was many times in our conversation during the years of our marriage. On the dresser in a bedroom Cecilia had a portrait of Mabel Forbes and attached to it, a newsclip announcing Maitland Hardyman's death with a head-and-shoulders picture of him in uniform. His eyes fairly stare out of it, eyes that have seen too much agony, suffering, and heroism, eyes that could hardly bear to see more. Both pictures are still there, and the eyes still haunt one.

This young woman from a late Victorian background learned much and quickly of a different world: that a person was to be judged by one standard only, *his quality as a person*, that sex, religion, race, social class or "family" has really nothing to do with the evaluation in the end. This was her lifelong attitude as I was to see so often in the years ahead. To her father, I think, she owed thanks for those intimate, early years of love and friendship and the true education he gave her that enabled her with relative ease to break free of the late Victorian restraints upon her sex.

Her mother's ill health forced her to resign regretfully from the department in September 1917 after eighteen very happy months. G. D. H. Cole in a letter of recommendation wrote:

> During the time that she was with us she occupied a responsible position. . . . In addition to typing work, she had general charge of our accounts for some time, and she was also called upon to do much important special work of a responsible character. In all respects, what she did was excellent.

One evening at dinner after my retirement we were being very lazy over coffee and enjoying reminiscences. I mentioned the *Labour Year Book, 1916*, which we had on our shelves and which had been published during the time Cecilia was in the department. The book is a compilation of special contributions by various authors, statistics of importance to labor, and such. D. Loch's name appears in the list of contributors. I asked her who compiled the book. Very proudly she said, "I did."

Because of her mother's illness, which required Cecilia's presence at home part of the day, she turned to part-time work and held a series of appointments—private secretary, research assistant, and so on. Her first position in this situation was as a private secretary to Victor Branford, a financier, much concerned with the social issues of the time, especially those foreseen for the postwar world. He was a friend of Patrick Geddes, and it was most important for Cecilia that he was president of the British Sociological Society. This appointment was to have far-reaching effects on her life and mine, too, as it turned out. Let Victor Branford speak about her work and performance:

The Sociological Society
President: The Right Hon. The Earl of Balfour, K.G., O.M.
Le Play House, 65, Belgrave Road, S.W. 1

27th December, 1923

I have much pleasure in bearing testimony to Miss D. C. Loch's unusual combination of qualities. Six years' association with her has made me familiar with these qualities. Miss Loch came to me as Secretary in 1917, and until 1921 helped me with business correspondence and activities, as well as with scientific and literary ones.

In 1921 Miss Loch was appointed Secretary of the Sociological Society. For more than two years she has not only conducted the bulk of its correspondence, but has taken a large and initiating share in organising its meetings and its research. That Miss Loch has administered the affairs of the Society to the entire satisfaction of the Council the following extract from the Minutes of the 13th November, 1923 will make plain:

"that the Council record its deep indebtedness to Miss Loch for her services in restoring the Society to active functioning after its period of comparative inactivity during the later stages of the war; and the Council greatly regrets Miss Loch's inability to continue in the office of Secretary."

(signed) Victor C. Branford
Chairman of Council

At a meeting in 1920 the council had instructed its secretary, Miss D. C. Loch, to see that the three small rooms on the top floor of Le Play House, headquarters of the Sociological Society, were prepared for occupancy by a young American, Lewis Mumford, who was coming to accept the post of assistant editor of the *Sociological Review*. Once Cecilia recalled in our conversation that when she looked at those bleak rooms she thought it would take some very bright curtains and furnishings to make them habitable. But she went to work to carry out her instructions.

Not long ago, while reading Mumford's *My Works and Days, A Personal Chronicle* (1979), on page 70 I was startled to find:

> . . . but however austere the furnishings of my cell were, it was bright and cheerful, for it faced west, and there was a glass of flowers—five narcissus and a tulip!—with a note on the mantelshelf. The young woman who left them, Branford's part time secretary, began with that gesture a life long friendship.

Mumford, perceptive, imaginative, and articulate, came to know this "young woman" very well during his short stay in England in which they were associated in the workings of the Sociological Society. In his *Little Testament of Bernard Martin* (1926) he wrote poetically of his friendship with "Charlotte." The *Little Testament* is reproduced in his *My Works and Days*, where I first saw it and was greatly moved, for it contains his portrait of that "young woman" I had first met in 1925–26 and later at the British Museum in 1927. I wrote him, requesting permission to use those stanzas here. He replied:

> I . . . am deeply touched by your plan to use three Stanzas about her [Cecilia] in my *"Little Testament"* and though you don't need any permission for this from anyone I'll give you my blessing! . . .
>
> These three Stanzas tenderly recall our friendship. After I wrote them in 1926 she married you!

In thanking me for a photograph of Cecilia I sent him and his wife, he wrote, "Her beauty of spirit reveals her in both her face and her posture, so animated, so inwardly serene."

For the cast of characters in these Stanzas, read Lewis for Bernard; Sophia, later Mrs. Mumford, for Eunice; Cecilia for Charlotte. Comte House is Le Play House.

62
Charlotte came from Aberdeen to help fallen women before she knew exactly what fallen women were. That was seven

years before she found a post in Comte House and left a
posy of tulips over the fireplace in Bernard's room when he
arrived. Charlotte plumbed the depths of other people's
tragedies so successfully she made them forget her own was
deeper: but love, despair, suicide, jealousy had singed the
hem of every garment that she wore. She had watched her
youngest friends go bitterly and unconvinced to death in
France: she had worked with labor men and conscientious
objectors in the face of a family that took comfort in the
editorial certitudes of the Morning Post: her sweetness
tartened as one side of her clutched loyalty, the other love.
. . . She says: Oh dear: I thought so! when Bernard tells her
about Eunice. She says: Remember to wear your evening
clothes, when he almost goes to a dinner in Notting Hill
Gate without a dinner coat. She says: They have Maids of
Honor tarts some people call nice at Richmond: and there is
an old tree in the park that was meant to shelter lovers or
conversation. We have plenty to talk about she adds firmly.
Charlotte dresses with the ambiguous primness of a private
secretary. Her tweeds are a little too heavy and her shirt-
waists not less serviceable than ugly. Her voice is a clear
Northern voice. Her face and her body are a fine landscape,
shorn by a November storm: her mind is a lake in the midst
of the landscape, agitated but deep. When one sees her
mind gleaming through a copse of hazel eyes one finds that
her face is beautiful. Like a blindman, poor young Bernard
plucks at the heavy tweeds and the assertiveness of metallic
dress supporters, and takes a long time to discover that her
face is beautiful.

63

Charlotte gently wipes clear the foggy patches in Bernard's
mind. Charlotte smiles at Bernard's rages against old England: she finds the southern English funny, too, and likes
the gaunt dank air of Edinburgh, drinking terror in black
closes, more than the slatternly complacence of London. A
Sunday spent discussing Eunice in the greenwet silence of
the Chiltern beeches almost removes the thought of Eunice
from Bernard's heart. When Charlotte recites patches of
Chaucer from a northern Downtop near the grassy Pilgrim's
Way, Bernard swoops with her to Canterbury, quite forgetting ties of Franco-German-American ancestry. The smell of

marjoram and mignonette: the blush of Charlotte's prim-dancing face: almost make England a possibility if ten years and many customs did not come between their pairing. In complementary qualities, Bernard and Charlotte are well-married: but the parish register does not recognize marriages made in Heaven unless they come down to earth. Charlotte feels too tender toward Bernard to let him come down to earth. She has an uncle who was a general in Afghanistan, and her father retired from the Hongkong Customs Service with honors: Oxford, Cambridge, Eton, or Cheltenham are the prerequisites for marriage in her family. Charlotte has five equally maiden sisters.

97

When Bernard faces Charlotte in a restaurant in Greek Street, Charlotte's eyes snuggle into Bernard's broad shoulders. Three years ago I knew what hell was like, says Charlotte: I'm past that now: I'm thirty-nine. But you look strong and confident. I've danced on fiery stones and had my fill of nettles too, says Bernard: my letters about Eunice and myself did not begin to tell you half of it. The baby and my being thirty have made me feel mature: having lived through a first day in the Navy, first year of marriage, and a first hour of childbirth, I'm fit for anything. Do I look strong? You do, says Charlotte: and you, says Bernard suddenly, are beautiful: how is it that I've never kissed you yet? At thirty happy married lads, though anchored fast, begin to realize another woman's worth. I'm glad you came and glad you're going, says Charlotte. A month of seeing you might bring an ache.

Thank you, Lewis Mumford.

And so Dorothy-Charlotte-Cecilia and Luther-Sheeleigh went to Uckfield as planned in the cab. There we walked on the Downs and talked, and ate our picnic lunches and talked, and found a tree for shelter and support in a shallow wash and talked, while a farmer and his helpers hauled in the harvest from the adjoining field with a pair of good horses and a wagon. How did we find a refuge so peaceful, quiet, and relaxing for friends' and lovers' talk? We drank tea and ate delicious cookies and talked and talked some more in the tearoom where Cecilia's sister worked. As we joined each other at breakfast

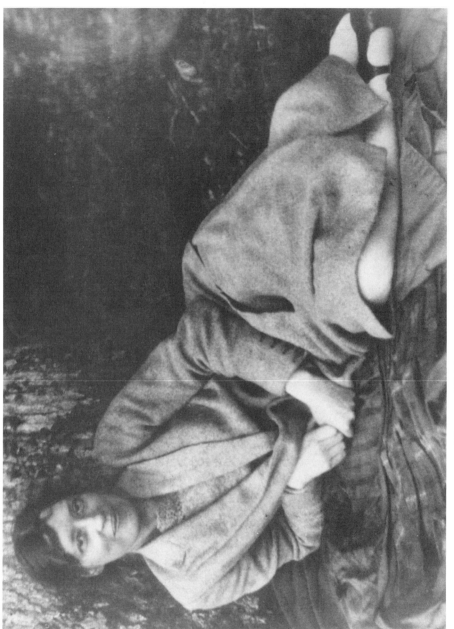

Cecilia at Uckfield, 1927. Photo by L. S. Cressman.

each day, our talk started anew for we had so much to talk about: past, present, and hoped-for future, although at first only hesitantly made explicit.

By the time we returned to London we both knew that we hoped to spend the rest of our lives together, but we held back from making the desire a firm commitment. Cecilia wanted to be sure that a childhood illness, diagnosed as tuberculosis, was absolutely cured or had been erroneously diagnosed. We let it stand; I would ask her later.

The last thing I remember of this trip was our farewell at London's grimy Waterloo Station. Cecilia had come to see me off on the boat train for Southampton. We talked a few minutes on the platform, said our good-byes, hoping they were au revoirs; Cecilia turned back on the platform, I boarded the train. From the steps I watched her small, disciplined back as she walked further and further away, never looking back. It is not good luck to look back after parting from a lover, a friend, or a guest. Those days with Cecilia were so emotionally overwhelming that I have absolutely no memory of any other part of the return trip or my arrival in New York.

My life's course now took a sharply different tack; maritally, I was separated with a divorce in my future; I had changed my place of residence from the Columbia University neighborhood to Greenwich Village, a spatial change inevitably resulting in a change of association; I had no longer any connection with the church, and I was a full-time, successful college teacher—all in the new ambience of my desperate longing to marry Cecilia.

In the fall I again asked Cecilia to marry me. She replied that her problems had not yet been cleared up and that I should write later. I thought I sensed in her letter also a slight feeling that perhaps Margaret and I might change our minds and that a short postponement would finally settle the problem.

My 1927–28 experience was demonstrating that I was a good teacher, that I could do sound research publishable in reputable journals, and that I could make crucial decisions affecting my life. Through these accomplishments I had developed a strong sense of self-confidence. I now knew that my professional future lay in college-university teaching. The only question was: where? But place didn't seem important to me.

So, in the late winter, I again wrote Cecilia, asking her to marry me. This time her reply came, warm and carrying total commitment even though marrying me meant she would have to leave her beloved England, her family and friends, and be faced with building an entirely new life with me.

I knew that our new life together would require a new environment outside of New York with its associations and people in order to unfold and grow on its own terms. Shortly after I told the Columbia University Appointments Bureau of my desire for a change, I was asked to confer with President Black of the Washington State Normal School at Ellensburg, Washington, who was in New York looking for a social science teacher. Although I was favorably impressed by President Black and even though the salary would have been twice what I received at CCNY, I refused his offer primarily, I suppose, because I thought normal-school teaching lacked the prestige of college teaching and Ellensburg seemed so terribly isolated after New York City and London. In a few days he asked to talk with me again. By that time I had thought about the matter, talked it over with friends, and shed my silly snobbishness. At the second conference I accepted President Black's renewed invitation and thereby made another commitment without the least idea of where Ellensburg was located or what normal-school teaching would be like. The decision certainly met the need to start our new life outside New York and its environs!

I wrote Cecilia about the new position to which we would be going in the Far West, new to both of us. She was thrilled at the idea of "going west," in part perhaps because of her exciting, surreptitious reading of Bret Harte's stories of California's gold-rush days that she had found in her grandfather's library at Cameron, though not quite intended for the edification of young ladies. At any rate we were to be together now; and the place, as long as we were away from New York, was of little importance. I made reservations, student class, on the *Empress of France*, Southampton to Quebec, for September 28.

Cecilia had had a wretched winter: a bad attack of measles; the death of her father on June 24, although his death eased the pain she would have suffered by leaving him at the time of our marriage; the breakup of the family home at 46 Harcourt Terrace after her father's death; and, of course, her decision to marry me, which meant leaving her family and friends and her England. When I met her as I got off the boat train in London, I was almost shocked by how fatigued and thin she was. Only an inner strength and sense of discipline had carried her through. Having taken lodgings for me, she was staying with Lady Acland.

The few days before our wedding were taken up with last-minute preparations: my call on the American Consul in London to verify the completion of papers for Cecilia's entry as a nonquota alien into the United States; our purchase of a rather plain but necessary wedding ring—a very informal affair on a late afternoon at a small jewelry shop Cecilia knew; blessed private teas provided for us by Lady Acland each afternoon; finally, a reception Cecilia had arranged for forty or more members of her family "to meet her young man." I remember particularly from that pleasant affair the advice given me by a second cousin of Cecilia: "Give her lots of strawberries and cream for breakfasts, and plenty of silk stockings." When I told Cecilia about it later, she said, "Poor Maud, I am sure she never had much of either."

All arrangements were now in order and our next move would be to the registrar's office for our marriage.

Homeward Bound

How blest am I in this discovering thee!
To enter in these bonds, is to be free; . . .

(John Donne, *Elegie*)

August 31, 1928, found us breakfasting at Lady Acland's. From there, later in the morning, Cecilia's close and long-time friend, Mamie Bovenschen (née Acland), drove us to the registrar's office in South Kensington, where we were to be married.

The registrar's office was on the second floor, up a flight of well-worn stairs. I recall this experience much as a stage scene with controlled lighting. I remember the large room as quite dark as one moved from the window where the elderly, slightly stooped registrar had a desk under a hanging, bare light bulb. Cecilia's mother, two sisters, and Mamie were indistinct in the semidarkness close to the wall near the door through which we had entered.

The gray-haired registrar, with his steel-rimmed spectacles, gave the sense that we were enacting a scene straight out of Dickens. He took up our papers, established our identities, asked me if I accepted the divorce decree, and on my affirmation began to fill out the necessary form for the marriage certificate. But right then he hit a snag. My father had no middle name, only the lonely letter S.

"What is your father's middle name? There is only the letter S."

"That is quite right."

"It can't be, one never has only a letter. I must have a name."

"I am terribly sorry, but the S is correct. Years ago I asked Dad what the letter S stood for and he replied, 'Nothing; it is just the letter S. My parents thought I ought to have either a middle name or letter; so they gave me the letter S instead of a name.' I am sorry, sir, but that's the way it is."

He shook his head sadly as though again defeated by life or an odd American and signed the certificate without a middle name, only the letter S for Dad.

Cecilia and I took our vows in the presence of the witnesses I mentioned. No other ceremony validated our marriage, only the jointly held commitment that it was to be, as it so beautifully turned out, "until death do us part," almost fifty years later. As the dear old registrar pronounced us man and wife, an air of melancholy seemed to pervade the room and enfold the occupants. To dispel the apparent gloom, I took my bride in a whole-hearted embrace with the same kind of kiss to conclude the ceremony. My temerity and strange American, really undisciplined, behavior almost shocked the registrar and Cecilia's family, but with appropriate restraint they gave no overt sign. The ancient building still stood, even if slightly shaken, and we departed in Mamie's little Austin for the United States consulate.

As we arrived at the consul's office to have our papers completed, we found him leaving for a two-hour lunch. He disregarded our consternation and waved us off, telling us to return at two o'clock.

"But we have to take a train at one o'clock."

"Come back at two." And out he walked.

The gods must have been on our side, for at that moment a subordinate walked into the room and, seeing our discomfiture, said, "Bring your papers and come with me."

That kind and thoughtful chap always had a warm place in our memories, and after all the years I still remember his name, Callahan—a *good* name that. He needed but a few minutes to complete the forms, and then took us to another room for Cecilia's physical examination.

Fortunately, she had papers to prove her freedom from communicable disease and mental deficiency and had satisfactorily answered the questions: Have you ever been a prostitute? Have you ever been in jail? among others.

When the physician in his white coat, with a stethoscope, appeared, Cecilia reached to her throat to unbutton her blouse. "Where did you say you were going? Seattle? A beautiful city and country. Be happy; good-bye." And that was her physical examination!

Minutes later Mamie had us on our way to Paddington to take the train for Bath. A helpful porter took our bags and found us a compartment with a single occupant, a male, perhaps in his fifties. Cecilia had received, too late for packing, two silver gravy boats. These she had put in an ancient but very strong, hard leather hatbox, veteran of many a voyage to India and return. The porter, having arranged our bags in the overhead racks, was putting the hatbox in a space above our fellow passenger's head when he objected strongly, saying that it might fall and injure him.

"It's light as a feather, sir, see?" The porter shook the box up and down.

Out came horrible thumps as the gravy boats bounced about inside. Our fellow passenger cringed, as did Cecilia, but she for fear of what had happened to her lovely gravy boats. The porter found another place for the box.

We followed him outside the compartment to tip him, and said, "We're sorry about the box."

"'ardly 'uman, I calls it, 'ardly, 'uman," he said as he tipped his cap.

At Bath we went to the Landsdowne Grove Hotel on a hillside with a lovely garden where tea was served on sunny days. In our room a huge bouquet of flame-colored gladiolas greeted us. The manager told me that, though I had ordered them, she wanted them to be a gift. She, in her late thirties, lingered a few moments with us in our sunny room, regarding us with warm friendliness, perhaps, I thought, sadly envious since she knew we were on our honeymoon. Had her husband or lover, I wondered, been one of the "killed in action," 1914–18? But here we were, after all the days' adventures, welcomed with flowers, sunshine, and the announcement by our hostess that tea would be served in the garden.

The weather was kind to us that week, and so the downs saw much of us. One day we spent, I think the whole day, in a well-known coffee house, Theobald's, made for drinking coffee, lingering, and talking. Some thirty years later, in 1958, when in Bath, we looked in on Theobald's for old time's sake, but it had been renovated, "prettied up," into a coffee and pastry shop. We didn't go in.

This leisurely, happy honeymoon started us on a life of emotional fulfillment, as Donne so aptly wrote in *The Ecstasy*:

> Loves mysteries on soules doe grow,
>   But yet the body is his booke.

This book we would continue to read until it was no more after fifty years together.

We spent a few days in London clearing up last details, saying farewell to the family and favorite relatives who could not be at the prewedding reception, then to old Waterloo Station again, only this time together to take the boat train to Southampton to board the *Empress of France*, Southampton to Quebec.

On board, some bon voyage letters awaited Cecilia—and a telegram from her very close and long-time friend, Mabel Forbes: "Splendid wishes for journey Homeward Bound on High Adventure, not Outward Bound. —Comrade." In Britain "outward bound" always meant going away from "home" to distant service in the Empire, but the departing person always looked forward to returning "home" to England or Scotland. Cecilia's departure, however, had just the opposite meaning for her, and only someone with the family background she rightly claimed could appreciate the real thrust of Mabel Forbes's telegram. Mabel's reassurance and confidence in Cecilia's future certainly eased the ache she could not help but feel as the *Empress* was slowly warped into the channel.

A stormy ocean crossing made the *Empress* four or five hours late when she picked up her river pilot and customs officials at the mouth of the St. Lawrence River to take her on to Quebec. She carried the royal mail, and her owners faced a fine, we understood, for each hour she was overdue; so the trip up the river seemed to us one long vibration as the engines were pushed to safety's limit. Customs were cleared en route. We debarked at Quebec after dark to a boat train for a night ride to Montreal, to be followed after some two hours on a train that would take us to New York. A stop at Rouse's Point across the border in New York provided Cecilia with her entry permit as a nonquota alien and a card she would be expected to carry at all times in the United States until she might be naturalized.

At Grand Central Station in New York, again long after dark, Cecilia first set foot on American soil, albeit only the station concrete, but reassuringly it was not moving; and to our delight there was Dorothy Thomas to meet us. Yes, Dorothy Thomas, who had introduced us by letter almost to the day three years ago in London. She eased our fatigue by taking us across the city to the Pennsylvania Railroad Station. Here we would take still another train to West Philadelphia to be met by someone with the family car to drive us on that last wearisome stretch to my family's home in the peaceful Pennsylvania countryside. On the ride to Philadelphia we were both so tired that we fell asleep in each other's arms, to be awakened by a solicitous conductor telling us that we were coming into the station.

It must have been near midnight when we arrived, happy to find my mother and youngest brother, Fred, awaiting us with the car, an Overland touring car. It was so characteristic of Mother to understand the importance, for all her sixty years and the late hour, of making the long trip to welcome to our family and country the young woman who had chosen to come so far and had left so much to be the wife of her son Luther.

I rode in the front with Fred, and Cecilia in back with Mother. While still in the city we had a flat tire, and as Fred and I repaired it Mother said, partly from hunger and partly to make conversation with Cecilia, "I sure could do with a hot dog right now."

"Yes, that would be nice," replied the courteous Cecilia.

Hot dogs were not to be found at that time of night; so, with the tire repaired, we headed for home, where we knew Dad and other members of the family were gathered to welcome the new member with food and conversation. Even deaf, old Mr. Harkness, who, that August day fourteen years before, had announced as Charlie and I ate lunch, "War, war, war!" came down to join in the welcome. It was about 3:00 A.M. before Cecilia and I, dazed with fatigue, were shown to our room.

"Your family is wonderful, Sheeleigh, and I am nearly asleep on my feet and need desperately to get to bed, but what is a 'hot dog'? Your mother said that she could do with a 'hot dog.' I said that would be nice, thinking she should have what she thought would be nice, but why should we or anybody have a dog, and hot at that, in the car with us and at that time of night?"

"It's a kind of sausage we have in this country, dear, very popular and usually eaten sandwiched between two halves of a long roll. You will see lots of them."

"Ohhhhh, that's a 'hot dog'! Now to bed."

The next day Cecilia was introduced to more Americana, fried chicken and corn on the cob. Mother had gathered all available sons, their wives, and children to meet Cecilia at Sunday dinner. Much refreshed and rested, she easily met the guests with her usual gracious friendliness. Fried chicken, however, was something else, indeed. Roasted, yes, but fried was something new. And corn on the cob! One really needed a letter of introduction to something so disconcertingly new. My kind and perceptive Dad, noting the wariness with which Cecilia approached both booby traps, provided the introduction. "Dorothy"—using the name my family always used for her, he took an ear of corn in his hands and holding it between his fingers, he lifted it to his mouth—"it's done like this." As for the fried chicken, he explained some portions like wings and legs could be quite properly held in the fingers much more effectively than by a fork, as she could observe around the table. Dear Cecilia never did become acculturated to corn on the cob, and I, even though a native, shared her lack of enthusiasm.

In the four happy, sunny, autumn days that Cecilia spent with my family a mutual lifelong relation of love and respect was engendered. Much too soon we had to board the overnight train to Chicago and then the *Olympian*, the crack train of the Milwaukee line, which would carry us to Ellensburg, Washington.

In those days railroads catered to passengers. For this portion of the trip we enjoyed a compartment, a small room with its comfort and privacy. Here we could talk, read, and together experience for the first time the wonderful newness of our life, a significant sharing as we rolled farther and farther west through North Dakota, Montana, northern Idaho, and into Washington. We passed through rich farming country, the country of the wheat ranches, and then cattle country as we neared the Rocky Mountains and climbed over that barrier.

On the sunny morning of our last day, as our train rushed through the Montana Canyon, we saw our first sheepherder with his horse, dog, and band of sheep grazing down an opposite slope.

"The sheep on a thousand hills," exclaimed Cecilia, and we felt that we were truly in a new country, the Far West.

Then across the "scabland" of eastern Washington, the Columbia River, and through endless miles of sagebrush. Sagebrush, more sagebrush! A pall of forest-fire smoke shut out any view of the distant landscape with its snowcapped peaks. Then across a large irrigation canal into a gardenlike landscape—our first vivid evidence of the life-giving power of water.

In a few minutes the train rolled to a stop. We were at Ellensburg, our new home, at least for the time being. That was where our concern lay, for we had a job to do and that was the "first order of the day." The Normal School would provide us with an intellectual base, a condition of the utmost importance and, fortunately, as I came to see later, in a nonurban area, where we could learn to know the basic character of so much of this vast and strikingly different land into which we had come. It would be our home for now; we would get on with our job and see what the future held.

The question, however, kept coming back to us: "Is this the same world as the one we knew that October evening in 1925, just three years previous, where we had met in Previtali's restaurant in Soho because Dorothy Thomas had given Luther a letter of introduction to 'a nice girl she knew in London'?" Yes and no.

Here we were at least at our destination in a really new world for both of us, even more so for Cecilia than for me. Yet, in all that time, with its inevitable fatigue, I saw Cecilia only twice give way to any sign of grief at her departure from England, although I knew it lay heavily on her. On the lighter taking us down the Solent at Southampton to board our ship, we stood together at the rail watching the green fields of England slip past in the late afternoon light. Sobs shook her slight figure momentarily. I put my arm around her shoulders. She steadied and that was the end of it. Later, desperately weary on the morning train from Montreal to New York City, we passed for miles under heavy overcast through scrub evergreen forests, a truly forlorn landscape. For a few moments she sobbed, then smiled at me appealingly through her tears as though to say, "Now, it's all over, Sheeleigh." We were both confident that new life lay ahead, and each succeeding day gave us further assurance.

Imagine, if you can, the cultural chasm separating the urban centers of London and New York, from which we had just come, and the isolated town of Ellensburg with some three thousand persons, approximately half of which were students, in the range country of east-central Washington! We were always glad, however, that we spent our first year in the Far West in this particular environment.

President and Mrs. Black and colleagues took us on long drives and picnics introducing us to, what were to Cecilia and me at any rate, wonders of the new country. They made us feel they were glad we had come.

Toward spring we were taken on a very exciting trip to the Columbia River just north of where interstate highway 90 crosses the Columbia River to see something very special in my field of study that would quicken my interest. After leaving the highway, we drove down

Whiskey Dick Canyon, with angles, not curves, so sharp I had to back the car to make some turns; then we walked down a difficult trail above the river because our Normal School friends felt the river was too high and swift to take the boat with an outboard motor offered by the rancher, who was to be our guide. After perhaps a half-mile walk, there they were, what we had come to see! Indian paintings of human figures in brilliant red, hematite, on the dark basalt cliff!

This was my first experience with and my introduction to the pre-historic life of the Far West. The experience is as sharp in my memory as though it happened but a few days ago. The excitement of the experience continued as Cecilia and I accepted the rancher's invita-tion to ride with him on the return. The high point was our trip in the small boat up that swift-running river under the high cliffs, with our beautiful Irish setter, Pat—acquired during the winter—standing in the bow with his ears "streaming like banners" in the wind. Our boatman knew his river and brought us safely in. Could it have been anything more than chance that my first significant archaeological work three years later would be concerned with Indian "rock writings" in Oregon?

We suffered no culture shock. Cecilia and I, having met many new challenges, knew that the new, even if at first forbidding, often offers unanticipated rewards. So, we found our situation an attractive challenge. In contrast to the urban, nonresidential students I had known at Columbia University and the College of the City of New York, the Normal School's students were mostly "in residence" in dormitories. As a whole, they were not intellectual, profession-bound types, but rather unspoiled kids, boys and girls from ranches and small towns. In some cases, they were interested in securing a teach-ing certificate; in others, in "testing the water" to see if they wanted to go on to college, or just in expanding their intellectual horizons. I found them eager to learn, not bored by the experience.

After we had been at the Normal School a short time, Cecilia sug-gested, and I agreed, to invite groups of students to our apartment for tea—"After all, if it is the custom at Oxford, I don't know why we can't do it here."

Cecilia's cooking skills were extremely limited, so we ordered cakes at the campus restaurant run for the benefit of the home economics program and as a training source for students. She did know how tea *should be made*, although she disliked it, and could brew coffee, and, of course, there was plenty of milk. We treated these boys and girls as guests, as persons, and as a gracious hostess Cecilia was at her best. She laid the table with a linen cloth from her dowry and used silver where appropriate.

The first invitation to ''tea with the Cressmans'' was so new that it was greeted among friends with a shrug of the shoulders and ''If it has to be it has to be; we can live through it once. Teaaa!''

But after word of the first experience got around, the invitations were eagerly accepted. What boy or girl could resist a slice, and often a second, or chocolate fudge, devil's food, or even angel food cake with something to drink? Cecilia and I directed the conversation to their life on the ranches, their homes, to hunting and fishing as well as other local matters, but always to *their* lives. After we got to know one another better, they asked about our lives, and we talked openly and freely with them about the East Coast and England. Our success in developing informal student-faculty relationships would stand us in good stead in our many years at Oregon that lay ahead, although at the time we were unaware of it.

Sometime after the first of the year, 1929, I received a letter from the head of the Sociology Department at the University of Oregon at Eugene, Dr. Phillip Parsons, saying that I had been highly recommended by Professor W. F. Ogburn for a position as professor in the department at Oregon. The contemplated position was temporary, but there was a chance that it would be made permanent. The purpose of the appointment was to secure someone to handle advanced research in social science and to develop the field of cultural anthropology. Would I be interested? I replied that I had a commitment to the Normal School and, of course, would not break it. But I would be interested in a permanent position that could be held open until the following fall. The answers to both conditions were affirmative, and a visit to the Eugene campus was arranged.

Both Cecilia and I had felt that I should get back into college-university work, so we welcomed this opportunity. I talked the matter over with President Black. Even though he was not happy with the idea of losing me as a staff member, he thought that if I were offered the position and it was to my liking, for my own professional career, I should take it. He was kind enough to add that he already knew they would not be able to hold me long at Ellensburg. Cecilia and I were shortly invited to the university, where we underwent the usual ritual

Cecilia at Cressman home in Pughtown, Pennsylvania, holding Gem, born September 22, 1929. Photo by George R. Cressman.

The Cressman family at Pughtown house about 1932. Cecilia and Gem were not with me. In addition to Mother, Dad, two grandchildren, and we six brothers, Mr. Harkness stands far left, partially in shadow, and Sara, a first cousin adopted at six after the death of her mother, stands next to Martha, George's wife.

Mother and Dad at George's house, probably prior to Dad's birthday, January 1, 1941. Photo by George R. Cressman.

of observation—in those days much simpler than now—and, to our great pleasure, I was offered the position, Professor of Sociology, starting with the academic year 1929–30.

Our lives now took a fresh turn as we faced the academic change that awaited us in the autumn. While we had been happy at Ellensburg, we had begun to feel that our marriage was still lacking something to complete it—something that would be bone of our bone, flesh of our flesh. In February, Cecilia had sensed some new stirrings in her body apparently trying to give her some message. She made an appointment with the doctor to decode the message. I hurried home from my office on the afternoon of her appointment, disappointed to find she had not returned. All I could do was wait, but not for long. I heard her at the door and jumped to greet her.

I didn't need to ask; her shining eyes told me as, with pretended shyness, she said, "I'm going to have a baby."

I put my arms around her and ever so tenderly said, "A blue-eyed, fair-haired baby girl." My wish, expressed so precisely to Cecilia, may not have seemed very polite to her with her brown eyes and dark hair, but her father, whom she adored, had had blue eyes and fair hair. She smiled, but volunteered no promises, as she sat down to contemplate the *wonder* of her new state. I excused myself, hurried to the florist, and returned with a pot of bright red tulips, symbol of spring and new life, for this new Cecilia.

At the close of summer school, we said farewell to the Blacks and our other colleagues at the Normal School and boarded the train east to Pennsylvania to be with my family. I left Cecilia there to await our baby's arrival and to stay for the following few weeks to adjust to her new relationship—mother and child. I was afraid to move her to Eugene—she would soon be forty-one—and try to settle her there so short a time before the expected birth. She would come to Eugene as soon as she felt it wise to travel. I returned to Ellensburg, packed our few remaining belongings in our little Ford coupe, and drove alone to Eugene. There, on September 22, I received a telegram: "Blue-eyed, fair-haired girl arrived as ordered. Mother and baby excellent."

Some six week later I drove to Portland to meet Cecilia and see with my very own eyes our daughter, Gem, for the first time. I awaited their train at the Union Station. It arrived on time at 8:00 A.M. I hurried to the platform of their pullman, saw through the open door a very harassed-looking Cecilia, and heard angry and loud wails coming from a basket she so carefully carried. I embraced and kissed Cecilia, then looked down at the very small source of the loud complaints in the basket; Gem looked up at me, smiled, and promptly went to sleep.

"That little wretch! What did you do to her, Sheeleigh? Here she was yelling her lovely head off and looked up at you, and blessed silence settled down!"

"Oh, it's just a way I have."

Cecilia had made her transcontinental journey alone with our treasure before any of the remarkably helpful devices for transporting infants had been invented. Cecilia's mother had made many much more arduous journeys, however, some really harsh experiences in the long voyages to India and return, often with infants—as had all the wives of the men in the Indian services. It was a way of life for them, something to be expected. In keeping with her family tradition, Cecilia took her long journey in stride even though the same train on its run only the week before had been held up by a masked bandit and the passengers robbed as it neared the Rocky Mountains.

My older brother, Charlie, had foreseen her major problem and had put his engineer's skill to work. He had taken one of the strong wide-splint market baskets then in use, strengthened it by interlacing it and its wide handle with wire, and heavily padded the inside. The padding kept the baby snug and warm and made it possible for Cecilia to take her out to bathe and nurse. Dad had given her a Masonic emblem, a tiny golden slipper, to wear on the lapel of her coat, a symbol to tell any Mason to provide any help that might facilitate the wearer's way. At Chicago the conductor at the check-in station saw this golden slipper and, true to his obligation, took Cecilia and her small charge in his care and passed her through the gates to her pullman berth before they opened to the public.

The tired but happy mother, happy father, and sleeping infant returned to the hotel, where, after a few moments of chatting and the sheer pleasure of being together again, we went down to breakfast with our baby in her basket. The waitress purred over the sleeping Gem to the pleasure of the proud parents.

It was a beautiful, Indian-summer-like day as we left for Eugene. At a small town, about halfway to Eugene, the ladies agreed and announced to me that it was time for the young one to have lunch. I found a wide side street lined with great maple trees, their leaves golden in the sunshine, and parked under them. There Cecilia proceeded to nurse our blue-eyed one, who knew exactly what she wanted and needed no map to find the source. The absolute peace and comfort as Gem satisfied her need and the happiness in her fulfilled maternity so clear on Cecilia's face was replete with a very special meaning for our relationship. Even though only a poor male onlooker—albeit the father—I felt now that the incompleteness in our marriage, sensed at Ellensburg, had been turned into completeness and the new Cressman-Loch family was truly bone of our bone and flesh of our flesh. Our lives now, whatever happened, would be different from that we had known before.

The hunger of our young one satisfied and the mother comfortably settled, we proceeded to Eugene and our little two-room apartment we had rented on our visit in the spring. Family life and university life would now become an integrated whole.

The journey, "homeward bound," on which Cecilia and I had embarked on the *Empress of France* from Southampton a year earlier had now come to an end in Eugene. Here we would set up our lares and penates. One hot August afternoon in 1931 we moved into the house where we would spend the rest of our lives together. Our household gods served us well. It is where I now sit in their company writing these memoirs. Your bon voyage greeting from Mabel Forbes, Cecilia, has been fulfilled.

Journey's End

Here a star, and there a star,
Some lose their way.
Here a mist, and there a mist:
Afterwards—Day!

Emily Dickinson, *Life, I, Success*

DAY dawned for Cecilia, Gem, and me as we carefully placed our lares and penates in our two small rooms in the Osburn Apartments, Eugene, Oregon, that lovely midautumn afternoon in 1929.

Eugene, a small town of about 20,000 persons within its environs, lay at the southern end of the Willamette Valley—through which the Willamette River flows—a trough varying in width from 20 to 40 miles between the Cascade and Coast ranges and extending 125 miles to the north to the confluence of the Columbia and the Willamette rivers where Portland, the major city of the state, is located. A quiet city of wide streets lined with gracious maple and oak shade trees was our new home.[1] The presence of the University of Oregon, a state-supported, liberal arts university, gave a cultural quality to the town, linking it intellectually more with Portland than any other in the state. Support services for the university provided a large segment of the town's economy, but beyond these it had a Southern Pacific Railroad roundhouse and served as a service center for a few wood-products industries and thriving agricultural activities, mostly garden, orchard and seed production. Springfield, with a population of about 2,500, a mile or more to the east, was an important industrial center based on the lumber industry.

The Oregon Agricultural College, also state-supported, at Corvallis, a small town of about 8,000 persons, was forty miles north of Eugene on the west side of the valley. The unfortunate—in my opinion—separation of these two land-grant institutions was a result of certain local historical processes in the newly settled state. I remember an anecdote—perhaps apocryphal—I heard shortly after my arrival about an early president of the university, a classical scholar, when offered in the interest of economy the addition of the agricultural college to the university, had snorted almost as though insulted: "What has a university to do with cows and pigs?" And would have none of it.

I soon learned that regardless of its origins the hostility between the two institutions was a situation boding no good for their future relations. At the university, the common, informal name for the Corvallis college was "The Cow College," a piece of snobbishness that would pay poor dividends. I don't know what corresponding epithet was used by the Agricultural College people to characterize the university, but I am sure it was whatever they saw as appropriate. The frightening, to me at least, reality of the hostility became clear that first fall with the annual football game between the two institutions' teams, called the "Civil War." A deep-seated rivalry with strong overtones of disdain and hostility found an opportunity to vent itself as a kind of safety valve, but when carried over into the political and legislative arenas, unfortunate results would be sure to erupt.

Eugene in 1929 was certainly isolated almost as much as Penn State was in 1914 when I arrived there as a freshman. It was an overnight train journey via the Southern Pacific Railroad to San Francisco and three or more hours by the same means to Portland, so the traveler desiring to go to the east had to start his journey by first going to either of these two cities. Of course one does that now if one wishes to travel by train, but that has been changed by the direct air connections from Eugene to major cities in the United States and by one change of planes to intercontinental travel.

Eighty miles of narrow, winding roads across the Coast Range took one to the magnificent Pacific coast with its rocky headlands, "where the mountains come down to the sea," interspersed with beautiful sandy beaches, where the water is always cold. Winter saw the few roads across the Cascade Mountains to the semiarid plateau, characteristic of much of the eastern part of the state, closed by snow. Only the Columbia River highway through the gorge could be kept open. The narrow but blacktopped Pacific highway, U.S. 99, ran south to San Francisco, approximately six hundred miles with long stretches of tortuous mountain roads.

Well before our marriage, Cecilia and I had planned to start our new life together preferably far from New York. We wanted a total break with the past. We did not know the place, only that it would have to be a world providing intellectual freedom at some university. We were experienced enough to know that that freedom would have to be exercised with discretion but never compromise, for academic institutions everywhere tend to place a high priority on the preservation of long-established values often to the extent of not considering them appropriate subjects for questioning. So, when I came to the University of Oregon, it was not primarily to hold a job or a position—that would, of course, provide the necessary economic base—but to start a new phase of my career in the comradeship of the deeply understanding and sympathetic Cecilia.

We were not shaken by the apparent isolation of our new home, even though we were separated by only that first year at Ellensburg from our years in London and New York with all the diverse cultural riches these cities offered. We were always glad that we had had our first year in Ellensburg and the associations shared there for the insight it gave us into the open-ranch and range-style life so much more characteristic of the traditional western values than was the case in the large cities. Cecilia and I, as time permitted, explored the range and mountain country and came to love it, an attitude we would find to our great advantage in the years ahead, although at the time we were unaware of it.

Our first year had been an important transitional time for us. From areas of population congestion we had come to a country of vast spaces and few people; from an educational establishment based upon long-standing institutions well aware of their prestige and how to use it to their own advantage; from an intellectual world where too often knowledge was organized into a series of accepted, almost taken-for-granted theories or propositions—to which all new ones or ideas had to be referred for evaluation by their degree of conformance—instead of probabilities derived from the pertinent information.

One day that first year Cecilia and I stood on a low hill high above the Columbia River and gazed in amazement to the west, where in the crystal-clear air the massive summit of Mt. Rainier gleamed brilliantly white under new-fallen snow, seemingly almost close enough to touch. Our car map showed that 150 miles then separated us from that shining snowfield with very few people in the intervening space. Fifth Avenue and 42nd Street and Picadilly Circus seemed far away and somehow lacking in reality.

Our knowledge of Indians, too, moved from books and museum exhibits in London and New York to living Indians as we saw them on the streets of Yakima (a small town about thirty miles south of Ellensburg), close to the reservation of that name. Some Indians were distinguishable from whites only by their physical appearance, whereas others wore their hair in long plaits decorated with porcupine quills and shells or were wearing perhaps some specially decorated articles of clothing.

Western history and prehistory became real for us that Sunday morning as we looked in wonder at the ancient pictographs on the cliff above the Columbia River, just as it had that long-ago morning when as a small boy I found the 1776 English shilling in my Dad's cornfield. The "River of the West" of history books and explorers' journals became a sensational, near-frightening reality as the rancher-boatman brought us from the pictograph site up the river, almost in flood, with his little boat and outboard motor.

How unaware we were that morning in our elation how our lives would soon be intertwined with pictographs and the River of the West! We did know that we were discovering basic realities about our new world, realities from past and present, but new in our experience. We were going to have to ask a lot of questions and search for answers wherever the sources of information might draw us, for we had already learned that much of what we sought could not be found in the books then at one's disposal. Most important, our year at Ellensburg confirmed what Professor Ogburn had written us,[2] and we, too, found in the West a willingness to explore new ideas, less restriction on intellectual adventure, a fact to be repeatedly impressed on us in the years ahead.[3]

From the anguish of my 1925–27 years I made my final decision for my career, a decision certainly not lightly arrived at, to be a teacher of the young: to be a DISCOVERER OF KNOWLEDGE, not a TRANSMITTER OF REVELATION. I saw then, and the years since have done nothing to change my opinion, that teaching is the most challenging and most responsible of careers and, indeed, the most honorable. I would be helping the young to use their minds, the most complex and awesome instrument developed in the long evolutionary stream of life: NOT WHAT TO THINK, BUT HOW TO THINK.

To teach HOW TO THINK would require me to reevaluate continually my own performance as a teacher; to replenish my intellectual resources by significant research, a spring drawing on a great aquifer to maintain its flow of fresh water; to inform colleagues by publication of my results and invite their criticism in the interest of improving my performance; and as a teacher in our democratically supported educational institutions, I would have to share my work with lay people by appropriate publication, lecture, and public service as a decent gesture of appreciation to those whose taxes support that system and who send their children to be our students. The teacher who deserves that respected name is as much driven by his demon as is the artist and in the same way. These were the values I had chosen as my ideals during my first two years of teaching in defining the obligations and opportunities of the teacher; and now, after more than a half century in their service, I remain firmly convinced of their validity, for they have served me and my students well.

As a participant in the University of Oregon community I accepted my obligation to work toward the realization of the university's educational objectives through the smooth functioning of my department, any department, toward that end. My own contribution could be achieved by working within this framework so long as no significant conflict of values occurred.

Further, I saw teaching as a mutual-aid activity with both student and teacher receiving and giving to each other in the process, one in which Cecilia and I would share jointly to make OUR CAREER, OUR DAY, a joint enterprise best expressed in a few words by "AE" in a poem to which Cecilia introduced me during my *Wandeljahre*:

No blazoned banner we unfurl,
One charge alone we lay on youth,
Against the sceptered myth
To hold the golden heresy of truth.

(*To Some Irishmen Not Followers of Tradition*)

As mentioned, in 1929 the University of Oregon was about the size of Penn State when I arrived there as a freshman in 1914, with similarities, but important differences. In origin, both were land-grant institutions and geographically isolated; both were coeducational and residential with limited dormitory space, so that each relied to a great extent on the town to provide lodging. They differed sharply in the focus of instruction: Penn State was mainly science oriented with major focus on engineering and agriculture and with the liberal arts, although a college, holding a very minor position in the curriculum; the University of Oregon was a balanced, liberal arts institution. Both were small, a situation resulting in low-enrollment classes and close student-instructor relations. In spite of Penn State's low accent on the liberal arts, I majored in the classics and English poetry and enjoyed the most significant formal education experience of my career in my Greek class, where for four years two of us made up the class and sat across a table in his office from Dr. Harris, an inspired teacher. I never heard any suggestion that our class failed to meet some cost-benefit evaluation of management budgeting. Neither institution had been affected by the ''publish or perish'' syndrome, and both placed emphasis on good teaching. At Penn State I was a student; at Oregon I was a faculty member, a full professor.

The intellectual world of 1929, however, was vastly changed from that of 1914–18. As a student at Penn State I saw the war clouds approach and finally envelop us; as a faculty member at Oregon, I saw my students leave for service and empathized with their feelings even though the war atmosphere on campus was not the same as in 1917–18. I would see some of those who came back answer the call a second time in Korea. After my retirement came Vietnam. Always the young, the loss of leaders in the generation to replace us. Will we ever learn?

' The College of the City of New York where I enjoyed my first college teaching experience in 1925, 1926 to 1928, had provided a very different setting. CCNY students, in my experience, were on the whole brilliant, the best I ever taught for sheer intellectual drive and ability. Many of them were sons of first- or second-generation immigrant families with an intense motivation to achieve and escape from the slum environment of their parental homes. It was strictly urban and nonresidential. The teaching staff, at least our department, Government, had no individual offices, only a single one with a couple of desks for the staff. When our classes were over we went home. CCNY was not coeducational—Hunter was the women's college—and the sense of community was lacking at both faculty and student levels. My association with those lads was a stimulating, intellectual experience.

I do not intend to write a history of the University of Oregon in the following pages; that will fall to another. I wish to share with you, as I relive them, those significant elements in the development of my professional career as a teacher in the full range of appropriate activities and member of the faculty from September 1, 1929, until my retirement June 30, 1963, and as an emeritus professor after that date. It is a record of personal relations, friendly and hostile; planning and the lack of it; the ability to see an opportunity and to grasp it; the willingness to accept responsibility; the defiance of power when necessary; serendipity and pure chance providing critical opportunities to be seized; successes and disappointment; lifelong friendships with students, teachers and others—a career always jointly shared with Cecilia.

I found the university a community consisting of about 3,000 students and 150 faculty, separate, to be sure, but complementary and not juxtaposed, internally coherent and ideationally separate from the "town." The focus of university life in an area well removed from the business district, the common purpose of its members, the isolation from the distractions of large population centers, together with its residential character and the grouping of fraternities and sororities close to the university all contributed to the sense of community. The president's house was on the campus, really centrally located next to the administration building, and several senior faculty members had houses immediately adjacent to the campus. I never had any sense in those early years of either administration and faculty as competing elements or president and teaching faculty as separates. Such confrontations that did occur were on a personal level. The university's geographic isolation, however, and keen sense of community could, unless carefully nurtured in the right direction by wise administrative leadership, grow into an intellect-damaging state of provincialism.

The faculty, though small, was on the whole good, with some distinctly outstanding members.

Looking down my long perspective of more than a half century, I find that certain of my associates of those years appear vividly for some distinguishing trait, a capability of personality or performance significant enough to have given each deserved recognition in any above-average university.

I think first of Dr. C. Valentine Boyer, professor of English literature, dean of the College of Literature, Art and Sciences, with a Ph.D. degree from Princeton, a law degree, and study in Europe. He was educated, civilized, a product of the wise use of wealth, an excellent teacher, especially of the English social novel. An anecdote from one of his students comes to mind of the time when he returned to his class after several weeks of illness and his students gave him a standing ovation and prolonged applause. A tall, spare man, he gave the impression that he lacked any great reserve of physical strength. Dr. Boyer always drove a Packard sedan, but the significance of that trait may be lost on the present generation. Mrs. Boyer and he were gracious hosts to both town and gown at their red-brick Georgian house on Twenty-second Street not far from the campus.

Ed—he probably had a related name but I never, never heard it used—Lesch, also with a Ph.D. degree from Princeton, professor of English literature, was an exciting and interesting teacher, especially in this annual, brilliant course in Shakespeare. He was sharp-tongued and impersonally defiant of authority, when such was needed or Ed thought so, with a bitter sense of humor and a deeply founded sensitivity to the importance of intellectual integrity. He and I were very good friends who joshed each other in private and at time in faculty meetings, and we always understood the nature of the joshing. One warm spring day I had come out on the campus to walk home to lunch; I saw Ed coming to go to his home not far from mine, so I stopped to wait for him. His greeting as he came up to me was, "The warm sun doth bring forth the adders."

Dr. Henry Sheldon, dean of the School of Education, had been associated with G. Stanley Hall, the famous authority on adolescence who tried to develop, but rather unsuccessfully, Clark University on the model of the German university. Lack of funding was his major obstacle. Dean Sheldon, a spare, tall man, was well toward the end of his service, broadly educated, sophisticated, ironic, and very wise in the ways of men, especially in academia. Dr. Orin Stafford, professor of chemistry, pushed research into new fields, such as the utilization of wood waste and the production of "heavy water." Harvey G. Townsend, professor of philosophy, had come to Oregon from Smith College, was a distinguished authority on American philosophical

thought and one of the country's leading authorities on Cotton
Mather. I always have thought Townsend had the most brilliant
intellect on the campus. He was educationally conservative with
impeccably high standards of personal and social ethics. Professor of
philosophy, Dr. George Rebec, of Czech extraction, dean of the
Graduate School, could be irascible and kindly. He was deeply educated and insisted on high levels of scholarly performance. Eric Allen
was founder and dean of the School of Journalism, where many of the
coming young men in Oregon journalism received their training. He
was a leader and an innovator, and his opinions were always worth listening to. Dr. Warren D. Smith, professor of geology and geography,
I found to be a very fertile source of ideas, too fertile some said, but I
soon learned if I listened and filtered them a bit, some very stimulating and helpful ones came through. He was always happiest in the
field, as long as there were not too many snakes about. I rather
quickly got to know him. I found him invaluable as a source of help
and information in my fieldwork, always generous with his time if he
could help and with an exciting interest in my work. Wayne Morse,
who became dean of the Law School, was a dynamic force on the campus, but I can't think of him as a scholar.

I am sure another person from my period might differ with my
evaluations of these men, accepting some, rejecting others. The men I
have named were the intellectual core of the university. I was fortunate to be associated with them.

Cecilia and Gem did not arrive in Eugene until after the president's annual reception for the faculty and so did not have the opportunity to meet other faculty members. Her year with all its new
challenges would be difficult. We lived in a small apartment downtown some distance from the campus. Cecilia faced not only a new
society and culture but also a new family situation with our small
Gem and all the necessary details of taking her place in the university
community as well as learning the details of household management
her American counterparts grew up with. Her year would be one of
continuous challenges. I, of course, helped all I could, but I had to be
on the campus most of each day. Mrs. Parsons, the wife of my department head, had died shortly after we had been in Eugene for our
preappointment interview or she would have taken the responsibility
of being Cecilia's first line of support and would have given it graciously and successfully. As it was, there was no help from the depart-

ment in any way. The other senior professor was unmarried, and the other two were also new.

Wives of senior faculty members made a point of calling on Cecilia. Mrs. Sheldon, Mrs. Boyer, Mrs. Smith, Mrs. Stafford, and Mrs. Townsend were most solicitous in calling on her and offering their friendship, starting associations to last many years. Mrs. Townsend put us in touch with a charming graduate student of her husband's who came for the evening for twenty-five cents—yes, that's right—so we could have dinner out one night a week and give Cecilia a "break," since she was really just learning to cook. On those magic nights we used to get a complete T-bone steak dinner for one dollar at the Eugene Hotel and then walk the streets and window-shop, for we had little money to buy with. Gem's young efforts to use her sitter's name resulted in something we elders fancifully said was "Gi-Gi," and so she always was to us over the long years of our association. My status as a full professor and the assumption of social responsibility by these gracious ladies inevitably drew us into a closer relation with that group than with any other.

Our first year obviously had to be a time of finding our way and place in the department, the university, and the town. To use a contemporary idiom: we had to locate the minefields in the university community, learn how to defuse a dangerous situation, and make our way through with minimum damage. Minefields could be of different kinds.

Near the end of our first year Cecilia and I gave a dinner to return social obligations incurred during the year. We arranged for the dinner at the Eugene Hotel in a special second-floor room requiring the use of the elevator. I met our guests at the street door, escorted them to the elevator and to Cecilia, who received them at our room. I met Dean Rebec at the street door—Mrs. Rebec had come separately —and as I was escorting him to the elevator, he inquired who the other guests were. When I mentioned, among others, the Sheldons, he started to make a kind of low moaning noise to my consternation, which I managed to conceal.

The dinner was a great success. Mrs. Boyer lingered after all the other guests had gone, then said to Cecilia, "My dear Cecilia, what a delightful evening, and I must congratulate you on your skill."

"You are very kind, Mrs. Boyer, but I didn't know I was being skillful. Our guests were very gracious and kept everything going smoothly."

"We wondered, Cecilia, with some anxiety, what would happen with both the Sheldons and the Rebecs as guests, for they are not on speaking terms. But you had seated them so that they were not near each other. That was clever."

"But, Mrs. Boyer, how in the world was I to know they were not on speaking terms? I just seated guests so that they would not be next to someone each had probably been seeing during the day. It was just sheer good luck."

That night Cecilia and I learned about one kind of faculty minefield, annoying but not dangerous, that could be easily defused or passed through without damage; not all were so harmless.

I got the impression that first year that the university community, and it was a community, seemed to be held together by some inertial force which was effective so long as no disturbing influence erupted in its course. The basic structure of the university was centrifugal, with no unifying central organization to hold the related units into some mutually supporting subdivisions, such as a college of liberal arts. The College of Literature, Art and Sciences under Dean Boyer was the largest and perhaps represented the original subject matter making up the university's area of study. Other areas of study were organized into "schools," each under a dean: education, social science, physical education, business administration, journalism, architecture and allied arts, applied social science, and home economics. The organization suggests that the college was the original unit, and when it seemed wise to the president, or some individual or group convinced him of the desirability of adding a new field, a "school" was set up for that purpose and with a dean. This was certainly the case with the School of Applied Social Science. It was not that the concept of applied social science was bad, quite the contrary in my opinion, but the organization was not capable of doing it. The Sociology Department should certainly have been organizationally with economics, political science, etc., but it apparently was in the School of Applied Social Science as a core for that concept and had Dean Parsons as its head. The result was that the Sociology Department was organizationally of dubious parentage and parental supervision, a situation that could cause discomfiture to its members.

Late in my first year I found myself nearly victimized by this faulty situation. I was working in my office, which I shared with another newcomer, one Saturday morning, fortunately alone, when a knock came at the door. The door opened to my "Come in," and Dr. Parsons entered and accepted with a somewhat uncertain air my invitation to have a chair. The stiffness about him, his not looking at me, but letting his glance settle on my bookcase, put me on the alert. Still without really looking at me, he started abruptly, "Cressman, we are going to renew your appointment for another year, but I must tell you that your teaching is not entirely satisfactory."

This statement was really a shock to me, for all my experience with students and faculty had given me quite the opposite impression.

"This information is a great surprise, Dr. Parsons," I said, trying to avoid a confrontation, "and if there is some deficiency I should like to know so that I may take the necessary steps to correct it. Just what is the problem?"

"Dean Gilbert told me that he had been talking with President Hall about new staff and the president had told him that the students felt that you were too critical; I am passing that information on to you to consider."

We talked a few minutes, avoiding arguments, and I asked if I might talk with Dean Gilbert. Of course he could not refuse, but my reaction was not what he expected. I thanked Dr. Parsons and said that I would talk with Dean Gilbert.

I got an appointment with Dean Gilbert, told him of the situation, and said that I was anxious to do everything possible to improve my teaching, but that this was the first sign of negative criticism I had encountered.

"I usually call in certain students from the classes of new instructors, Cressman," he said, "but I haven't in your case because you seemed to be more under Dean Parsons than me."

"I wish you would follow your practice with me, Dean Gilbert, for I am anxious to have the information."

Then he told me essentially the same thing Dr. Parsons had about his conversation with President Hall.

"May I call on President Hall to follow up on this?"

"Of course, and I think you should. I shall call in students and let you know."

"Thank you, Dean Gilbert."

I got my appointment with President Hall and told him the reason for my taking his time. He made a gesture of frustration with both hands, saying, "My God, Cressman, has it come to this? I was at a fraternity dinner the other night and I asked a boy next to me about his teachers, and your name came up. He said that he thought you were a very good teacher but too critical. I passed the information along to Dean Gilbert without any idea he would make this use out of it."

"I come from a hard school, President Hall, Columbia University and the rigorous standards of Boas and Ogburn, where nothing could be presented as fact unless documented."

"Humph," replied President Hall, a political scientist, "if Ogburn were on a coon hunt and the hounds had the animal treed, he wouldn't accept it as a coon until it was on the ground where he could see it."

"True, President Hall, and he would shoot it on the way down so it would not escape before identification."

"I had no idea this would happen, Cressman, and didn't mean it to."

"Will you please clarify this matter with both Dean Gilbert and Dean Parsons?"

"I certainly will, and thank you for coming in, Cressman."

When I told Cecilia of the interview I said that Hall's explosive comment was the same as Ogburn's when I told him of the refusal of my adviser to let me change to him. I wondered if it was a favorite academic response to frustrating situations of this kind.

Dean Gilbert called in the students from the A and B groups and, as he told me later, received excellent reports.

Parsons learned a very important fact from this confrontation: that I was not timid and did not scare easily. I learned of a very dangerous minefield I would have to negotiate in the time ahead. Parsons's misuse of information with which he could damage my reputation was either stupid or malicious; in either case it was dangerous, a warning to be on the alert.

I came to Oregon at a salary $600 less than I received at Ellensburg, but there I was on a twelve-month appointment. At Oregon I was promised teaching in the Extension Division in addition to my regular schedule or in summer session to make up the difference in income. My first year I taught an extension course in Portland, leaving the summer vacation period free for work.

For the summer of 1930 I accepted an invitation from the Institute of Social and Religious Research in New York, which had made available to me the raw data for my dissertation research, to repeat a series of surveys of small, rural communities in western Oregon and Washington using duplicates of the original schedules. This was part of a national program to assess the amount of social change in the five-year period following the original study. The project offered me, in addition to the financial benefit, the opportunity of gaining at least an acquaintance with a new and significant area of our new world; there was a suitable community on the western border of the great wheat ranches of north-central Oregon and another in Washington a few miles south of the United States–Canadian border.

I started my survey with a community not far south of Eugene. I finished that and returned to Eugene on Saturday afternoon to spend a quiet period with the family before starting on the balance of the survey requiring three to four weeks. I had planned for Sunday morning a short fishing trip to an exciting riffle near Eugene—Cecilia called one of these short outings of a few hours or days taken for their immediate benefit and pleasure an *Ausflug*, a word she had learned from a German tutor when she was in Wiesbaden, Germany, in 1912 with her parents for her mother's treatment at the famous Augenklinik—then spend the rest of the time with the family until my Monday departure.

My late-Saturday-afternoon homecoming was exciting, as expected, for all concerned. Gem and I had much to tell each other in our language in the short time before dinner. Cecilia and I always followed the English custom of separate dinners for children and the parents; in our case, Gem's dinner preceded ours so we could have ours uninterrupted by any claims for attention. With Gem tucked snugly in her bed watching my approach eagerly, I sat down on the side of her bed to tell her the story for the night, one I conjured up for the occasion or an appropriate one from a book. This always ended in a ritual roughhouse, a good-night kiss, and the light out.

Cecilia and I were enjoying our dinner, savoring again the pleasure of each other's company, when the phone rang. I answered.

"This is Western Union. We have a telegram for Professor Cressman."

"This is he," I said with that sense of trepidation one always felt with a telegram. "Please read it."

"Opening first tomb tomorrow at eight, Sunday. Please come supervise excavation. Can you take over direction starting Tuesday?"

I repeated the telegram for verification and then asked the operator to deliver a copy, telling him I would have to think about my answer.

Cecilia looked at me inquiringly and puzzled, completely mystified by what she had heard. I, as puzzled as she, remarked that "tombs" reminded me of Egypt or Mesopotamia, but certainly not Oregon. Compounding my confusion was the fact that I never had a course in archaeology, nor ever in my wildest fantasies had I been an archaeologist. That riffle at Black Canyon in the Willamette River with its waiting trout was providing very enticing images. Gold Hill, Oregon, the location of the "tombs," was about two hundred miles south, many over uninviting mountain segments. I would lose the whole day and evening I had planned with the family. The Western Union messenger delivered the telegram while we lingered over our after-dinner coffee. We were not yet ready for an answer. Time to clear the table; a decision had to be made.

"I guess this is why we came, isn't it," said Cecilia.

I heard her words like an echo of her father's in India to his men: "The exigencies of the Service require that. . . ." The Service, not the individual's desire, commanded one's devotion. "You know, Lutie, you are supposed to . . . ," the gentle but firm voice of my parents.

"You're right, Cecilia. The fishing can wait."

"Please take a telegram," I said to the answering Western Union operator.

"Go ahead, please."

"Arriving at eight o'clock tomorrow, Sunday."

With that decision Cecilia and I crossed another Rubicon, an act to affect not only our own future lives but also those of many others, even in distant places, for an unknown number of years. The date? June 7, 1930.

I was apparently the first customer that Sunday morning, June 8, 1930, when I sat at the counter before eight o'clock in Gold Hill's lone, small cafe after my long, nonstop drive from Eugene. The owner-cook-waiter, wise from long experience, put a mug of hot coffee before me without waiting for my order.

I think both my eyes and voice thanked him as I ordered breakfast. It was a sturdy breakfast, one for hungry men that he prepared as he carried on some exploratory conversation to discover who this stranger might be. Gold Hill didn't have many strangers, especially so early in the morning.

As I relaxed with my good breakfast and chatty host, two men entered with a hearty "Mornin', Ed" to the proprietor, who acknowledged their greeting with a wave of one hand as he deftly reached under the counter with the other to bring out two mugs, his fingers through the looped handles, filled them with hot coffee and put them out for his friends. Before starting their coffee the men turned to me and one asked, "Are you Professor Cressman? We saw the unfamiliar car outside and hoped it would be you."

"You're right and call me Doc."

"I'm Alex Woolverton and this is Eric Wold, Alex and Eric, and we want to welcome you. Ed, this is Professor Cressman from the University of Oregon at Eugene. He has come down to help excavate the tombs. Take good care of him and give me the check."

"While we enjoy our coffee, I wish you men would tell me what is ahead, but if the place is close by we can go after we finish and you can explain everything there. This rest feels good; I left home at four o'clock."

We finished our coffee, and then I followed their car a very short distance over the Rogue River bridge to a side road off to the right, where after perhaps a hundred yards we came to a very unimpressive and small wheat-stubble field. It was just across the river from the cafe. We pulled into the field from the road and stopped. I had already sensed that Alex was the leader, when he came to me and said, "Here we are." I wondered where the tombs were, but politely waited to have that explained. I said that I would like to walk over the site first to get an idea of the place as a whole, then we could talk about the details. My suggestion was agreeable to the men, so we followed up on it. The field ended on the north or village side about forty-five feet above the river in a rather sharp slope showing a series of three terraces down to the river level. Kane Creek, bordered by bushes, ran along the west side to the river. A cultivated field was on the south side, and the road over which we came was on the east side. The field was about a hundred yards, north-south, and nearly the same on the east-west axis. After this quick examination I asked my guides to tell me briefly, before anyone else came, just what they had here in this field.

Their story was simple enough in its details, but I thought from what I heard that they really had an important prehistoric site on their hands. The rancher (a Mr. Hittle) had planted wheat in the field, but the lack of sufficient water resulted in a poor crop. He was struck, however, by something he did not understand, something new; there were spots in the field where the wheat grew higher and more thickly than elsewhere. Puzzling over this, he decided to try to find the answer later in the season when his work load became lighter.

At his first opportunity, he chose one of the spots and started to dig, for he felt sure there must be some explanation common to all spots. Here I was seeing again what I had observed my first year in Washington: how curious and observant the country people, the ranchers, were about their environment; how they satisfied that curiosity rather than let it pass as something of no concern. To succeed in that country they had to be observant and knowledgeable, and they shared their information with interested scientists, making a contribution too often unrecognized.

After digging about one and a half to two feet, Hittle struck a fist-sized rock. Stones of this size were unusual in the plow depth, and finding this novelty made him dig carefully, even using his hands. He found a layer of stones, some broken apparently by fire, forming a generally oval pattern. As he removed these he noticed that the soil was darker than that outside the oval area. Continuing his careful removal of the dirt, he was startled by uncovering a human bone. With great care he uncovered other bones of a skeleton and with them a pair of obsidian knives. Hittle was sure now that he had uncovered an Indian burial, but even though he was familiar with much of the Indian lore of the area, he had never heard of any relating to this field as a burial ground. During the next few weeks, he dug several other "spots," and in every one there were the remains of a human skeleton in varying degrees of completeness, some with but a few fragments of bones. What he found with some of the burials was to him more exciting than the human remains: large obsidian blades, some nearly a foot long; shells of marine animals; some long, ground-stone tubular objects he thought must have been pipes; pine-nut seeds drilled apparently for suspension; but nothing of metal. This was exciting news. Then Alex said, "Come on, Doc, let's go and see the things; Hittle likes to show them." As we went to his house I thought of the lines:

> I sometimes think that never blows so red
> The Rose as where some buried Caesar bled.

> (Omar Kayyám, *Rubáiyát*)

Hittle was expecting us, for Alex had, as I surmised, informed him of my coming, and he had his most impressive finds ready to show. Taking us into a special room, not the family living room, he pointed proudly to his exhibit, "Here they are, Doc. What do you think of them?"

I couldn't answer for a moment because they were so far beyond what I had expected to see.

"They're beautiful. I have never seen any specimens of this kind nearly as beautiful as these. Do you mind if I handle them?"

"No, just so you don't drop and break them."

There were solid black obsidian blades and some red and black mixed, "mahogany," certainly a foot long and other smaller ones; long, smoothly ground, tubular stone pipes; a variety of shell beads and one flat square of abalone shell that had been an ornament of some kind; and other more usual objects, such as grinding stones. We discussed these and the conditions of the finding. I hefted the blades, trying to imagine who had handled them in life. Those pipes had some particular significance, for I believe Hittle said that he found six or seven with the same burial. I was completely unaware of any literature at the moment that illustrated similar blades or explained the use of the pipes. Our talk finally drifted off to other subjects, especially since this was my first trip to the area. I explained that I had given up a planned fishing trip to come down to see if I could help.

"Don't give it another thought," said Eric. "The Rogue is the best steelhead river in the country, and I have a few private rapids I'll take you to on one of your trips if you come again, and you shall catch a Rogue River steelhead."

"I'll take you up on that, Eric."

With this foreknowledge of what might be awaiting me, my fatigue from the drive seemed to disappear. As we returned to the site, Alex said that the families would join us for dinner with me as their guest at Rogue River, a small village three miles west through which I had passed earlier.

It was well past mid-morning when we chose one of the "spots" for me to do my first archaeological dig. Inexperienced I surely was and could not help but feel some apprehension with the gallery of observers now assembled to watch the professor from the university. I had been in lots of worse spots before and knew I had to proceed with complete confidence even if I didn't feel it.

My luck held! Shortly, I exposed and uncovered a flexed skeleton, but the sole artifacts were a few shells, apparently once on small wrists by their location on the bones. After I had written some notes and removed the bones and artifacts, Alex said with some emphasis that it was time to go to dinner at Rogue River. I look back nostalgically on that fried-chicken dinner served on a porch, home-cooked by an expert, as the most satisfying meal I ever ate as a member of a field party, and I have eaten many in a great variety of circumstances. I heard a lot about the people and the country of the Rogue River that noon, all new and interesting. I am afraid we did not make haste to return to the site, but finally did, where I excavated two or three more burials. By this time it was getting late in the afternoon and I thought I should start the long drive home; I was beginning to feel tired.

I was convinced this was an important archaeological site that was certainly worth further study. My summer commitments made my return impossible before September. The rancher-owner hoped to prepare the field for irrigation and planting by removing sufficient portions of the upper part to permit use of water from Kane Creek. There were still burials in the area he had prepared for my coming. I suggested that he proceed with their excavation; I would try to get a small research grant to return and hire help to remove the overburden. I felt confident that he would do a responsible piece of work on the basis of what he had demonstrated, and he had watched me work. It was agreed that I would return in September.

Since I planned to ask for a research grant, I knew how important in supporting my request a sample of those beautiful blades and pipes would be. Furthermore, these objects were so impressive that I would get some kudos favorable to my own work from showing them. Hittle graciously let me take back some of the more striking blades and pipes and some shell beads. I promised to take good care of them and return with them in September, hopefully with some money.

With warm expressions of friendship and thanks for my coming and my promise to return in September, I said "Good-bye" and with my precious trophies, even though borrowed, started my two-hundred-mile drive home.

At Grant's Pass, fifteen miles into my homeward drive, I turned on the long grade up Sexton Mountain, the first of three, and for the next sixty miles would drive through mostly coniferous forest past places like Skull Creek, Grave Creek, Cow Creek, and Wolf Creek with its lonely service station, general store, and owner's house in a single complex. My body had settled into the rhythm of my car, and I could begin to reflect on my experiences of the day and their import. Today, after these last years of reflecting on and analyzing my life, I can understand the origins and the depths of those experiences far better and more meaningfully than I could or even dared to try on that lonely drive, tired as I was.

Then I felt a certain sense of euphoria, a new experience — inchoate, but exciting and certainly challenging in a poorly understood way. But is was definitely discovery; and the subject was human beings and their works, even though but partially and pathetically revealed in their graves. Everything was new. Where would it take me? It didn't seem to be cultural anthropology, although certainly closely related. And how would it fit into my field of sociology? I had no answers at the time, but I was sure of one thing: my experience that day had a promise of great significance. I would go on from there.

Today I am sure that June 8, 1930, provided the experiences, the force to pry off the lid from that abyss of my subconscious life into which events had forced so much of my childhood experiences, then seemingly casual but really deeply significant. That lid had dropped shut when I left home to enter Penn State as a freshman in 1914 to be successively followed by military service, preparation for the priesthood, and graduate study at Columbia University and a short, meaningful, but unhappy marriage. Census tables of populations, community survey schedules, pages of information gathered by others to be statistically analyzed and evaluated provided the raw data with which I worked in my graduate studies in sociology, but they left me somehow unsatisfied; the human beings from which these studies derived didn't seem to exist. Whoever saw the "average man" or the census "family of four"? These fictional concepts lacked humanity and were indeed too fragile to restrain for long the struggle of my early values to emerge, pressing with increasing force since that decisive year in my life, 1925–26, in Europe. Now I can equate parallels: the small boy holding the Revolutionary War bayonet dug up on his father's farm, feeling its lethal point and edges, and the grown man holding at Gold Hill beautiful obsidian blades, pointed and with sharp edges, and—both times—wondering about them and the people who used them; the soldier forever trapped in the cave with his musket and belt buckle and letter to his fiancée and the skeletons with telltale beads from clothing long since gone. These experiences from my childhood derived from objects dug out of the earth as did those of Gold Hill; and the work to discover these objects was all done in the open air. I am quite sure that during the Sunday at Gold Hill and on the drive home—though I am equally sure that I was then quite unaware of the process under way—I had loosed the lid over my long-suppressed, significant childhood experiences to permit their memories to push their way into my conscious life. It was not a sudden, blinding light, but the seed or the bulb pushing its way slowly and surely through the earth's surface into the sunlight to carry out the imperatives of growth and fulfillment inherent in its own being.

As the miles slipped behind, I thought of how the day had introduced me to wholly new facets of experience and accompanying challenges. Skeletal material: I knew precious little about the human skeleton; shells: my knowledge in that field was zero; stone artifacts and the rock from which they were made: they were absolutely new to me. To study this material I would have to acquire a lot of new knowledge. That was the challenge of discovery, and I never doubted my ability or my drive to do it. I accepted the challenge.

It was dark well before I arrived home to find Gem in bed, sound asleep, and Cecilia very anxiously waiting to share dinner with me.

"Oh, Sheeleigh, I am so glad to see you. I have wondered all day if perhaps I had helped you go on a fool's errand. I didn't, did I?"

"Don't worry, dear. Wait till you see what I have brought back in these boxes."

"Shouldn't we have some dinner first? You must be tired and hungry."

"I am both, but not that much; dinner will just have to wait until

I show you the trophies your husband has brought back. Close your eyes; don't peek.''

I spread some blades and pipes on a paper on the table. ''Now open.''

''Oh-h-h Sheeleigh, what beautiful things! I have never seen anything like them.''

''Hold them in your hands.'' I gave her a blade, warning, ''But don't run your finger along the edges; they cut.''

''And these long, smooth tubes, are they stone? They are beautiful.''

''I'll explain as much as I can later, but let's have dinner now. Oh, by the way, Cecilia, I am promised a substitute fishing trip for steelhead in the Rogue. Thank you, dear, for helping me to remember the word, *duty*.''

''Oh, Sheeleigh''—she threw her arms around me—''I am so happy I can hardly keep back my tears.''

All this on June 8, 1930!

My day at Gold Hill had been an exciting and pleasant experience, but since I was planning to continue the work it had to be something more than a pleasant, personal *Ausflug*. It must be made a recognized part of my professional program. Since the schedule for my survey was flexible, I postponed my departure for two days to devote the first exclusively to initiating the integration of my archaeological project into my sociology and cultural anthropology fields.

With my boxes of specimens in hand, I first reported my work to two friends in the Geology Department interested in archaeology and anthropology, Dr. Warren D. Smith—we always called him W. D.—and Dr. Packard. I first showed my specimens to W. D., who responded even more enthusiastically than I had anticipated: ''Luther, you've really got something important here. Tell me about it. This is the first I have heard of it, and how I can help.''

''I am afraid, W. D., I shall be calling on you for a lot of help, because what I shall need to know, the geology and related areas, I simply don't.''

I explained that this whole thing had come as a surprise to me with the Saturday-night telegram, that I had no opportunity to talk it over with anyone, and that I knew now I wanted to go on with the work as an additional part of my university duties. I also indicated that when I returned to the site in September my work would be greatly assisted by a small research grant to hire earth-moving labor and pay some small personal expenses.

W. D. suggested that we see Dr. Packard, who was in his office next door, explain the situation to him and, since he was chairman of the Research Council, inquire about a possible grant.

Dr. Packard asked us in, following our knock, and with a surprised look at my boxes, asked, "What have you there, Cressman?"

I proudly showed my trophies, explaining what happened and what I hoped to do. W. D. commented on the importance of the specimens and the work, pointing out my need for a small amount of money to continue, and suggested that as chairman of the Research Council perhaps he could explain the availability of funds.

Packard, so different in temperament from W. D., was almost as enthusiastic in his restrained way. The council, he said, did have a small budget and probably could find $200 if that would help me. I assured him that it most certainly would and asked instructions for making my application.

"Write me a letter," he said, "addressed to the Research Council, not over a page in length"—present day applicants take note—"stating the amount of your requested grant, what it would be used for, why the work is important, and when you will do the work. The university is now in recess, but I think I can get the council together in a week or two and give you our response."

He could not, of course, commit the council, but I felt reassured by his very positive and supportive attitude.

Then I took my boxes to find the head of my department, Dr. Parsons, and seek his support. I brought out my specimens and briefed him on the matter. The artifacts were as new to him as to me, and he was equally impressed. He also saw the opportunity for establishing a good public-relations situation and urged me to continue my work. I now had the support of my department head. Thanking him, I stopped in the departmental office to dictate my letter of application to the Research Council. Mary Galey, the secretary, said that she would have it ready for my signature in a few minutes. Promising Mary to return shortly, I continued on my "show-and-tell" course. After several successful "showings," I returned to sign my letter, thanking Mary and asking her to put it in the campus mail.

By midafternoon, June 9, 1930, I had secured the support of critical faculty members and the endorsement of the head of the Department of Sociology; and the submission of my research grant application to the Research Council involved the university, an action to be validated by the approval of my request. My career as an archaeologist had this modest beginning, firmly rooted in the university structure, from which it would develop into a significant, new program of discovery and personal fulfillment.

The next day Cecilia and I made preliminary plans for our move later in the summer to a nice house in the country rented from a colleague going on sabbatical leave. After the move we would take a short vacation at an inexpensive cottage in the mountains. I completed my community survey late in July and the next day took advantage of my nearness to Vancouver, British Columbia, with its famous Hudson's Bay Company store, to buy a few useful and unusual trophies to take home for the family waiting in Eugene.

I started my long drive home, between 350 and 400 miles, about four o'clock in the morning and found it uneventful after a near mishap with a prowling skunk at a sharp curve in the road soon after leaving. Evasive action by both prevented disaster, and the drive then gave me the first real opportunity to reflect on my new situation with my archaeological commitment and its meaning for my program.

It was clear that I would have to integrate my new work into, but in no way substitute it for the sound student research and teaching I had already well established in the Department of Sociology. The archaeology program, at least for the time being, appeared to have a limited life expectancy, so I would carry it strictly as an extra without the customary student participation. During the summer I had received word that the Research Council had approved my request for the grant of $200 and thus insured institutional support.

During the fall I made several weekend trips to Gold Hill to continue my excavation, and in May 1931 W. D. accompanied me to check the site for significant geological information and give me needed support. I now had sufficient artifactual and skeletal material at hand to formulate my problem and organize the descriptive process I would follow. Although my work at the site was far from finished, I decided to report on it to Section H, Anthropology, of the Pacific Division of the American Association for the Advancement of Science meeting at Pasadena at the California Institute of Technology in June 1931.

My participation would renew my contact with the western anthropologists with whom I had a fleeting acquaintance at Columbia University and introduce me to others as I brought my message that archaeological work was under way at Oregon. It also provided the opportunity to visit the Southwest Museum in Los Angeles and the Los Angeles County Museum with exhibits of the world-famous Rancho La Brea Tar Pits. The Southwest Museum under Mark R. Harrington's direction had recently completed the excavation of Gypsum Cave in southern Nevada with evidence, although questioned by some, indicating the association of humans with an extinct Pleistocene fauna. A specially prepared exhibit of the stratigraphy was a feature of the meetings. My paper, of necessity, was limited to a simple progress report, but, at that, what was "in progress" was new. The meetings and my trip in the company of colleagues from the science departments held promise of considerable rewards.

My fledgling paper, well received by a small but interested and courteous group, was an experience of considerable importance for my self-confidence. It indicated my work would be judged on its own terms, what I had to say, without regard to my antecedents or present or past associations. I met archaeologists with whom I would be associated to my great advantage in the years ahead, and I heard discussed for the first time problems of climatic variation in relation to human occupation of the Great Basin and adjacent areas. Seeds were falling on receptive ground.

As measured by results, I think the most important event for me was a luncheon engagement with Ruth Benedict, my close friend from the Columbia days, and our subsequent conversation. We had last seen each other in 1928, and we had a lot of catching-up to do as we relaxed in the warm sun on a patio. Naturally, I asked about Margaret, her fieldwork and health. Ruth filled in some of the gaps and then said, "She also had a miscarriage; did you know that?"

"No. What was she up to?" I asked, imagining some extreme physical effort as the cause.

"You knew, Luther, didn't you, that she had a tipped uterus and was not likely to carry a baby to term?"

"Ruth, to the best of my knowledge, this is the first time I have heard of it. Since I remember Margaret telling me before our marriage that she had an ovary removed because of a cyst, this information, had I known it during our marriage, is not the kind of thing I would have so easily forgotten and in so short a time." That closed the matter and we talked of other things.

One of the "other things" proved to be very important. She asked, "What are you going to do after you finish this Gold Hill project?"

"I have no plans now, for I have heavy commitments in my sociology program, where I have some fine stimulating students."

"You like archaeology, don't you?"

"Very much, indeed, but this has been so new and taken me into such entirely new fields of work requiring exceptional effort that I have had neither time nor inclination to think ahead."

"I think, Luther, you might enjoy making a study of petroglyphs in Oregon; it hasn't been done. You told me about the time you and Cecilia went to see those along the Columbia. Kidder made this kind of study in the Southwest and was able to use some for stratigraphic and chronological purposes. Why not think it over?"

By design or simple kindness—I think the latter—she was offering me very enticing bait. A. V. Kidder was then the leading light in Southwest American archaeology. If the subject was important enough for him to study, it was a compliment to me for her to think I would be up to the challenge of the same kind of study.

"You make it sound very interesting, Ruth, and I shall certainly give it serious thought."

A couple of years later Ruth stopped to visit us overnight. We were vacationing at the coast; I met her train in Eugene and took her to our cottage. The fieldwork for my petroglyph study was history. It was during that fieldwork in 1932 that I saw the vistas upon which I laid the foundation of the basic problems in prehistory to occupy the rest of my life. Thank you, Ruth, for that afternoon at Pasadena.

The meetings also introduced me to a quite new and significant experience: groups of scientists from different but related fields cooperating in the attempt to solve a scientific problem. Gypsum Cave and the La Brea Tar Pits presented complex situations involving the use of scientists and specialists from anthropology, geology, chemistry, biology, and paleontology. My driving companions as we passed through the fascinating western country were a geologist, a chemist, and a physicist; and much of our conversation was not of campus politics but of the environment through which we passed, of its coming into being. My work so far at Gold Hill with its diverse material had shown me the need for cooperation. The Pasadena meetings threw on a large screen the same kinds of problems I had recognized on a microscale in my own work at Oregon. The realization I gained at these meetings, of the necessity of cooperative effort to solve these complex problems, became basic to my whole professional career.

After my return to Eugene, happy with the warm reception I had experienced at Pasadena, I mailed a copy of my paper to the American Anthropological Association. In a short time I had the exhilarating news of its acceptance—and in the official journal of the association![4] I could go on with confidence.

I continued short weekend field trips to Gold Hill in September and October in 1931. To meet the rancher's convenience I had to complete my excavations in 1932. An additional research grant of $200 from the university and one of $400 from the National Research Council facilitated my work by enabling me to rent a pair of horses and a Fresno (an enlarged scoop shovel) and hire an operator to remove overburden. These research grants seem minuscule when compared with the five- and six-digit grants made today. I, too, have had large grants; but I will not let anyone denigrate the quality of our work in those early days, for we laid then the solid foundation on which all later work was built.[5]

My last trip to Gold Hill in August 1932 carried with it Eric's promise of the fishing trip for steelhead in the Rogue, and so I had my fishing gear with me. Closing out my work late in the morning, I met Eric for lunch at his home at Central Point. Lunch disposed of and important business on the Rogue ahead, we started in Eric's four-cylinder, Chevrolet panel truck, a veteran of many such trips as the scars vividly showed. We headed up the road running much of the way beside the Rogue River, eventually to cross the Cascade Mountains and descend into the Klamath Lake Basin. We rattled along, with Eric entertaining me with the countryman's story of his much-loved river and mountains. We also passed what seemed to me to be some very good riffles, but to my queries he kept reassuring me that the best one, the one he had for me, was still ahead. We passed a vision of pure destruction: fire-blackened trees tossed willy-nilly along and even in and across the river.

"No, that wasn't a forest fire," he answered to my question. "They're trees burned and turned to charcoal by the eruption which made Crater Lake. Pumice covered them once but has been washed off by flood waters."

I could see it had been a catastrophe all right, but what had it to do with steelhead fishing? He had asked some distance back if I had ever seen Crater Lake. I noticed that he slipped that query into our conversation more than once. I had to admit that I had never seen Crater Lake, nor did I mention that I had never heard of it. Since he was the guide, I preferred to defer to his judgment. When I again raised the question of our riffle, his comment lacked enthusiasm in great contrast to the conviction in his following statement, "You really ought to see Crater Lake."

"OK, Eric," I said, "let's go see Crater Lake."

Eric must have shoved the gas pedal to the floor the way that ancient panel job lurched forward full-speed toward Crater Lake. He knew exactly where to take his first-time visitor for the most effective impression. We stopped at 7,000 feet, air crystal clear.

"There, Professor, look!"

The beauty, the grandeur, strictly nature's work, were so far beyond my wildest imaginings, even as stirred by Eric's anticipatory praises as we approached the lake, that silence could be my only fitting response. I turned to Eric with a murmured "thanks" as I stood in silent awe and marveled.

Darkness was approaching when I finally stashed my unused fishing gear in my car at Central Point to start my long drive home — no, I never became a fisherman, but I did become an archaeologist.

Somehow a brooding sense of loneliness seemed to settle over me as, with my headlights on, I started up the long grade of Sexton Mountain. A car overtook and passed me. For the next seventy-five miles to Roseburg I followed that friendly red taillight, never permitting it out of my sight for long, for I could not feel at ease without it. I had traveled that road so many times in the last two years in daylight and darkness, but never, never with this sense of solitariness. Had that beautiful, mysterious lake cast some spell over me?

Some six years later in collaboration with a volcanologist, Dr. Howel Williams from the University of California at Berkeley, I would discover evidence to make this eruption, on whose effect I had gazed, take its rightful place of monumental importance in Far Western North American prehistory.

I began the challenging description and analysis of artifacts and skeletal material during the winter of 1930–31, although my fieldwork was still in progress. A young archaeologist trained in modern methods of archaeology in standard university courses and summer fieldwork training recently asked me, "If you had not had a course in archaeology, how did you know how to go about the work?"

"I used my head," I replied. "I had had an excellent education with a wide range of significant experience. I could start out clean with no school to follow, nothing to prove."

My boyhood in the country, with our life following the rhythms of nature and with my experience in hunting, trapping, and fishing, taught me how to read messages the earth carried about the creatures who lived on it. All my archaeological evidence was gathered from and had to be interpreted in part in the context of the earth in which it was embedded. As we boys hunted and trapped, we knew what it meant in our tracking when the footprints of one animal were impressed upon those of another, even though we had never heard the word "stratigraphy."

To locate points on a flat surface, "plan of the site," I used training from the days in gunnery instruction in the Field Artillery Officers' Training School in 1918. I bought a good timber cruiser's compass and a fifty-foot steel tape. I established control-point stakes, datum points, and located my find by reading the azimuth and the distance. This I could do alone with a little legwork. Depth of a find below the surface was matter-of-factly measured by tape from the surface. A transit and rod would have provided little improvement, for the site had been farmed and the original surface destroyed.

I had a good sense of problem and how to go about analysis. My major problem I reduced to several smaller ones: (1) What do I have? (2) How is it arranged in the earth? (3) How did it get there and why? (4) What is its age? (5) Can my material be fitted into the presently known prehistory of the coastal-interior peoples? At Columbia I had learned under Boas the essentials of the method of cultural-historical reconstruction. Here, I had the opportunity to use it.

I had to draw on information from the earth sciences and biology to prepare my report. Geology was then an unknown to me, but I had a basic knowledge in biology. A smattering of information in physical anthropological methods carried over from my Columbia days, but I would have to go far beyond that into the techniques of description and measurement. I could get this information from books, but my main difficulty was the lack of anthropometric instruments. I needed outlines of skulls I had excavated and, in the absence of instruments, interested a geology student to use the department's pantograph to provide the necessary craniograms, the outline of a skull in side view. From these I could make satisfactory measurements for description and comparison. I imposed on my dentist, a young, alert, recent graduate of the Dental School, for help with my study of the teeth. He not only gave me much help but also even small instruments to help in my lab work. To learn about our western forest trees and the mollusks of fresh- and saltwater environments, I used books and the help of friends in the Geology Department. Friends in the School of Architecture and Art gave me a crash course in modeling, casting, and the use of plaster in the repair of broken skulls. I did not sit down and whine at the really shocking amount of things I needed to do and know; I used my head to discover what I needed to know but didn't and then found ways to find out, often to improvise.

The University of Oregon Press in 1933 published my modest final report on the Gold Hill site.[6] The report's small size is inversely proportional to the importance of the Gold Hill experience in my professional life. *It was seminal.* I came away from this experience firmly convinced of the necessity of cooperative relations with scholars from the earth and life sciences, for I saw human behavior as a product of more than sociocultural and psychological forces; we humans are a part of the living world — and always have been — and our relation to it at a given past time and place in space is a part of the information the archaeologist has to consider. I had found out in practice in a small way what I had observed at Pasadena. It became a basic part of my professional ethos.

W. D. found a small room with a sink in his building, Condon Hall, to serve as a lab for me, and my archaeological work went on there. This new space was of considerable significance, for it brought me into close contact with science members of the faculty. These new areas of interest into which I was now making my way were a rounding out of my intellectual life. In my undergraduate years I had humanistic training in the classics, in graduate school I gained competence in social science, and now I was completing the triad by adding earth and life sciences. My scientific career would reflect this triadic approach to problems.

While I worked on my Gold Hill project during the winter of 1931–32 Cecilia and I discussed Ruth Benedict's suggestion for my study of petroglyphs. We decided that I should undertake the project. In addition to my other work, I now had to plan this: gain information on locations, decide what kinds of information I should attempt to secure, lay out a plan of travel to sites, and consider other logistic details. By the summer of 1932 my plans were complete, but before starting the fieldwork I had to complete my excavations at Gold Hill. Since I was carrying a full-time load in the Sociology Department, I had to find the time to do my archaeology, really peripheral to my regular duties, at the expense of my personal and family life. Cecilia always loyally supported me, even though she faced long periods alone in a world new and in many ways difficult for her. She never chafed at being a fieldman's widow.

The new vantage point on my Journey, the completion of my Gold Hill project, gave me a view ahead more valuable than my earlier, random glimpses of a road I might choose to follow. The challenging and mysterious landscape into which the road led was becoming more and more exciting.

I found my students that first year at Oregon more sophisticated and better prepared than those at Ellensburg Normal School, but certainly as a whole far less intensely driven intellectually than those at CCNY. My first year with new colleagues, a new administration, and a completely different environment was inevitably devoted in large part to finding my way through and along new roads. Above all I had to establish rapport with my students in large beginning classes, small advanced courses, and individual advanced instruction. I tried to follow my ideal of the genuine teacher from my first experience at CCNY, but adapted to the demands of my new situation. An excerpt from a recent letter from a former CCNY student recounts his recollection of our student-teacher relation:

> He [Cressman] soon created a warm rapport with the class. He made the class assignments on various problems interesting and significant by lucidly explaining the nature of the problems and by giving vivid statements on the real life situations and social conditions that created these problems. He treated each student as a responsible individual with a mind of his own, and often got students to work out their own approach and solution to a problem, by use of the Socratic method.[7]

As a teaching sociologist I had noticed that the ongoing social scene provides a perfectly good source of research problems, especially for those involving student assistants. Experience of this kind made them participants in the social process, but not activists. Since teaching students how to think was my commitment, not obeisance to a distribution curve, I was concerned with any factor that might influence their progress. I discovered, for example, that at Oregon many of my students came from the "goiter belt," and I wondered if this environmental factor might influence their performance.

At Ellensburg and Eugene I had frequently noticed women with surgical scars on their throats, something quite new to my eastern background. Discreet inquiry informed me that the states of Utah, Oregon, and Washington, because of the very high incidence of goiter in the population, formed the "goiter belt" on the distribution maps of the public health cartographers.

The thyroid gland, located in the neck, produces and passes directly into the bloodstream a chemical to regulate the body's metabolism. At Columbia University, as a graduate student, I had shared in the post-World War I explosive development of new knowledge about endocrinology, vitamins, and the relation of both to health and disease and behavior problems. Roughly, one may say that hypo- or subthyroid functioning results in a sluggish rate of metabolism, accompanied by a lowering of the normal, expected level for the particular age and sex under observation. The opposite traits appear with the hyper- or above-normal level of thyroid functioning. The malfunctioning thyroid gland generally showed an enlargement, the goiter, developing sometimes to a very disfiguring stage. The state of the art of medicine and surgery offered only the nonreversible solution: surgery to remove the gland. If the removal of the gland was complete, the patient faced sometimes a disfiguring scar, depending in part on the surgery. All this was before the present practice of preventive nutrition.

I have always thought of the human organism as a unified system of diverse but interrelated complementary subsystems, so I wondered, since so many of my students came from the "goiter belt," if there might be any evidence of resulting below-level academic performance. Intellectual activity in the widest sense certainly is a part of the general metabolic process of the organism. Concerned as I was with student performance I felt the idea was worth further exploration.

The doctor in charge of the University Health Service proved a sympathetic listener, agreeing that the study provided the possibility of discovering information of value in student counseling. No relevant information was available. He offered to cooperate by providing, on an anonymous basis, the physical examination records of 375 women students of the freshman class of 1933–34. At that time all entering students were required to take a rather full, uniform physical examination given by advanced students from the university's medical school in Portland. The examination records would be separated into "normal" and "abnormal" groups and the data then statistically analyzed "to discover whether any significant differences exist between a group of women with thyroid disorder and one in which the gland functions normally; and if there are differences, what they may be."[8]

I asked two of my advanced women students, after giving them a full explanation of the project, if they would be interested in conducting this research. They enthusiastically accepted the opportunity and carried out the whole study, coming to me for regular consultation and advice at special times. These students gained a lot of substantive information and put in practice the procedures studied in our social statistics class. Together we wrote our conclusion: "The evidence of faulty metabolism, greater inconvenience during menstruation and lower academic achievement is all cumulative. The results are not final but are surely indicative of points deserving further study."[9] Grateful acknowledgment was made to the student assistants who made the analysis.

I accepted the invitation of the faculty Social Science Club to read our paper at its 1930–31 meeting. Only one person dissented from the warm reception given the paper: Howard Taylor, professor of psychology in charge of personnel studies and much involved with psychological testing. Howard was really upset, indicating his displeasure during his comments by physical effort as he twisted about on his chair. He completely misinterpreted our paper as a personal attack on his personnel policies because no one had thought of doing this kind of a study before. It was nothing of the sort. Howard had no reasonable, substantive criticism to offer, only this final expression of opinion: "You should stay in your own field!" I thought to myself: "Another minefield, Cressman; be careful when you boundary jump." Time showed my opinion was correct. Unfortunately no follow-up on our study was ever done.

I always thought that boundary lines between fields in the learning process were a delusion, and because we had apparently found some interesting relations, I believed the paper deserved presentation to a wider public than just to our club. I sent our manuscript to Dr. Raymond Pearl at Johns Hopkins University, then editor of the journal, *Human Biology*, where it was published in the December 1931 issue. A spin-off study of an idea suggested by our study was carried out by Edna Spenker, one of the two students working on the first project, and published under our joint authorship in the September 1933 issue of the same journal.[10]

Bess Templeton's experience (Oregon 1931) as one of my senior students illustrates how I considered my students as distinctive individuals, not faceless statistics, and tried to meet their needs accordingly. She was a person of real intellectual ability, but very shy, lacking in self-confidence, and without a sharp focus in her intellectual interests. Through a series of conversations I drew from her the statement that she really wished after graduation to become a dean of girls in a high school. Further conversations led her to formulate the information she would need to know to prepare for her work: how little was known, how to go about getting it, and what to do with the information when she got it. My shy young student had become interested and excited, and I gave her needed support and advice, but put the responsibility for decision making primarily on her. Bess completed her project on time, an excellent piece of work, and it was published under our joint authorship in *The Commonwealth Review*;[11] it could well serve as a guide for college counseling.

I urged her during her work to apply for a scholarship at Syracuse University in a new program designed to train graduate students in her field of interest. She received her scholarship, completing her work for the master's degree in 1933, and served two years as assistant dean of women at Syracuse in 1933–35. In a letter to me dated February 1, 1985, providing me with some information I had requested, she wrote, "I want to thank you again for being one of the professors who helped guide my life."[12]

My pattern of student involvement, observed by Sidney Ratner at CCNY in 1925, was thus continued with these and other students as my deeply felt, appropriate teacher-student relation. It was my hallmark at the University of Oregon.

Cecilia and I in our second year, 1930–31, found in our spacious rented house in the country the facility to carry out one of our most cherished desires, the development of family and student relations transcending the limits possible in formal classroom contacts. My senior seminar met one afternoon weekly at our home from two to four o'clock in our large living room. At the close, Cecilia always joined us with coffee, tea, or milk and cookies and cake. Our small Gem came too as a matter of course. This manner of sharing our lives produced not only excellent academic results but also friendships, some of which lasted over lifetimes.

During that second year, an event occurred of great personal significance: I was invited to membership in the newly organized Social Science Research Council of the Pacific Coast States. The Social Science Research Council, the parent organization in New York, had initiated and funded the council as a project of its Pacific Coast Regional Committee to offset the disadvantages inherent in the great distances separating the western area from the population centers of the East. Membership was by invitation, I believe from the regional committee, and limited to a small number of social scientists, rather loosely defined, considered to be leaders in their respective fields from each of the major universities. Total membership varied with attendance usually in the high fifties and sixties (sixty-six were present at the Fourth Annual Meeting, 1933–34),[13] a manageable size to keep the meetings unified and intimate.

Meetings were usually held in the San Francisco area because it was the most convenient for the majority of members to reach by train. The conference was not broken up into sections of economists, sociologists, etc., because the emphasis was on social science as a body of knowledge made up of constituent fields. To achieve this ideal each annual meeting was devoted to a single topic or subject, with a lead-off paper followed by others by members from different fields approaching the subject from their points of view. General discussion followed each paper. The atmosphere was always friendly and warm, though by no means lacking in disputation. Lunch was open, and friends and acquaintances met together for conversation. As I recall, the last meeting in the afternoon closed the day. The entire milieu of the conference promoted friendship and the formation of new acquaintances and the cementing of old. I think the project succeeded remarkably well in giving a sense of unity, dignity, and importance to the intellectual life of the social scientists of the Far West.

The University of Oregon provided only three members to the council as far as I can remember, Wayne Morse in law, Donald G. Barnes in history, and me in sociology. I was secretary-treasurer of the council in 1937–39, and a member of the regional committee in 1937–38 and 1938–39. The final meeting of the council, the twelfth annual conference, was held in San Francisco, March 26–28, 1942.

The continuity of the association of the membership through the annual meetings not only developed new friendships, but also acquainted each of us with programs at other institutions and those engaged in them. I became acquainted with practically all the social scientists of any standing in the Pacific coast states and British Columbia, and they in turn got to know me as a person and a sociologist.

In contrast, the meetings of the A.A.A.S., Pacific Region that I attended in 1931 at Pasadena were broken up into sections composed of members from a specific discipline, Section H - Anthropology, for example. Although A.A.A.S. had a continuity in annual meetings, it differed from the conference with its stability of membership. Development of acquaintance into friendship at Pasadena depended entirely on a shared interest in a common problem, such as an archaeologist and a paleontologist interested in Early Man studies—I know from personal experience. As I reflect on the two types of meetings I perceive a subtle but significant difference in the method of study pursued in archaeology at Pasadena and that in the conference, a difference I probably sensed and responded to, but never made conceptually explicit. I just accepted it as the appropriate way to proceed; it made sense to me. The archaeologists with colleagues from appropriate fields of expertise were involved in the solution of a particular problem: the determination of relations in time and space of components of a particular site thought to be evidence of human activity. All participants were fieldmen to some degree and some held academic appointments, but in their academic duties they usually worked with the material collected by their field projects. These scientists were bringing individual expertise to bear by first-hand evidence on a total problem, the validity of the site, for which they were jointly seeking a solution.

Conference meetings were subject, not problem oriented, focusing on a concept, a historical process, or a social event. Their data came from books, reports, surveys, all of which were at least secondary in contrast with the objective field evidence of the archaeologist and colleagues. I think the most apt description is that each conference participant was trying to describe, perhaps evaluate the subject as seen from his particular field of expertise, not find a solution to a particular problem. Consensus was not sought, only a subject explored. It was the individual point of view that counted. Solely academic people (as the social scientists were) by their very life-style are individualists, each of whom is recognized as an expert or at least a specialist in a particular field; and I fear we all share the tendency to generalize into other fields from one's specialty. Perhaps this trait should be called the "academic syndrome." Good hard fieldwork is the prescribed antidote.

During my first few years at Oregon, my separation by distance and locale from the East where all my rich past was rooted could not help but produce some sense of isolation. My participation, however, as member and officer in these two groups was a very significant countering influence. It gave me intellectual and personal status in the West, new and valued friends and acquaintances, and set my professional and personal life course on a westerly bearing to the meaningful life Cecilia and I enjoyed for all our years.

Even in the peaceful atmosphere of the conference, events far afield could intrude. On the third day of the conference in early August 1932, I was lunching with some friends in the coffee shop of the Clift Hotel in San Francisco, when Wayne Morse from Oregon entered briskly, took a seat at the counter, swiveled his chair to see who was in the room and, seeing me, motioned to me to come to him.

"Have you heard, L. S." —he always called me by those initials—"about what's going on on the campus?"

"I've been down here, Wayne, and haven't heard anything about the place. What has happened?"

He told me that John Mueller, my senior colleague in the Sociology Department and unmarried, had allegedly been observed by boys of the fraternity adjacent to his boarding house in some personal sexual peccadilloes, and they had spread the word on the campus. Perhaps there had been more than one occurrence and a kind of voyeurs' party. At any rate, John's position was badly compromised by the gossip and he would probably have to resign.

"This is all news to me, Wayne, but I am not interested in Mueller's affairs, and where do I come in?"

"Parsons [the head of the Sociology Department] is spreading the word, L. S., that you have started these false rumors as gossip about Mueller to damage him and get him out of the department."

"That's a blatant lie, Wayne. I don't care what Mueller does as long as he doesn't interfere with my work."

"I know that, but Parsons is creating a very dangerous situation for you; and since people are likely to believe him as your department head, you had better see him and get things straight as soon as you get home."

"Thanks for the information, Wayne. I shall take care of it, but I am afraid your message hasn't helped my appetite."

I arrived home Sunday afternoon and, after settling in a bit, told Cecilia what I had come home to. She was livid, for she had had a very low opinion of Parsons even before this episode.

"Sheeleigh, you have to go tonight and get this thing cleared up and get a written statement from him."

I phoned Parsons and found him at home, but he wanted to put our meeting off to the next day. I insisted that I had to see him then. He told me to come over to his house, where he would be working in his rear yard. To take care of possible eventualities I put a small note pad and a working fountain pen in my pocket before leaving the house. As I was leaving, Cecilia's firm command was: "Don't come back to this house without that written statement!"

Her final charge to me sounded like that given by the Spartan women to their men leaving for battle: "Come back with your shield or on one!"

I was going to have to tell my department head that he was a liar and malicious, but obviously not in those terms. It was certainly a confrontation I had little zest for. I found Parsons in his backyard, puttering about in a desultory manner, picking up fallen branches to drop on his patio fireplace. After our greetings I came right to the point, telling him that I had heard of the Mueller matter from Wayne in San Francisco, that I had nothing whatever to do with it, and that I wanted him to tell anyone who raised the question that I was quite in the clear, blameless. He agreed rather easily with my statement, I was pleased to discover, and bemoaned the fact that the thing had happened. Then came the hard part, for I wanted to get into my house when I returned.

"Dr. Parsons, I am grateful for what you have just said, but I would like something on paper that I could show to anyone who questioned me to the effect that you are convinced of my innocence."

"Won't my word do, Cressman?"

"It will with me, Dr. Parsons, but if I tell someone who accuses me that I have your word clearing me, he can reply, 'That's what you say, but how do I know you are telling the truth?' If I have a statement I can say, 'Read this.' "

"But I don't have any paper."

"I have some right here," producing my note pad.

"I don't have a pen."

"Here's one."

"Thank you, Dr. Parsons. I can't tell you how much I regret all this happening."

I arrived home and entered to meet a stern, expectant Cecilia. I handed her my precious pieces of paper.

"Here, my dear, is my shield."

Eugene, Aug. 12, '32

My Dear Cressman:

I am deeply grateful for having had an opportunity to talk over the situation relative to the department and the unfortunate rumors concerning Dr. Mueller and the future adjustments. You may tell anyone concerned that I am confident of your complete cooperation and loyalty, and that you are not in any way engaged in promulgating any rumors or in any way trying to injure Dr. Mueller or his reputation.

Yours sincerely,

(signed) Phil. A. Parsons

Cecilia's and my decision that I should undertake Ruth Benedict's suggestion, a study of the petroglyphs of Oregon, not only promised a continuation of my archaeological interests but also forced me to

Summit of the Cascade Mountains, view to north from Batchelor Butte west of Bend, Oregon. Photo by L. S. Cressman.

assume full responsibility for designing and carrying out an archaeological study, another first in my experience. The Gold Hill experience was pure serendipity. I viewed the petroglyph project as a continuation of my new interests developed so rewardingly at Gold Hill and, therefore, thought it important to avoid any hiatus in the continuation of the exploitation of this experience. As a result the winter of 1931–32 found me facing a new challenge in addition to my other obligations.

I first had to define my problem, its parameters of subject matter and the area to be searched. Scanty literature on the subject and almost none on Oregon used up little time in the research of literary sources. My real problem was going to be logistical. That alluring expression, "eastern Oregon," covered a diversity of highly contrasting landscapes when seen against the gentle country I knew in the Willamette Valley west of the Cascade Mountains. My exploring conversations with my geologist friend, W. D., promised that I would discover not only petroglyphs but also a new landscape, varied, often frightening, always fascinating, and sometimes on a stupendous scale. This prospect increased the appeal. Little did I foresee how the

The Columbia Plateau, Oregon, view to southwest; depth of the canyon is from 800 to 1,000 feet. Confluence of the Crooked River (left) and the Deschutes River. Photo by L. S. Cressman.

seductive mystery and grandeur of my new country would entice me into a love relationship still rich and vibrant after more than fifty years!

The eastern Oregon country, for purposes of my study, could reasonably be considered as falling into three main divisions: The first one is the eastern slope of the Cascade Mountains for some 150 miles south from the Columbia as they drop gently to a high lava plateau averaging between 3,000 and 4,000 feet in elevation and incised by deep, sheer canyons. This plateau with its drainage system to the Columbia River, like its western neighbor, is the second division and comprises most of northeastern Oregon. The third division is an area across the southern part of the state from the Cascade Mountains nearly to the Idaho border consisting of living and dried lakes, sometimes covering a vast area. Each is, in general, extended on a north-south axis and separated from its neighbor by a high tableland, igneous in origin. Some thirty-five or more miles of the eastern flank of the Cascade Mountains in the south lay in the Klamath Lake — the living lake in the series — system, an area with drainage to the Pacific

Ocean via the Klamath River. This area was the northern extension of the Great Basin from Nevada and Utah and designated the Northern Great Basin. Its system of interior drainage gave it special significance as a human habitat. The vastness and diversity of the area into which I would have to go awed and challenged me rather than deterred.

It was perfectly clear that I would need a reliable, responsible, and companionable associate. I asked Howard Stafford, the son of Professor Stafford of the Chemistry Department, to go with me. The only reward I could offer in addition to expenses was the satisfaction in fieldwork and what we might give in companionship and knowledge to each other. We were good friends. I had no financial support for the project other than a grant of $100 from the National Research Council for photographic supplies and another from the University Research Council of $125, based on a mileage allowance at $.05 per mile, to be paid after filing a travel claim on our return. Howard accepted my invitation eagerly. He had been a graduate student in geology, but when the advanced and graduate work in science at the university was transferred to Oregon State College, he was financially unable — other reasons aside — to continue by transferring there. The Great Depression was already making itself felt. Howard's interest in geology — and he had done summer fieldwork in some of the areas where we would go — was a strong motivating factor and of great help to me, ignorant of the field. Howard and I now made it our project and worked together on the planning: our first objective was location of any petroglyphs, and the second was how to get to them to record and study.

We discussed our problem with W. D., who, from his geological studies, was familiar with the geography of the state and had detailed geological knowledge of various parts. We could not just write letters of inquiry to ranchers; in many potentially promising parts of the area there were no ranchers. We decided on certain categories of activity in which there would likely be persons with detailed knowledge of petroglyphs in sparsely settled areas. I counted on the traits I knew and admired: keen observation so characteristic of the men and women who lived in the great range country and their generosity of spirit and willingness to help. I drew up a short letter, less than a page, explaining my project and requesting the recipient's help with information. To facilitate a reply I enclosed a single page of a few questions: knowledge of any "rock writings," the folk name for petroglyphs; their location; how to get to them; and willingness to provide further information, if available, if I called. I also enclosed a stamped, return-addressed envelope. We mailed over four hundred copies of my letter to postmasters, forest rangers, state police, game wardens, newspaper editors, and highway engineers east of the Cascade Mountains. Other sources of information were available west of the Cascade Mountains, so that area was not included in this part of the project.

The category "postmaster" needs explaining. In some areas of very few settlers, the post office was a ranch house bearing the name of the owner. Since anyone claiming a particular address had to come to that ranch house for his mail, the postmaster-rancher was familiar with the people in his area. When anyone came for mail, there was always time and really the social necessity for gossip. Information about the country spread through this network.

I also wrote personal letters to special persons (for example, Lewis A. McArthur, author of *Oregon Geographic Names*) seeking their help and was seldom disappointed.

When we thought most of our expectable replies were in, we collated them for information available and location. We used an Oregon highway map and plotted as accurately as possible the location of each reported petroglyph site. The official Oregon State Highway Map of 1931–32 was certainly a different specimen from today's with all our roads.

After careful examination of the distribution of our reported sites, we planned a route to give us the maximum coverage with the greatest economy of time and mileage. A minimum of backtracking would be involved. Our route from Eugene would take us first to Bend about 150 miles almost due east of Eugene in our area number 1. The short period here would be a kind of shakedown experience. Then east to the John Day country in the southern part of area number 2. From here, our course took us south to Burns, our jumping-off place for the Northern Great Basin, the land of the ancient lakes, area number 3. After a swing eastward nearly to the Idaho state line, we would return to Burns again by way of the John Day country, for there was no connecting road to Burns. Then we would go west and south again to the Warner Valley, an ancient lake bed, and from there, return via Bend to Eugene.

In all that vast area I can recall but two blacktop-surfaced roads: U.S. 97, the north-south highway from the Columbia River to San Francisco running along the east side of the Cascade Mountains in

Oregon; and the present U.S. 26, the east-west highway entering Oregon from Boise, Idaho, through Vale to the John Day country and west to intersect U.S. 97 at Redmond. Other roads were gravel-surfaced, some just scraped; and in still others, one followed tracks of one's predecessor through often miles of sagebrush toward an objective, such as a "gap in that mountain." Mile after mile was often through almost blinding dust if there was any wind, and almost always there was abrasive dust to scour the car and its exposed working parts as well as the passengers.

My car, a Model-A Ford sedan with about 3,000 to 4,000 miles on the odometer, provided our transportation, and it never let us down, even when we exercised bad judgment. Outside of mileage and N.R.C. grants I have mentioned, all other expenses were out of pocket, covered by Cecilia and me. I put a baggage rack on the back of the car to hold our beds, bedding rolls, and a folding, portable table. All other gear was stashed in the back of the car. A Coleman gas lantern and a two-burner, portable gasoline stove proved invaluable. Cecilia and I collected a supply of canned foods—dehydrated foods had not yet arrived—which we thought would be ample for the trip. To give body to our canned foods Cecilia prepared a large roast of beef, well done, from which we could draw as we wished to add to our soups. Bread could be bought at stores, and if we forgot when our supply was low and passed up the chance, we had nobody to blame but ourselves, a fact we had to realize. First aid consisted of a basic, portable kit and another especially for rattlesnake bite, a use we sincerely hoped to avoid. Following a rancher's advice to carry firearms because of rabies among the coyotes, Howard carried a .22 revolver and I, a .38. A new towrope completed our equipment. We packed our gear for ease of access to the materials most likely to be needed as work proceeded, and Howard and I were "ready to roll," planning to camp each night at some "wide spot in the road."

In the brisk, early morning of a late August day, 1932, with the Gold Hill dig history, Howard and I said au revoir to Cecilia and the small Gem, roused from her sleep for the occasion, and headed out across the Cascade Mountains into EASTERN OREGON and our great adventure.

How fortunate I was to have Howard as my companion—I think we were soon more comrades than companions—on this field trip!

His vastly superior knowledge of the nature of the country where we were going gave him a position of authority to which I deferred; in certain other areas the relationship was reversed. Coming from an old, established faculty family—two generations—and uninhibited by stuffy conventions, he shared with me much history and folklore about various faculty members as seen by a senior, superior student. Our gravel-surfaced road, the McKenzie highway, now Oregon 126 and 242, paralleled the beautiful river from which it takes its name, but after about sixty miles it left the river to climb sharply up the west face of the Cascade Range by a series of switchbacks, taking us in the next fifteen miles up some 2,000 feet in elevation to the McKenzie Pass across black, treeless, ancient, lava flows at 5,324 feet elevation. Beyond lay eastern Oregon, with scattered mountains rising blue in the distance, mysterious and inviting.

Howard was in his element as we climbed those switchbacks with the road cuts revealing the history of the mountains. They were built mostly by fiery volcanoes, with the lava flows at the top as evidence of the most recent activity. As we climbed higher the flora changed in response to the environmental changes in temperature and precipitation. I was a willing and eager student and Howard was my equally eager and fascinating teacher. After a short rest at the summit we proceeded on our way, but now through a different flora: ponderosa pine mixed with juniper. Then, after a few miles the pine gave way entirely to the juniper in the arid environment. On the ground were sagebrush, rabbit brush, various grasses, and other products of the arid soil. It was a different world from that of the moist, lush Willamette Valley, and we would find that different lifeways marked the two environments. We were now in our first area of planned study, the eastern flank of the Cascade Range.

We went on to Bend on U.S. 97 as a base of operations for the first days of our trip. I wished to meet the publisher, Robert W. Sawyer, of *The Bend Bulletin* (a remarkably good paper for a town the size of Bend, about 5,000 population), and his editor, Phil Brogan. Both were very knowledgeable about the country and generous with their information. Phil, a native of eastern Oregon, had come to the University of Oregon to study geology as a supporting source for his journalism, for he expected to spend his life in the eastern Oregon country and help in the interpretation of its earth history. These two men became my lifelong friends, each assisting my professional career in different ways. Bob Sawyer's maps were not to be relied upon too closely, as I found out, but without harm to our work. I wanted to get more specific directions to a series of sites recorded around Bend and further information from Phil about campsites. Both desires were satisfied.

Our first site was about twenty-five miles out of Bend on U.S. 26 in Horse Ridge canyon, a dry watercourse except for storms and spring runoff, between two rims, the vertical surface marking the edge and end of a lava flow. The smooth, vertical face of the rock provided the decorative field for the Indian artist. We parked our car on the shoulder of the road, took our photographic gear, notebooks, and compass and started through the dry grass and sagebrush, to walk perhaps a hundred yards to the spot we were informed we would find the designs. I had taken only a step or two when a sharp, loud rattle almost at my feet made me jump straight up, then "freeze" to try to locate the source of the rattle. I was chagrined, but certainly relieved to discover that the source of my fright was a lonely locust. I would later learn the sound of a rattlesnake and never confuse the two again. Try as we might, we could not find the drawings. We finally gave up and returned to Bend and Phil. That kind man said that he had time and would go out with us and help find them. We retraced the miles, following his car, and he took us right to them, but they were not in the place we thought our guide had told us.

These were paintings of various figures and designs in both red and yellow pigment. There were no carved elements. Phil decided not to wait for us because he had work requiring his attention, but before he left he told us of a place at the north end of town where we could camp close by the Deschutes River, which flowed through Bend. It was getting fairly late by the time we returned to Bend, and our campsite was all Phil had promised us. We were able to take stock that night and lay plans for the next day, Sunday. Our campsite that night is now the lovely Pioneers' Park in Bend.

Sunday, a beautiful, early autumn day at that elevation, 3,500 feet or thereabouts, found us late in the morning at a site on Tumalo Creek, a few miles north and west of Bend on the east side of the Cascade Range. Several hundred yards below the remains of a beaver dam, a number of lava boulders lay strewn in the grass among large, yellow pine trees (*Pinus ponderosa*) on the north side of the small stream. In this idyllic place, Indians had lived and used the smooth surfaces of the boulders for their painted designs. Like most of the others seen so far, these too were in red pigment, hematite. I, busy with my photography and note taking, was making certain that I had not overlooked any and turned to go back to Howard making his observations. I saw him slap at something and then wipe the back of his right hand on the leg of his jeans. I couldn't hear, perhaps fortunately, his comments. Reluctantly, we had to drive to another site well down the creek near the village of Tumalo.

To reach the Tumalo site, we had to return to the main road and then turn north toward Sisters. The road soon dropped sharply from the surface with its lava exposure down a cliff showing an underlying series of strata quite new in my experience, a series of clearly demarcated alluvial deposits. The stratigraphic significance I understood, but the nature of the deposition and the kind of materials composing them I clearly did not. Here, Howard gladly and expertly came to my assistance with his explanation of the stratigraphy of the fill exposed by the road cut and stratigraphy in general. This was the first of many lessons we would share as our trip progressed.

We collected all our scientific information relevant to the designs on a cliff exposed by the creek in its meanders and then decided to lunch, for it was well past time for it. I noticed that Howard kept looking rather often at his hand, but not as secretly as he hoped. I asked him about it and he explained that he thought a bald-faced hornet had stung him at our first Tumalo Creek site. The sting, whatever it was, was beginning to annoy him and was rather painful at times. Before leaving we painted the spot, now inflamed, with an antiseptic and hoped for the best. We had two sites to study to complete the Bend area of our study, one near Prineville and the other some forty miles farther. We decided to go on to find a good campsite for the night since it would be too late to do any work.

We took the road to Redmond, a matter of a dozen miles, but up again on the lava surface. At Redmond we turned east toward Prineville, near where our first site the next day would be found. Now we were clearly in a new environmental zone: the juniper-sagebrush, with yellow pine found only at higher elevations in areas of greater precipitation. None of the junipers was very tall, most of them twisted in their growth by the high winds; and between Redmond and Prineville, we saw some of the largest-in-diameter trees in this forest that stretches clear into Idaho.

Our first site to examine was on McKay Creek, on a side road some five miles out of Prineville. It was getting late when we reached the general area to hunt for our "wide place in the road" to camp, and since it was open-range country, cattle seemed to have found the wide places before we got to them. Finally, we, too, found enough clear space for our simple needs and decided to make our camp. All we had to do was get our sleeping gear and folding table from the baggage rack, the stove and lantern and whatever we were going to eat for dinner from the car, and get on with it. I noticed Howard favoring his right hand and I asked to see it. It was clearly inflamed and had started to swell. He tried to make light of it, but I knew Howard and was concerned; he, fortunately, had a good night undisturbed by wandering cattle or predators.

Morning was a different story. Howard's hand was clearly worse, and the swelling had started to move up to his forearm. It was painful, too, as I saw when we had to load our gear and he dared to use only his left hand. I obviously had a problem on my hands. I told him I thought he needed medical attention, but where to get it in that country I didn't know. The alternative was to finish what we had to do that day and then return to Eugene, where he would have medical and any follow-up care. He chose this option, and I said that we would go to the McKay Creek site, then on to Beaver Creek some forty miles or more east of Prineville if he felt able, then back to Eugene.

At McKay Creek we found only pictographs in red pigment on an exposed lava surface in a road cut. On our way to Beaver Creek, we turned off the main road on to one following up the Crooked River through a flat, wind-swept area with a badly weathered, lonely, large ranch house. Our map showed it was the Lister ranch. By this time, I was truly worried by Howard's condition. His hand was swollen so that his fingers were spread apart and would not bend, and his forearm was swollen to his elbow. I said, "Howard, if it is all right with you, I am going to stop and see if the people here will keep you until I can get up to Beaver Creek and come back for you. It's twenty or thirty miles, but I can hurry and then we shall go for Eugene."

"That's fine with me," said Howard. "We don't want to have to go over this route a second time."

I drove up to the ranch house, which was sandblasted by the winds and had its fences and outbuildings in a sad state of disrepair. In answer to my knock, the door was opened by a large, motherly person obviously engaged in housework. I introduced myself and told her my problem, asking if I might leave Howard to rest there until I returned from my task on Beaver Creek and then take him to Eugene. I called Howard to come to the house. Mrs. Lister had introduced herself, and I introduced Howard and showed her his problem. She said of course she would help and that he should come right in. So I left him and drove to the site on Beaver Creek, passing at a Y in the road a fingerboard, put up by some practical, local joker who knew what he was talking about, declaring as it pointed up the hill on what passed as a road: "Burns a helluva long ways." I found the ranch house I was told to come to on the edge of the pine forest on the southern section of the Ochoco Mountains. A couple of young men lounged on a porch. I got out of my car, introduced myself, told them of Howard, and asked if someone would take me to the "rock writing" site to save time. Without any hesitation, one got up and said as he climbed in the front seat that we could drive. I found more red painted designs but no carvings, hurriedly finished my work, and returned to the house with my guide, where I thanked them for their help and headed back toward the Lister ranch, wondering as I drove out why anyone would choose such an isolated spot to build a house and life, unless perhaps one did not want to be found.

At the Lister ranch I found Howard and his motherly nurse very reassuring. She had packed his forearm and hand with hot Epsom-salts the whole time I was away, and Howard had clearly felt relief, both physical and mental. She said she thought it was a local infection and would respond, but it was better for him to have medical care. We thanked her, and then I said, "Are you perhaps descended from the Lister family of Scotland and Dr. Lister?"

"You are quite right," she said, "but it's a long way here from Scotland, isn't it?"

"My wife is a Scots, of the Loch family."

"How nice; the Loch family is a well-known and an honorable one, too; we Scots do get around for a small country. I am so glad I could help. Don't drive too fast now, but try to get past that storm building ahead. Good luck."

"Our thanks from our hearts to you, Mrs. Lister, and good luck. Good-bye."

Howard and I, with that storm building on our left front, started our 150 miles to Eugene; most of it would be in the dark and over the mountain roads we had traveled a few days before in the opposite direction. My driving now was purposeful, for I had to get out of that low area before any rain fell; it would turn the roads to a slippery mass. Howard was more or less asleep as I drove fast, keeping alert for cattle or any other obstruction on the road. A slightly rising curve in the road cut through one of the colorful John Day formations, giving the surface, especially in the yellowish light of the approaching storm, a greenish color, characteristic of the formation. Howard woke just as we came up to that spot in the road and almost shouted, "What's the color of the road?" "Green," I replied. He settled back, relaxed, and drowsed off again. We stopped at Redmond for a hurried dinner and to phone home. I called Cecilia, told her the situation and that I would arrive near midnight, asking her to phone Howard's family and alert them. I would drop Howard off with them on our way in.

We finished our dinner and I settled Howard comfortably and started our 125-mile-drive for Eugene. It was dark when we crossed the lava beds, and the switchbacks were ahead. I found night driving on the switchbacks easier than day driving; at night, a car could be seen by its approaching lights. We were making good progress without traffic, when, as I made one hairpin turn, there in the center of the road ahead was the biggest, buck mule deer I had ever seen, with a magnificent spread of antlers, staring defiantly at me, an unwelcome intruder. We were on a collision course with no hope of stopping on that gravel-surfaced road. Then that beautiful animal, as though his legs were all springs, gave a magnificent leap sideways up the slope from the road and disappeared into the brush. I pulled myself together, relaxed, and kept going. Without further excitement, we arrived at Howard's home, and I turned him over to his parents. I explained hastily what had happened and then went on home. After I relaxed with some hot chocolate that kind Cecilia had ready for me, I found bed a good place to be; the Staffords would call as soon as they had Howard examined in the morning.

Morning found Howard with the family doctor, who assured him that Mrs. Lister had given him the exact treatment he would have prescribed; he should go on with it for three or four days, when he would be ready again to go across the mountains.

Four or five days later, Howard and his doctor felt that his condition was sufficiently improved for us to start out again. Cecilia and I had checked over our supplies and made up deficiencies. Fresh fruits in particular and an added piece of roast beef replenished our supplies. This time we started as veterans, a bit swanky perhaps, but we had had some significant experiences those first days with which we had coped successfully.

Our first day's destination was a ranch house at Opal City — a lovely name, but a developer's dream gone bad. We planned to visit a site on the Crooked River, then swing across into the John Day country, from which we would go into the Northern Great Basin.

A young man in his twenties and his widowed father welcomed us at the ranch house, inviting us to bring our beds inside and be their guests; after breakfast the next morning, one of them would show us how to get to the site in the gorge of the Crooked River.

Opal City derived its name from Opal Spring, a large, freshwater spring, where small opals washed out in the sands of the spring's flow. Reality disabused my fantasy that the name derived from the lovely opalescence of the atmosphere as one looked westward in the late afternoon sunlight toward the Cascade Mountains not many miles distant.

That night was a night for good stories from our hosts, one of which I remember vividly. I had asked about rattlesnakes down along the river where we had to go. Our elder host drawled, "Yes, they're among the tussocks, but they're not all bad."

"What do you mean?" I asked. That was the first good word I had heard about rattlesnakes.

"I heard this story the other day about a fisherman a little further down river than you're going. Seems the follow was a dyed-in-the-wool fly fisherman and usually preferred to go home with nothing rather than use bait. The day I heard about he was having a real bad day, not a strike. Finally he broke down and this time, for some reason, he didn't want to go home skunked. He looked around for a grasshopper or a small frog, willing to use anything, for he was desperate. Then he saw this snake with a small frog's hind legs and part of its body sticking out of its mouth. He quickly put his foot on the snake just back of its head and tried to pull the frog out, but the snake's teeth were hooked in it and he couldn't budge it. He had an idea: he took from his hip pocket the small flask he always carried in case of snakebite, and poured a few drops into the snake's mouth as he held the frog's feet with his other hand. The snake shuddered, choking, and coughed up the frog.

"The fisherman let the snake go, for he didn't want to hurt it after it had helped him out. Using part of the frog for bait he cast again, had a strike but missed. As he reeled in to see if he had lost his bait, he felt a tap, tap, tap against his boot and looked down to see his friendly snake back with another frog in its mouth.

"We'll see you boys in the morning; have a good sleep, for you have quite a climb ahead of you, and remember not all snakes are bad."

Following breakfast, the young man was preparing to go in to Bend on some business and shaved in the large kitchen, using a straightedge razor. Finishing, he walked around talking and shaving the back of his neck as Howard and I sat, horrified, waiting to see the blood spurt, but never a nick did he put in his neck. He finished his preparations for his trip and, as he had promised, on his way to Bend he took us to where the trail went down into the gorge. We thanked him warmly for their hospitality and went our separate ways.

The gorge's maximum depth where our very narrow path descended to the river on the left side going downstream must have been about eight-hundred feet, so we had a fairly long, slanting walk. As our hosts had told us, the river was low at that time of the year and apparently easy to cross, which we had to do since the paintings were on the opposite side at the base of the sheer cliff. Failing to find enough wood to make a bridge from rock to rock, we decided that the only way to get across without getting wet was to leave our clothes until we returned, not wanting to wear wet clothes for the long drive we faced after climbing out of the gorge. Since we were below a bend in the river and well concealed from the view of anyone but some rare fisherman who might come along, we decided to risk it and leave our clothes and cross the river with our notebooks and cameras and our boots slung about our necks to wear to protect our feet. We felt that, even among the local friendly snakes, it would be disconcerting to have any tapping at our bare ankles and, too, we had no flasks. We crossed the river, got our photos and notes, and saw never a snake. After the long climb up that trail, we needed a rest before starting toward our next stop, the small village of Antelope, to see the village wise man, John Silvertooth. We arrived late in the afternoon after a long drive over dirt roads.

John had answered one of our letters and had asked us to be their guests that night. He was a barber with a drowsy customer in the chair when we arrived, a driver of a grain truck, hauling wheat from a ranch to The Dalles on the Columbia River for shipment, but on his way home from a long, hard day. The main room of John's place of business opened into the barbershop, but he sold varieties of confections in the main room. Here was a counter, open at the back. I heard it rumored later that John did a bit of bootlegging, but the charitable man explained it was just western hospitality to have a little something under the counter where a friend could get a nip after a hard day and perhaps leave a bit of something in a cigar box in appreciation. He told us to go up to the house and put our bedrolls down in a grassy spot against the side of the house and go in, where we would find his wife getting dinner.

After a hearty dinner, the last of that kind Howard and I would have for some time, John thought he should go back to his shop and check on his customer, whom he had left sound asleep; he hadn't been able to wake him, so he had locked the door leading to the main room and left him. He returned shortly to report that his sleeper had apparently come to and couldn't get out the locked door, so had broken out the window and gone home. Our host knew the man and didn't seem to think his behavior was anything to get upset over.

He then brought out a cigar box containing not cigars but some small, strange-looking objects that turned out to be fossil nuts he had dug out of the Clarno formation, the name given to one of the early formations in the John Day rock system, something Howard knew about, but about which I was quite ignorant. Here in that small village was this man with almost no schooling—his father had run a saloon in 1905 at Summer Lake—showing us these pieces of evidence of an environment with characteristic life-forms of millions of years ago. What was important was that he knew what he was showing us and the meaning they had for earth history. These he had found a few miles from his home. That night John Silvertooth gave me a most important introduction to a new aspect of experience that would become a very part of me. Aeons of time and change!

The next morning he took us to the pictograph site with its red designs, and told us more about the country and the roads we would take across the John Day River at Clarno and then up through the great exposures of that world-famous fossil area to our next stop at Sheep Rock.

I met John many years later at a meeting of the Wasco County Museum Commission, where he was a valuable member. Little did he know how, that night in that lonely village of Antelope, he had ignited a flame in my mind that still glows with memories of many experiences, of which those fossil nuts in his cigar box were an initial spark.

After fifteen miles of dirt road, Howard and I crossed the John Day River at the little village of Clarno, where we moved back intellectually into a world many millions of years earlier in time, vastly different in appearance from that of our pictographs, but ancestral to it. Howard had studied this world, but it was utterly new to me until my glimpse of those fossil nuts in Silvertooth's cigar box. Now, for our next sixty-five miles, Howard would interpret the main outlines of the story the rocks preserved. It was a story of volcanic eruption, erosion, preservation of deposits in different places by overlying lava flows, mineralized bones, fossils, casts and impressions of plants and animals preserved in the sediments, with sections overlapping so that eventually the geologists had been able to piece together a remarkable story of the evolution of life. The first white man to discover a fossil was a trooper, an observant and curious member of a U.S. Army cavalry patrol out from Fort Dalles, maintaining peace in the Indian country. He turned his find over to his patrol C.O., who, on the patrol's return, showed it to the Congregational minister at The Dalles, Thomas Condon, an easterner and an educated person. Dr. Condon immediately recognized the specimen as a fossil bone and understood its significance.

Over the years, he collected for eastern paleontologists, who wrote up and published their findings. Then in 1899 a young professor of geology at the University of California in Berkeley, Dr. John C. Merriam, fresh from a Ph.D. degree under the famous Munich professor, Dr. Karl Alfred Zittel (whose recent paper had proved that the Sahara was once a friendly land for man), decided to organize a program of study of the John Day area with a group of graduate students.[14] The professor later became the president of the Carnegie Institution of Washington, D.C., the most important source of scientific research support in the United States before the National Science Foundation existed.

Dr. Merriam came to the University of Oregon to confer with Dr. Condon, then professor of geology, and lay out plans for his program. Each student would have a special field and the work of all would be coordinated. Dr. Merriam's interest in the John Day story became a lifelong passion with him. As Howard unfolded the story of the John Day, I found myself fascinated and completely involved. As we passed exposures in the cliffs with their different colors, Howard explained the chemical processes and mineral sources represented by the record. All this record was long before any possible time for the arrival of *Homo sapiens* anywhere in the world.

It was a story of change, but in the continuation of life processes. Here was a story of the evolution of the horse from a small animal about the size of a fox to its present size, its migration to Asia across a two-way land bridge, its extinction in this continent, its later reintroduction here by Spanish and English settlers and brought again to the John Day country by Indians and United States cavalrymen.

I had never had a course in geology or paleontology, and Howard introduced me that afternoon to a whole new and immensely important range of knowledge. It came as a crash experience, with all the significance such an event could convey. I did not read about this first in a book in a distant library, but *saw it*, the *places* and *formations* and the record of earth-building processes that told the story. Books would come later in my life to help me understand the record more fully. Dark was approaching when Howard and I picked a nice level spot off the road behind some logs for our night's camp, no matter that it had been a sheep corral shortly before. Just across the river from us was a high, massive, remnant formation called "Sheep Rock," preserving under its lava cap an almost complete sequence of the John Day formation.

That night as we prepared "to hit the sack" we were both very tired but deeply happy. Howard had been in his element — earth history and its explanation — while I, on the receiving end of the communication link, was being introduced by an enthusiastic and excellent teacher to a whole new world of experience. Unlike Howard, I could not sleep with all the strangeness of the day dazzling my mind, so got up, pulled on my boots and a jacket and walked out to where I could look toward the moon riding high in the sky and outlining the massive profile of Sheep Rock. In the clear air the reflection of bright stars came back from the river flowing silently just below me. My mind had been a tumult of ideas as we passed mile after mile through this wonderland of the past stretching even to the present, but a past so far back in time that my mind, versed in the short span of a few thousand years of human history, found it difficult to contemplate.

Out of the tumult of newness as I gazed at Sheep Rock, ideas, concepts began to take shape: time, origins, life cycles, catastrophe, destruction, renewal, continuity, growth, change, nothing static,

Sheep Rock, petroglyph survey, John Day country, September 1932. Photo by L. S. Cressman.

interdependence, and Man, I, a part of it all. Man the minuscule, yet the only creature in the whole scheme of things to be able to do what I was doing then, to reflect on the process, to hope to understand. As order began to emerge in my thinking, I sensed how a real void in my education, knowledge of earth history and its significance, would be filled by the continuation and expansion of what I had seen so strikingly that day.

How could I dare to dream that night, and I certainly didn't, that within ten years Dr. John C. Merriam, whom I then didn't even know by name, would compliment me by including me among his highly respected scientist friends, or that some of his students of those early days in the John Day program, now internationally known scholars, would favor me with their collaboration and friendship, or that at the close of World War II he would successfully urge my appointment to develop and direct under the Oregon State Board of Higher Education a program of lectures and publications he initiated to "interpret the results of specialized scientific research to the public"? Fortunately, none of these thoughts ever entered my mind as, with some of its tumult stilled, I returned to my bedroll.

Now, in 1985, I understand that, as in 1925–26 in the cities and museums of western Europe I found my spiritual identity and integrity, in those September days of 1932, as I viewed the vivid record of earth history, I was starting on a course of knowledge leading to my intellectual integrity and wholeness that would fill the void. I would learn to appreciate Man as a part of the natural world, a world of change—always change—but woven by threads—often broken —from the past, providing continuity. Man now was an inescapable part of this natural world. Humanities, social science and natural history merged into a unity, and the person I never dreamed I would be that night at Sheep Rock was in the making.

The next morning, after recording our information from the red pictographs close by the river a short distance upstream from Sheep Rock, we decided on a bit of further exploration of the area before turning away from our fascinating landscape. The near-treeless John Day valley ended in an oblong-shaped section extending about twenty miles east and half as many miles wide into the forested Wallowa Blue Mountains, a great ridge from the northeast trending southwest for nearly a hundred miles to enclose the Great Basin on the north. Howard and I would return to John Day later after our work in southeastern Oregon and the adjacent Great Basin was completed, for there was no direct road then from Vale, our easternmost point, to Burns, where our planned course would bring us again to start the last stage of our study, Warner Valley and west.

Early afternoon found us driving south from John Day along Canyon Creek, a small mountain stream rushing down some ten miles along the road, the only one to Burns from the north, now U.S. 395. Canyon City, a flattering name, boasted in 1971 a population of 625 souls, but in the gold-rush days of the 1860s[15] it was a boomtown with all that meant of a mixed population of miners, gamblers, Chinese miners and laborers, shopkeepers and the usual collection of camp followers. In 1932 we noticed that every gravel bar had someone eagerly and, as we were told, fairly successfully panning for gold. A miner could make a day's wages, not to be ignored in 1932 as the Great Depression deepened. The old scales for weighing the miners' take at the day's end had been brought out and put to use again. But only the wraith of the boomtown of folklore and history remained.

Neither of us had ever been over this road or in Burns, so we were savoring the difference and beauty of the forest after the beautiful but rugged, treeless country we had just left. The road, although called an "other all-weather road," was as I recall mostly gravel and dusty, not conducive to speed, with grades taking us to the summit of the Strawberry Range of the Blue Mountains, 5,158 feet in about fifteen miles from John Day, some 1,000 to 2,000 feet lower. Seneca, population in 1971 of 405, the only settlement in the seventy miles separating John Day and Burns, had an importance in the area quite beyond that suggested by its small size; it was the center for much of the activity providing logs hauled by truck and company railroad to the lumber mills of the Burns area.

In that short September day, night seemed to come early. As we approached Seneca the forest crowded our road on one side and on the other, log trucks, both loaded and empty, filled the open space. The dust of the road and the last grayness of daylight seemed to form a slow-moving mass coming toward us. We slowed and then came to a full stop as we saw the cause of the apparent mirage: a very real, and to us enormous, band of sheep moving toward us with their dusty gray backs merging into the cloud of dust they raised from the road. We kept our windows closed as that bleating, dust-raising flock flowed past and around us. The little dogs skillfully kept the sheep on the move, turning back any attempt to stray out from the mass and nipping at those not moving fast enough. The dust-covered horse and herder followed. Last was the chuck wagon carrying the supplies. The band of sheep, probably not less than 2,500, was being moved to another grazing area in the national forest. When the air cleared, we started on toward Burns, not at all unhappy to leave that dusty, shabby-appearing village behind us.

We faced a drive of forty to fifty miles to Burns, and it was probably going to be dark when we arrived. We would worry about a place for our bedrolls when we got there. It was pitch-dark when we arrived, and after a bit of an "explore," we returned to a Richfield gas station we had passed as we entered town. Fortunately, it was open. A young attendant came out to us as we arrived. We asked if there was any place we could put down our bedrolls for the night out of people's way. He said there was a small stream up along the Silvies River coming in from the mountain we had just crossed. To my questions, he replied that there was no road, only grassland and barbed-wire fences; also there were snakes. The whole prospect sounded most uninviting, so I asked, "Are there any cheap cabins in town?"

"I have some, just over the hill there, the way you fellows came in."

"How much is one for the night?"

"The usual price is a dollar fifty, and that includes light, water, gas stove, toilet, bed and mattress, but no bedding."

"That sounds fine, but a little more than I wanted to pay. We have our own beds and bedrolls, Coleman stove and lantern, so we would not use your facilities. We just want a place to get in out of the night and sleep, to go south in the morning."

"Who are you fellows, Forest Service people?"

"No, we're from the University of Oregon, with practically no budget, making a study of rock writings and trying to get along with the least expense as possible."

"Oh, hell, you fellows can have it for seventy-five cents."

"Is it clean?" I asked, and have been embarrassed ever since at what seemed to be my ingratitude.

"I haven't seen any bugs in them this summer; if you want it I'll get the key."

"Thanks a lot, and we are very glad to take it," I said as I gave him the money.

He returned with a key and said it was the second one in from the street and if anything wasn't right to let him know.

Here we were, our first night in the Northern Great Basin after entering in pitch-black night. What would the morning show?

We did not push ourselves for an early start the next morning. Going into a country absolutely different from anything we had been in, we wanted to get all possible information about roads, water, and such before we drove ahead. We checked our maps carefully and the reports we had of sites, and when we turned in our key, asked some details of our helpful attendant at the gas station. If anyone knew road conditions, we thought he would because he was constantly in touch with traveling people.

We showed him on our map where we planned to go in the southeastern part of the state. He took one look and said, "Do you fellows *have* to go there? That's a God-awful rough country."

"We have reports of rock writings in those places and we have to get there if we can."

"Your first hundred miles will be easy, but after that it will be mighty rough. Go down to Blitzen about eighty-five miles south out in the old lake bed and stop there for the night. You can get further information there. That's the way to *do*: always get local information. After you leave Blitzen, you will have to go across the south end of

Steens Mountain and then north through another dry lake bed, Alvord, to Folly Farm. There you will turn east, but ask there, for it gets really rough. Be sure you keep your gas tank and water jug full, and good luck. Stop in on your way back.''

Before leaving Burns we replaced the supplies we had used on our last four days out. After a few miles out on the gravel road south, we came to a Y with no fingerboard to guide us. We chose the left road as the more likely correct one, but after a few miles were pretty sure we had made a mistake. I decided to go up to a ranch house we saw, but had not been told was there, and ask directions. There was a cattle guard and a big gate with a large, thick clump of willows in the field just to the side of the gate. As I got out to open the gate—the custom of the country was, and I think still is, always to leave a gate as one found it—a middle-aged, stern-faced woman in a long, black skirt and white blouse, cradling a 12-gauge automatic shotgun in her left arm, with her right hand on the stock and trigger finger in place—I recognized the type of gun since I had one exactly like it at home—stepped out into the open to my shocked surprise. Quickly I introduced myself and Howard in the car, explaining that we wanted to go to Blitzen and had apparently taken the wrong road and had stopped to ask directions. She accepted my explanation with a friendly comment that she was shooting crows, that we had taken the wrong fork at the Y, that the other fork would take us over a long, rock formation and down into the old Harney Lake basin, now dry. That road would take us down to Frenchglen along the Blitzen River, where the road turned right to go up over the rim and south again in another lake basin, Catlow Valley. It would be about eighty-five miles or more, but we ought to make it by dark. I wished her good crow shooting—I am sure she had suspected us of being rustlers after calves—thanked her, and turned around to head for Blitzen.

We came down into a lake basin, then over a slight rise at a place called ''The Narrows,'' a neck of land joining the dry Lake Malheur and Lake Harney basins. This was the first of our lake basins and, although it was characteristically different from any of the tumbled landscape we had known, it did not appear at all impressive or marked by any prominent beachlines.

Darkness was coming down when we reached Frenchglen, but the road to Blitzen was clearly marked, and we moved on to climb about five miles up a rim and out into the old lake bed we had been promised. Some fifteen or twenty miles ahead was Blitzen, with nothing taller than the two-feet-high sagebrush to interrupt our view. Shortly, we saw the lights of Blitzen, where we knew the store had acetylene gas. It was dark as Howard and I pulled up to the store with its welcoming lights in all that darkness. The store was partly below ground for storage, so a raised, wooden slab deck reached by stairs ran across the front entrance. A long, hitching rail stood at the side with one end by the steps. Along the western horizon stretched a line of golden light promising a clear, cold night. A breeze I would come to associate with the desert nightfall came in softly, pungent with the smell of sage. As we sat for a moment in our car savoring our experience, a cowboy rode up, threw his reins over the hitching rail, walked up to the steps to the door, and as he went his spurs *did* go jingle jangle jingle. What an introduction to our first desert night!

In the store we found a teenage boy, the son of the owner, told him who we were, and asked about a place to put down our bedrolls and camp for the night.

"There's the old hotel across the road you could use. Nobody's used it for a long time and it's dusty, but it's out of the weather. There may be some mice. Don't try to use any of the water; we'll give you all you want. I'll take you over if it sounds all right. No, it won't cost you anything."

And out of the weather in the dusty, old, abandoned Hotel Blitzen, Howard and I spent our first night in the desert. With such an arrival and welcome, who would not be full of happy excitement?

After cleaning our breakfast gear and preparing to load the car, we took our maps and went outside to look at the country into which we had come so romantically the night before, but in pitch-darkness. A crisp, clear autumn day with excellent visibility greeted us. Three or four houses appeared north of our hotel on the same side of the street; the other side held the store-residence and gas pump of the owner in a unit.

We moved beyond our hotel to avoid any obstruction to our view and stopped. We just stared, first in one direction and then another, speechless. To no one in particular I said: "I apologize abjectly for the derogatory comments made yesterday when I saw the unimpressive Harney-Malheur lake basin." Now space and distance challenged us. Ten or more miles to the east, a mountain range, with Steens Mountain rising at its highest point to nearly 11,000 feet, formed the shore-

Blitzen, Oregon, Main Street, 1935.

line. To the south, the mountain sloped to a low gap, where our map showed another range, the Pueblo, starting. The road that we should follow passed through the gap some twenty-five miles south of where we stood. On the west, the lake bed extended seemingly almost flat, to end in a blue mass, Hart Mountain, 7,710 feet in elevation, the highest point in the tableland thirty to forty miles distant. The map showed another lake bed, the Warner Valley, at the western base of Hart Mountain that, of course, was not visible to us. Farther south, about twenty-five miles from us, Beatys Butte broke the skyline at 7,916 feet in elevation to terminate the northern extension of the lava plateau forming the western shoreline in that section and separating the Catlow and Guano Valleys. Lone Grave Butte, some ten miles south of Beatys, rose to 6,507 feet.

We also could see a series of what appeared to be terraces, beachlines of ancient lake-water levels, cut into the cliffs of the Steens-Pueblo shoreline. When we focused my field glasses on them, they stood out with sharp clarity to confirm our first impressions — our measurements in a later year would show the lake's maximum depth had been about 150 feet. Howard and I that September morning in 1932 were almost silent as the full significance of our experience slowly involved us: here we stood on the floor of a once-monstrous lake, fifty miles in length, thirty-five in width, and very deep.

Our map showed another lake bed, the Alvord, bordering the eastern side of Steens Mountain. Then came that ''God-awful

rough" country our service-station attendant in Burns had warned us
about, but it was in the Owyhee Upland, not the Northern Great
Basin. From the Alvord in the east to the Cascade Mountains in the
west, this series of north-south trending, ancient lake basins separated by lava tablelands or plateaus terminate the Great Basin and
meet the vast drainage area of the Columbia River system in the
north, which in turn abuts on the Yukon and Mackenzie drainages to
the Arctic. As Howard and I stood with our maps, understanding
something of the potential of their message for human and natural
history, we felt that we had arrived at the cornerstone of something
very significant, but exactly what we didn't know. We would talk
about it as we drove on and continued with our work. It was a hesitant, a very tentative idea.

> There ariseth a little cloud out of the sea, like a man's
> hand.
>
> (1 Kings 18:44)

Did perhaps these people I heard about in 1931 at Pasadena,
coming south from their land bridge in the Arctic to live in the
Southwest at the same time as the extinct horse and bison, pass
through this land of lakes on their way south and leave their spoor
here? In the conventional archaeological wisdom of the time, such a
thought was heretical, better not even mentioned. But Howard and I,
after our journey through the John Day country, were putting
together ideas that earth and reason suggested, regardless of conventional book-wisdom, and we saw a "little cloud, out of the sea." We
would watch that cloud in the days ahead.

Before leaving for our "God-awful" country, we went to the store
to thank our hosts for their courtesy, pick up some odds and ends of
food, and fill our gas tank and water jug. In reply to our query about
Blitzen's past, the boy told us that years past, in the days of the great
cattle ranches, buyers came from Burns to meet and bargain with the
ranchers for their cattle; the hotel had been built for them. Big deals
were often made. Sheep ranching, after some violence, replaced the
great cattle ranches as well as the kind of men and women involved.
Fortunes declined. A wave of enthusiasm for dry farming swept
through the country, and in 1917 a General Land Office of the U.S.
Government was set up west of town. In 1935 I searched out and
found the ruined walls of one of the buildings covered by sagebrush

and the drifting sand. World War I took its toll of the country, and changing laws brought about different land uses and a different population. In 1932 Blitzen still had a post office to which the mail came on alternate days from Burns and, as the boy said, "Raised the population overnight from twelve to thirteen." Some of the ranchers on the Steens, Guano Valley to the west, and occasional government operatives or explorers like us were about the only people to be serviced; of course, they were always glad to see any of us.

That morning I did not dream that in 1934 I would pass through Blitzen, but not stopping, on our way to Home Creek on the Steens searching for caves in the Catlow beachlines, nor that in that same summer I would ride to the top of Lone Grave Butte from the Guano ranch with a companion and rancher guide as a part of our survey of the Guano Lake bed and would be able with field glasses to see Blitzen. In 1935 the hotel would provide shelter for my field party for the season, and in 1937 and 1938 Blitzen was our post office and source of some supplies for our mess while we camped at Home Creek. In 1949, with a colleague on a three-day trip of collecting and exploring, I spent the night in the old Hotel Blitzen, but by then moved board-and-beam from its home to Frenchglen and reconstructed in the newly established National Malheur Wildlife Refuge. The State of Oregon map I have been using during this writing was issued in 1972, and Blitzen, along with several other places we visited and found located on our 1932 map, is not mentioned. Perhaps it is just as well that "old men dream dreams."

Our young friend at the store told us the road ended a couple of miles down past the lakes — water holes rather flatteringly called the Garrison Lakes, but water holes in that country were almost priceless and these were on public land — and then we should just follow the car tracks through the sagebrush.

"But how will we know which one to take to get the road to Fields?" Fields was the very small village across the Steens where we turned north.

"Just head for the gap in the mountain; they all go there."

And they did; and what a road the "gap" provided! It served as the drainage ditch for any spring runoff and summer-storm downpours. Fortunately, the base was solid rock and, as we would soon find out, not the only one of the kind ahead.

At Fields we turned north along the eastern escarpment of the

Steens, on a great fault line, rising for some thousand feet and so steep my friend W. D., who had studied the geology of the Steens, said, "A goat could not get up." The Alvord Lake bed, the most easterly of the lake system, provided for several miles on its hard, flat playa the finest road we had been on since the main street of Burns, but it gave way to gravel and sand at times until we reached the store and filling station, Folly Farm. It does not appear on my 1972 map and no wonder, but the road junction, unnamed, is there. We stopped to get our road information, ice cream cones, and enough gas to fill our tank. The road information corroborated what we had been given at Burns. We were going into absolutely new country, and where we would stop for the night would be where we felt it wise and could find a place.

Howard was tired and I took over the driving, which had to be at a very slow speed since we were in country marked by the menacing sight of black, rough lava fields and little else that I remember. I high-centered three times on that road, but the only damage was to my pride and Howard's effort to sleep, for he was very tired. He was bothered with sinus problems, and I remember how he waked several times that afternoon to nosebleeds from the dry air and jarring ride.

Where we stopped that night I haven't the least idea, but it was approximately a hundred long, hard miles from Blitzen. We had to examine sites at Arock and Danner on Jordan Creek, a small stream flowing into the Owyhee River. To reach these places we had to ford Crooked Creek, although we didn't know it beforehand, to get to Rome—population in 1972 too small to be listed—and then down an unimproved road to take us to our sites. Morning of that day started well as we moved on to the unexpected ford at Crooked Creek. Apparently the stream had been deepened, with dirt piled like a dike on the side we approached. Car tracks appeared to cross the creek at various places, and we chose a likely looking spot. Then potential disaster struck. We high-centered with both front and rear wheels too high off the creek bed for traction. As we were puzzling how to get our car off that teeter-totter, a Model-T touring car full of youngsters with a young woman driver came splashing easily through the creek a few yards from us. Seeing our plight, she stopped the car and everyone piled out to see if they could help. We assured them they certainly could.

"Do you have a towrope?" the young woman asked.

"We do that," I answered and got it out.

"I'll fasten it to your bumper and mine; then you start your motor, put it in reverse, and I'll have you right out."

And so she did. I explained who we were and what we were doing, and had a very interested audience. No wonder, for the driver explained she was the teacher from the school and had been told that it was planned to drain a reservoir upstream and that the school should close and the children come up and get the fish before the birds and animals picked them up from the mud. She said they would wait to make sure we got across all right before going on. Again our thanks. We crossed where she had and without difficulty.

W. D. had told us before we left that southeast of the Steens we would find Basques among the ranchers, a spilling over from the large Spanish-Basque population of Nevada and Idaho (we were in extreme southeastern Oregon, very close to both Nevada and Idaho). These people we found to be small ranchers, owning the land. Under Federal laws, land ownership gave the rancher certain perquisites in using the public domain, such as grazing sheep on it. The families were mutually very supportive and provided a solid, dependable population. Since more males than females immigrated to work the mines and do the herding, intermarriage with local families, many of Scots-Irish descent, gradually dissipated the original Basque component. I was told the language was rapidly dying out.

A Scots-Irish lad from a ranch took us to a neighboring Basque place to record some petroglyphs. There we met a charming, young, native-born girl of Basque parents who had been through high school in one of the towns. (It was fairly obvious that these two young people were going to add to the mixed-marriage process.) They told us about the difficulty some of the older folks had with the English language. In the girl's story an older immigrant man was well versed in the facts of life, but the intricacies of English were a little too much for him. He had learned quite well the words relating to cattle, but poultry was something else. He wanted to start a small poultry business and went to a neighbor who had promised to sell him some to start his flock. One day he came, saying he wanted his hens, and had some burlap bags in which to carry them home. The rancher, taking him at his word, was giving him hens, when the man very excitedly started jumping around, saying, "Some bull hens, some bull hens; hens have to have bull hens, too."

"Oh, you mean roosters." And he then went home happily with his "bull hens, too."

These ranches were all small and included a section of one bank of the creek or river. There was precious little farmland, for the lava fields and outcrops were perilously close in. Large lava boulders along the creek provided surfaces for the Indian petroglyphs, designs made by pecking the base rock with another to cut through or at least into the dark, surface patina or desert varnish to produce figures of varying contrasting shades of gray. We had seen so far only painted designs; here there was none. We sensed an important difference in the aboriginal culture, but just what it might mean we didn't then know.

After checking out our sites in the Arock and Danner area, we had our most important one in the whole southeastern area remaining, that at Watson down in the Owyhee River canyon. We went back to the main north-south road at the Basque village, Jordan Valley (population in 1971 of 200), and found the road was important for truck traffic even in 1932 as the main road—though unpaved in Oregon—from San Francisco, Reno, Winnemucca, Boise, and points north and east. Inquiries at the gas station resulted in advice to wait morning before trying to go down to Watson. There was plenty of space up the road to get off and sleep, we were told, and then have daylight to go on. We were also advised to get back from the road some distance in the sagebrush, because the trucks ran all night and there was both the noise and dust. We found such an area some twenty miles north toward Watson outside Sheaville. There we spent the night and found the advice to stay back from the road most helpful. Morning would take us on some ten or twelve miles to Leslie Gulch, which led off from the left side of our road, and that would take us down to Watson.

Turning at the fingerboard identifying Leslie Gulch, we drove a few hundred yards on a dirt road in the sagebrush, then stopped to look at the sight ahead of us down into the canyon where we were going. I remembered reading many years before how a French field marshall, Marshal Turenne, while observing from the saddle the progress of a major battle in which his command was involved, felt his knees shaking and remarked, "Stop that, for if you knew where you're going in a few minutes you would save it for then." The road was on solid rock with all kinds of bumps and breaks. All the runoff water from time immemorial used Leslie Gulch as the bed to reach the Owyhee River at the bottom. I put the car in lower gear and told Howard not to let it "kick out." With careful use of the brake, we were making our jolting way slowly down when we saw a cowboy on his pony coming up, but not on the road. I said to Howard, "Even the cowboys won't risk their horses on this thing."

We finally reached bottom with both car and contents relatively intact. The ranch house and post office, Watson, was close, and we pulled up there to introduce ourselves and ask the exact location of the petroglyph site. The postmaster-rancher met us warmly.

"Yes, I remember your letter and answering it. I was hoping you would come. I have time and will take you to the rocks where the writings are."

He was a tall, well-built man with a full, red beard and red hair; and when we got outside the building in the daylight I saw a pair of the bluest eyes I had ever seen. His speech was an Irish brogue, so broad that Howard said, "We could cross the river on it." Here was one of the Irish not replaced by the Basques—perhaps being the postmaster had something to do with it. He told us he was going to have to move; in a year the corner of his house would be under thirty-six feet of water as the Owyhee reservoir filled. Watson thus disappeared from the map, and its absence on my 1972 map reflects that bit of history.

Here on the tumbled mass of huge boulders was the richest and most interesting of the series of "rock writing" we had seen. All were petroglyphs. Our guide stayed with us until we had finished, then rode back to the house with us—we could always find room on the front seat for a friend.

"Where do you boys go from here?" he asked.

"To Vale to get back to Burns; but isn't there any way out of here except that God-awful Leslie Gulch?"

"Oh, hell, don't go that way; nobody does. We cross the river at the bridge you saw near the writings. Just go right up through the sagebrush and junipers, follow the tracks, and you can't get lost. It's about forty-five miles or more and brings you out a few miles from Vale. Bring your sandwiches in the house and I'll have hot coffee in a couple of minutes. The rest will do you good."

So we had our lunch and some more good conversation about the people and the country as the hot, strong coffee warmed us. How far we would go that night we didn't know, for our next scheduled stopping place was Burns and it was a long way there: 230 to 240 or more very long miles. After a decent rest we thanked our new friend, and with mutual good wishes for good luck took off over the bridge to pick up the tracks through the sagebrush on our way to Vale. The "sagebrush road" here, as in Catlow, did not always run in a straight line since a storm might leave a mudhole and the next driver, to be followed by others, would go around it and eventually pull back to join the pack.

Our road ran for some miles along a dry watercourse—in the arid Southwest called an arroyo—about thirty-five to forty feet wide and three to four deep, capable of carrying heavy, floodwater runoff. Suddenly the tracks stopped and there was no place to get down into the arroyo. "Let's circle around," I said, "and see if the tracks do that from someone through since the last storm."

We found someone had and followed that track to the place where the bank was broken away to get down into the arroyo, drove in it up to another break, then up and out on the other side and on through more sagebrush and juniper. The sky had become overcast and the day was shortening when we suddenly emerged from the sagebrush-juniper world onto a dirt road running through the greenest field we had ever seen—at least so that field of alfalfa under irrigation with its service road seemed to us. At the edge of the field, a big gate hung from a heavy post. Howard opened the gate, and across a blacktopped road we faced a wonderful fingerboard: Vale 4 miles. Properly closing the gate, we headed for Vale feeling "we had it made," and on a blacktopped road!

To John Day, where our blacktop road from Vale ended, was 116 miles beyond the Blue Mountains, most of the way through coniferous forest and with no settlements until Prairie City, fifteen miles out of John Day. Vale offered a general store, service station and gasoline, and the houses of a small settlement. Before going on, we had our car well checked and the gas tank filled. After our equipment, we turned our attention to ourselves. Able to buy some fresh fruit, the first in some time, and with some other oddments we made that our dinner. Our discussions with the service station operator and others at the store warned us that the road was easy to drive, but it was narrow and it would be very dark with the forest. Ditches would make it difficult in the dark to find our usual "wide place" for the night. It was getting late, and we decided with all the miles still ahead of us to drive just as far as possible on our good road.

I don't recall passing a vehicle or an animal on the road that night as mile after mile passed behind us. We changed drivers and still the road ran on in darkness, a darkness that pressed in to the very side of the car. There was no suggestion of a "wide place," and we kept on. We had been going downgrade for some time and had covered a lot of miles when I said that we ought to be coming out into the John Day valley where we could see a light at any rate. Then ahead on the right was our light! What a welcome sight! It was a confectionary store with a soda counter, a young lad on duty, and a few teenage customers who eyed us a little skeptically, unkempt as we were, as we came in. We ordered cones and explained who we were and asked the lad at the counter if there was a place we could put down our beds for the night. He thought a moment then told us of two places and gave directions how to reach them.

Finishing our cones, we thanked him and started out for the first one he told us about. That was a large house with all the windows lighted, obviously a much-occupied place and the "wide place" for our beds would have been the front yard.

"This is not the place," I said. "Let's try the other."

Howard agreed, and we went on to try to find the turnoff our boy had told us about. We did and drove over a wooden bridge across a ditch, through some willows ten to fifteen feet high, into a field, up a slight grade to a quite large level space. It was completely concealed from the road by surrounding willows and there was no sign of a light anywhere. I said to Howard as we stepped out of the car, "This is it," a sentiment with which he heartily agreed. We soon had our bedrolls down, sound asleep in them, to have a completely undisturbed night. I woke at dawn, but lay in bed watching the day come on. Shortly, Howard joined me. With the full light we could look around at our sleeping quarters for the night. We discovered that we had been peacefully sleeping in the city dump, probably Prairie City's. Who cared? We had had a wonderful night's rest after all the places we had been and where we had tried to sleep the last few nights.

Fifteen miles separated us from John Day, where we would say good-bye to blacktop again for seventy miles of gravel through Seneca once more to Burns. We had work to do that afternoon well southeast of Burns on Riddle Creek and near Crane. We breakfasted and pushed on to Burns, where we took our cabin again for the night ahead at the original price. Our young host of our previous visit was pleased to see car and passengers back relatively intact from that "God-awful country" he had warned us of.

We now would start the last segment of our project, still requiring at least six hundred miles of driving. We hoped the worst roads were behind us; there would be little chance for the rest we needed. Our first day would take us from Burns to a site some sixty miles southeast on Riddle Creek, a small stream from the west slope of the Steens. Leaving all our sleeping and cooking gear in our cabin, we traveled light since we would return with no worry about a place to put down our beds.

The Riddle Creek trip should have been easy, but things happened, as they have a way of doing. We found the rancher where we were told to call sitting in an easy chair in the shade in front of his house. He welcomed us without leaving his chair, for some reason, and said the "writings" were easy to find on large boulders on the slope up the field a ways from the house. Unfortunately, a working irrigation ditch with no bridge required us to leave our car and walk into the field up to the location he indicated. The field bordering the service road we were on was swampy. On the other side of the road a boulder-strewn slope stretched up fifty to seventy-five yards to a low rim. A well-used trail probably made by sheep and cattle wove among the boulders along the slope. The rancher said we could easily see the "writings" from the trail since they were on a large rock.

When we left the car at the ditch we also left everything we thought we could do without to travel light, including shirts and first-aid kit, carrying only our notebooks, camera, and guns. That slope was made for snakes with its excellent habitat for small rodents on which snakes could feed. We had trouble finding the designs and were becoming frustrated, impatient and, in turn, careless. I was going down a slope in the trail, looking right and left for our petroglyphs when, as I raised my foot to step ahead, a menacing rattle and the strike of a snake on the trail where my foot would come down jarred my reflexes. I never before thought I could change my step to a jump, but I did. Fortunately, the snake could not reach my boot sole, the target. Even if it had, I probably would not have been in danger because of the heavy sole and sock. As I landed from my jump I turned and shot that snake five times before I could stop.

In psychology classes I had heard and talked about how an aggressive response to fright often occurred as a completely irrational reflex act. My five shots into that snake above Riddle Creek demonstrated the actuality of the response in me. The realization of what had happened, that I could and would do such a completely irrational act, taught me a very disturbing fact about myself—probably a valuable lesson—and I could watch for it now in the future. Never after that experience did I confuse the rattle of a snake, as I had done the first day out, with the sound of a locust. No, I don't like rattlesnakes or any kind of snakes. I learned over the years in eastern Oregon the ways and nature of rattlesnakes; I learned to respect and not fear them, but no, I don't like them.

Shortly after my rattlesnake lesson we found our petroglyphs, returned to the car without further incident, and started for the site near Crane. Our directions took us to the house of a railroad hand, whose young wife with her two children drove her car to guide us to the site. She said we might find some snakes, so "be prepared." As we got out of our car, right at the site, a warning rattle sounded. We had to kill two with rocks to get our pictures and notes. Our guide explained the snakes were bad around there. Just that morning she had come out of her house to see what her two small children were doing and found them sitting playing some children's game on the wooden steps coming up to the porch of the house. As was often the case, the tread and the rise of the next step above did not meet, and there between the two children was a rattler's head protruding through the open space. She backed away quietly without speaking to the children, afraid that any movement might cause the snake to strike. Fortunately, it pulled back under the porch and she got her girls from there in a hurry. We thanked her and returned for the night to our cabin at Burns.

Our next objective was Stone Bridge in Warner Valley at the base of Hart Mountain, over 150 miles because we had to go by The Narrows to pick up a site passed on our earlier swing. Our road that afternoon, as we turned for the Warner Valley stretch, took us over eighty miles of graded dirt road, a part of the project for building the highway, now U.S. 395, down the east side of Abert Lake along the world-famous fault scarp 2,000 feet high. Driving that road, I had to save my detailed study of the formation for later times—and there were many. Because of our slow progress, the afternoon had worn on. At Valley Falls at the south end of the Abert Lake basin we picked up a better road, but darkness overtook us soon after we had turned east eighteen miles farther on to the road over the Warner Mountains. Adel, the village we wished to reach, was some twenty-five to thirty miles farther and the road, well over 6,000 feet at the pass, ran through mostly ponderosa pine forest.

We descended into a pitch-dark valley with not a light in sight. We were south of Adel, a jog not shown on our map, and could not see it. We drove slowly, looking for our usual sleeping space, but all we could see with our car lights and flashlight were drainage ditches with water and tules or cattails. Finally we saw a light, seemingly a long walk in from the road, but I was desperate enough to take a chance on dogs and try to get information. I was not greeted by any dogs, but by a friendly man who told me of a place just ahead where a service road started up the slope, and if we weren't too particular we could make do there. Adel, he told us, was up the valley from where our road had come in and that was why we hadn't seen it. Thanking him warmly, I returned with my information to Howard, and we said, "Let's go."

That was a miserable night. We could "make do" with the space even though it was not level, but we were probably at over 6,000 feet elevation and the water did not want to boil for our coffee. We got the soup to appear to boil, but the contents refused to respond. Peas we could mash by sheer force, but spaghetti! That was something else, and there was a lot of it in that can of soup. The stuff just stayed slippery and hard. I vividly remember sitting with our Coleman lantern providing the light as I used my fork to remove that stuff, forkful by forkful. We had to do with what we had, for we couldn't run out and pick up a substitute. Not a bad lesson at all. For the first time, I was cold that night, probably because of fatigue and insufficient food. Finally, as the morning came I saw the sunshine start to move down the east-facing slope above us—we had no idea of what was around us in the dark—and sensing that there was at least the idea of warmth there, I got up, put on my boots and jacket—having tried to sleep in everything else—climbed up the slope, and sat down in the sunshine. As it moved down, I got warmer and returned to the car and Howard, who was stirring.

We managed some breakfast and then turned back toward Adel and information on the location of Stone Bridge. A helpful person at the gas station told us to take a road that would get us close to the site, where we would find a cabin occupied by a coyote trapper named False Morgan. "Stop there and ask him."

"Why is he called False Morgan?" I asked, wondering about his reliability.

"He has a bit of a reputation for tall stories and knows quite well why we call him False, but he won't give you any unreliable information on a matter like this. He uses his cabin to dry and stretch his coyote skins, so the smell may be pretty strong; but he lives in it."

A drive of about twenty miles took us to False's cabin. It was by then a warm, sunny midday, and he opened the door to our knock. We were lucky to have been warned about the atmosphere in his cabin; of course, we stepped in in response to his invitation. The cabin, built of plain boards and two-by-fours without insulation, was very hot, and the sunshine streaming through the windows showed a large number of stretched coyote skins, from freshly skinned to quite dry.

"Maybe we ought to step outside. The air may be a little strong in here for you boys. And then tell me what you want."

I explained our coming and asked directions. He told us quite clearly, but particularly warned us that the "writings" were on the other side of a narrow peat bog. Grass grew through the water, and it was three or four inches deep to firm soil. He said we would have no trouble if we got a good start, hit it, and made sure not to stop. He wished us good luck.

We found the place and, following his directions, made the crossing with no trouble. Here was the finest series of petroglyphs we had seen, rivaled only by those at Watson. Several showed use of red paint as a kind of border to the pecked figure. We wondered if we were in a boundary zone between the pictographs we had seen earlier and the petroglyphs of this southeastern part of the state. It was something else to think about, possibly important.

We finished our work and started our return crossing of the bog with all the speed we could muster in the short run available, and it was our bad luck, perhaps twenty feet from the edge, to lose traction and stop. We tried every means of getting traction under at least one rear wheel, one of us at the driver's position and the other pushing. Our progress was heartbreakingly slow and the afternoon was slipping past very fast. Just as we were almost ready to call it hopeless, a cowboy rode up on his pony.

"You boys in trouble? Can I help?"

"You're right both times," I said. "I am sure you can help us."

"Do you have a towrope? I heard your motor running and thought you might be in trouble."

He fastened the towrope and then the other end to the saddle horn and took his pony by the reins to lead him. The pony lunged and broke the towrope. It was a new standard towrope for small cars.

"Let's see the rope, see if it's long enough to tie." The expert with ropes soon had it knotted into a satisfactory length and one end attached to our front bumper.

"Let's try it this way." He mounted his pony, wrapped the end of the rope in his hand around the saddle horn, spoke to his mount by voice and knee. The pony leaned gently but firmly into his pull as Howard used the motor and I pushed, and out we came. Our rescuer patted his pony's neck and tossed us the rope.

"He's a cow pony, not a draft horse, and good luck, boys," he said as he rode away.

His final remark as he rode away taught me a lesson to use in administration that helped me all my life—not that it pleased everyone I had to apply it to, but it served to secure efficient performance. I hired persons for special fields and held them to it.

"Now we're out of here," said Howard, "let's keep going."

And so we did, finally to stop for our last night out at an available spot we had passed the day before some few miles south of Valley Falls. It was already getting dark when we pulled into the waist-high grass. Out of the car, we kicked around to make a noise and stir things up to be sure we were not going to share the spot with snakes. It was all clear, and there—now the Chandler Roadside—we spent a quiet night hoping the next one would find us in Eugene.

It was about 225 miles from this last stop to Eugene, which we expected to reach that day. Our route took us up through the long Summer Lake bed through Paisley and Summer Lake to Picture Rock Pass, elevation at 4,830 feet, where one of the large boulders on the south side of the road provided our last petroglyph site. Finishing that chore, Howard and I posed with evident satisfaction, side arms clearly visible and no makeup, for our only photograph. I set the timer so we both were in it. We looked pretty tough, too, against our travel-scarred car. This picture has appeared in at least one national TV program, and I am afraid the script did not always make clear that

Howard Stafford and I at Picture Rock Pass, Oregon, on petroglyph survey, September 1932. Time-release photo.

the side arms were protection from rabid coyotes or from rattlesnakes when a rock could not be found.

From Picture Rock Pass we looked down on another lake bed, Silver Lake, and soon were passing through a small part of that. A few miles beyond, the ground fell away slightly to reveal another lake bed, at one time shared with Silver Lake, with large, circular, rock formations rising starkly from the level floor of the valley. A fingerboard pointed down a dusty side road to Fort Rock. Howard explained that the rock formations we had seen were the remnants of old volcanoes. No wisp of even a dream entered our heads as we continued out of the basin onto the high, level plateau we had known at Bend that my life in a few years ahead would become entwined with the history of the Fort Rock area and the lives of the Indians who once lived there, a record to force revisions not only in the prehistory of Oregon but also in Far West prehistory.

A few miles out of La Pine, where we would pick up U.S. 97 and blacktop, twenty-seven miles south of Bend, we stopped to change drivers, for Howard was feeling sleepy. As I walked around to take the wheel, I checked the tires and saw the left rear was soft. I could not detect any signs of leakage and, hoping it was a slow leak, said that we would try to make it to La Pine where there was a service station. We had a dirt road with a bad washboard surface and so hoped for the best without too much confidence. But luck held and we made it to La Pine. Checking at the gas station would not reveal a leak without dismounting the tire, something we didn't want to do until Bend if we could help it. There we could get some dinner while the tire was repaired for our drive across the Cascades to Eugene, another 128 miles. We decided to try it after getting the tire fully inflated. I drove as fast as was safe on that nice blacktop because, if it was a slow leak, time was our ally. We pulled into a Texaco service station in Bend, our tire still up, alongside the building housing *The Bend Bulletin* where my friend Phil Brogan worked.

We were just leaving for a restaurant that would accept us in our unkempt condition, after arranging for the tire to be taken off and repaired, when Phil appeared.

"Have the state police found you boys?"

"No, Phil, and what would the state police want with us? We haven't been in any trouble that I know of."

"Howard's grandfather, old Dean Straub, has died and Howard is wanted to be a pallbearer tomorrow. Bill Tugman called me to help find you. The state police thought they had at Hart Mountain, but found it was a party making moving pictures of antelope."

"We came up from below Valley Falls, Phil, and have not been off the main road, but have never seen an officer. If we hadn't wanted to see one, I'm afraid they would have been all over the place. Please call Bill at the guard and have him call the Staffords to tell them, and pass the word on to Cecilia that, with luck holding, we shall be in about midnight or earlier."

And we were! Mission accomplished!

The next morning after breakfast I began to unload the car—I had been too tired the night before to bother with anything but my immediate toilet articles. Cecilia was in the kitchen going about her chores when I brought up and set down on the floor by the door a sturdy wooden box in which we had once carried perishable food. As I returned with another armload I found Cecilia standing looking in a puzzled way, and with some distaste, about the kitchen.

"What on earth is that awful smell?" she asked. Her keen sense of smell was obviously offended.

"What smell? I don't smell anything wrong."

"Don't smell anything wrong?"

With that incredulous remark, she turned, sniffing (I said "like our Irish setter"), and went straight to my good wooden box. She took out two or three oddments and then—victorious!—held at arm's length a small, badly worn and torn brown bag, showing through the tear a green remnant of a once-delicious roast she had sent out with us. As she held the thing out even I could tell how right she was, and I opened the garbage can for her to drop it like some contaminant.

"Do you mean to tell me that you two have been riding all these days with that stench and could smell nothing?"

"Well, dear, we haven't seen much water except what we needed for cooking and shaving for a long time. This morning was my first real shower since we left; but you were never in False Morgan's cabin. That was something! That roast, though, while it lasted was delicious."

I thought that afternoon, as we joined the funeral party for Howard's grandfather, what an entirely fitting close it was for our long trip through prehistory: Howard, the young grandson, a pallbearer honoring his distinguished grandfather, and we among the friends showing our reverence for the dead and support for the living. My mind flashed back to the night with Sheep Rock silhouetted against the moon and the silent river below me, and again came the thought, change and continuity, continuity and change, as we two on our return became participants in the visible demonstration of the timeless reality.

At first glance I appear to have devoted an excessive amount of attention to our field trip to locate and record petroglyphs, but when one relates the importance of this experience to the major purpose of my writing, how I became the kind of archaeologist I am, the significance of our work becomes clear. A host of new and quite unanticipated experiences had made a profound impression on me. Although I had wide experience and training in humanistic and social science fields, I lacked any intimate knowledge of natural or earth history. Howard skillfully introduced me to this neglected field as we moved from site to site, beginning to fill this intellectual void and give me as well as emotional appreciation of earth history to lead toward a deeper understanding of life's unified nature.

I was then in my mid-thirties, probably the most creative period of my life. I was intellectually a discoverer, not a supporter of any "school" or established theory. I could learn, and did, at firsthand from what I saw, not at secondhand from books, although they would later amplify and explain in much detail what I saw in the course of those memorable days and nights with Howard. My mind was an intellectual field ready for seeding, the visions of landscapes, often monumental, and reflection on their significance were the seeds being planted. In fertile soil they would germinate and grow. The field trip was seminal, for it proved to be basic to my development as an archaeologist. I would have to view the human experience as a process of change in a changing world of nature. All my archaeological work in the years ahead would reflect this intellectual stance.

> I am a part of all that I have met;
> Yet all experience is an arch wherethro'
> Gleams that untravelled world whose margin fades
> Forever and forever when I move.
> (Alfred Lord Tennyson, *Ulysses*)

To follow the new direction I saw my professional life inevitably taking would require a different academic situation from that provided by the department I was in. Of course, I carried out my full departmental duties, but also found the time to continue the fascinating exploration of my new world. After about two years, without the slightest intimation that a solution was near, it would come.

Stress was a way of life at the University of Oregon during the 1932–33 academic year—real distress, affecting the whole life pattern for families of faculty members and many in the town. The full impact of the Great Depression was beginning to be felt. Upper division and graduate work in the sciences, some of the best departments of the university, had been transferred with personnel and equipment to the State College at Corvallis; corresponding levels of instruction in the humanities and social science at the college had been transferred to Eugene, an exchange by any measure of comparison to the deprivation of the university. The action produced a deep and long-lasting trauma among the university faculty. Even though the voters had soundly defeated the Zorn-McPherson bill to move the entire university to Corvallis, the bitterness of that confrontation was very fresh in our memories. A widely believed, but uncorroborated report that President William J. Kerr of the college had secretly contributed heavily in support of the bill fired the intensity of the interinstitutional and intertown hostility.

A federally appointed commission to study and make recommendations for the development of higher education in Oregon had not only recommended the shift in academic responsibilities, but also recommended the appointment of a chancellor to administer the two institutions through a kind of super dean at each. The appointment of a chancellor, given the history of interinstitutional relations, was clearly crucial to the success of the experiment. I think it fair to say that most thoughtful people believed that an outsider should be appointed by the state board. President Hall clearly believed this solution to be necessary and, after discussions with President Kerr, thought it was mutually acceptable: each would resign and withdraw his name from consideration in the morning before the state board convened for its meeting in Eugene to consider the whole matter of appointments. Hall and Kerr validated their agreement by a handshake, then an acceptable method among honorable men, the morning before the board's meeting. Hall resigned and boarded the train for Washington, D.C. Kerr, however, did not resign, but joined the board as its guest for lunch. Kerr, by conniving with individual members of the board, had tricked Hall and the public.

Shock and incredulity greeted the board's news release: (1) the appointment of Kerr as the chancellor of the system of higher education, (2) he would retain the presidency of the Oregon State College and serve as the chief administrative officer of the University of Oregon, and (3) Chancellor Kerr would move to Eugene and take up residence in the president's house on the university campus adjacent to the administration building, Johnson Hall. The first two decisions were bad enough, but the third appeared almost to be an effort to humiliate the university. Kerr in the president's house! It was incredible, scandalous! The triumph of personal ambition by whatever method necessary boded ill for the smooth effort necessary to put the new organization into being.

Campus life turned into an uneasy, armed truce.

April 3, 1933, Kerr called a special faculty meeting, which I attended, to *tell us* what fiscal economies would be made. That economies had to be made was certainly no news, but the faculty had a long tradition, derived from its charter, of *sharing* with the president the administration of the university, a relationship the Advisory Council had been organized to implement. Kerr's autocratic method so long used at the college, *telling* us what economies had to be made, was utterly alien to our traditions. Harvey Townsend, professor of philosophy, rose and moved that the faculty adjourn. The motion was immediately seconded and, not subject to debate, was put to the vote and enthusiastically passed. Kerr was livid. He instructed all budget officers to meet with him immediately in his office. For good or ill, we had crossed our Rubicon; there was now no turning back.

The Advisory Council, at its regular meeting a few days after our act of defiance, voted to collect suggestions from the faculty on how economies could be effected both within the university and the state system as a part of a larger part of a full report to be presented to the chancellor.

Either that night or the next I received a phone call asking me to a secret meeting of a small group to deal with an important matter of faculty concern. I found Stephenson (Steve) Smith of the English Department in charge, with Harold Noble (I believe) of the History Department, Major Roscius Back of the Military Department, in addition to myself, making up the group meeting at Roscius's house. I am not certain about Steve, but the others were members of the Executive Committee of the American Association of University Professors, but not, as far as I know, chosen for that reason.

Each night Steve brought a copy of the chancellor's budget, with all of his proposed cuts marked in red ink, with which we could work. None of us ever asked where he got his copy of the official, proposed budget; I still don't know, but I believe it was Dean Boyer's copy. Steve had to return it to the appropriate office by 8:00 A.M. Our group spent some four to five hours of intensive work for as many nights, drew up a report over our signatures to assume responsibility, and Steve handed the report to Dean Boyer for the Advisory Council.

The full report of the Advisory Council was read by Dean Boyer at a special faculty meeting called to receive the report the afternoon of April 10, 1933. I remember vividly recognizing with much pleasure that our report, improved by a few cosmetic changes, composed a significant part of the full report. The faculty approved the report and instructed the council to forward it to the chancellor. With this action we demonstrated firmly to Chancellor Kerr that we intended to continue our long-established prerogative of participating in the administration of the university.

Early in his administration I had my only personal contact with the chancellor, an appointment at my request. It was businesslike and I got what I wanted. I explained to him that the university had one large and several small ethnological collections of very good quality which had been donated over the years by friends of the university. These collections, because I taught anthropology, simply drifted into my care as they came to light, sometimes from closets, where they had been casually stored when accepted, but often neglected afterwards. I pointed out to him that, in addition to the inherent quality of the collections, there was one very important consideration, the relationship of the university to the public, an institutional tie that I knew Kerr valued highly, and rightly so, but one that the university administration ignored. I assured him that I was very glad to have the responsibility for the collections, but I lacked the authority to carry out the appropriate duties, something I should have.

He listened attentively, then asked, ''What do you have in mind, Professor?''

''I believe, Chancellor, the situation could be adequately taken care of by giving me an official title indicating I had the necessary authority.''

''Do you have a suggestion?''

''Yes, sir; I propose the title, 'Curator of Ethnological Collections.' ''

''I see no problem with that, Professor, but I must make it clear that with the present budget stringency there cannot be any increase in salary or reduction in teaching load.''

''I understand the conditions, Chancellor; they are acceptable.''

''In that case I shall process your appointment. Thank you for coming in.''

''Thank you, sir.''

I shortly had my promised appointment as Curator of Ethnological Collections with the appropriate budgetary caveats, a condition almost religiously adhered to by the university during my long tenure.

This achievement was not just another piece of academic trivia or bric-a-brac; quite the contrary is the case. This appointment by Chancellor Kerr officially recognized my anthropological work in the structure and function of the university. It set in motion a process of development leading in 1935 to the establishment by legislative action of the Oregon State Museum of Anthropology at the University of Oregon.

The latent hostility smoldering in the truce between the faculty and the chancellor was utterly alien to the thoughts of the carefree visitor that warm, Indian summer day of the 1933 annual homecoming at the University of Oregon. Even Bill (William) Tugman, editor of *The Register-Guard*, Eugene's highly respected and widely influential daily paper — Bill was the best friend in the press the university ever had — had acquiesced, if grumpily, in the advice of both his doctor and his publisher-owner, Alton Baker, to take a leisurely voyage down the West Coast on a freighter to "get away from it all." He was in a state of near exhaustion from his successful leadership of the statewide program to defeat the Zorn-McPherson bill to move the university in toto to Corvallis and at the same time trying desperately and successfully to keep the paper afloat in the depths of the Great Depression. Saturday, November 4, found Bill stretched out on a deck chair, his slouched, weather-beaten had resting lightly on his face protecting his eyes from the sun.

Saturday, November 4th, was also the day of the alumni luncheon before the football game with the University of Idaho. Luncheon guests in addition to the loyal alumni included Chancellor Kerr, members of the State Board of Higher Education, the press, and various other notables. The announced speaker for the luncheon was the ambitious young dean of the Law School, Wayne Morse, appointed in 1931 by President Hall in spite of negative recommendations from various members of the Oregon bar whose opinion he had sought. The young dean was an enthusiastic follower of Robert La Follette, the Progressive Party senator from Wisconsin; Wayne had his degree from the University of Wisconsin. At the university he had been but one of the opponents to the Kerr appointment. He was president of the University of Oregon chapter of the American Association of University Professors, the watchdog group devoted to the protection of faculty rights and, by virtue of his position, chairman of the Executive Committee of which I was a member. At the close of the luncheon, the guests, in a well-fed genial mood, settled back to hear the young dean before moving on to the really important event in the afternoon, the football game.

The young dean had his own thoughts and ideas, shared with no one to the best of my knowledge. Wayne rose to speak after a generous introduction, but his stance warned those of us who knew him well that something quite unexpected was about to happen. Mincing no words, Wayne attacked the chancellor; the state board and its president, a distinguished trial lawyer from Portland, for trickery in the appointment of Kerr to the chancellorship; Kerr's lack of qualifications for the position; and so on for his whole speech. It was a bombshell. As he finished, Chancellor Kerr, the state board members, all supportive of Kerr, and members of the press rushed from the hall to meetings and, the latter, to phones to contact their papers. We who had been working slowly but with some success toward a solution saw a new parameter to our problem. Morse had obviously taken over the leadership of the anti-Kerr forces, and the nature of his seizure of the position meant that we now had Morse to defend in addition to riddance eventually of Kerr. Many of the press, especially the Portland dailies, demanded that Morse be fired; others recommended his resignation as dean. We obviously would stand up for our own.

On the freighter slowly moving down the coast toward its next port of call on November 4, 1933, a ship's officer came to the rangy figure asleep under his slouch hat in the warm, afternoon sunshine. "You're William Tugman, aren't you?" he asked as he waked the comfortable Bill.

"Yes, why?"

"We have just received this radiogram for you. Will you accept it?"

"Of course; let me have it. Oh my God, not that." The radiogram read: "All hell's broken loose on the campus. Return at once. Alton Baker."

"What's your next stop, Officer, and when do we arrive?"

"San Francisco, sir, and we arrive about midmorning tomorrow."

"Thank you. I'll be leaving the ship there; no, there's no reply."

"We shall be sorry to have you go, sir."

"Thank you, for that makes it unanimous," grimly replied Bill.

Bill arrived in Eugene early on Monday morning on the Southern Pacific's overnight train, the Cascade, to find out that Alton Baker's radiogram had not in the least overstated the new campus situation.

Wayne's attempted leadership coup was only partially successful. Although we worked to protect him as "one of our own," not all of us were willing to follow unquestioningly in his train. He dismissed Harvey Townsend, one of his staunchest protectors when possible, from the Executive Committee of the A.A.U.P. for "undercutting" him, when Harve's only offense was to give information over the phone when requested by the A.A.U.P. investigator, a professor of philosophy at the University of California at Berkeley, because he felt that Wayne was so emotional he could not get reliable information; and he replaced me by a phone call, and the only reason he gave was that they needed new blood on the committee. I suppose I acquired guilt by association as a close friend and tenant of Harve's. Wayne never wanted comrades, only followers in his wars.

As a participant in the events I was convinced, and all my subsequent experience confirms that belief, that Wayne's action led to traumatic results for both the university and the sciences on campus since they were woven into the fabric of the university's life patterns. The old sense of community so reassuring to Cecilia and me when we arrived in 1929 now began to disintegrate; it was the beginning of factionalism, faculty group against faculty group, faculty against administration. Coming home to lunch one day in a very blue mood, I expressed my fears to Cecilia. Cecilia, always perceptive, closed our conversation with this wise remark: "I suppose this is Kerr's legacy to the university."

The American Association of University Professors came in 1933 in response to our request and, after extensive hearings, presented its report to the board in a private session. To not disturb further the tense campus atmosphere and besmirch the public image of the board and the chancellor, the A.A.U.P. postponed publication of its report to give the board time to correct the problems. When, in 1935, the board had failed to keep its agreement, the A.A.U.P. published its report.

Dean Boyer was appointed acting president in 1933 and president in 1934. Dean Gilbert had adamantly refused to be considered for the post, but Morse, quite characteristically insisting that he was not a candidate, made it clear that he would not interfere if any of his friends pushed his candidacy. Morse had, however, so antagonized influential opinion throughout the state and even among many faculty on the campus by the violence of his attempted coup that he could never have been given serious consideration.

Morse became a bitter opponent of President Boyer, using his position as chairman of the faculty Advisory Council to which he had been elected. How well I remember one very tense faculty meeting in which Morse launched such a vitriolic attack on Boyer that he felt it necessary to turn the chair over pro tem while Boyer took the floor to answer Morse. I seem to recall that the attitude of the faculty that afternoon was that Morse had overstepped the bounds of common courtesy. Morse criticized the budget submitted to the Advisory Council for their ''advisory'' opinions. He took the position, without any justification in custom or faculty legislation, that the Advisory Council should prepare the final budget.

I knew Wayne intimately during his years at the university and followed his subsequent career, presiding over a large meeting at the University of Oregon at which he spoke as ''your junior senator from Oregon''; and years later, I benefited from his knowledge of how to get through a piece of legislation to appropriate money to salvage petroglyphs from being inundated by the rising waters of The Dallas Dam. I have always thought Wayne was happiest in the opposition; he certainly was at the University of Oregon.

I remember a meeting one night of some genial, fellow faculty members, when Bill Tugman, our lone nonfaculty member, joined us thirty minutes late and in an unusually somber mood. After taking a comfortable seat and being supplied with appropriate refreshments, he explained his late arrival; he had just dropped off the dean at his law school office, having brought him from a joint meeting. In the half-hour discussion in Bill's car, Morse had said that he and Jim Gilbert were going to break Boyer. I have been told that there is correspondence to this effect, but I have not seen it nor do I know where it might be. I think they succeeded in their objective.

Gilbert, in contrast to Morse, always played behind the scenes. I never knew him to be in the front rank on any issue. At a dinner one night at the Sheldons with the Warren Smiths, W. D. and I had joined our host in his study for a brief talk before ''joining the ladies.'' His anchoritic study had walls lined with books and a few etchings. He was at his desk, chair tilted back, feet on his desk as we chatted about this and that, when W. D. finally asked him, "Why does Gilbert hate Boyer so much?"

"That's easy," said the dean. "Boyer's an aristocrat and Gilbert's a peasant."

Bang! And bull's-eye!

There was a network of old close friends and relatives in the university community to which the Gilberts belonged and whose mutual support in a personal cause could be counted on. Gilbert, as dean, always administered his school as a personal fief where "favors went by kissing."

Both Townsend and I had staunchly defended Wayne before A.A.U.P. investigators, but it was after one such session that Morse dispensed with our services — perhaps because of our defense of him; who knows? At any rate we continued to be used individually from time to time as counselors to the university administration. We both worked for the expansion and validation of faculty rights to be administered through the Advisory Council, but strictly in its advisory capacity to the president, any president. As president of the University of Oregon chapter of Sigma Xi, the national Science Research Society, I was involved in the continuing effort at first just to maintain the little science left on the campus; later we would work for the return of science. Oregon State College had only a council rather than a full chapter of the society and, following the transfer of science, tried to get the chapter moved to Corvallis. Such a move would have been a further disaster for the university. The Medical School was an integral part of the university, and the Sigma Xi members on that faculty belonged to the university chapter. None of them had any desire to be counted for any reason in the faculty of the "agricultural college." Professor Stafford held the nominal position of dean of science on the university campus — "straw boss," he always called it — and in that position was the main correspondent with the national office on the matter of the location of the chapter. He and I worked together with the Medical School faculty and the national office and were successful. At a later date the university chapter asked me to appear before a meeting of the national council to seek its support for the return of full work in science to the university; of course, I did. I was on leave at the time on a Guggenheim Foundation fellowship, working at the University of Pennsylvania museum in the fall of 1940. This activity in support of science at the university was an important bond strengthening the personal relations between the scientists and myself as well as between our two fields.

In the Sociology Department, too, my 1932 year was bad for me. My department head, Dr. Parsons, for whatever reason, decided that he could get money to raise the salary of a part-time unmarried woman teacher by forcing me to accept a much larger salary cut than the faculty as a whole had to take on the excuse that I had the smallest teaching load and, therefore, the highest per-student-hour cost. How he came to this absurd conclusion I could only guess. I was sure he was wrong, but after one brief conference I knew he meant to maintain his position. I went to the registrar's office, got the class enrollment for each member of the department, then went to the business office to get the salary for each one (public document information), and used the university's method of computing student-hour cost. I prepared a full report with comparative figures for each member, complete with effective graphs, and gave a copy with an appropriate covering letter to Dr. Parsons and another copy to Dean Gilbert, informing Parsons of the fact. The report, as I knew it would, showed quite the opposite to be true from what Parsons had insisted. I did not have to take the extra cut. The dean's daughter, one of my brightest students, told me some years later that her father had commented on the affair at dinner the night he received my statement and said that my report had convinced him that Parsons was wrong.

I also had the promise of Parsons to recommend me for indefinite tenure in the department's budget in the spring of 1933. I came in later in the summer from a field trip and asked him about the action on his recommendation. "By God, I forgot that, Cressman," was his reply. As a result, the next year, the year I was given tenure, the state board terminated its program of automatically joining with the Carnegie teachers' annuity program for new appointees. As a result of Parsons's duplicity or "forgetting," when I retired my first monthly retirement check, including Cecilia's portion, from the State of Oregon for July 1963, after service as a full professor from 1929, was a munificent $170.28!

The year 1933 into 1934 was the low point in the long curve of my academic career. It should, on the contrary, have been a year of promise and hope, for the appointment of Dean Boyer to the presidency indicated that the faculty was winning the struggle against the board and Chancellor Kerr by quiet pressure through the A.A.U.P. But the unfortunate spin-off from the main issue, the power struggle led by Morse against Boyer, augured ill for our desired larger aims. There was even talk by a dissident group of Morse adherents to boycott the inauguration ceremony of President Boyer, but it fortunately never got beyond the talk stage and the ill-will it provoked.

I began to look around for another position to escape the turmoil, but the economy was in such a shambles that there were no positions open. If one were lucky enough to have a position, no matter how bad, just so it provided basic economic support, it was the better part of wisdom to swallow a lot of unpleasantness and keep it so long as no compromise of moral values was involved. As I have reflected carefully on my academic experience, I am convinced that President Boyer, of the seven presidents and four acting-presidents I served under, measured up best in his office in the qualities to be expected of the president of a university. I think my developing interest in my new field, archaeology, and the intellectual commitment it required provided me an escape hatch to avoid the psychological trauma suffered by less fortunate faculty members exposed in one way or another in the campus turmoil.

Writing up my petroglyph report, with the help of a number of students hired under student work-relief programs, took up much of my time and attention. Further information on a rich area of petroglyphs, unknown to us in 1932, between the Guano and Warner valleys came in from a government trapper at Adel, Merle Jacobs, who offered to guide us to them. Merle highlighted the summer of 1933 by guiding Joel Berreman, a graduate student in the Sociology Department doing his master's research, "Tribal Distribution in Oregon," under my direction, and me to the new area. Our short survey had very important results; it showed that we had to return to that area to complete my petroglyph study. The new information suggested aspects of areal relations with the American Southwest and occupation of the petroglyph area through a very long period of time, ideas theoretically much in our minds at the time, but until then lacking substantial field support.

The chairmanship of two important committees, extending from the latter part of 1933 through 1934, required much time, but were valuable to me for the experience in studying and planning programs in the total context of the university's function. The dean of the

Graduate School, Professor George W. Rebec, set up the first committee with a very general charge "to recommend action to improve the graduate program at the university." Our committee recommended an entirely new program, the establishment of a terminal master's designed for public school teachers, with appropriate administrative organization.

The other committee, appointed by President Boyer, was charged to report its recommendation to the faculty on whether "to require or not require R.O.T.C. for undergraduate males." It was required at that time. The partisan feeling on this issue was so strong among both faculty and students that it seemed wise to me, and my committee agreed, to safeguard our record by having my departmental secretary take verbatim notes on all hearings or witnesses and having the subsequent reports available to any responsible inquirer, but only within the departmental office. Our precaution was indeed very wise, as we discovered during our deliberations. We recommended continuation of the present requirement, but with many loopholes available to a responsible student who could present his claim to a special faculty committee. Actually, the committee's action made the requirement practically optional.

The reports of both committees were accepted by faculty action.

In spite of the time these committees required from my research program, the assignment provided valuable experience in familiarizing me with administrative responsibilities and faculty response in the larger context of total university aims, and I appreciated the respect I gained from my colleagues for demonstrating leadership ability and management skills. I would find the experience useful in the days ahead.

Just as my developing archaeological program in close association with my student assistants and one or two faculty members provided a world apart from the academic chaos, my summer field trips, I am sure (as I told Cecilia much later), shielded me from the psychological trauma affecting so many of the faculty by offering a sanctuary of constructive, exploratory work. As we studied our 1932 data, patterns of designs and their areal distributions were beginning to emerge. Exciting suggestions of possible Southwest connections came from designs found in the brief survey of 1933 in the region between Warner and Guano valleys together with positive evidence of a great expanse of time represented by the different degrees of weathering of superimposed petroglyph designs. And that daring thought Howard and I hesitantly shared that morning at Blitzen about the possibility of our eastern Oregon area having shared in the southward migration of the ancient ones, "a little cloud out of the sea, like a man's hand," became much larger as we learned that winter to control much more information from archaeology, geology, paleontology, and climatology. We knew we must go next and soon to the Guano Valley. There we hoped to sharpen and clarify the nature and meaning of the cloud. We started to make our plans, but wondered how we could support the undertaking.

One of my students, hearing of our planned trip, came to tell me he had a relative, a great-uncle or something like that, Joe Shirk, who had been born in Catlow Valley, had spent all his life there as a cowboy, knew the country like his hand, and was now living as the manager of the California and Oregon Power Company ranch at Modoc Point on the east side of Klamath Lake. He was sure his uncle(?) would be glad to see us and help in any way he could.

"That's the best piece of news I've had. Will you please ask him if he will see us, you and me, and if so we'll drive over."

"Sure, I'll be glad to see you and the professor," he phoned back. "Come over with your bedding rolls and stay in a bunkhouse, but have your meals in the house with us. We'll have a good time."

That, too, was a night for stories! Joe's father had made three drives of cattle from Texas over the Chisolm Trail, the third for himself to start his own ranch in Catlow Valley at Home Creek.

At an appropriate point I asked, "Are there any caves in Catlow Valley or Guano?"

"Yes, there are some big ones in Catlow, but I don't remember much in Guano. There's one big one in particular south of the road crossing over to Fields, and then there are some smaller ones."

"Did you ever dig in any of them?" I asked.

"Yes, I dug in the big one. There was where it was thought the highwayman who held up the stage and got away with the gold coins stashed the loot."

"Did you find any coins? And how much did you dig?"

"Didn't find a darn one, and I dug three holes, each nine feet deep."

"That was a lot of digging, and to find nothing. Did you find any Indian things, like arrowpoints or basketry?"

"I sure did. You name it: chipped stones, good arrowpoints, bones, bits of baskets, pieces of arrows, and a couple of pieces of pottery."

"That's the kind of stuff we're interested in. Is there much of the cave left?"

"I'm sure there is; people don't dig for that Indian stuff. They pick it up if they see it, but now not many people go into that country."

In addition to this exciting information, he told us that his sister and her husband, the Spauldings, now lived on the Guano Valley ranch, his father's second ranch—he owned three when he retired—and would be glad to see us and probably be happy to feed us cheaply if our party was not too large. What an unexpected break this night had turned out to be! Fortunately, I did not know our host's reputation that night. Some years later I heard a man say, "That Shirk is the biggest damn liar east of the Cascades." There was, however, enough truth in what he told us to send us down an immensely rewarding road.

Serious planning now required our attention. Berreman, who had accompanied me on the 1933 survey, was a graduate student at Stanford University in the Department of Sociology, but still hoping to complete his Ph.D. degree in anthropology by linking courses at California. He found he could get some money by way of a grant to a fellow department member, who arranged to have it put at Joel's disposal providing we took his twelve-year-old son along for the experience. I had a small amount left from my petroglyph grant, and I was able to get a small grant from the University Research Council. To provide transportation we had my car and a Model-A Ford pickup I begged without cost from the Ford agency in Eugene. Tents and surveying equipment I scrounged from the Geology Department. The Spauldings had graciously invited us to pitch our tents near the house and offered to furnish us meals with the family at a very modest price. At dusk, July 29, 1934, our two-car caravan pulled up to the Spaulding ranch house just as they were finishing dinner, for they had expected us much earlier. A hot, full dinner was soon ready for us, and so started one of the most memorable months of my field experiences.

Our small party, in addition to Berreman and myself, consisted of four volunteers: Howard Stafford; Roscius Back, my close friend from

A participant in the "Trail to Rail" parade in Eugene, Oregon, 1934, as a courtesy repayment for loan of the truck by the Ford agency. Clockwise from Gem, on running board: Howard Stafford, Fred Hoffstead, Carl Reynolds, and I.

the Military Department interested in mapping; Fred Hoffstead, a geology student who had worked on my project on campus; and Carl Reynolds, a nice lad of twelve, the son of the Stanford staff member who made the grant money available to Berreman. No one received a cent of compensation, only food and shelter; and I shared the same conditions. Direct and indirect costs as a feature of research grants were far in the future.

Our very happy, successful party returned to the campus on August 29, 1934. A day or two after my return, I was walking to my office when a colleague caught up with me and, as we walked together, asked me to serve on the Honors Council for the 1934–35 academic year. I said that I would be honored to serve, but would first have to ask my department head's permission before giving a final answer. Since I was going to the department then, I promised a quick reply.

I found Dr. Parsons in his office and, after our customary exchange of civilities, told him of my invitation to serve on the Honors Council and requested permission to accept the invitation. He complimented me and told me I should accept the appointment. Then, to my complete surprise, he asked, "Cressman, are you still interested in your department of ethnology? [He meant anthropology.] I can't do anything for you without having _____ [mentioning his name] on my back for taking something away from him and giving it to you, something he will probably do with this Honors Council business. Then, too, your work in anthropology has progressed beyond my capacity to direct it. If you are still interested, I'll recommend it to Dean Gilbert.''

I was momentarily speechless, for I had never heard or even thought such a thought, and this question, ''Are you still interested . . . ?'' threw me. Even though I had never before thought of it, I was not one to let this golden opportunity escape my grasp. Keeping as poker-faced as possible, allowing only my appreciation to show, I assured him of my strong continuing interest. I thanked him warmly and honestly.

''In that case I'll recommend it to the dean, Cressman.''

''Thank you very much, Dr. Parsons.''

I hurried home to share my incredibly good news with Cecilia. Skeptical about the man's integrity, she rejoiced with me, but warned me to be sure I had the plum before I risked my happiness. When after a month nothing had happened, I began to fear Cecilia's skepticism was going to be warranted and went to Parsons to ask about the status of the proposal. He had not yet taken the matter up with the dean, but would in a day or two. I shortly had his assurance that Dean Gilbert had accepted his recommendation and would be in touch with me.

Dean Gilbert next told me to present the proposal with supporting documentary data to the social science faculty on a certain date. The proposal was accepted after a brief discussion, including a very candid expression of opinion by a member of the History Department that he was in favor of the proposal, but opposed to giving me any new courses because there was only so much money and any money given to me would be money taken from him. It didn't bother him that he was assuming the dean's responsibility, budget, which was certainly not his. The dean told me to prepare a budget for the academic year 1935–36 and a proposed first-year curriculum.

That different academic situation I knew after my 1932 field trip to be necessary, for the course I saw my professional life taking was now completely and unexpectedly at hand; now I had the authority and the responsibility for planning my program with the intellectual freedom and personal and professional responsibility for its achievement. My future now was my own responsibility, one I accepted gladly but not lightly.

The year 1934 was crucial in my personal and professional life: it was then that I first tentatively formulated my hypothesis that the eastern Oregon country held an important part of the record of the prehistory of the Far West. A lifelong work of hypothesis verification by field and laboratory activity developed, a program of problem-oriented archaeology, the first in the Far West.

In the report on the Guano Valley region I wrote:

> The discovery of artifact bearing caves, which give prom-
> ise of the stratification of culture . . . was reward in itself
> sufficient to compensate the expedition. This discovery has
> pushed the problem ahead to the point where we may look
> forward with some confidence to answers to many of the
> questions raised by the survey concerning the significance of
> the culture, its relationship to those of the surrounding
> areas, and the time at which the various developments in
> the culture took place.
>
> The best hope, therefore, of finally solving the general
> problems of this area, the relationship of the culture to that
> of the surrounding areas, and the effect of the climactic
> changes upon it, seems to lie in the correlated study, by
> archaeological and climatological methods, of the human
> habitats, the historic and paleoclimates, and the evidence of
> the clay varves and the fossil pollen.[16]

The establishment of a Department of Anthropology with me its head gave my work a fully recognized status in the university program. I would have to face some envious colleagues, an annoying situation I would rather not have had to deal with, but it was not new in my experience. A department at Oregon brought the university into line, at least organizationally, with Washington and California in the Pacific coast states and New Mexico and Arizona in the Southwest. To join this group was not only an honor but also a risk; I lacked the "imprimatur" of the Ph.D. degree in anthropology.

It took me some time to avoid having a sense of temerity in participating in strictly anthropological meetings. Because of strictures on travel and for great distances, most of the meetings available to me were in western states, where I was already known to a certain extent and where I found a warm welcome. I was already aware of the tendency of the "eastern establishment" to rely heavily on the status of the promoter of a theory or idea, often to the extent of ignoring the content of the idea expressed. Some of my discoveries were already impinging perilously close to questioning the validity of some of the "accepted" theories in my field held tenaciously by the academic fraternity in the East, and the East had many more anthropologists than did the West. Since my Guano Valley report was my first to present, even in a rather nascent form, my hypothesis and plans for verification, I looked forward with some anxiety for any review in a professional journal. My anxiety was relieved when I read the review in *American Anthropologist* by Florence Hawley, a well-known archaeologist at the University of New Mexico, who wrote:

> Dr. Cressman and his associates have put out a paper which makes the fashionable attitude of scathing criticism impossible. Caution and lack of dogmatism are everywhere evident. . . .
>
> In a period when poor and inadequate photographs and lack of caution and of outside consultants on the technical aspects of questions touching sciences outside one's own field have damned the publications of work which otherwise carried some merit, the authors of this monograph can be congratulated on their carefully selected illustrations and on their perspicacity in quoting the opinions of the numerous experts who have examined their artifacts, basketry, and fossilized wood, and have commented on the geology, tree rings, and climatology which outline the Guano Valley problems. Future aid from various studies and from identification of fossil pollen is planned. . . . If this type of well rounded work can come from a region where the problems are difficult and cultural material scanty, workers in richer fields will have to look to their laurels if they would compete.[17]

Dr. Hawley's generous review gave me much-needed support, for it was clearly judging my work strictly on its merits. It also set a high level for our future work to strive for.

Our Guano Valley Survey produced extremely significant results both in scientific data and the knowledge it gave me of the country and the resulting insight into the problems of fielding an archaeological party in this arid, sparsely settled land with Burns, the nearest town, a hundred miles distant over a dirt and gravel road. It was the Spauldings' limitless kindness and desire to help with no expectation of reward that was the basis of our party's success that summer of 1934.

Zete (Mr. Spaulding) provided saddle horses for Joel and me to cover many miles of rugged country otherwise inaccessible to us. Mine was a magnificent animal named Traveler, a wonderfully appropriate name, and I used Joe Shirk's work saddle with its heavy tapaderos, so heavy I could barely throw it on. Another time he provided three saddle horses and a skittish, young packhorse and guided us to the top of Lone Grave Butte so Roscius and I could establish necessary controls for his survey of the west shoreline area of Guano Lake, or Valley. He took Joel and me in our little pickup on a two-day trip to Big Spring,[18] a name it hardly deserved in 1934, although in that arid period any water hole might seem *big*. The spring was actually a small, remnant body of water approximately ten by five feet and perhaps two feet deep drawing on some aquifer that maintained it at the level we saw. On the north side was an unsavory-looking mound two to three feet high, blackened with ash and charred pieces of sagebrush sticks and the carcasses of dead rattlesnakes, occupants of the den burned out by the driver of a tank truck who hauled water from four o'clock in the afternoon to four in the morning for several thousand head of sheep summering in the rough country to the south on the Dufferino(?) ranch.

Zete told us how he and other buckeroos riding for wild horses twenty-one years earlier used to dive into what was then a lake from the bank, now appearing as the top of a shoreline some eight or more feet above the present floor, mute evidence of the affect of the period of arid years.

On our approach to Big Spring, we drove over several smaller, dry beds, probably originally a single large body of water. In the exposed face of one butte were beds of both black and red obsidian from which chunks had eroded to the base and scattered the length of the now-dry bed. We picked up a good number of artifacts from these exposures,[19] some of which, after a great deal more work had been done in areas north and south, were recognized as having a considerable antiquity. Oddly enough, we found no artifacts at Big Spring itself, perhaps an indication that when the Indians were hunting along the areas close to the north, Big Spring occupied the whole basin, which would account for the name.

On our return we stopped at South Corral—water holes in 1934 were twenty-five to thirty miles apart—where we had lunch, with

Zete cooking the meat over an open fire, buckaroo fashion.[20] It provided a striking example of the effect of a common experience, such as lack of water, on living creatures often hostile to one another. It was a "sanctuary" where mingled, along the waterline and a short distance back, range cattle, wild horses and domestic stock that had turned wild, and even a coyote sniffing the ground for food as it moved among the others. Our arrival caused little concern, for apparently we were accepted like all the others, something in need of water. When we left; though, the band of wild horses took off to the safety of their range, tails and manes flying as they galloped, their stallion driving them from behind through the rock-strewn, sage-covered landscape. That was a real sight, something worth seeing.

The Spauldings' most important single act of assistance was to take us to Catlow Valley to look for the caves Joe had said were there; and the Spauldings remembered them. They made a three-day picnic of the trip, camping at Three-Mile Creek where, as it turned out, my party would camp in 1937 and 1938. We made camp the first day. The next morning we drove the fifteen miles to Joe's cave, stopping at the base of the slope. As Zete and I climbed the terraces Howard and I had looked at through my field glasses that morning in 1932 from Blitzen, he asked me, "How many holes did Joe say he dug and how deep?"

"Three holes, each nine feet deep," I replied.

"That means he dug one hole three feet deep," said his knowledgeable brother-in-law.

That was exactly what we found. And in defense of Joe's reporting, I am delighted to say that we saw in the face of the hole, after gently cleaning it, the same kinds of artifacts he reported having found. Here was our dry cave, probably with stratified fill.

We stopped at Roaring Springs on our way home, fifteen miles north of our camp, where a cave above a thicket of fire nettles could be seen. It was deep and narrow, very dry, and contained artifacts.

Through the generous help of these kind people, we now had real knowledge of the dry caves, the very thing we had most hoped to find.

I knew I would now try to find out what stories the contents of those caves would tell us; but my experience that month in becoming acquainted with the landscape and its problems alerted me to the tremendous problem of logistics that would be involved to set up and maintain a field camp in the Catlow Valley, with the nearest source of supplies and help in case of disaster at Burns, a hundred miles away. I did not know how I would solve the problem when the time came, but I had faith that I would. My future was involved in the program of reading the stories of those caves. I never doubted I would learn to do just that.

Two harbingers of future events enriched our anthropological calendar in 1934. Two weeks after our return from the Guano Valley Survey, Phil Brogan of *The Bend Bulletin* called me to report that a potentially important discovery had been made by a fieldman of the U.S. Corps of Engineers that should be examined by scientists; would we please come? Indian artifacts, stone knives, had been found apparently under volcanic ash from the eruption that had formed Crater Lake. If the claimed relationship of the knives and the ash reported by the fieldman could be verified, it would be of extraordinary importance for both archaeology and geology. Something of the importance attributed to the find is shown by the sequence of response: discovery by John F. Isackson of September 13, 1934; turned over to the project engineer, Mr. C. A. Fisher, on September 14, who at once phoned Brogan: Phil phoned me immediately, bringing W. D. Smith and me to the site September 15, where we were joined, in addition to the men just mentioned, by Mr. A. C. Spenser of the U.S. Geological Survey, geologist in charge of the Deschutes Project Survey.

All evidence from examination of the site by our party pointed to the very strong possibility that Isackson's report was valid and showed the presence of humans at the place well before the deposition of the volcanic ash, probably in the late terminal glacial stage; geological opinion at the time, however, held that the terminal glaciation was about 20,000 to 25,000 years ago. The artifacts (scrapers) were well below the pumice and covered by what was thought to be glacial outwash. If the chronology of the geologists was correct and the position of the knives was valid, we were facing a shockingly new fact. W. D. and I returned that night to Eugene with a lot of new possibilities swirling in our minds.

I agreed to return the following summer to excavate at the place of the discovery to try to verify the report by finding, if possible, undisturbed artifacts in place (in situ) and to turn what was now an exciting but unproven possibility into a historical event. The project engineer promised to fence and protect the site for our 1935 excavation.

This accidental discovery by a workman, like so many in archaeology and paleontology, if verified, had far-reaching implications for both geology and archaeology; their interlocking relationship was clear. That incredibly beautiful lake I had gazed upon in awed silence that afternoon after finishing my Gold Hill work was now inexorably weaving its web of mystery to involve me in its violent history. The cloud I saw now was much larger than a man's hand.

A second important incident was a by-product of the 1933 planning by the U.S. Corps of Engineers for the Bonneville Dam, the first in the series of great hydroelectric dams planned and now built on the Columbia River and its tributaries. Interested persons, I among them, were finally successful in persuading the Smithsonian Institution to send a staff member, Dr. Herbert W. Krieger, to carry out salvage operations—some fifteen years before the River Basin Surveys and subsequent salvage programs were initiated on a national scale after World War II by the Federal government.

My interest in pushing this project took me to the corps' office in Portland, where we established a warm working relationship that was to help me with my work until I retired. I was given a set of large-scale maps of the Columbia River from its confluence with the Snake River to the sea. I had a graduate student record on these maps every site, occupied and unoccupied, mentioned by Captain Meriwether Lewis in his journal of the famous 1805–6 expedition from St. Louis to the Pacific Ocean and return. I wrote the Smithsonian that I would be glad to make these maps available to Dr. Krieger, asking in return that, since the University of Oregon offered the only regular work in anthropology, he hire student help from the university in case he planned to use such.

My next information was from a news item in the Portland newspaper, *The Oregonian*, that Dr. Krieger had arrived, hired one or more students from Oregon State College, and was planning to start excavation immediately. To say I was upset would be a gross understatement. I was trying to get our Guano Valley party ready to leave, and with that plus campus duties, I perhaps overreacted somewhat excessively. I thought my offer generous, and it would save Krieger a lot of time that could be used in actual excavation. My letter to the appropriate Smithsonian official was very explicit in what I thought of the bureaucracy, dependent on taxpayers for support, but thoughtlessly acting in a way that seemed calculated to ignore that very important relationship.

While in the field in the isolated Guano Valley I received two telegrams, each fortunately having been held at the Adel Village post office for about a week, then sent out with the first person to come through by car or on horseback. To have delivered them by Western Union messenger would have cost me twenty-five dollars each time. There was no phone, and it was the custom of the country to do exactly what the postmaster at Adel had done — he probably knew the contents and made a sound decision. Both telegrams were addressed from Krieger to me in Eugene, but forwarded to Adel, saying he wanted to come to Eugene and clear up the difficult situation with me. I wrote him a note telling him when we would return and inviting him to Eugene. The "flap" was easily resolved to everybody's satisfaction. A couple of weeks in the desert helps clear one's mind. A letter from the Smithsonian soon arrived, promising to deposit with the State of Oregon one specimen of any artifacts of which there were more than one and, in the case of important artifacts, a cast of those represented by only one specimen.

That promise was fine, but this question was open: where, to what organization, would these specimens go when sent to the "state"? It was important for our developing program in anthropology, the only one in the state, that we be the recipients. I already had the title Curator of Ethnological Collections given by Chancellor Kerr. In the fall of 1934, I persuaded Dean Gilbert and President Boyer — a little effort was required — that the university should ask the legislature in the 1935 session to designate by official act that the collections at the university should be declared the Oregon State Museum of Anthropology and be the official depository for all future acquisitions. President Boyer shepherded the proposal through the legislature, and in 1935 it passed a bill, signed by the governor, establishing the museum at the university, including an Antiquities Act (Oregon Laws, 1935, ch. 380). The anthropology program under the new department was getting off to a quick and sound start.

When our field party in 1935 rolled out of Eugene to excavate at the Wikiup Damsite and then at Catlow Cave, I had faith that the little cloud would increase in size and bring its life-giving waters to the parched earth. Discoverer that I was, I knew I would accept the challenge of the problems presented as the changing, parched land revealed its riches. The nadir of 1933 was behind me, and I was the stronger for my record of participation. I would never again think of leaving the University of Oregon and the opportunities it offered me for discovery.

Our 1935 field season of four weeks had two objectives: first, to spend a week attempting to verify, if possible, the reported association of artifacts under the volcanic ash deposited by the explosion that made the basin in which Crater Lake formed; then, to use the remaining three weeks to make our exploratory excavation of Catlow Cave to determine the nature and the implications of the deposits for further study. The implications of the reported association at the Wikiup Damsite were profoundly significant for Pacific Northwest prehistory. If it could be verified and dated, it would serve as a "horizon marker" wherever it might be found, since any artifact under it would be earlier and those above it later in time. And what we found at Catlow Cave, together with the nature of the work, would determine to a large extent our program for years ahead.

For transportation, our small party of four,[21] in addition to myself as "Chief-of-Party," had my car, a survivor of the petroglyph survey of 1932, and a used International pickup furnished by the Ford agency in Eugene as a contribution. For tents, I again went to the Geology Department. We carried our own cooking gear, even to the cooks, for we took turns at that chore, where, as may be inferred, the results were highly uneven.

Our work at the Wikiup site failed to answer our question of the possible association,[22] so the potentials of that problem remained ahead of us. Although disappointed with the negative results, we were not discouraged as we moved toward what we felt was certainly a more promising situation at the cave.

For the Catlow Valley work, we turned from outdoor camping to the comparative luxury of the hotel at Blitzen where Howard and I had found refuge from the enveloping desert night in 1932. After a rather hasty rough-and-ready cleaning, mostly removal of dust deposited by the desert winds along with dessicated remains of small rodents, we were, in terms of a field camp, quite luxuriously settled. Although we had to carry water for drinking and cooking from a neighbor's well, we had a roof over our heads in the unlikely case of rain, and the absence of glass in the windows was no hardship.

A watering hole for range cattle had been prepared by a governmental agency downhill from but close to the road to Blitzen to alleviate drought-caused hardship for animals on the open range, a situation vividly recalling similar conditions from the previous summer in the Guano Valley. Two large, heavy, wooden troughs, the source for the name of the place, The Troughs, were kept filled by the flow of water through an underground pipe from a spring at the base of the cliff. Water overflowed from the lower trough through a short pipe into an excavated hole some forty to fifty feet in diameter, providing a depth of probably two and a half feet of water. Cattle drank from the troughs and wallowed in the hole. Some of these animals had come as much as fifteen miles to this hole, the nearest, yet known somehow in animal lore. Here they would drink, lie around, and chew their cuds for about four days, then drift out slowly for two days to find what pasturage they could over a distance of possibly fifteen miles, and again slowly move back to the water hole to repeat the rhythm. (This information on range life came from Spaulding in 1934.)

We used these troughs as a remedy for the lack of water at our hotel in the interest of personal cleanliness, but use of soap was not permitted since that would have spoiled the water for the cattles' use and that had priority. Each morning we filled out canteens for the day with cool water from the upper pipe, and on our return after work we stopped to clean ourselves and engaged in some inevitable horseplay, evidence that my crew continued in good health and spirits. We learned in our first stop at The Troughs that rattlesnakes, too, liked the place because of its coolness and the small rodents there, so each time we stopped to take a quick look-see to make sure of our safety before turning to our particular needs. We were learning to adapt to the needs of our new environment, the makings of a good field party.

While settling in on our first full day at Blitzen, we were very pleased to be welcomed by one of the twelve inhabitants, called by his neighbors "Old Joe Butler," who had strolled over from the little house he occupied alone a short distance north from the store on Blitzen's main and only street.

"I'm Joe," he said. "Heard at the store you fellers were comin' and I dropped over to tell you we are glad to see you."

"Thank you, Joe, we are glad to be here and to meet you," I assured him as we took turns in shaking his hand, twisted with rheumatism and a lifetime of very hard work.

"As soon as we get settled in," I told him, "we'll want to learn a lot about the country, and I suppose you can help us with that. Can you?"

"That's right down my line, and I sure can if I don't have to walk. I can ride in your truck and show you from there. I know this country, but most from horseback, sometimes on foot, 'specially above the lavvy rocks"—Joe never did say "lava," only "lavvy"—"and be glad to help you boys."

After some desultory conversation, he was off with a cheerful "Be seein' you." We did see him and take him with us to point out both details and large aspects of the landscapes, and he gave us excellent instructions on how to follow some of those desert roads to isolated places and caves. Our thanks to you, Old Joe Butler.[23]

Catlow Cave No. 1, as we decided to call our first cave to be excavated in the Catlow Valley, presented us with fresh problems of excavation techniques, mainly because of its size and structure. I had, probably fortunately, been unable to find any prototype in the literature, so we had to devise our own methods of horizontal and vertical controls of our excavations. Roscius and I set up a very simple grid system so that any point could be located by the intersection of two lines or axes. The grid could be laid out by two persons with a good compass and a steel tape or by use of a transit and tape or rod. Further, our method would be equally applicable to a cave or open site. I made a slight change in 1938 and then changed again to the internationally used, scientific metric scale.

Our first couple of days showed that in the time available we could hardly do more than "scratch the surface." Our party, individually and as a group, never doubted that we would be back, even if we didn't know when. So, to have a continuous series of reference points to tie in any future work with our 1935 season, Roscius and a couple of boys ran a level line from a U.S.G.S survey stake about three miles north where the road crossed over to Fields to provide a true elevation, a bench mark, that we established in hard rock in the rear wall of the cave at 4,761.07 feet elevation. The position of the horizontal line across the front from which interior cave measurements started was indicated by a spike driven at each end into solid rock. In our later work after Catlow, we simply assigned an arbitrary value, 100.00 meters elevation, to a selected bench mark and measured all elevations in the excavation from that level to establish comparable data for any artifact or observation. Since there was no topographic map available for our area in 1935, Roscius and the boys found enough iron-pipe stakes with brass caps giving range and township and section lines to enable him to locate our cave precisely on the landscape.

Our much-desired dry cave, with a long sequence of human occupation, preserved both organic and inorganic material in addition to that left by the human occupants: wind-blown debris and dessicated and skeletal remains of large and small animals that had died between periods of human use; feces of animals and occasionally of humans, too, especially in Catlow Cave; remains of materials brought in but never used by the inhabitants; and artifacts — the mute and sometimes touching story of the lives of the men, women, and children whose day-to-day lives in all their humanness ran their courses in this environment — were all mixed in a confused continuum. From this kind of fill the archaeologist has to derive knowledge of the lifeways of the ancient ones.

We quickly discovered that the kind of rock containing the cave markedly affected the character of the fill. In volcanic country many caves are remains of bubbles in the original lava flow, with very hard surrounding walls. Others have been cut by wave action of a lake in initially soft material, such as a now-indurated mudflow down a drainage source. Following the lowering of the lake level, the weathering of the exposed mudflow continues by normal means to drop its contained rocks of different sizes building up the cave fill. Catlow Cave's north end had developed in a mudflow, and the ceiling was rough with rocks of differing sizes weathering out even during the time we worked there, which caused difficult and sometimes dangerous situations. At the south end the exterior wall and part of the roof were hard and smooth, the telltale evidence of wave action. The south-end fill contained much less roof fall, and excavation there in 1937 posed different and less troublesome problems than those in the other end.

Howard Stafford, my mentor in the petroglyph survey in 1932, and Lloyd Ruff, instructor in geology at the University of Oregon, with extensive field experience — the two geologists in our party — carried me beyond my John Day experience in historical geology into the complexities of the structural and dynamic features of Catlow Valley and its bordering ranges, helping me to grasp more fully the dynamics of the natural environment of our particular unit of study, Catlow Valley. Since Catlow was fairly typical of the larger Great Basin—characterized by vast areas of great crustal displacement causing fault basins, which in moist periods of climate held lakes without external drainage—it could be used as a model to understand much of the environmental nature of the basin as a whole.

Simple mechanical problems of digging in dry cave fill make it difficult to keep faces of a trench straight and neat for study. A loose stone exposed in a trench wall may fall out bringing surrounding material with it or an accidental jar of a workman's shovel may do the same. Clear-cut distinctions between strata, we discovered, are difficult to assign in dry cave fill, but we could turn, and did, to the geologists' concept of "bed" and "bedding."

Then there is the dust! But that is the price paid for artifact preservation. I would discover, however, in 1937 and 1938 that Catlow Cave was practically free from dust by comparison with Roaring Springs. After a few days of experience, it was the general opinion of the crew that to be a cave archaeologist one must either be crazy or an unusually committed archaeologist or a little of both. After several years of this work, even with a protective mask, I told Cecilia I thought my lungs and sinuses still carried cave dust, but if one has to have respiratory problems, what better way than ours to get them.

I think the one disappointing aspect of our field camp was the limited and resulting monotony of our mess, or in contemporary idiom, the delivery of food services. We were limited by our stringent budget, the supplies available in the Blitzen general store, and the limited cookery skill possessed by different members of the party who took turns at the task. Breakfast, which I seemed to have taken over, was easy with standard hotcakes, bacon (and perhaps eggs), jam, and coffee. Peanut butter and more peanut butter, cheese, and jam sandwiches supported by oranges, citrus juices, and pickles composed our lunches. Dinners were likely to be more of the same, with a bit of variation based on the cook's skill and imagination for what he could do with the contents of a can. I remember only one complaint, not really a protest but rather a plaintive query, one morning when some of my good hotcakes were not eaten.

"Chief, do we really have to have cold hotcakes for lunch?"

"We can't afford to waste anything because of our budget. I can cut down on the morning issue, but I suggest you just take plenty of jam."

One wonderful Sunday, however, is historic for breaking the monotony of our meals. One of the boys' family and friends came, eight of them, and brought a complete dinner for all. I remember especially a huge, so it seemed, chocolate-covered layer cake, three or four strata high, and decorated — I don't remember if the beautiful creation recognized a birthday; it well could have. Roscius, easily our best problem solver, naturally took charge of the proceedings. Actually, he rather let his imagination carry him off the deep end at one point, but the only harm was to his feelings. Roscius apparently, all the while, had been harboring a secret yearning for some nice, firm Jell-O, but the conditions at Hotel Blitzen were not favorable in the time available, especially after returning from a day of hard, dirty work. So, he decided that we should go the whole way this Sunday and have Jell-O with our dinner.

To cool the concoction from liquid to a gelatinous consistency required all his military engineering skill and imagination. He responded appropriately to the challenge. Since a strong wind was blowing, he could turn on the pump at our next-door well and run a hose into the bathtub, undoubtedly the first time it had held water for a long time. But there was no intention that it should hold water, only provide a cooling medium about the kettle containing the lovely liquid jelly as the water, a constant flow, discharged through an outlet to run down a hole in the floor into the ground, quite possibly the original design. The theory that provided the basis for Roscius's project — quite correct, too, for the usual well — was that as the water level in the well lowered, the water drawn would be cooler and eventually produce the much-desired, firm Jell-O. He constructed a support mechanism to keep the kettle from spilling and to hold it steady in the running water even if the outlet got stopped up. At last all was ready. "Go out and turn on the pump," he commanded one of his onlookers. With creaks and groans the long-unused machinery started to work, soon running smoothly, and the water flowed into the tub, around the kettle and through the outlet, maintaining its level as planned. Roscius, with all the pride of an Edison, graciously acknowledged the plaudits of his onlookers.

Then the boy setting the table came to Roscius to report that there were thirteen people; how could he cut the cake into that many equal parts? "No problem," clipped Roscius. "Bring my slide rule and protractor from my table." He made a couple of manipulations with his slide rule and determined that "each piece should be a weak twenty-eight degrees. Bring the cake and a piece of string." So, after fixing a center point with his two strings, he took the protractor and a knife and shortly had the cutting marks indicated on the cake. Any ordinary cutter could take over from there.

A certain anxiety, generated by repeated inquisitive visits of inspection, had developed over the apparent failure of the liquid Jell-O to reach its desired state of firm but quivering mass with the lowering water temperature as we all expected to happen. Roscius's assumption of the lowering temperature of the water, however, had proved erroneous; our long-unused Blitzen well was not the usual run-of-the-mill well, for its water temperature remained constant. Remembering that we could not afford to waste anything, good fieldmen that we had become, we took cups and glasses and drank the stuff, assuring the crestfallen Roscius, "You can't win them all, even in the field." But, what a day to remember!

We fortunately avoided any physical damage beyond what a Band-Aid with a bit of antisepsis could treat. A severe case of sun-burn taught a lesson: that the sun was extremely dangerous even on an overcast day. The application of three treatments with Unguentine over the body from belt to neck between dinner and midnight gave enough relief that the victim, Fred Voget, could finally sleep and was ready to work the next day, but wearing his shirt.

I had our only experience with the worrisome tick, about which we had been warned. One Sunday morning in the Blitzen store, I found two Basque sheepherders in from their camp on the Steens Mountain relaxing from their herding. One, as he moved about with a partially consumed bottle of beer in one hand, was in a singing mood, although the words were painfully doleful. As he paced back and forth he sang and repeated time and again:

> They cut down the old pine tree and hauled it away to the mill,
> They made a coffin of pine for that sweetheart of mine when they cut down the old pine tree.

At one of his rest stops, I engaged him in conversation and in the course of it asked if there were any ticks still about on the Steens.

"Yes, around the junipers and the aspens," he replied.

"What's a tick look like? I've never seen one," I asked.

"Never seen one!" He looked at me incredulously, then loosened another button on his shirt and began to scratch purposefully in the

1935 field party returning to Hotel Blitzen at end of day. From left to right: Roscius Back, Howard Stafford, Fred Voget, Lloyd Ruff, and I. Time-release photo.

dark, curly mass of chest hair. Triumphantly, with the obviously experienced nails of his thumb and forefinger, he deftly extracted the shiny, small, black specimen. ''Here's one of the little bastards.'' He held it out for my inspection and then expertly crushed, as though from long experience, the tiny creature between his nails. During the next few years I helped dispose of many ticks on myself and other members of my parties, but none stands out with the vivid imagery of my first, my Basque-Blitzen specimen.

A busy last day we spent, first, in a visit to our old friend Catlow Cave to give it a final closing checkup to be sure no equipment was inadvertently left behind, something very easy to do, especially small tools; pick up any carelessly dropped papers and such; and finally break down one end of our trench so that if any stupid sheep—all sheep are stupid as any rancher or herder will tell you—fell into it the animal could get out. Permits to excavate on public lands, as we had, always require that a site be left clean and no danger to livestock.

Then we made a short stop for an exploratory dig at Roaring Springs cave. It was drier then Catlow, held more artifacts in a better state of preservation, and was shockingly more dusty. I knew where our first post-Catlow dig would be.

Cleaning our equipment, packing specimens, and preparing our gear for early morning loading and takeoff, along with a lot of good-natured chatter and banter, took up the rest of the day. After a light breakfast—we would compensate for its lightness in Burns—it was load the vehicles and go across the street to say goodbye to our friends and give our thanks for their hospitality, balanced with the warm and urgent invitation to return, for they had enjoyed having us, and we were ready to roll on our long, 350 miles to Eugene. Happy as we were to be going home, there was a certain sense of melancholy, a feeling that something important had come to an end, and more than one throat had a lump in it as Blitzen, our home for three significant weeks, gradually disappeared in the dust of the lake bed raised by our little caravan. We arrived safely in Eugene, a veteran group, tired but happy and full of stories—many to call our veracity into question—to tell of our days in the desert, a first of its kind.

As our work drew to a close I kept trying to evaluate the real significance of our summer's work. The most important result, as I saw it then and now, too, was not in the artifacts and other specimens, important as they were, but when seen as a whole the summer's work was fundamental in helping me to plan more comprehendingly and thus effectively the organization of my future research.

Our four-week field trip to the Wikiup Damsite and Catlow Cave in 1935 was the land-based equivalent of the shakedown cruise of a ship before it is commissioned and reported ready for service. I learned through the summer's experience most of the conditions and operational procedures I would need for my future archaeological program. These fell into three separate but interrelated categories: the continual refinement of the definition of my problem, the logistical requirements for the work, and the recognition that my scientific program by its very nature would be a cooperative enterprise shared with colleagues from related fields of science.

My basic scientific problem, hypothesis, had grown from that "little cloud like a man's hand" Howard and I saw but dimly that morning at Blitzen in 1932 to the PROBABILITY THAT EASTERN OREGON, THE LAND OF THE NOW-DRY LAKES, WAS ONCE A SEGMENT OF A MIGRATION CORRIDOR OF THE EARLY INDIAN POPULATIONS IN THEIR MOVEMENTS FROM THE

NORTHERN BERING LAND BRIDGE AREA INTO THE AMERI-
CAN SOUTHWEST. By the end of our 1935 field season I was breaking my major problem into smaller components, each a formative
part of the larger mosaic. I saw, too, how new discoveries added new
parameters that opened vistas until then unseen or corrected what I
thought I saw along an old one, which emphasized that my problem-
oriented research had to respond in kind to this dynamic characteristic.

The provision of logistic support for a party of ten for six weeks in
the field in the arid, isolated country of our caves I now appreciated as
posing forbidding obstacles, such that I could not field a party in
1936. Transportation was the most difficult. Eugene to Blitzen
(Three-Mile Creek our future campsite) was 345 miles mostly over dirt
and gravel roads. Burns, our only supply center, was a hundred miles
from camp and would require a pickup truck and two men for once-a-
week replenishment of supplies. Although I had been so far successful in getting a pickup as a contribution to our party, there was no
large truck available, nor with the country in the depth of the Great
Depression did there seem to be any possibility of getting one.

I needed tents, mess gear, a cooler to keep cooked meats for a day
or two, and a full-time cook to provide good meals and avoid taking
men from our digging crew to cook, with very indifferent results.
Inoculation against Rocky Mountain spotted fever (nearly always fatal
then without the shots), tetanus (always a danger in horse country),
and typhoid fever, along with the ever-present danger of rattlesnake
bites, were part of the preventive planning. I held to the tenet drilled
into us in officer training for World War I that it was the responsibility of an officer to see that his men had the best possible mess and
living conditions if one expected maximum performance, and I tried
to do that for my field crews. Before I could field a party of ten to continue research on my problem, I faced a long period of planning,
searching for financial support in a world where it was very scarce, but
I always hoped for good luck.

Cooperation between different fields of knowledge had always
been a cardinal point in my teaching and research, so when I describe
my program as a ''cooperative enterprise'' I am not really introducing
a new element, only placing the proper emphasis on it in this new
context. My introduction to it had occurred at Gold Hill; the Guano
Valley Survey had expanded it. The Wikiup site and Catlow Cave

produced new problems requiring study by scientists from different fields of natural history, prehistory, and other areas in universities and museums, and at appropriate points I would have to request their aid, as I did, and was never disappointed. My search for financial support would take me to eastern foundations, and we thus became acquainted. Further, I would have to involve my collaborators for support in my applications, and the wide-ranging fields from which this help would come gave my work a rather distinctive flavor among archaeologists. Our collaboration I have called ''Our Cooperative Enterprise,'' for the help these people gave, from the simplest ranch hand reporting a site to the internationally known scientists contributing their expertise toward a problem's solution, was basic to my future success.

Aside from the professional cooperation, and even more significant, was Cecilia's continuous and unwavering enthusiasm and support. No matter how lonely her summers when I was in the field, and they were lonely, she never complained at being a ''fieldman's widow.'' She and I made a pact in our hearts and minds that Saturday night in June 1930 when we took up the challenge by the people of Gold Hill, and through all the ensuing years she was a staunchly core figure, absolutely critical to my success, as we stood side by side in Our Cooperative Enterprise.

My return to the campus from our 1935 field trip brought me into a significantly new situation. I had always returned to my office in the Sociology Department with anthropology a minor part of my official responsibility, but that year I returned in my new position as head of the Department of Anthropology to my office in the limited laboratory space I had enjoyed in Condon Hall with the geologists—a result of W. D. Smith's kindness at the time of my Gold Hill work when I needed laboratory space. Even such a small relationship as this carried a sense of continuity of my archaeological work. My change in status, however, carried consequences far beyond that symbolized by the new spatial separation.

My appointment as curator of the Oregon State Museum of Anthropology in 1935 and in 1936 as director of the Museum of Natural History,[24] incorporating the museum of anthropology, required that I report directly to the president's office, for the M.N.H. budget was allocated as a separate account and thus provided me certain freedom of action and its accompanying responsibility.

Now, as head of the Department of Anthropology I was drawn into the administrative structure of the university to face new responsibilities. I had direct contact with my dean instead of through a department head, a very significant advantage even in such seemingly simple matters as applying for student assignments under work-relief programs. That I was at the time a one-man department was of little importance; I attended all meetings of heads of departments, participated fully in all discussions, and like the head of a large department had one vote. I now had the duty and opportunity to develop my new field, as my appointment implied, keeping in mind that my objectives must remain congruent with the educational goals of the university. My breadth of experience in the humanities and social and natural sciences made this objective not only desirable but also pleasurable to attempt to achieve. My change in status had moved me professionally into a new and challenging world, a challenge I accepted enthusiastically.

I now, in addition to the new academic housekeeping for which I was responsible, had to set up a cataloging system for the Oregon State Museum of Anthropology to meet the needs of past and future accessions. After consulting with the museum of anthropology at the University of California at Berkeley I adopted in the main that system. I secured students from a student relief project to aid in the processing of our summer materials from Catlow. During the winter of 1936 I began to make plans for my next trip to Catlow Valley, and my overriding problem was to secure nonuniversity financial support. The university would provide a small grant, but not nearly enough. It is important to remember all field-party members were volunteers, serving without wages and paying a mess fee for their board. We had never heard of the forty-hour work week and the eight-hour day. I received no salary. To make the summer work more attractive and give it an educational emphasis I succeeded in having the summer fieldwork incorporated in the Summer Session curriculum. This obligated the student to pay the Summer Session fee for the number of academic credits granted. When the university adopted this practice and received the students' fees for work done under my direction, I felt that I deserved an appropriate salary for my contribution. I succeeded in getting, if I remember correctly, a three-quarters of full-time salary. The support for research in the 1930s was minuscule when compared with the generous sources today, but we did fine work; we had a commitment to the project and did not see it as often appears to be the case today as a source of summer income under rather pleasant conditions.

I applied to two eastern sources for research grants, a few hundred dollars each. My first application was to the Carnegie Institution of Washington, D.C., which, under the presidency of the distinguished paleontologist, Dr. John C. Merriam, had become the premier source of research support in science and science-related fields. Remember, this was before the National Science Foundation was established by the Federal government. My other application went to the American Philosophical Society in Philadelphia. I had been told by Harvey Townsend that this society made small grants.

I received a letter saying that Dr. Merriam was interested in discussing my application further and would be in Florence, Oregon, the very small, coastal town west of Eugene at the mouth of the Siuslaw River, on his annual visitation of projects funded by the Carnegie Institution. He would be glad to meet with me at the Florence Hotel on a certain date if that were convenient for me. Our family, including Cecilia's sister from England, had arranged to spend our vacation at Siltcoos Lake, a few miles from Florence, and at the time Dr. Merriam set for our meeting. The driver of his and Mrs. Merriam's Packard sedan was also a kind of executive secretary, a general factotum. Mrs. Merriam always accompanied her husband.

I met Dr. Merriam, as arranged, in the weather-beaten hotel, Florence's one and only, after dinner. We had a very pleasant conference exploring my program, its prospects, my need for support, and he made a clear expression of interest and a promise of modest support. He was impressed with the possibilities my program suggested for development. Our conference closed with warm inquiries about my family and our vacation and well-wishes. Here in this drab hotel in this brief conference without a lot of paper work began perhaps the most important personal-professional relationship of all my later years. Our association continued until his death in 1945, ten years of personal association.

My application to the American Philosophical Society was also favorably acted upon, providing a small grant of a few hundred dollars for the 1937 field season. The following anecdote is worth repeating for the benefit of those who fume, as I have done, at the nature of a contemporary application for funds.

Shortly after my return from our 1935 field season in Catlow Valley, Cecilia and I were invited to dinner by the Yocoms, a husband and wife team from the Biology Department, to meet some summer guests from the East, a professor of history at the University of Pennsylvania and his wife. The ladies were sisters. I remember a very pleasant evening with dinner on their shaded patio and good conversation, then a regretful good-night since we thought in all likelihood we should not again see these gracious visitors from the East. The Yocoms later told us this interesting story. Their guest that night, the professor of history, was a member of the American Philosophical Society and, as it later turned out, a member of the committee on grants-in-aid the year I applied, the late spring of 1937. He was examining applications for the committee, going through an ordered pile, when he picked up one from a man named Cressman at the University of Oregon. The coincidence of name and place sparked somehow a sense of something familiar about the application. Then he recalled the pleasant evening in Eugene that August of 1935. Picking up the phone, he called the Yocoms to inquire if, perhaps, this Cressman of the application was the young man they had met with his wife that pleasant evening of the previous summer, and, if so, what did they think of his work and should it be supported. The Yocoms apparently gave a good recommendation, and I received my grant, the first of many, and the A.P.S. became my most generous supporter both with funds and with excellent publication of research results.

As spring of 1937 moved ahead I had most of my logistical requirements arranged for except the terribly important matter of transportation. This continued to trouble me. I answered the phone one afternoon in my office, to hear Bill Tugman, my close friend from *The Register-Guard*, say, "Lute, I think if we play our cards right, I know how we can get you a truck."

"Bill, that would be wonderful! What do I do?"

Now Bill, as a member of our group of genial fellows who met at suitable and regular intervals for conversation and appropriate libation, had listened to my many complaints about the difficulty in getting on with my work because transportation was so limited and difficult to provide. In addition, he was very much interested in the work, both for its own character and as a part of the university's program that really reached out to a wide public. So, with the veteran reporter's practical wisdom of the ways of many politicians and office holders, he applied that knowledge to the Oregon situation and Lute's truck.

"Here's what you do right now, Lute. Go down to the Ford people; Ed Laurence is there and knows your work and has helped you with pickups; tell him what you want and get the cost of that kind of a truck to the state and the possibility of delivery, when and if ordered. Then call me back. Get back to me as soon as you can."

"Thanks, Bill, and I'll get right on the job."

I was ready the next day with the information: a Ford V-8, stake-body truck with compound low gear, duals in rear and special wheels to give added clearance in rocky country was in stock except for the larger wheels—and they could be brought up from Roseburg (a small town seventy-five miles south), where they were in stock, and mounted—and delivery to the state would be $809, if my memory serves me well. I called Bill and gave him the information.

"I'll take over for a couple of days and you wait to hear from me and don't tell anybody."

Bill's carefully thought-out plan started with a call to President Boyer.

"Val (familiar for Valentine), a lot of people are interested in Cressman's work in eastern Oregon, but it is hampered by his inability to get a truck needed for that rough country. Why can't the university buy him a truck?"

"I just don't have the money in my budget, and can't get it from the chancellor."

"If you could get the money you would buy a truck?"

"I surely would."

"Thank you very much, Val."

Bill, now well under way, called Chancellor Hunter.

"Good morning, Bill, what can I do for you this morning?"

"Chancellor, I have just talked to President Boyer about the importance of Cressman's work and how that work is being held up because he can't get a truck for his summer field parties. President Boyer said he doesn't have the money in his budget, but if he could get it he would certainly buy the truck."

"Well, Bill," interrupted the chancellor, "I would be very glad to appropriate the money to President Boyer's budget, but I simply can't get such a requisition through the Board of Control."

"But, if they would approve a requisition, you would appropriate the money?"

"Of course, Bill."

So after thanking the chancellor and wishing him well, Bill, now hot on the trail, put in a call to State Treasurer Holman. The Board of Control, referred to by Chancellor Hunter, consisted of the governor, the secretary of state and the state treasurer, all elected officials. This body, believe it or not, had to pass on every requisition for any purchase using state funds. All university requisitions had to clear the chancellor's office, then go for further checking to the system controller at Corvallis, and then once a month the whole pile went to the Board of Control for final approval or rejection, and then some things would have to be let out for bids. Yet, somehow the business of the state stumbled along. Bill's call to Treasurer Holman was carefully chosen; Holman was planning to run for the United States Senate in the near future and, with his eye on that, he was very sensitive to the fact that Bill's paper carried a lot of clout.

"Good morning, Bill, how are things with that fine paper of yours? What can I do for you?" The treasurer's secretary had announced Bill's name when making the connection.

"Just a little matter of business that won't take much of your time, Treasurer."

"What's on your mind, Bill?"

"I'm sure you know about Professor Cressman's archaeological work in eastern Oregon, how important it is for the state and the university, but it's getting almost impossible to get on with it because he needs a truck."

"Why doesn't the university buy him a truck?"

"The chancellor won't appropriate the money because he says that the board will not approve a requisition for one."

"What does he mean? He's never turned one in. Tell him to get one in here and I'll see personally that it is approved. I take it there is some urgency; am I right?"

"Yes. He needs to have the truck for his planned field trip late in June."

"Tell the chancellor to mark the requisition 'URGENT' and tell the Corvallis office to send it through by special letter mail and not let it get lost in the pile they send in. I'll watch for it and get it through at once. Glad to be of help, Bill; call me any time."

"Thank you very much, Treasurer Holman."

Bill reported the treasurer's instructions with appropriate emendations at once to Chancellor Hunter. Hunter promised to appropriate promptly the necessary funds to President Boyer and Boyer assured Bill that he would act promptly, for the money would have to be assigned to Cressman's budget for the Museum of Natural History so he could prepare the requisition. Bill suggested to Val that he thought it would be appropriate for him to tell me that he had the money and take over from there.

Apparently the Corvallis office did not follow instructions, and Bill got an annoyed call from Treasurer Holman: "Where the hell, Bill, is that requisition for Cressman's truck? It was supposed to be sent in separately for our consideration. Find out, will you?"

"I'll get right on it, Treasurer. Thanks for your concern. I'll call back."

Inquiry at the chancellor's office confirmed that the Corvallis office had followed its own devices and sent the requisition in with all the rest.

"I'm sorry to have to tell you, Treasurer Holman, that the error was in the Corvallis office; it was sent in from there with all the rest, but I hope something can be done so the truck can be bought in time."

"I'll tell you what I'll do, Bill: we will approve the requisition in absentia, those university fellows will know what that means, and I'll call the chancellor and tell him to release the money to the appropriate budget so Cressman can complete the deal and his arrangements for the summer."

"Thank you, Treasurer Holman."

In a very short time I was able to take my purchase order to the Ford agency in Eugene and pick up our truck strictly according to specifications. We thought it would be nice to call it "The Tugman Special," but refrained from pushing the bureaucracy too far. Bill suggested that it might be a good idea for me to drop in, quite casually, on the board members in Salem, especially on Treasurer Holman, both a courtesy I was glad to show and as an investment in the future.

To complete our transport facilities for 1937 I arranged with the Ford agency in Burns, the owner was a friend of the university, for a second pickup, but when I stopped to pick it up one tire was in such bad shape that I didn't dare take it out. No replacement was available until the manager came and arranged for another. I started out in that with one of my men, but found it had no brakes and the tires were worse than those on the other. We returned it, and the student with me called his father, a lumberman from near Lakeview, who had brought him in his pickup to Burns to meet me and was still at the motel, to ask if he could spare his pickup. He could let us have it if I would let him use my car. So my car worked in the woods for the summer and his pickup kept us operational.

Our party now rolled on to our Three-Mile-Creek campsite, courtesy of Western Properties, Inc., a subsidiary of Swifts, and our 1937 field season was under way.

The new library, built with Federal funds as a relief project, was to be finished and go into service during President Boyer's administration. This achievement would release the second floor of Condon Hall, originally assigned to a museum — the original Condon cabinet in Johnson Hall had been dismantled, with much of the collection in the basement under Villard Hall — but taken over in the meantime by the library for a reserve-book reading room. I and many others thought the space should be used for its original purpose, to house a museum, now the Museum of Natural History, and office space for the director and an additional anthropologist, also carried as a curator. The Psychology Department, housed on the top (third) floor of Condon, mounted a strong drive for the space and lobbied very aggressively to persuade the Advisory Council to give the space to psychology.

The showdown came at a night meeting of the Advisory Council to make a final decision. I represented the museum interest, but it seemed to me that there was some agreement between the head of the Psychology Department and his supporters on the council, who obviously had been effectively lobbied, none of whom had had museum experience or knew anything about the role of a museum in the university of about teaching in general. The council voted in a body to recommend assignment of the space to the Psychology Department. President Boyer with his sophisticated background knew the value of museums, and he also had a sense of the importance of a previous commitment to the long-range plan of the university. He wasted no time; after a very few explanatory remarks, he overruled the council and assigned the space to the Museum of Natural History.

President Boyer's decision had a dynamic effect, for it gave me both the opportunity and obligation to develop the museum to make the most effective use of the space in the university's program. Along with my colleagues, W. D. Smith, Ralph Huestis and Mr. Henderson, we agreed on a floor plan of space—subject matter allocation. At the suggestion of Lance Hart of the School of Architecture and Allied Arts I had small blocks made to scale for both flat and vertical cases, and he and I experimented by shifting these models around, considering such things as light sources, the type of objects to be exposed, effects of light, and so on. We arrived at a plan that met with my colleagues' approval. I then went to the Physical Plant and set up a program of construction under a Federal grant to use some of the best cabinet makers in Eugene, now unemployed, to modify old cases and construct new ones. Two graduate students in the Art School working on their Master of Fine Arts degree painted two large murals, appropriate to the fieldwork that produced the specimens, on canvas on the east walls. In a simple ceremony, President Boyer, obviously very tired but sitting relaxed by one of the front cases, accepted the paintings on behalf of the university and in his short remarks spoke of Giotto and the early beautification of wall and altar spaces. I wondered how many members of the Advisory Council had ever heard of Giotto.

We luckily secured a very competent, retired, former high school teacher of Greek, a Mr. Robe with a wide knowledge of natural history as an attendant under one of the Federal programs. School teachers with eager but undirected pupils quickly started to use the museum. To organize this public function and make it more effective, I worked out an arrangement with the Eugene Public School District to put one of its teachers—she had been a very competent graduate student working in anthropology and natural history—on a half-time assignment to correlate the school visits with the appropriate study projects in the students' programs and then as a docent lead the visits with their teacher. I felt it was the university's responsibility to provide the resource material, but the school system's responsibility to provide for the proper use of it in its instruction. We provided a room almost adjacent to the museum display area to which the children were brought with their teacher, and for ten minutes the docent explained how what they were going to see was part of their current study program at school. The docent then led the tour, followed by a short, free period to move about the museum with their pals to look at different exhibits, then back to the classroom, where they were given a short test with questions on their conducted tour that were previously prepared by the docent. Class size was limited to twenty pupils.

Our very successful scheme of university–public school cooperation in teaching unfortunately ended for this program when our docent was awarded a fellowship by Cornell University to work toward her Ph.D. degree, an end I am happy to say she achieved. I was making progress toward setting up an expanded program to involve both the Eugene and Lane County school systems since schools from outside the Eugene area had found the museum program beneficial when the outbreak of World War II brought the work to a halt.

By the end of our 1937 field season, after two and a half years, I had laid the foundation and sketched out the basic blueprints for the development at the University of Oregon of a program of teaching, research, and publication based upon a cooperative relationship of the fields of anthropology, natural history, and related areas, some of which I saw had to be humanistic.

The totally unexpected action in 1934 establishing a Department of Anthropology in 1935 with me as its head was one of those climactic events that sometimes mark a point in a life, as this did mine. I had never been one to sit down and whine because something I considered important had been rejected or seemed impossible to get. After a reasonable period of damage assessment, I would attempt to achieve essentially the same end but by a different and perhaps less conspicuous effort. I had to "find out things," an essential personality trait from the time as a small boy I stuck the pin into Dad's beagle hound "to see what he would do" and was not chided for it by my observing dad. I was taught from my boyhood to seize opportunities. The unexpected and sudden change in my status released all my pent-up emotional, intellectual, and physical potential. Eagerly, with Cecilia's understanding and happy cooperation, I took full advantage of the opportunities not only explicitly expected but also, as we saw it, duties implicit for anyone holding such a university position. The vision we shared of our future of discovery was inspiring, but as we well knew it promised nothing but the requirement of our full commitment to an end and hard work to bring our vision into the world of reality. We thought what we saw was worth the cost.

Our three summers of field research, starting with 1937, provided the validation of my hypothesis, in 1932 no "bigger than a man's hand," that south-central Oregon had been a part of the north-south corridor of migration from the Alaskan land bridge into southwestern North America. The conclusion rested on the state of the art of geoarchaeological-chronological dating.

Starting with 1937 I established a completely independent field camp with our party of nine students in tents, a cook who shared a tent with our food supplies, while I had my own tent. The program had been accepted as a part of the Summer Session curriculum,[25] insuring that the work was not just some odd interest of mine, but a recognized function of the university's program. Our new truck transported us the fifteen miles from camp at Three-Mile to Catlow Cave, and I sent two boys once a week in our pickup the hundred miles to Burns for supplies, practically a day's drive. Mail came to Blitzen every other day from Burns and could be picked up there when anyone came out or we sent someone in. We had no radio, no newspapers, only something sent in by mail from home.

I made it a policy never to send one man alone out on a project so that in case of accident there would be someone to help or go for help. I later changed the number of persons to three so one could stay with the injured person and the third go for help. I also made it a policy never to ask a student to do any task I could not do or was not willing to do; if there was any doubt, I always did it first and then let others take it on.[26] This was simply my code of leadership by which confidence and camaraderie were built up and maintained. I tried to fit people to appropriate assignments for which they might have a special aptitude, for example, a cartographer or a bone identification specialist. There would be discussions of the work as it proceeded, of a special artifact discovered, and always there was the question of the significance of what we were considering. Sometimes there were discussions at night. This was the model of our summer field camp for the whole period of our lake bed studies, except for the period of about ten days at Fork Rock in 1938 when the Deschutes National Forest ranger graciously permitted us to use the abandoned C.C.C. mess hall at Cabin Lake for our living quarters and the amenities of a shower, with other smaller rooms for me and as the occasion might need. At McDermitt, for a few days in 1938, we found a couple of vacant houses that we were permitted to use instead of our tents.

As we continued our preparation of work for the 1937 field season shortly after the New Year, I was surprised and elated to receive a letter from the Philadelphia Academy of Natural Sciences over the signature of Edgar B. Howard inviting me to attend the International Symposium on Early Man to be held in Philadelphia, March 17–20, 1937, to commemorate the 125th anniversary of the founding of the academy. Although the academy could not pay guests' travel expenses, we could attend without charge all lectures, discussions, and social events. I knew Dr. Howard by name and was familiar with his work on Early Man sites in New Mexico.

The symposium would seek the following objectives:

1. To bring together a group of eminent world authorities on, and students of, prehistory.
2. Through papers read at the Symposium, to further the correlation of important new discoveries throughout the world.
3. Through special exhibits of specimens representing major new discoveries, to facilitate the study and correlation of new data.
4. To stimulate cooperation among anthropologists, paleontologists, Pleistocene stratigraphers and prehistorians in furthering our knowledge of early man, his environment, and his culture.
5. To make available in published form the results of the Symposium.[27]

I brought the invitation home at noon and showed it to Cecilia. She read it and, with eyes shining, threw her arms around my neck. "Oh Sheeleigh, I am so happy; you must go."

"How can we afford it, dear? My salary is about $2,900, and with the loss of our investments where is the money coming from?"

"I don't know now, but you have to go; you must go, Sheeleigh; this is a once-in-a-lifetime chance for you and your work. We'll work it out."

Since my museum appointment gave me direct contact with the president, I went in that capacity with my invitation to President Boyer to ask if there was any possibility of a grant of coach fare, round trip, and we would personally cover the rest. After some discussion of the importance of attending these meetings as a significant invest-ment in my future work and its benefit to the university Dr. Boyer said he would find the money for the coach fare.

Dr. John C. Merriam, then president of the Carnegie Institution of Washington, opened the symposium with brief introductory remarks, and a selection shows why this symposium was of such importance to me as my work was shaping up:

> Consideration of major problems from the point of view of geology, paleontology, geography, climatology, general biol-ogy, anthropology, archaeology, and a general distribution of organisms associated with man, enables us to develop a perspective which will be of great importance in all efforts to understand early human history. . . . And it is important that ultimately we examine the meaning of these facts with relation to the present and future of the human world.[28]

With his closing sentence Dr. Merriam brought to the attention of the participants the importance of considering the humanistic aspect of their studies, a value he never lost sight of and which, in my subsequent association with him, I would find influencing my own perceptions.

I arrived at the symposium without incident, somewhat weary after the long coach trip, but excited and eager to see and hear the internationally known scientists. All lectures were held in the large auditorium, and smaller meetings were provided for in adjoining rooms. Social events, such as receptions, were held in the large hall, and the whole symposium moved with well-organized management.

All papers, even from sometimes apparently unrelated fields—certainly as customarily considered—were oriented toward the one objective, Early Man, and as the meetings progressed the interrelatedness of fields became clear. Try to imagine what this series of meetings meant to me, a young neophyte, to sit before these inter-nationally known scientists whose writings I had read, but now to see them in person and hear them presenting their thoughts in a manner that communicated meaningfully to a common theme. Here was scientific cooperation at its best. Each paper was a stone in an arch in which the keystone holding it together was the concept, the fuller understanding of Early Man. My mind today flips back to those semi-

Field party at Three-Mile camp, 1937.

nal days in 1931 at Pasadena and the discussions on Early Man when I saw the first faint glimmer of light now glowing at Philadelphia in full force to lighten the area into which I had chosen to come. Cecilia was right that I should go, no matter the cost, for it *was* a "once-in-a-lifetime chance" for me.

The symposium alerted me to men in different fields who were interested in my area of study and willing to provide help when asked. Within the next three or four years, six men whom I saw and heard there would answer my request for professional help, and another, several years later, I would have the pleasure of inviting to give a three weeks' lecture series at the Oregon institutions of higher education. President Boyer's investment would provide generous returns.

Three months after the Philadelphia meetings we began our 1937 season of excavation in Catlow Cave to complete the work begun in 1935. Near the close of our work, we unexpectedly exposed portions of a human skeleton in the top of the bottom level of the fill composed of beach gravel and fallen roof debris. Our excavation was meticulously careful because of the potential importance of the find. If the body had been deposited when the waves were still breaking into the cave, then the age of the deposition would be that of the gravel and the terrace with which it was associated. This cave, as I pointed out above, had no clear-cut stratification, only bedding. If the deposition was not entombed as the gravel was being deposited, but by some human effort, such as a burial, then the question of stratigraphic determination of the age was irrelevant. There was much other evidence that could be considered in an effort to solve the problem as we worked in the laboratory, but the geological stratigraphic potential had to be fully examined.

I wrote Dr. Merriam after our return from the field telling him of our find and asking him to please send Dr. Ernst Antevs, whom I had heard at the symposium, so he could give us the expert opinion I needed. He graciously agreed, writing that he would send Dr. Antevs, who would come in a few weeks after he had completed an assignment in New York. Since he was going to visit some deposits at San Diego, he could combine the two tasks in one swing. He thanked Mrs. Cressman and me for offering hospitality in our home for Dr. Antevs and said that he would communicate with me as soon as the date of Dr. Antevs's schedule was clear.

I had been very fortunate to have as a member of the 1937 field party, on a strictly volunteer basic, Walter (Walt) J. Perry of the staff of the Deschutes National Forest, who was kept on two or three years after his retirement age because no real replacement, only a follower, could be found to replace the valuable Walt. He was an excellent amateur paleontologist and geologist, always reporting his discoveries to scientists for their study. He knew the country widely, had many friends, and his probity was above question. His evidence presented at a jury trial for an arsonist would always result in a conviction, when the same evidence coming from the superintendent of the forest would be disregarded, partly because of the dislike of the country people for the bureaucracy. He was anxious to expand his knowledge into the field of archaeology and so offered his services, which I gladly accepted. What an addition! Walt's experience with us that summer alerted him to the importance of caves for my program, so after the field season he used his available time to inquire among his widely scattered friends about the availability of caves. His search paid off and he wrote me saying he had found two dry caves with occupation layers clearly separated by sharply defined beds of pumice; would I please come and check the caves; he would take us to them. What a break!

I wrote him at once, congratulating him, to say that I would come with Dr. Antevs and party and let him know as soon as I had firm word of our visitor's schedule. Walt was one of those rare people born to and almost a part of the very landscape: rancher, buckaroo, forester, trapper, miner—I have met them all—who know the land and have shared their knowledge unselfishly with questing paleontologists, geologists, and archaeologists, knowledge often crucial for the scientist to carry on his studies. Too often not even a mention of the person's name occurs other than a small footnote at the bottom of the page. How much I and Far West prehistory owe to Walt!

Our meeting as Dr. Antevs got off the train was our first, but I had heard him give his paper at the symposium, and his arrival in Eugene marked the beginning of a lifelong, cooperative friendship. At home, Cecilia welcomed him to his room, brightened by a small bouquet of flowers on a bedside table, a custom she had brought from England and followed all her life. She told him to rest up after his long train journey and come out when he was ready. He had become host to a nasty cold on his trip west, but worried little about it.

This week I knew would be a difficult one for me, since I had arranged to have an outside expert come as a consultant basically to check the validity of my work. It was a week in which I saw scientific rigor at work.

To benefit as many persons as possible, I took our big new truck and lashed inside against the stake racks on both sides long wooden benches I found in a more or less abandoned building on campus. Fred Voget, who had carefully guided our truck during the 1937 season to maturity, was chauffeur. In back on the benches were W. D. Smith, who had aided us in 1937; Howard Stafford, my companion and mentor on the petroglyph study and a member of the Guano party as well as the 1937 season; Howard's father, Dr. Orin Stafford, professor of chemistry and dean of what science was left on the Eugene campus; Carl Huffaker, a member of the 1937 party and my cartographer, and I. Dr. Antevs, because of his cold, and the place of honor in the cab with Fred. On a lovely September day we rolled out of Eugene, destination Three-Mile-Creek campsite.

Our expert's first assignment was to determine if our lake bed with its terraces was really that and, if so, a part of the Great Basin system of pluvial lakes without outlet to the sea. His second assignment was to determine if the Catlow Cave skeleton could be dated by its geological stratigraphic position.

As we moved down the familiar road in the bed of the ancient lake we knew so well, we riders in the rear were on the lookout for a good example of a terrace for Antevs's inspection. Then we saw what we thought was our quarry and pounded our fists on the top of the cab, our customary signal to the driver to stop. After all had dismounted I pointed out to Dr. Antevs our supposed terrace. "It might be or it might not be," said our expert. "It might be a structural terrace as often occurs in this volcanic country. If it is a beach terrace there will be gravel. We shall go up and see."

Up the forty-five-meter climb to the supposed beach we all went, and there was a beautiful, curving, barrier beach with its gravel, over which the water had spilled into a channel between exposures of lava formations.[29]

"It is a beach and a typical Great Basin lake terrace and shows that this lake belongs in the Great Basin system." Question number one was answered in the affirmative. The point was, don't act on assumptions, verify—a very good point, too. No automobile geology in this field!

The next day we went to the cave to examine the stratigraphic problem of the skeleton and the gravel. Dr. Antevs wanted our earlier trench enlarged where we had found the skeleton so he would have a clear view of the character of the fill on each side of the exposure. I did this work, uncovering a few bone fragments. His judgment, after a careful examination of the character of the fill at the level of the skeleton and on each face of the trench, was that the bones were undoubtedly in a bed containing gravel, but because the bed was so mixed with fallen roof debris it could not be said that stratigraphically the skeleton was naturally associated with the deposition of the gravel. He pointed all this out clearly and convincingly in his discussion. Here was scientific rigor at its best, forcing me to accept a negative conclusion on a matter very important to me, just the opposite of the day before when the evidence supported my opinion. This field training in scientific discipline was painful but good experience indeed.

Dr. Antevs's opinion was related only to the question of the stratigraphic evidence. My later laboratory study produced a series of pieces of related information tending to support the temporal association of the skeleton's entombment and the deposition of the gravel. I have published every detail of these studies but the only response has been to ignore the problem, to sweep it under the academic rug, and pretend it doesn't exist. It is one of the many lumps under that rug, difficult matters better ignored. My final effort to obtain a carbon-14 determination has so far been futile.[30]

Following the examination of the cave, we drove to the north rim of the lake bed to verify the opinion arrived at by W. D. and Ruff that the lake had never had an outlet. Our visitor confirmed our previous conclusion.

Our last night at Three-Mile camp provided me with one of the most pleasant and nostalgic memories of all my many field trips. Ernst and I had arrived at a first-name relationship. He and I, the only ones still up, were sitting on folding camp stools, talking on either side of a small but cheery fire. Our fire threw dancing shadows on the encircling grove of aspen, ghostly in their mottled white bark against the pitch-black, enveloping night. How long we sat and talked I haven't the least idea, for it was one of those rare experiences of complete, uninhibited communication two persons are sometimes fortunate enough to enjoy, not arguing but differing, agreeing, questioning, always communicating. Occasionally one of us would rise to push a branch into our fire to hold our perimeter of light against the pressing night. We had been discussing the problem of correlating the lake terraces in a synchronous system; for example, highest terrace here is essentially the same age as the highest terrace there, based on the theory that the rise and fall of the lakes' levels was the product of a common cause, a meteorological condition. A final question of mine brought our pleasantest of evenings to a close. As devil's advocate I said, "But, Ernst, is it not possible that local geological differences will effectively interfere with this synchroneity? For example, can one equate a lake bed once holding a relatively shallow lake and a small drainage basin with a deep lake drawing on a large drainage basin, since the temperature of the water in the two lakes would be quite different, thus affecting evaporation rates of the two bodies of water to be reflected in the geological features? Perhaps the history of each should be studied on its own terms?"

"Ahhh" [it was a long, drawn out "Ah"], "that is a very logical question, Luther, but let us not make a noose and stick our necks into it."

With that sage advice we drowned our friendly little fire to find our bedrolls, surrendering our enchanted island of light to the pall of the surrounding darkness.

In planning our trip I thought we should get all the possible expert help Antevs would give us and laid out our route west from Catlow across very rough country, but easy for our truck, to take us into the north end of the Warner Valley close to the peat bog Howard and I nearly foundered in in 1932 to make it pay its tribute for our trouble. I borrowed from my friend at Oregon State College, Dr. Henry Hansen, who was engaged in a study of the postglacial forest succession in the Pacific Northwest, his Swedish peat sampler for extracting samples to form a complete sequence of specimens at measured intervals clear to the base of the bog and thus get a record of vegetation changes through time that would reflect the corresponding climate. I would ask our guest to demonstrate the proper method of using this instrument—later we would have our own sampler. Dr. Antevs was pleased to demonstrate its use. But before going to the bog we stopped at Plush, the service station–store–dwelling complex for gasoline and to give us a chance to stretch our legs. As our truck's tank was being filled Ernst came out of the store with bottles of cold beer for all. As we raised our bottles he said, "This is on my wife, who supports both me and science." With thirsts assuaged we drove the short distance to the bog, being sure to keep our truck on the road. At a sunken causeway called Stone Bridge, Ernst said, "Stop here."

He showed us how to extract the sample, enclose it in a sterile bottle, label it for date, place and depth in centimeters until we encountered blue-gray lake sediment free of peat at a depth of some twenty-four feet. We now had added a new method of securing data available to us, one we had all read about since it was widely used in Europe and was gaining in acceptance in this country.

It was well after dark when we arrived at Lakeview in Goose Lake Valley, the next lake bed west of Warner. We checked in for the night at a series of cabins, taking advantage of the various kinds of benefits provided by the hot-water spring, which in one place had been capped to form a very impressive geyser. The water carried a heavy odor of sulphur, and when we emerged from our showers we carried a rather distressing aura of sulphur with us, reminiscent of my boyhood when we had to burn sulphur to fumigate for infectious disease. Leaving the next morning, smelling disgustingly sanitary, we picked up Walt Perry at Paisley, some fifty miles on our route home.

Walt now took us to something that would be absolutely new in our experience if our examination corroborated his inspection. His cave was at Five-Mile Point outside of Paisley on the high terrace on the east side of Summer Lake. Uncovering the small test hole he had dug, perhaps fifteen inches across, he cleaned it out with his hands and then cleaned the sides of all loose material. Kneeling, he looked up at us and said, ''There it is.''

It was clear that there was a level of occupation fill, then the clean undisturbed pumice resting on another bed of cave fill with bits of pieces of artifacts clearly in situ in the wall. Ernst examined the test pit with his usual care and said, ''If this stratigraphy, for that is what you have here, holds when you excavate, you will have one of the most important sites for Early Man in the whole West.'' He didn't say ''if'' but ''when'' you excavate. It would be important and necessary, he pointed out, to have the pumice identified for source, have that dated by the geological methods then in use, and the result would date the occupation of the Paisley Cave. I realized we were facing the same problem of interrelatedness of fields of learning as we had at Wikiup.

Walt then took us another fifty miles to a cave called variously ''Cow Cave'' and ''Menkeimer Cave'' from the name of the ranching family renting the property. Later we would call it Fort Rock Cave, and that is its name today. Following the same routine at this cave, Antevs confirmed the accuracy of Walt's conclusion: cave fill of human occupation separated by a stratum of clean pumice. We knew now where we would have to work in our 1938 field season, although we had ''unfinished'' business to change to ''finished'' in Catlow first.

What a week this had been in the field with Ernst! How grateful I was that Cecilia had insisted I go to the Philadelphia symposium, ''a once-in-a-lifetime chance.''

Ernst and I closed out our field trip as I took him to his Pullman on the midnight train for San Diego. I expressed my gratitude for his coming and the great help he had given me and my colleagues. As I stood waiting for his train to pull out I little realized how deeply he had entered my life as friend and colleague.

I read a paper in 1939 at the Sixth Pacific Science Congress of the Pacific Science Association at Stanford University reporting on our discovery of the association of humans and extinct fauna at a shelter, Paisley Five-Mile Point Cave No. 3, together with other material. A. L. Kroeber was in the chair and made some remarks to introduce the general subject of the meetings, in the course of which he spoke rather denigratingly of the Oregon discoveries. At the close of his remarks, Ernst took the floor for comments and made a very strong statement to the effect that the Paisley site was one of the best Early Man sites in North America.

In the summer of 1940 Dr. Merriam again sent him to help. He joined W. D. Smith and Dr. Ira Allison, professor of geology at Oregon State, as my guest at our camp at Laird's Landing on Lower Klamath Lake, where we worked together for nearly a week trying to decipher the involved history of the lake to interpret the significance of our lake bed finds of the summer. We beat miles and miles of brush and rock-strewn landscape and finally walked almost the whole western shoreline of Klamath Lake, the mother lake, searching for terraces as evidence of pluvial history. This was a tough as well as a good week.

In 1941 I was on leave, working up the report on my research under a Guggenheim fellowship. Ernst had promised to show me the Early Man sites and related manifestations in southern Arizona if I would stop on our way back from Santa Fe where I had been working. I seized this generous offer and stopped at Globe, the Antevs's home. Ernst and I would be gone in my car for nearly a week, so he and Mrs. Antevs asked Cecilia and Gem to be her guests while I was away. It was a wonderful kindness, for it relieved me of worry about their welfare.

We visited all of the sites across southern Arizona from Double Adobe on the east to Ventana Cave in the west. Ernst had been involved in the excavation of most of them and so his explanation in each case was exceptionally important. At Tucson we stopped to see the young archaeologist who was directing the excavation of Ventana Cave, a very important site. It was my introduction to Dr. Emil Haury. As we studied these sites, Ernst's acquaintance with my Oregon work helped me see a pattern beginning to emerge in the Far West differing from the prestigious Folsom record of the High Plains. This trip, like the Oregon one, was a concentrated research project with comparably important results.

Field party at Roaring Springs cave, 1938, at end of day. Cave visible over
truck rack.

In 1950 I read a paper, "Western Prehistory in the Light of
Carbon 14 Dating," that was subsequently published in the *South-
western Journal of Anthropology*. I find this note on page 289: "1-
Adapted from a paper, read by invitation, before the American
Anthropological Association and the Society for American Archae-
ology at Berkeley, December 30, 1950. *I am particularly indebted to
Dr. Ernst Antevs who read this paper and made valuable sugges-
tions.*" [Emphasis added.][31]

In the years following, our contacts were few as different commitments pulled us in different directions. Our friendship continued,
renewed by an occasional letter. Then I heard that he had been
seriously ill. Not daring to write without further information, I wrote
Emil to ask if Ernst would like a letter from his old friend. Emil
strongly urged me to write, for he was sure it would give Ernst
pleasure. So I wrote my old friend a warm letter of some length.
There was no answer or acknowledgment. A short obituary notice in a
newspaper sometime later told me why.

Our acquaintance turned into friendship that night of pleasant
memories at our fire at Three-Mile-Creek Camp, and through the

years our association became warmer and filled with mutual respect to greatly enrich my life, for which I am immeasurably thankful. So now, "Adieu, old Comrade, with love and gratitude."

As planned, the summer of 1938 found my party at Three-Mile, settled at our old camp, but with a new cook; ours of the year before lost his welcome when we found him, according to his own story, on probation from San Quentin, that unpleasant penitentiary in California (and he not supposed to be out of the state). We planned first to complete the excavation of Roaring Springs cave with its rich store of perishable artifacts, then move to the pumice-bearing caves at Paisley and Fort Rock, an ambitious program. Somehow, I can't remember now, I had scrounged up the money during the winter to buy a 16-mm. Bell and Howell movie camera to record our fieldwork, primarily for use in my classes as a teaching aid. A record of some of the incredibly difficult character of the work, the dust at Roaring Springs, has been preserved as a result.

Probably the most important event in the excavation of Roaring Springs cave occurred one morning quite unexpectedly when Willie Suver called from the two-meter square in which he was working: "Come see what I've found." When we gathered, Willie removed the dry grass he had put over his find to conceal it and there was a beautiful red atlatl or spear-thrower, the first ever found in Oregon. No firstborn to a long-childless couple was ever treated with greater care and tenderness than our specimen. The dry cave had preserved all the details except what was once attached, probably feathers, to two strings projecting from under the handle's hide wrapping. The weapon was 70.5 centimeters in overall length. After all the necessary treatment, photographing, and admiration it was tucked safely away for transport at day's end to camp. We returned to our work.

Scarcely had we settled into our working rhythm when another call came from Willie, perhaps just a bit blasé: "Oh, my God!"

"What's the matter now, Willie?" I asked as I and the others kept working.

"I have the little brother."

As we gathered around he exposed a second atlatl, smaller than the first, but of the same pattern.

We now knew the identity of some wood fragments we had found, a hook and parts of a slightly curved, flat piece; they were

Two complete atlatls from Roaring Springs cave, fragment from Plush cave.

parts of two broken weapons. We were now experiencing something very important to the archaeologist: how finding a whole specimen sometimes will help identify small, unimpressive fragments, often found and then long puzzled over. The small parts demonstrated as effectively as did the whole the presence of the artifact in the cultural inventory.

Since the atlatl was in use millennia before the bow and arrow displaced it, we now had convincing evidence of cultural stratigraphy in the cave, but no idea of the actual calendrical time. All the hard work in Roaring Springs now took on a new urgency. The pieces of the butt end of projectiles that we had been finding became meaningful. Even though we thought those with a small cup in a piece of hard wood were evidence of the atlatl, we did not have the necessary proof; we lacked the visual proof that Antevs had demanded to identify the terrace. Now we had it. The arrow with its cross slot, the nock, to receive the bowstring was familiar to us.

Toward the close of our dig against the rear wall, unfortunately slightly moist, we found a cache of pieces from worn-out baskets, too valuable to have been thrown away, so saved for some future use. This cache preserved some of the most beautiful specimens of the basket maker's skill. As we closed out our dig we were also pretty sure that there was a bed with stone implements, but lacking basketry, which would be further evidence of cultural stratigraphy. Our last day we breakfasted at the ranch house, then rolled out on the long drive to Paisley and camp three miles out on Chewaucan River.

Paisley Five-Mile Point Cave No. 1 certainly introduced a new parameter into our cave program, a strictly geological factor entirely

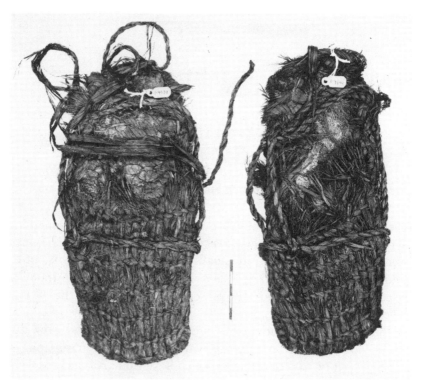

Pair of Fort Rock sandals from 1938 excavation. Lighter colored lining material is pine needles. Radiocarbon dated at 9,000 years old (average).

independent of the cultural, but one which could be of great chronological value in the interpretation of the cultural remains. The interbedding of the pumice in the occupation material demonstrated that the eruption had occurred while the cave was occupied. Atlatl shaft fragments similar to those found in Roaring Springs indicated that the occupants shared a similar culture and were contemporaries or roughly so. But when that time was remained a mystery. The eruption date of the Sunset Craters near Flagstaff in northern Arizona had been established by associated, dated pottery, but at Paisley there was no analogous situation. The problem remained a strictly geological one and now assumed a marked importance in Pacific Northwest prehistory; the ash deposit, once identified, would be a horizon marker for any stratigraphy in which it might be found.

Dr. Howel Williams, an internationally known volcanologist at the University of California at Berkeley, came at my request from his

Lake bed at Five-Mile Point caves, where discovery of Mt. Mazama volcanic ash separating occupation levels was made in 1938.

study of Mt. Mazama, where he had been engaged for four years and knew every detail of its history. We had in the meantime excavated the Fort Rock Cave with its pumice stratigraphy and its remarkable record of a unique type of sandal under the pumice stratum.

Dr. Williams's first response was to ask our aid as archaeologists in dating the pumice deposit. I declined with all possible grace and put the ball back in his court. Going first to the Paisley site, then to Fort Rock, he verified our stratigraphic evaluation and then took samples of the pumice to identify its source. He tentatively identified the Paisley source as the Mt. Mazama eruption and the Fort Rock as a Newberry Crater eruption, somewhat later in time than the Mt. Mazama event. His estimated date for Mt. Mazama furnished me later, based on all the geological evidence he could muster, was between 4,000 and 10,000 years ago, probably nearer the lower than the higher age, with the Fort Rock somewhat later.[32]

We now had some specific time reference to work with even though the bracket was very large for the archaeologist dealing in units of centuries or less. Independent evidence was now beginning to support my hypothesis of an early time frame for the lake bed culture of south-central Oregon.

Late in the summer Dr. Merriam sent Dr. E. B. Howard to Oregon to examine the reported Oregon manifestations and report to him. He had earlier appointed Howard to a special consultant post to evaluate all the reported sites of Early Man in North America. Dr. Merriam wrote, "In company with Dr. Cressman, Dr. E. B. Howard has examined the principal localities studied in south central Oregon, and agrees regarding the exceptional value of these finds. Dr. Howard has wide acquaintance with the problems of early man in America through intensive special studies at Clovis and other exceptional localities, and through examination of the principal sites available. His view of the problem has therefore high value."[33]

Neither Dr. Merriam nor Dr. Howard represented any academic institution with an entrenched interest in any particular theory of Early Man, but both were asking with open minds the same kind of question Antevs had asked, "What is the evidence?" to provide a basis for forming an opinion.

Since it was important to make our new information available to the public, I planned a publication with cooperating authors. I would prepare a general theoretical contribution, Williams would report his geological observations, and Alex Krieger, the analysis of the projectile data. The "establishment"'s theory of the origin of the Great Basin culture was that it was a product of diffusion from the American Southwest and dated no earlier than about A.D. 1000. I wrote on the basis of our evidence through 1938, "The Southwest origin and diffusion theory of the source of the culture with which we are dealing cannot be fitted into this geological framework; it is the writer's opinion that the geological evidence strongly points in the main toward an autochthonous origin for this Northern Great Basin Culture."[34]

Following President Boyer's resignation in 1938, Donald M. Erb was brought from his position as professor of economics at Stanford University—he had held a similar position at Oregon before going to Stanford—to succeed Boyer. A colleague for several years, I knew him as a teacher with a good reputation, but I never enjoyed close personal contact with him. Frankly, I was shocked at the appointment; I did not see Don as presidential timber. He had a certain reputation on campus as being Dean Gilbert's "fair-haired boy." Although Gilbert could have been Boyer's replacement, he would not accept the responsibility; he preferred to work behind the scenes. I'm afraid I saw the Erb appointment as a front for Gilbert so he could exercise the influence he wished without accepting the associated responsibility. My first and only face-to-face contact with President Erb until near his death was a surprising, even if successful experience.

Dean Stafford informed me that Mr. Henderson, curator of the herbarium, now a part of the Museum of Natural History, was paying the salary of his part-time assistant out of his own pocket, a situation obviously not to be tolerated. He suggested that we go to President Erb and request the small amount needed as an addition to the M.N.H. budget. I immediately agreed and we arranged a joint appointment with the president.

After we had waited a few minutes in the outer office, President Erb opened the door to let out Dean Eric Allen of the School of Journalism, one of the professional schools with a very high reputation, for which Allen was largely responsible — beyond the boundaries of the state as well as within.

The president invited us in, and as he closed the door after us, said something I could hardly believe I heard correctly but was later assured by my companion that surprisingly enough I had. The president's comment was: "There goes an idea man and, by God, I can't stand idea men." Dr. Stafford and I refrained from comment or any show of surprise, but explained our mission and quickly had the promise of the addition of the necessary money to the M.N.H. budget. We thanked the president and withdrew, but outside we gave way to our near state of shock at our new president's remark that he could not stand idea men. Regrettably, my experience with President Erb during the four years of his office convinced me that he knew what he was saying in his shocking remark to us.

Through a budget addition from the graduate school I had secured a student, Alex D. Kreiger, from the University of California as a graduate assistant. After taking his master's degree at Oregon in anthropology, he was advanced to the rank of instructor. Alex relieved me from some elementary teaching although his effectiveness was limited by the fact of his very marked deafness, a condition the faculty at California neglected to inform me of in its recommendations. He was a substantial member of our 1938 field party, but returned to Eugene at his own request before the excavation of the Fort Rock Cave. I offered him the opportunity of joint authorship of the paper on projectiles that, of course, included the atlatls if he would do the analysis while I provided all the illustrative material. He eagerly accepted the offer since it gave him the chance to get his name in print as well as write the first description of Oregon atlatls. That article would join those of Williams's and mine on the pumice stratigraphy and a general description of the effort.

I looked forward to the preparation of a full-length monograph to analyze and synthesize the results of my fieldwork on the completion of my lake basin studies. Laboratory study of the material and the preparation of illustrations was very time-consuming. My student assistants were promised appropriate recognition on publication. My graduate assistant, later instructor, Alex D. Kreiger, in addition to the joint authorship of the projectile paper for another proposed publication, made the first gross classification of the basketry. I was doing most of the photography with a 35-mm. camera in my office. I planned to complete my fieldwork in the seasons of 1939 and 1940. The amount of work in research and instruction along with other university duties was appallingly heavy. Even though my work load was constantly increasing, there seemed no hope for any relief under the Erb administration. I desperately needed a full-time assistant of staff rank, but that I considered only a fond hope.

In June 1939 a completely unexpected event came to my aid. The university gave Dr. Merriam an LL.D. degree, and for the few days he was on the campus I was asked to be an informal aide-de-camp to him, an opportunity I gladly accepted. President Erb may have entertained him and the other honored person at a luncheon, but if so I was not among the guests. Cecilia and I discovered that there was no entertainment in the form of a special dinner planned, so we took care of that as an opportunity and obligation implicit in our position. We honored Dr. Merriam with a special dinner at which, of course, the Erbs were the senior guests. From all points of view the dinner was apparently a considerable success.[35]

When I led my 1939 field party out of Eugene a couple of weeks later, I went with new assurance because President Erb had told me to secure an additional staff member, a Ph.D., starting in the autumn. I was sure that I recognized the hand of Dr. Merriam. During the summer Dr. Homer G. Barnett, Ph.D. from the University of California, accepted my offer of a position, the most important appointment I ever made. We were lifelong colleagues.

The first week of 1939 we camped at our old site on the Chewaucan to make further exploration of the Paisley Five-Mile Point area before going to the farthermost southeastern area of the pluvial

lakes, east of the Steens Mountain. I had veterans of 1938 in my party
and sent them the first full day in camp to do exploratory work while I
devoted my time to necessary paper work. In the late afternoon the
party returned in a jubilant mood, eager to show me what they had
found. They spread it out on clean paper.

A possible location some seventy-five meters along the rim from
our No. 1 cave caught their attention and it alone, among others
tested, really paid off. Clearing off the overburden of talus, they dug
through a stratified deposit with its pumice as we had done in 1938,
but here the deposit continued to the sand and gravel of the old
beachline. In this gravel and overlying wind-blown dust and small
fragments of roof fall, they found a site that was in many ways the
most significant in all our studies: a fire site with ash, charred sagebrush bark, animal bones thrown aside and onto the fire, and
artifacts, apparently some damaged hunting gear that had been
replaced with new. No wonder my boys and Walt Perry, with us again
that summer, were jubilant. This was a discovery far beyond my wildest hopes, the first of its kind in the Great Basin. I recognized and
pointed out to my rather "swanky" crew the bones of extinct forms
of animals, . . . but let Dr. Chester Stock, paleontologist at the California Institute of Technology and one of my collaborators who
shared the symposium at Philadelphia, tell what was found:

> The bird bones included in the collection represent pintail,
> teal, duck, hawk, and sage hen. The mammals represent
> bison, mountain sheep, camel (probably *Camelops*), horse, a
> large dog (wolf), a fox (perhaps red fox), and probably bear.
> *Among these mammals are two genera, namely horse and
> camel, that we generally regard as more characteristic of the
> Pleistocene than of the Recent epoch.* Some of the remaining
> forms do not range in the region where the cave is located at
> the present time. The avifauna suggests the presence of water.
> [Emphasis added.][36]

I spent the next day at the site (actually a hole) mostly on my
knees with trowel, brush, and fingers—I had no dust mask—expanding, collecting more specimens, and verifying. I, unfortunately,
carried with me the source for a short but violent attack of probably
dust pneumonia at McDermitt, our next camp. Liberal doses of
aspirin and lots of very hot tea helped break a fever, but I had to stay

quiet for several days while the boys did the surveying. Our information here was largely related to the further knowledge of the extension into Oregon of the great pluvial Lake Lahontan, covering many square miles of western and northern Nevada and thus important in Great Basin prehistory.

Closing out the McDermitt survey we moved to the Alvord Lake basin east of the Steens, where we examined surface sites and some caves that contributed little to our data.

A young couple, systematic collectors who lived at Klamath Falls, had gathered surface artifacts from the dry bed of Lower Klamath Lake, and they brought them to my attention because they thought their collection showed cultural development, which in their opinion could be correlated with periods in the lake history.

On his 1938 visit to our sites I took Dr. Howard to see the collectors, Mr. and Mrs. Payne, and the artifacts. Dr. Howard agreed that the Payne material warranted further field study. As a result and in cooperation with the Paynes, I planned the study for the 1940 season.

Lower Klamath Lake was not a typical pluvial lake, but a body of water symbiotic to Upper Klamath Lake and so shared at least in part that lake's history. This project would require much expert geological opinion in the fields of climatic history, sedimentation, and structural geology. So, as mentioned earlier, I arranged for the forthcoming season (1940) to have Dr. Antevs, W. D. Smith, and Dr. Ira Allison of Oregon State College, a sedimentation specialist, join me in my efforts in the Summer Lake and Fort Rock Basins.

As I worked over the mass of data recovered by our summer expeditions two things became clear: first, I needed a lot of free time to write my monograph, and to do that effectively I needed to visit museums and universities in the East and Southwest to examine related collections and talk with the men involved in their excavation and study. Now that I had Dr. Barnett as an assistant the instructional program could be arranged should I ask for sabbatical leave. To survive on half my salary while on sabbatical and do the required traveling was another matter and seemed an insurmountable obstacle. Cecilia and I decided that we would try some way to find the money and began to plan accordingly. Fellowships were very scarce, but I could try for one and hope to be a fortunate applicant. I asked Dr. Merriam if he would support my application to the Guggenheim Foundation for the comparative study I had in mind. He promised his enthusiastic support. I decided to make the application, feeling rather daring, for the Guggenheims were prize fellowships. I made my application for the 1940–41 academic year, then continued with my work and waited.

As I was preparing to leave for the office an airmail, special delivery letter arrived from the Guggenheim Foundation. Cecilia had received it, so I asked her to open it. Making clear that this letter was not to be taken as evidence of a grant, it asked for a very simple form of budget, mainly to see, I took it, that I knew what I was doing. We sent the information promptly, for we had gone over it so often in our planning. More waiting and keeping the information to ourselves. Then came the announcement that I had been appointed a John Simon Guggenheim Memorial Fellow for the year 1940-41! Again another world was opening to us. I received a congratulatory note from my volcanologist friend, Howel Williams, when the public announcements were made, but I can recall none from the administration of my own university; given the situation at the time, had there been such, I am sure I would have remembered.

After the dreaming came the planning, and it had to be done under the pressure of time. Fortunately, the budget request had alerted Cecilia and me to the strong possibility, if not certainty of the grant, so we had done some preliminary planning. I had also alerted my colleague, Homer, and we had secretly discussed the steps to take. My official announcement of the award sent me to Dean Gilbert to alert him and request sabbatical leave on half pay for the year 1940-41. My request was granted, to be forwarded through channels for certain acceptance. Homer's and my plans for him to replace me were accepted and could be finalized. Most of our important books and household objects we stored in a friend's house and our old dog, Pat, was placed in the care of a veterinarian who knew him. With our 1938 Ford loaded to the gunwales, Cecilia in a small reserved spot on the rear seat, and our daughter Gem beside me, the driver, the Cressmans moved out on the start of an exciting and remarkable adventure. The year? 1940–41.

Planning had been carefully done to have us first in the East through the New Year, then after a week in Chicago to go on to Santa Fe, New Mexico, where the Laboratory of Anthropology had invited us to stay as long as we could and make use of their facilities. July, our final month, we would probably spend at the University of California at Berkeley to tie up all loose ends. Our family in Pennsylvania had invited us to be their guests in their spacious home near Pughtown, and offered the family car for daily use in case I wished to work at the University of Pennsylvania in Philadelphia.

I stopped at the University of California on our way east to call on Dr. Alfred Kroeber, head of the Department of Anthropology, and show him some of the basketry specimens I had brought with me. He was very impressed and discussed them with me, repeating the invitation to stop on our return, and wished us well. Following a short stop at my brother's family in Whittier, California, we would drive to Santa Fe. What happened there entirely apart from our planning is worth recounting. Arriving late in the day with a rain-mixed-with-snow welcome, we were unloading for the night's lodging at the La Posada Inn when a large, dark-colored sedan pulled in alongside of us. To our mutual amazement and pleasure, here were old friends meeting: Professor and Mrs. Ogburn returning from a drive through the Pueblo country! Before saying their good-byes that night, the Ogburns told us to be sure to let them know when we would arrive in Chicago on our return trip and they would do all they could to help us. What good fortune again!

Stanley Stubbs, the curator at the laboratory in Santa Fe, took us in charge the next day, promising to store our car in a garage, keep the battery charged, etc. We met his family and a real estate agent, a woman who they said would be sensitive to our needs and help us with little trouble when we returned. The working space that would be available to me was shown, and how inviting it was. With matters well under control in Santa Fe, we boarded the Scout, the all-coach train to Chicago, then on to Paoli by means of Pennsylvania's outdated railroad equipment. My mother met us and took us to the gracious hospitality of the Cressman home at Pughtown.

My schedule called for an initial few days work at Penn's museum by daily drives from home; then a week at Washington, D.C., for work at the Smithsonian, followed by a short break at home; and next with the family to Boston to study basketry in the Peabody Museum. We would move on to New York, where my younger brother, Fred, a career medical officer in the U.S. Army, was on duty on Governor's Island; he and his wife had kindly asked us to stay with them. I planned to work at the American Museum of Natural History and study the basketry and other specimens from the "stratigraphic pit" excavated by Harrington and Loud in Lovelock Cave, Nevada,[37] stored in the warehouse of the Heye Foundation in the Bronx. This material had never been adequately described. While in New York we would use the opportunity for museum visiting not directly connected with my project. On the completion of this planned assignment we would return to the family at Pughtown to share some days in that pleasant company and get further acquainted, for this was the first time our whole western family and my parents had been together, and the first since Dad had helped bring the "fair-haired, blue-eyed baby as ordered" into the world. Christmas there would be a festive affair before we separated again for no one knew how long.

The only real disappointment in this happiest of years was in Washington, where Cecilia and I had gone, leaving Gem with the family in Pennsylvania, to make a rather special personal week of it. I was asked to lecture on my work to the Anthropological Society of Washington at the national museum. I welcomed the opportunity and gladly accepted. I had to have slides, the old glass variety, and found that I would have to arrange that myself; I was told where it could be done and I had them made. We were invited by my host and his wife to have dinner at their home before the lecture, a pleasant enough prospect. Time for dinner came but no hostess, while our host evidenced more and more stress symptoms. The black maid-cook came to announce that our hostess had called saying that the bridge party had run longer than expected, but she would arrive soon. When she did and dinner was served, it was a rather strange affair, with a long delay between the meat course and a baked potato, apparently meant by the cook to be treated as quite unrelated items. Cecilia and I always thought the cook was "paying off" her employer for upsetting her plans for the dinner by her lateness in returning from her own social afternoon.

Our host, Cecilia, and I eventually arrived at the lecture to find some late arrivals still coming in. Organization did not seem to be the order of the day, so perhaps I was thoughtless to ask my host, who would preside, just as a matter of course to avoid a flub in some ritual at the start, if there were any conventions to be followed in starting my lecture. "Just don't you try to tell these people how hard and dirty cave work is; most of them have worked in more caves than you ever have" was his amazing reply. It sounded as if I were some peasant from the hinterlands. I wondered what the rest of the night would bring.

After finishing my lecture with some very good slides showing our caves and the clean stratigraphy, I accepted questions from the audience. The upshot came when the projector operator, whose name, if I recall correctly and I think I do, was Julian Steward, practically accused me of falsifying my evidence. Rather curtly I replied, "I am not falsifying anything; if the evidence contradicts the present ideas then the ideas will just have to be changed." Two members of the Smithsonian staff, Steward and Frank H. H. Roberts (I don't know if he was present at my lecture), wrote articles in the *Festschrift* to Swanton, published in 1940,[38] vigorously attacking my conclusions and those of my geologist colleague, Howel Williams, in their attempt to uphold the old theory of the Southwestern origin of the Great Basin culture. Cecilia and I left Washington and its archaeological officialdom with bitter tastes in our mouths. But we had learned by a hard lesson about how old theories hate to die and the danger inherent in being the cause of their demise.

By the close of 1940 I had completed my strictly eastern studies, but I could not escape a sense of depressing intellectual stuffiness—with the exception of E. B. Howard at the University of Pennsylvania—arising from most of my contacts, especially in the Washington experience. Dad's birthday was New Year's Day, for which we stayed on with the family, and shortly after that, with Cecilia and Gem sufficiently recovered from influenza, we took the train to Chicago. There, Dr. Ogburn met us at a suburban station, as he had advised, and took us to an apartment he had rented for us close to the university. He told us to settle in and Mrs. Ogburn would be in touch with us and he would introduce me to the campus. The air already was fresher; we were intellectually home. Chicago, as Sandburg writes, "Where the low great winds arise, and tall trees flank the way, and shoulder toward the sky."

Our week to ten days at the University of Chicago brought Cecilia and me back into the intellectual orbit of new ideas with which we had been familiar. Dr. Cole, head of the Department of Anthropology, asked an advanced graduate student to see that I got what I wanted in the way of data, contacts, and anything which might further my project. He even went beyond the department to have me meet Dr. Paul Martin, at the Field Museum and doing exciting work excavating caves in the Southwest, to examine his material with him. The student prepared for my use an outline of the prehistory of the Illinois country as seen at that time, and discussed it with me. Dr. and Mrs. Cole entertained us at dinner at the Quadrangle Club, the faculty club, and Mrs. Ogburn drove Cecilia and Gem to various kinds of exhibits of interest to both. I was asked to lecture on my work to the Graduate Social Science Club and gave essentially the same talk as in Washington and with the same slides. Here, questions were asked and ideas discussed and no shock expressed that something new was being reported; on the contrary, here at Chicago was the acceptance and evaluation of the new as a way of life. Here was that same exciting intellectual curiosity and freedom to meet new ideas that had marked those exciting days at Columbia with Boas, Ogburn and Giddings. My feelings had not betrayed me; we had arrived back in a different intellectual world.

Reluctantly we said goodbye to our Chicago friends—and they were friends—and again took the overnight coach train, the Scout, toward Santa Fe. Since no rail connections existed between Albuquerque and Santa Fe, the last leg of the journey was completed by bus in a foggy, cold atmosphere to an apartment on Manhattan Street, which we accepted after a brief examination. Here we settled for a happy, productive period of writing until mid-June, when we again moved west.

Santa Fe in 1941, B.L.A. (before Los Alamos) could not have been improved upon as a place to do the kind of writing I had to do, analyzing and synthesizing. At 7,000 feet elevation in a mountain environment, the air was crystal clear, visibility practically unlimited except by the landscape. There was a favorable portent in the atmosphere, both meteorological and social, that here was going to be a place to get things done, that things would fall into place. And so it proved to be. How different it was from all the other dreary urban centers where I had worked, with their grime, competitive and often combative crowds, and too often people with matching minds.

The Laboratory of Anthropology provided me with an office-lab with a large picture window, through which I gazed in disbelief over hundreds of square miles of forested mountains, arid plains, and grassy prairies. Hidden in this vast area were whole Indian pueblos, ranches, and uninhabited areas. One afternoon I watched in amazement as that vast expanse was host simultaneously to three heavy thunderstorms moving across the sky, each separated by sun-filled space from the next, moving on its own course. Petty minds seemed out of place in such a world!

Fellow anthropologists came to Santa Fe, paused for a few days to exchange information, and passed on. There seemed to be, as the Chinese poet Li Po wrote in his *Exile's Letter*, "Nothing at cross-purpose."

The Stubbs family of three, whose small daughter was the same age as Gem, were the most helpful of friends; as families and as individuals we were extremely companionable. Stanley, curator of the laboratory, with his expert knowledge of the Southwest culture, helped me fill out my own comparatively limited familiarity with that noteworthy field, an important item in my research project. At one period we spent several days, he choosing the specimens and I doing the photography, constructing with 35-mm. colored slides a graphic history of Southwestern pottery development for instructional material in the department at the University of Oregon, where it has since been used, together with a large design exhibit constructed with prints made from the slides, as display panels in the MNH.

Mrs. Otero, our landlady, found a music teacher for Gem and graciously invited her to use their piano for practicing.

Stanley arranged with a resident artist interested in aboriginal design to work with me on my basketry for a small wage. Together we worked out the structure and the design as a functional part of it or as a superimposed design element. He then would isolate the design pattern for my illustration.[39]

Visits to nearby pueblos to observe their ceremonial dances enriched my ethnographic knowledge. We went to pueblos well known for their ceramics to observe potters making their beautiful products by hand with the crudest of tools and marveled at the skill so casually but effectively used. We saw the famous Maria of San Ildefonso at work and brought home a bowl or two made and signed by her.

Late spring found us driving to Boulder, Colorado, to confer with Earl Morris in connection with his work on the Basket Maker cave materials from the Durango region. I had met him some fifteen years before—it seemed in a different world that day in Boulder—in New York City when Margaret and I were married and we had dinner with

Earl and his wife, Ann, both of whom were working on the excavation and reconstruction of the Temple of the Warriors at Chichen Itza in Yucatan under the federal government of Mexico and Carnegie Institution of Washington, thanks to Dr. Merriam.

Earl loaned me a fragment of the bottom of a Basket Maker soft basket to study for comparative purpose with my specimens. After taking the specimen back with me to Santa Fe, that thing gave me nightmares trying to solve the intricacy of the fabricator's skill, a skill I am quite sure she exercised almost thoughtlessly as she sat and gossiped with her fellow workers.[40]

At Denver a brief stop at the Denver Museum of Natural History enabled me to see again Dr. Marie Wormington, the young anthropologist whom I met and listened to in one of the small meetings at the Philadelphia symposium. After spending the night at Las Vegas (New Mexico), we woke the next morning to six inches of snow, courtesy of the storm we had outdistanced after leaving Boulder. By afternoon we were back in warm sunshine and mud from melted snow at our apartment on Manhattan Street.

Late one afternoon in spring I returned to our apartment to find Cecilia with her arm around Gem's shoulders greeting me with the unexpected announcement: "We have a young woman in our family now." I gave Gem a kiss—I sensed it was her day—as she stood a little surprised and bewildered by this new and strange manifestation of womanhood so suddenly thrust upon her. I excused myself and hurried to a nearby florist where I picked up an armful of fresh, spring daffodils and took them home and presented them to her, sure that flowers in spring with their promise of growth would free her mind of any possible trauma associated with this, her first experience of budding womanhood.

June 10th (with a skiff of new-fallen snow on the ground—I remember that day well: it was Cecilia's birthday, an affair the family always took seriously; but we were in Mesa Verde and, in the excitement of the day, Gem and I, but not Cecilia, quite forgot the occasion until Gem reminded me two days later in Santa Fe. We had been in one of the most beautiful of the ruins of the Classic Pueblo culture, and the rangers at Mesa Verde, familiar with my work, took us in charge (as they did at Aztec and Pueblo Bonito where we stopped after leaving Mesa Verde). If there was anything more they could have done to facilitate my work and family pleasure, including a forgotten birthday, I have no idea what it was. A long drive brought us back to our apartment long after ten o'clock and all were exhausted. But who cared!

Time had run out, but the portent I sensed when we came was fulfilled, for my year's work was all falling together. My monograph was largely written; only details needed working over and adding to, which could be left to be done in July in Berkeley at the University of California.

Regretfully, now with our Ford fully loaded as we had come, we had to bid good-bye to our good friends and Santa Fe and move west. After a stop at Silver City, New Mexico, to see our dear friends, the Howard Staffords, where he was teaching, we next went to Globe, Arizona (I have told earlier of the Antevs's kindness there), then a short stop at Flagstaff at the Museum of Northern Arizona and to see the mountains and the volcanic ash that had been dated by associated pottery. The last day took us to Whittier again, where we rested for a few days with my younger brother, Wallace, and his family. He and his very small daughter drove me to San Diego to see the museum materials, including the San Dieguito stonework that Antevs had gone on to see after his stop that autumn in Oregon. Our next stop, our last, would be at Berkeley.

There the Department of Anthropology kindly provided an office and work space, where with the help of a hired typist and Cecilia's support I put together the last pages of my manuscript.

A ten-day vacation at a recommended spot on the Russian River on our route north to Eugene enabled us to rest up and "unwind" at least a bit. Then an unanticipated call from Dr. Merriam asked us to have dinner with him and his wife (he had recently remarried) at a hotel in Garberville in the redwood country. Of course we gladly accepted.

He listened with great interest to the story of our year. I had with me a carbon copy of my manuscript, and when he and I took a short walk after dinner I showed it to him. I told him I planned to submit it to the Carnegie Institution to consider for publication and said how honored I would be if he could write a foreword for me. He gave me some advice on how to submit the manuscript and asked to keep the copy overnight. In the morning he returned my manuscript with his congratulations and his promise to write a foreword.

On the second day, after a harassing drive up the coast highway caught in long lines of military vehicles returning to base camp in the north after army maneuvers in California, we arrived at 2064 Potter Street, so glad to be home, but more than grateful for the year made possible by the Guggenheim Foundation fellowship. There would be a few days of rest and unpacking our bags, bringing home our goods stored with our friends and settling down. Gem would return to school with her old classmates; we had kept up her studies on our trip. There would be much shaking down to do at 2064 to establish the old routines by which our academic lives moved. Then Homer and I would welcome the challenge of developing our new program together.

Life in the university as well as our department flowed smoothly. My manuscript had been accepted for publication by the Carnegie Institution, where it would be honored by inclusion in a distinguished series of monographs. My editor, Mrs. Margaret A. L. Harrison, and I were working smoothly together. On the campus the war in Europe seemed far away, with none of the urgency we students felt in 1916. In our immediate family, however, the reality of the fighting was a family affair. Cecilia's relatives were with the fighting forces on the Continent and elsewhere and the family in England was undergoing the bombing raids; front lines had disappeared in the holocaust. While at Berkeley, to keep somewhat better informed than was possible by the available press, we had rented a small portable radio, our first one. We brought it back to Eugene feeling able to afford it by crediting the rental to the purchase price.

I was doing some clean-up work in our back garden in the warm sunshine of a Sunday morning with the earth washed clean by a night shower, when Cecilia called, asking me to go to the small neighborhood store for her in the next block to pick up something she needed for Sunday dinner. As I walked in the kitchen door on my return, she looked at me almost in a state of shock. "The Japanese are bombing Pearl Harbor!"

It was December 7, 1941.

"It can't be; there must be some mistake," I almost cried.

"Listen." And she turned up the volume.

All doubt disappeared.

"Oh, Sheeleigh, what does it all mean?"

"We're all in it now, and everything changes."

Academic life would go on after a fashion, but somehow it had lost its sense of reality and importance. Classes would meet on schedule, but seats where lads sat last week would be empty this week. My book would continue on in its publication process, but I could not help the feeling of relative futility.

This was the second world war for Cecilia and me. The two scenarios of historical process, the world reel and the inner personal reel had lost their synchronization and the inner personal one now was caught up in the wild unwinding of the outer world one. Our lives at the university now would have to join in the wildly speeding outer reel. Yet, somehow we would have to maintain the core of our life values despite the turmoil, for this would not be forever and we would sometime have to come back and pick up the pieces of a lifeway we cherished.

Cecilia, choking back tears, said, "Oh, Sheeleigh, thank God, you, all of us had this past year together."

The declaration of war with Japan and the Axis powers brought the university clearly into the military orbit; many students were subject to the draft and others in the reserves and the National Guard were subject to call to active service, a call not long in coming. I remember a class of mine that was reduced to women, with the exception of one lonely lad sitting in the rear who had failed the physical examination because he was underweight. He returned home to correct the deficiency—to fatten up like beef cattle, I thought grimly. He succeeded and I was told much later that he had coxed a landing craft in one of the Rhine River crossings by United States forces. My classes continued with women students, but some of these would leave to join appropriate services; the remnant and I carried on.

War contracts for teaching special classes for fixed periods were executed between the university and the Defense Department for such things as "preflight training," etc. The only evidence of the war that these classes brought was the marching from one session to the next and compulsory attendance. Our regular faculty furnished the instructors. I had no sense of the "militarization of the campus," as it had been called for these groups of servicemen. Although studying special subjects relevant to the war, they wore civilian clothing, and when moving about the campus differed from the other students only by marching in formations of twos.

Some faculty members left for war service, mostly on secret missions, such as radar development, psychological warfare, and the

O.S.S. Oregon simply fitted into the change of life-style overtaking all universities and colleges.

Shortly after the declaration of war, the Ground Observers, an organization for reporting aircraft, was activated under the Fourth Fighter Command, U.S. Air Force. An announcement was made at a university assembly that volunteers were wanted for this purpose. I responded, reporting to the indicated office in Eugene, and found myself appointed Chief Observer for a certain post, a duty I was hearing of for the first time. This service was composed strictly of volunteers who provided their own method of transportation to the posts and their own gasoline without even an allocation of extra gasoline ration tickets. Each served a two-hour tour of duty in a twenty-four-hour period. The program was under the command of the military down to the Ground Observers. As a Chief Observer it was my duty to see that the post was manned at all times, day and night. I had a roster for the post and each observer had my phone number to alert me in case the relief failed to report or if any other circumstance arose that might interfere with the post's functioning. My roster, especially for the night hours, was composed largely of men from the university faculty and some from town, whereas women served during the day.

In the near hysteria over the possibility of air raids during the first few days, blackouts were ordered and cars were permitted to operate only if headlights were covered with four to six thicknesses of dark blue plastic. After leaving my office at the end of each day, always in the dark, I made a point of driving to the observation post on a ridge reached by the Old Dillard Road. I still feel a special animosity for that road with its loose gravel surface cut into the side of the ridge and its hairpin turns, the bank on the uphill side rising steeply and the edge on the downhill side, with little leeway from the gravel surface, dropping into trees, bushes, and rocks. Usually at that time of year the night fog settled in early, and coming down that hill with plastic-covered lights was an experience. More than once I drove it holding the door open wide enough to see the road surface beside the car as I steered with my free hand on the wheel.

The Ground Observers was a really devoted group. As the winter came on, the difficulties of reaching the post in snow or sleet greatly increased. My phone would ring at one or two o'clock in the morning, and I would be told that the relief had not arrived. My call to the person who should be reporting for duty usually revealed that he had left or, as happened more than once, his car had slipped off the road into the ditch and he needed help to get it out. It was my job if I didn't hear that he had reported in in a few minutes to go and try to help him get his car out and then on to the post. There was a National Guard unit stationed at the fairgrounds in Eugene with plenty of jeeps, drivers, and gasoline. My efforts through Lieutenant Richards, our ground observation officer, to try to get help in the form of transportation for the observers failed because the National Guard had no orders to do that and had no intention of seeking the authority. So much for bureaucracy!

To get an observation post located at a site as good and more easily reached than the one to which I was assigned, I went to the university for assistance; there were various locations on the campus that might serve if a small shelter were built. All I could secure was the use of a spot on the library roof, with a small platform and sections of plywood siding, leaving a wide-open space to the slightly V-shaped "roof." Open to the wind and rain it was barely a shelter, providing a really wretched condition for the observers, especially during storms. But it was so much more easily reached than the other post that we continued to use it.

Somebody at some headquarters who must have had time on his hands developed the great idea that the Chief Observers should attend an Aircraft Identification School to qualify to teach aircraft identification to the observers. I attended such a school as Chief Observer—I had no choice—and still have my certification of successfully completing the course. There was no possibility in the world that the observers would be required to identify the type of aircraft since many had to be reported by sound alone; this assignment was just "busy work," an imposition.

Shortly after the declaration of war, I was having a cup of coffee late in the afternoon with a friend at the College Side, a restaurant mostly supported by university faculty and students. Someone from the office came to tell me that Mrs. Cressman had called to say that there was an "airmail special delivery" letter from the Executive Offices of the White House. I called to tell Cecilia that I would be right home. The letter was notifying me of my appointment to the Oregon State Defense Council as chairman of the Committee for the Conservation of Cultural Resources, something I was hearing of for the first time, and that my appointment would be confirmed by the state coordinator.

In a few days, confirmation by the state coordinator arrived and he asked me to be in Salem on a certain date for a meeting of the entire council. There I was given my instructions: to locate and inventory with special reference to bulk all scientific, historical, and cultural materials in seventeen counties "threatened by enemy action" and arrange for storage in case of an evacuation of the area. I was instructed to recommend a small advisory committee, to be appointed by the coordinator. He gave me a telephone credit card, a travel authorization of five cents a mile when on council business, the authority to hire a full-time secretary, and a list of the seventeen counties "threatened by enemy action" as the means to carry out my assignment. And then he wished me "good luck." As I looked at my list of seventeen counties I understood why his smile, as we shook hands, carried an ironic twist.

My assignment was essentially a staff job: to collect the necessary information for each county and supply it to the State Defense Council, which, in case of evacuation orders, would activate the county councils to implement the orders to the prearranged places for storage. Fortunately, though completed, the program never had to be activated. This program plus my Chief Observer duties plus the responsibility for the department and the museum plus going through the editorial process of my book could not help but cause both physical and sometimes mental stress. I kept a pen and pad by my bed, and in my many periods of wakefulness I jotted down plans for the days ahead. One morning after a bad night, Lucille Day, my expert secretary, commented: "When you have insomnia, Dr. Cressman, we certainly get a lot of work done the next day." I filed my report on time with the State Coordinator and received his congratulations.

A very important side benefit accrued to the state from our mission. As I carried out the committee's work I was appalled by the deplorable conditions for preservation of the official papers of the state and its subdivisions, so I suggested to my committee that we should recommend to the governor the establishment of a state archives division to correct this condition. The committee instructed me to confer with Governor Sprague, an exceptionally well-informed person who, when not in politics, was the editor of an important daily paper, *The Salem Statesman*. The governor strongly supported our recommendation and asked that my committee draw up a plan for an archives department and submit it to him for use in his next term.

We made our report to the governor, but in the upcoming election he was defeated by his opponent, Earl Snell, then secretary of state.

We had to start all over with my going to see Governor Snell. I did this, got his support, and with his political "savvy" and guidance the State of Oregon set up its first archives program, established as part of the State Library.

Since I am writing a memoir, I think it advisable here to recount more fully the details of my part and that of certain colleagues in the accomplishment of our project, a fine example of serendipity at its best, as I see it.

I had met Earl Snell in 1932 when I was making my petroglyph survey and he was the owner(?) of the Ford automobile agency at Arlington, a small town in eastern Oregon, near the Columbia River. Now, ten years later, in his final term as secretary of state, he had defeated Governor Sprague. Robert Sawyer, my committee member from Bend and editor of *The Bend Bulletin*, was our expert on political matters, and he urged on me the need to confer with the governor-elect as soon as possible so that, if he accepted our recommendation, he could include it in his inaugural address and we would thus be "on the way." I very easily made my appointment, and a very pleasant one it was. He greeted me by name and recalled our meeting in 1932 about the petroglyphs. I don't know if he had a remarkable memory or a very competent appointment secretary who gathered information and briefed him on the person he was to see. Whatever the reason, he had the capacity to put one at ease at once.

As secretary of state he had inaugurated a Work Projects Administration program for inventorying the records under his jurisdiction, so he was informed from personal experience of some aspects of our discussion. I explained to him the background giving rise to our recommendation and left with him at his request a copy of our recommendation to Governor Sprague. He was entirely sympathetic to my proposal and said he wanted to study our plan. I thanked him and returned to Eugene.

On the day of his inaugural address, my watchdog in Bend, Bob Sawyer, called me: "Professor Cressman, I have just heard on the radio the governor's message to the legislature and he recommended our program, that is, the establishment of a program for the care of state records. Now you get an appointment as soon as possible and see where we go from here."

"That's wonderful, Mr. Sawyer. I shall get right on it and let you know. Thanks for the information."

I very shortly had my appointment with the governor-elect. He had read our report and very astutely complimented me: "Professor Cressman, your committee had made a very fine report. But I notice it calls for a board to set up and administer the program. Now, Oregon legislatures have become very board conscious and it would be very difficult if not impossible, in its present frame of mind, to persuade the legislature to set up another board. What you want is to get your plan adopted and functioning, isn't it? I have a suggestion that I think would solve our problem: forget the board and set up the program as a department of the State Library, a well-established institution, and then all that has to be done is to increase the library's budget for the new responsibility. The salary for a professional archivist and the operational funds needed would not stand out as new and separate items to be shot down. What do you think of it?"

"I think it is a completely satisfactory solution to our problem, Governor, for after the program is basically established the necessary legislative steps to broaden the archival functions can readily be added."

"Very good. I shall have the necessary steps taken to set up the program in the library. We shall have to have a small subcommittee to consider the recommendation and report to the main committee considering the library's budget. I shall want you to provide me by [such and such a date] a brief statement to support my recommendation, pointing out the need for the program and the availability of space in the library. The small committee will have to hold a hearing to discuss the proposal with you at a time to be set. Can you do this?"

"Yes sir, Governor. You shall have my statement and I shall await the call of the committee. Thank you."

I asked Robert Sawyer and Burt Brown Barker, vice president of the University of Oregon, two members of the subcommittee I appointed, to prepare short statements for me to use, the first on the general nature of archival needs and the second to emphasize historical and other documentary sources. Their statements came in as requested. Only the report from the State Librarian, Eleanor Stephens, was lacking. To expedite her report I asked her to lunch as my guest while I was in Salem, but she had to go home for her "daily lunch with her mother." When several days passed and no report came in, I called and made an appointment with her, for her report was critical. I arrived in Salem to find that she had gone to a meeting in Portland, leaving the message that her cataloger, Miss Blair, would see me. Miss Stephens's meeting, she explained, had been quite unexpected.

Miss Blair, a charming, elderly, graying lady met me, giving me Miss Stephens's message. I explained in a strictly noncontroversial way the purpose of my visit, to get information on the space availability in the library for the proposed archives program. I found Miss Blair strongly in sympathy with our main purpose and eager to help with it. She took me over the whole stack area of the library, indicating what space was available. Space in the library was important since the program visualized extensive microfilming of documents. I was very grateful to Miss Blair and expressed my appreciation. As I drove the seventy-five miles home to Eugene I tried to understand Miss Stephens's attitude and also plan my next step. I don't think she was against the idea of a state archives program, but she didn't want it trespassing on her bailiwick, the library building, so she just dragged her feet or evaded contact.

As soon as I arrived back at my office, I wrote in a brief statement that there was available space in the library to accommodate the needs of the archive proposal. I then mailed it to Miss Stephens with a covering letter saying that the governor required my full report on a certain date and her report was essential for me to comply. In its absence, therefore, I was submitting this statement to her for examination and prompt reply in case she wished to comment. If I did not hear from her by a specific date voicing her objections, I would assume it met with her approval. When no statement of disagreement arrived by the deadline I prepared my report and mailed it to Governor Snell, meeting the date he had set.

I shortly had a call to appear before the subcommittee of the Ways and Means Committee considering the library's proposed budget that included a provision for the archives section. I found myself at this meeting in a small, sunny room of the State Capitol building for a scheduled hearing of two hours. The hearing took on a quite unexpected character when I saw the two subcommittee members. One of them had recently donated, largely as a result of my urging, a valuable collection of authentic Oregon Indian artifacts to the museum; and the other I knew only by reputation, but that shifted when he asked if I knew his daughter, a graduate student in economics at the university. It happened that I did, and she was either expecting to marry or had recently married—I don't remember now—my close friend in the History Department, Gordon Wright. This man was also an avid deer hunter and knew from the documents at his disposal that I worked in southeastern Oregon in the Steens Mountain area, where he went on his annual deer hunt. The hunter of deer and the hunter of ancient cultures had a most enjoyable time sharing reminiscences. Then the other member of the committee shared his intimate reminiscences of how as a small boy he had gone in a buckboard with a pair of horses driven by his grandmother, I believe then the wife of the governor of the state, to buy up for pre-servation authentic Indian wares from remnant Indian families. And these items were now in the M.N.H. of the university. After more than an hour of this enjoyable sharing of experiences and memories, the question of the archives proposal came up. A few pertinent ques-tions were asked and easily answered. I was thanked for coming and I in turn thanked my friends for the opportunity. They assured me that they would give a strong, positive recommendation.

The subcommittee's report was approved by the full committee and the "Do pass" recommendation was approved by the legislature; Oregon was now on the way to the establishment of a statewide archives program. For future historians I published a simple but ade-quate account of the process.[41] It was a bare-bones report on the steps followed in the development of the program. This account here fleshes out the bare bones, describing the many steps involved, the people who contributed and how, and my part in it. The only acknowledgment or recognition of any kind from any university offi-cial or faculty member of this important achievement for the state came some four years later in a letter from then President Newburn.

I have always thought it ironic that an archaeologist, not a politi-cal scientist, nor a historian or any student of government, should have been responsible for the initiation and development of this important aspect of the state's polity. The crucial element in this situ-ation and in many others is the capacity to respond when one sees a problem or condition calling for correction and to take whatever action may be necessary to correct it. Too often the response is hand wringing or whining instead of action. I saw the deplorable condition of official state papers, responded, found strong support, and together we carried the program to correction of the unsatisfactory condition. The demand on my time and energy was heavy when added to all the other activities I was responsible for, but I sensed that this was the time to strike. The condition was favorable and, whatever the cost in effort, we gave the state this important asset. My detailed, intimate account shows clearly that these things don't just take care of themselves; somebody must assume the responsibility.

In the melange of activities demanding my attention during the year 1942 the forthcoming publication of my monograph describing my seven years of archaeological research in the Northern Great Basin was a homing signal to keep me intellectually on course in the competing demands of important but extraneous activities in which I was involved. I was reassured by the warmth of the reception given my manuscript. Dr. A. V. Kidder, director of the Division of Historical Research of the Carnegie Institution, wrote me early in the publication process about '' . . . your admirable report. Because of the significance of the material (this book is going to remain a classic in the field of the study of early man in the New World) I think it is essential that the illustrations should all be of the same high quality possessed by most of them.'' Who wouldn't have been pleased, after this kind of a letter, to bring the few errant illustrations into line.

There was a play running in New York called *Honey Chile*, and as the publication process neared its happy culmination, my editor Mrs. Harrison and I gave the book a kind of vitality by christening it ''Honey Chile.''

The morning mail of January 18, 1943, brought an airmail letter from Dr. Merriam in Pasadena at the California Institute of Technology stating: ''I have received, within the last five minutes, from the office of the Carnegie Institution, one of the first copies of your paper. . . .'' A very warm congratulatory letter followed. My own precious copy arrived soon after Dr. Merriam's. February 9, 1943, to my surprise and real pleasure, brought a very complimentary note from President Erb. My old teacher and friend at Columbia, Professor Ogburn, now at Chicago, on February 2, 1943, wrote: ''. . . my heartiest congratulations. As I look at the work done in this volume I realize how science grows.'' Of all the letters of congratulation I received I think the one I appreciated most, under the circumstances of my becoming an archaeologist, was the one from Dr. Kroeber at the University of California in Berkeley and, after Dr. Boas, certainly the dean of anthropologists in the United States. His letter follows:

Dear Cressman:

Thank you very much for Carnegie Publication 538. It is a fine job. I want to congratulate you particularly on the care and exhaustiveness of your study and on the way in which you have pressed interpretation to the limit of what the evidence allows without ever straining beyond it. The job is going to be fundamental.

Sincerely yours,

(signed) A. L. Kroeber

All this was heady praise for the young archaeologist, without a Ph.D. degree in that field, who had dared to present certain new points of view because "this was what the evidence showed to be the case" and face the attacks of many eastern anthropologists. As I write I can't help but marvel at the strange concatenation of circumstances involved in the chain of events leading to my achievement. That afternoon at Pasadena in 1931, Ruth Benedict had suggested I might do a study of the petroglyphs of Oregon like the one Kidder did for the Southwest. I did that study and found my professional future in the doing of it with Howard Stafford. And now, the role model, Dr. Kidder was congratulating me on my publication that he was happily presiding over. Perhaps in the Valhalla of archaeologists-anthropologists they are chuckling over my wonder.

With this work brought to a happy conclusion, I knew that I could not rest on my laurels, for implicit in the very nature of those laurels was the order to "carry on."

Cecilia and I luxuriated in the rich warmth of the compliments on my archaeological researches, but during those winter months of early 1943 we could not help but look with some trepidation at the months ahead and the kinds of demands that would be made on us. Homer would be away at the University of California in 1943, teaching in the Army Student Training Program, and I would be assisted by a deferred graduate student from the University of Chicago. My duties as Chief Observer in the aircraft warning program continued, as did my work with the State Defense Council. Early in the year, Dr. John C. Merriam arrived to take up residence for several months in Eugene and at the university to work out programs of common interest. It was quite clear that this would involve me. Although Dr. Merriam would focus his attention mainly on the immediate problems he planned to consider here, they would be an extra obligation for me. Yet, the two years that followed in close association with him would prove to be among the most fruitful of my experience.

While trying to keep an effective direction to my life caught in this maelstrom of activity, I was surprised to receive a call from the president's secretary saying that the president would like me to come in to discuss a matter of some importance. Since I was accustomed to his always writing me, sometimes long letters, I thought there must be something frightfully important in the air and replied I would come at the president's pleasure. His secretary set up an appointment for either later that morning or that afternoon.

I was careful to arrive on time, and after the usual amenities I waited expectantly for the important information to be discussed. But when it came, I was completely aghast, but hid my emotion, that the president of the university should take his time and mine with such trivia; it was clear, however, he regarded it differently. With all the seriousness of reporting a major disaster, he informed me that an observer on duty the night before had actually defecated over the side of the library and stained the building. I could hardly believe that we were taking up our time over such a matter. Here was the president, who should never have permitted himself to be involved with such trivia, the work of a janitor or a yardman with a hose, treating this affair as a major delinquency on somebody's part. And since I was called in as the Chief Observer, the reprimand seemed to be directed at me.

The only suitable response I could think of under the circumstances was to reply rather jokingly, if a bit crudely, "President Erb, I have heard many students express the desire to do this to the university, but this is the only one I know of who has succeeded in doing it." My response was inappropriate, in other words, *wrong*. The president began to "chew me out" for the sins of the observers, mostly concerned with their rather pitiful attempts to keep warm. He explained that there had been a number of times when small fires had been started, and once even the tar-paper flooring of the post had been ignited, burning a small hole. And now this matter. This couldn't go on.

When I got an opportunity to reply, it was with scarcely suppressed anger. I reminded him that when we moved the observation post to the campus, with the university's permission, the present location on the library roof was the only place the university would provide for this wartime service; that the conditions there were nearly intolerable on a wintry day and worse at night; that the observers were all volunteers with no compensation, even for expenses involved; that most of the night observers were students waiting to be called for military service, deferred, or men faculty members; that each tour of duty was two hours and no observer might leave the post until relieved by the next observer; that this observer was only trying to carry out orders despite an obvious period of sudden illness like the good soldier he was; that nobody seemed to worry that the observer might have been seriously ill; that the clean-up work was something at the janitorial level, certainly not the president's or mine; that I was trying, with only a graduate student, a 4-F deferred, from the University of Chicago, as my assistant to keep my department on course and not cheat what students we had and for museum work I had one part-time student assistant; that all through 1942, in addition, I had gone through the demanding editing process for my archaeological researches; and that beyond my academic work and Chief Observer duty I was chairman of the Committee for the Conservation of Cultural Resources of the State Defense Council and expected to locate, inventory, and arrange safe storage space in designated areas for the cultural, historical and scientific materials in seventeen counties threatened by enemy action. Yet I was having to discuss this trivia. I ended my tirade by saying that I thought it was time the university administration got involved and did something positive for the war effort besides sending its own men and women to wartime service and running courses under contract with the Defense Department. I thanked him, excused myself, and walked out and back to my office.

Later that afternoon or the next day I had a call from the Physical Plant saying that the president had instructed it to get in touch with me to locate and construct an observation post at some suitable spot on the campus. Someone I was used to working with was sent over, and we carried out the president's instructions, producing probably the best observation post in the region.

My interview with President Erb was, as far as I can remember, the last contact of any kind I had with him.

My colleague Homer Barnett and I had felt that, for some reason we could not understand, we had come to a dead end for the department and museum under President Erb. This situation was especially striking after the dynamic period under President Boyer. Any suggestion for development or improvement seemed to be rejected on the face of it. The status quo was the ideal, but it was not what Homer and I were content with.

President Erb died of viral pneumonia December 23, 1943.

Orlando John Hollis, dean of the Law School, was appointed acting president, serving for two years until replaced by President Newburn. One of the acting president's first actions was related to the budget, and it was of the greatest importance. He instructed all budgetary officers to forward to the president's office a carbon copy of the budget submitted to their deans. Dean Gilbert had a reputation of appearing before the Advisory Council and the president in budget discussions and arguing against the budget proposed by a department head, who would have thought that his budget proposals had been accepted by Dean Gilbert, only to have him report back to the department head that he could not get the budget approved by the president; it would be necessary to accept the revised statement with its cuts or lack of increases. The negative action was always attributed to the president, when he apparently had not seen the budget prior to the meetings. But now, the acting president would have the chance to study the budget and be in a position to make some rational decisions.

Sensing that a new wind was blowing through academia, I rather daringly recommended a small salary increase for myself, the only time I ever asked such in my whole career. I pointed out that I had been at Oregon for fifteen years, had an excellent series of scholarly researches and publications, etc., and I felt that I deserved at least some evidence of the university's appreciation of my services. One morning I received a call from the acting president.

"Professor Cressman, I have been going over the budget requests and notice that you say you have not had a single increase since coming to Oregon. Is that correct?"

"I have had the cost of living adjustments given to the whole faculty."

"No, I don't mean that; I mean a salary increase directly related to the quality of your service."

"I have not had any kind of merit increase. As a matter of fact there was one effort to reduce my salary on the basis of faulty evidence and another to adjust it to length of service, but at a rate to result in a net decrease."

"Thank you very much, Professor Cressman; we shall give your request very careful consideration."

My recommendation was acted on to the extent of a $200 merit increase. This, when added to the across-the-board increases, made my salary for 1945 $4,270. Dean Gilbert no longer held his faculty in fief. A fresh wind was truly sweeping through the campus. I rejoiced in the "fresh wind," but I knew in the days ahead I would need what my former dean, Eldon Johnson, the best I ever worked under, would call at my retirement my "enviable enterprise, scholarly example, and managerial skill. His capacity for parlaying small funds into large enterprises was always the envy of campus and colleagues." My expectations were well founded.

My colleague Homer Barnett and I, in spite of the sense of hopelessness we felt under the Erb administration had talked much about how we thought the department should develop with the museum as a teaching adjunct. Our minds "clicked," for Homer had been a philosophy major at Stanford and came into anthropology after a year of preparatory study to qualify for graduate study in his new field at the University of California. He had a broad training in the humanities. As a graduate student he had done some archaeology directing digs under the Work Projects Administration, and although he had some experience in that field, his real interest was in ethnology, with a derivative interest in culture dynamics or cultural change. This was closely allied to my archaeological concerns and gave us a strong sense of community of interest.

Dr. Merriam's influence on my thinking was both direct and indirect. The former concerned the actualities of our research projects and the second developed in many conversations over lunch, in long drives, and during informal discussions from time to time and where and when the opportunity offered itself. He was a world-famous scientist and was aware of his position. He had foibles, and I experienced both pleasure and disappointment when they appeared. But he was a great man, rich in experience of the world and nature and in the knowledge of how to get things done. When he came here in 1943 his second marriage had been terminated, leaving him with a sense of great bitterness, expressed to me in confidential talks, but never made obvious to the public. The dinner at Gerberville in the redwoods on our way home from the East is where he proudly introduced Cecilia and me to his new wife. I often had to become a confidant, an experience I would have gladly avoided. In 1945 he was terminally ill with cancer, but stubbornly refused to move from the hotel to a hospital. Finally, like conspirators, Professor Ralph Chaney at the University of California, a friend of Dr. Merriam's and his student studying the flora of the John Day Formation, arranged with W. D. Smith and me to ask Dr. Merriam to come to Berkeley during the meetings at San Francisco drawing up the United Nations Charter to lead a group of visiting delegates to see his beloved redwoods, the one way Ralph thought might work. Ralph met his train and took him in charge, telling him that because he was ill he had made a reservation for him at a very good sanitarium for a checkup. The poor old man went with Ralph without complaint. He never left the sanitarium; he died shortly after his admission, probably happy at last to surrender his stubborn will and broken old body to the responsibility of others.

My last service to my old and greatly respected mentor was to observe, but at a proper distance from the actual incident, the legal "burglarizing" of a large safe-deposit box in his name at a local bank—the holder's key had been lost. The appropriate bank officers stood around watching eagerly to see what the large box in the name of this great man might contain. The sole object was a lovely gold chain for a locket! What part of this man's life and what were the events that gave this elegant piece of jewelry its emotional value? Was it too precious to him to permit it to share space in the box with anything else? Whatever the story, it passed on with the dreamer. My close association with this man involved me in experiences often painful but always rewarding as I was asked to share his life past and present and his dreams for the future of humanity, many of them now, I fear, having passed or are passing into the same limbo as those linked to the lady and the locket.

Dr. Merriam's association with the University of Oregon started in 1938, the year before he received his honorary degree, when the chancellor made him "Consultant and Lecturer on the Human Values of Science and Nature," an appointment without compensation but importantly did permit the provision of office space and, I believe, a part-time secretary when he was in residence. Dr. Merriam always believed that the most rigorous scientific work fell short of its goal unless the results were made available to the general population. He had a profound belief in the capacity of the average man or woman to improve the mind and behavior if the opportunity were presented to the person in terms of facts and their meaning.

As president of the Carnegie Institution of Washington he not only devoted his attention and administrative skill to providing financial support of scientific work but also inaugurated a distinctive program of interpretation of the results. He believed if a researcher said that he could not explain his research to the average taxpayer, who in the final analysis supported it, he really did not know what he was doing. Recognizing the existence of the attitude of intellectual arrogance, he organized under the inspired editorship of Dr. Frank Bunker the publication and distribution of the *News Service Bulletin*. Every grantee could be expected to prepare a short article explaining his work in terms suitable for high school students, for it was these sources that provided the future scientists, the supporters of research, and the friends as well as the enemies of scientific work. Dr. Bunker had the magic touch in translating the often scientific jargon for the final article for publication. I am greatly pleased that my report on Catlow Cave appeared in the series.

When radio developed he used that as an educational medium.

As a student of earth history and of life entombed in the rocks, he saw more than the mere record revealed there. He saw the story of the unfolding of natural law with its continuity and change through the resolution of contending forces, and nature he saw not only as a source of beauty in its manifold aspects but also as a great teacher of individuals as well as collective groups striving to live in a democratic society.

He threw his energy, therefore, into the educational program of the National Park System, and the developments at Yavapai Point in the Grand Canyon and the Sinnott Memorial at Crater Lake National Park are monuments to his beliefs and energy. I remember his telling me how in Oregon he went to Robert Sawyer in Bend—his name has appeared before in my story in another context—then, I think, the chairman of the State Highway Commission, to urge him to start a program of state parks by acquiring desirable areas while they were available. The next year he stopped in Bend to see Mr. Sawyer, who said, "Dr. Merriam, we have started the state park acquisition; now, what do we do next?"

"Get people to use them," was the reply.

He became a consultant to Mr. Sam Boardman, the superintendent of state parks, whom I knew, until his death. Although Dr. Merriam's influence is reflected in the excellent state park system, I don't know of a single memorial to him. May my statement have that privilege.

To carry out his ideas at the University of Oregon, he initiated and saw through the organization of two groups of men from West Coast universities and colleges to develop a program of research and education. The parent organization was The Advisory Board on Educational Problems of Oregon Parks, which was officially created by the State Board of Higher Education on July 22, 1941. The second group, derivative of the Advisory Board, was the research arm of the parent body and was approved by the State Board as a separate entity under the name, The John Day Associates, June 12, 1943. I was a member of both groups and the executive officer of the associates. This latter group ". . . as research scholars would be eligible to receive subventions and donations from foundations, philanthropic organizations, and others for the projects undertaken in this field." I was secretary of the Advisory Board, and Dean Ralph Leighton was chairman. My appointment as executive officer of the associates was to last until the membership either made the appointment permanent or replaced me, an act that never occurred.

Although the activity made heavy demands on my time, nothing but benefits accrued to me. Both programs were examples of cooperative enterprise at its best, not only cooperation within a university but also between universities and colleges in different states, Oregon, Washington, California, and the U.S. Geological Survey. This was not lip service to cooperation, but the real thing. I had known many of the men involved earlier in connection with my research program in the Northern Great Basin, but my acquaintance deepened, and others of whom I had heard but not met now came into my ken. As an officer in the organizations I also demonstrated managerial ability, which did not go unnoticed.

Several actions of the Advisory Board resulted in initiating active programs, but one in particular became a significant achievement. Dr. Merriam had suggested the desirability of a lectureship, to be set up in a manner to give it distinction, to be statewide in its reach, to interpret for the intelligent laymen the results of specialized research in science, the lectures to be published and distributed widely. The Advisory Board approved the proposal for a lectureship directed, certainly at first, toward earth history so strikingly exhibited in Oregon and agreed that the name of the lectureship should be the Condon Lectures. A note from the Minutes of the Meeting of the Advisory Board of February 17, 1945 reads: "It was moved and seconded that Dr. Cressman head a Committee composed of himself, Dr. Packard, and Dr. Larsell to make the arrangements and attend to the details that are necessary. It was passed unanimously. Howel Williams was suggested to inaugurate the Condon Lecture series. . . . The meeting was adjourned." And with my acceptance of the charge, I took over one of the most important and satisfying responsibilities of my career and carried it on until I retired.[42] The first lecture, by Howel Williams as suggested, was finally scheduled for 1946. Since there was no 35-mm. projector on the Oregon campus, I had to correct that deficiency by purchase of a Golde, but at present cannot remember how—other than it was by reasonably honest methods—since the budget lacked funds for equipment. I presided at Howel's lecture and dedicated it as a reasonable gesture of recognition ". . . to the memory of Doctor John Campbell Merriam, Teacher, Scientist, Administrator."

To say "I carried it on" is far from true. Cecilia, immediately recognizing the importance to be attached to this lectureship, felt that it should be made a distinctive university event on this campus since I would be responsible. We were never provided a cent toward entertaining or anything connected with the lectures, gladly bearing all expenses personally. Cecilia's social *savoir faire* helped make the lectures the outstanding success they were.

I found as I went through her papers after her death a few letters expressing appreciation for her contribution, unexpected gestures of friendship she shared briefly with me then placed among her treasured memorabilia. I should like to share excerpts—although she would have shrugged off the compliments saying, "It was just my job, my duty"—from three letters in chronological order of their writing. The first is from Robert Oppenheimer, the second from Jean Dubos, wife of René, the last lecturer in my tenure as chairman of the Condon Lecture Committee, and the third from Mrs. Hansen,

the wife of my fellow committeeman from Oregon State at Corvallis.
Under date of May 25, 1955, Robert Oppenheim wrote:

Dear Luther:

When I left Eugene, and again when I left Oregon, it
was clear to me that I would want to write a note to you
about the Condon Lectures. . . . I had a sense at the time,
and I have kept it, that perhaps in an unexpected way they
were useful; and I am grateful to you, and to all who acted
as my hosts, for asking me, and for bringing such warmth
and patience to the undertaking.

They went as well, I think, in Corvallis as in Eugene,
though it is a very different sort of place, and even in
Portland probably they were all right. During my visit there
I met a good many men and women whom I had not
known before whom it was a pleasure to meet, and who
may count in some way as my friends. I have had a very special sense about the week in Eugene, and about the hours
with you and Mrs. Cressman, and my thoughts have come
back again and again with warmth and affection as well as
gratitude. I hope that our paths will cross, and that for one
reason or another you will be able to visit us here in Princeton; but whether they do or not, I shall keep with me an
indelible sense of deep respect and friendship along with my
gratitude.

Very sincerely,

(signed) Robert Oppenheimer

Jean Dubos wrote from New York City, February 14, 1963:

Dear Friends,

We thoroughly enjoyed our weeks in Oregon and I know
that our lives have been enriched by the experience. We
appreciate all that you did to make our visit a happy
one—those things don't happen fortuitously. As we proceeded to Corvallis and Portland one remark we heard
repeatedly was that the Condon Lectures could never be
quite the same again without the guiding hands of the
Cressmans.

This evening I am going to hear Geo. G. Simpson lecture at the Rockefeller Institute. I am sure I am going less
out of an interest in the subject but more because he
belongs to the "Condon fraternity."

I am sure that in the days to come we shall often recall our Oregon experiences and many times, in fantasy, will walk on the dunes in the Honeyman Park.

Our sincere thanks,
(signed) Jean Dubos

Mrs. Helen Hansen wrote from Corvallis on February 18, 1963:

Dear Mrs. Cressman,

Today I am writing this so long contemplated note to you.

. . . .

I wanted so much to tell you how nice it has been knowing you, and being your guest at the annual Condon dinners. We have met so many fine Eugene people, and so many illustrious men. We consider their visits the high spot of each year. Dr. and Mrs. Dubos were especially lovely people and the times they spent with us were most congenial. . . .

Thank you, Mrs. Cressman, for the pleasant times we have spent with you, for your kind hospitality, and for being the wonderful person you are. I hope we may continue to see you often and that you and Dr. Cressman will find the retirement year pleasant and rewarding.

Sincerely,
(signed) Helen S. Hansen

One program recommended by the associates of a quite different kind was the preparation of an inventory of the John Day specimens in the various institutions as a means of facilitating research. Some of these were kept up-to-date and filed with my office, but the situation at Oregon was deplorable after years of near neglect and the travesty of dividing the collections when graduate and upper-division work in science was transferred from Eugene to Corvallis. W. D. Smith and I checked the collection, much of it still in cardboard boxes in various stages of disintegration in the basement of Villard Hall where they had been stored when they were removed from Johnson Hall. Also, much of what was left was still in the matrix of rock in which it had originally been brought from the field. Everything was covered with the kind of filth characteristic of a basement dirt floor. I know; I helped get the stuff out for study.

It was clear that to get Oregon back into the mainstream of verte-brate paleontology, where it once held an important position, a real job of specimen preparation would be required. We had found that a preparator at California Institute of Technology, Mr. E. L. Furlong, had retired and would be available to do the work for a reasonable sti-pend. As the executive officer of the associates and with Dr. Mer-riam's support, I requested a grant from the chancellor in the sum of $3,000. Chancellor Hunter approved the grant, to be administered through the Museum of Natural History—for some reason I can't now recall the Department of Geology wanted nothing to do with the project—and so with that, the museum brought back to Oregon the research in vertebrate paleontology. It unfortunately came to a tragic close when Mr. Furlong was struck by a car and so severely injured that he could no longer engage in any work. But when vertebrate paleontological research was again taken up after World War II in Oregon by the university, it was as a part of the museum program that had performed the brief rescue operation in 1945.

During the course of these other varied activities I had to think about and plan the structure and direction of the departmental pro-gram and my own archaeological research.

In the brief period of Homer's association on the campus and also while he was away on war-related service, he and I had discussed often, at length and in detail, our ideas of how the department should develop. We agreed that we should have a basic, general pro-gram of study, with specialization a function of advanced study. Our four basic fields were cultural anthropology, archaeology, linguistics, and physical anthropology. All candidates for advanced degrees should have a minimal knowledge of the four fields, both for their own training and for their own protection when they went out to teach. In all likelihood, they would be teaching introductory courses, not just an area of specialization. Each one, however, would have to have demonstrated competence in one area of specialization from the four basic fields. Barnett and I could start with the fields of cultural anthropology and archaeology, but staff additions would have to be made and we set a priority on them. Our first staff addition should be in linguistics, with physical anthropology next to complete the four basic fields. Each specialist would be expected to have a secondary field of interest for teaching and research; for example, we visualized our linguist having a competence in East Asiatic culture to teach courses in that field. This was a guiding program that could be modified as occasion required. A case in point: after some experience, to get better balance for our students, we temporarily reduced the importance of physical anthropology and moved into the field of African studies, having the good fortune to find an excellent candidate with an M.A. degree in physical anthropology and his Ph.D. degree in African studies.

Along with our definition of the developmental program of the department I fleshed out what I saw my role to be as the department head. The words "administration" and "administrator" are often to the teaching faculty member terms of derogation. I suppose it is because there is often justification, as my own personal experience with department heads certainly proved, and because the faculty member is so much an individualist as well as a specialist in one field, he tends to extend his area of expertise generally — what I have referred to as the "academic syndrome." The administrator, the department head, who in the end must make the final decision, is often seen as a "paper pusher," and, true, some are just that. Actually, department head is a very important position in the administration hierarchy, with heavy responsibilities of leadership in which one represents both the higher administrative levels and the faculty of one's department. I had tried to learn the principles and practice of leadership from my experience in the military service, and, as an undergraduate and graduate student, from political and other areas of intergroup relationship. I thought it was my duty as the "leader" of the staff composing my department to provide all facilities desirable for each to do the teaching and research along with other expected, legitimate duties; and if I was neglectful, it was the person's duty to call my attention to the situation.

Our family life had, of course, been dominated to a certain extent by our commitment to the war effort. Gem, in junior high school, joined the army of young workers in the fields around Eugene, furnishing vast amounts of vegetables and cherries for the local cannery. She continued this summer work through 1945, concerned then mostly with picking string beans on the same ranch she had worked on since starting. The last year, she and three others at fields elsewhere each picked four tons of beans and received a personal letter of commendation from the governor. But she lost her taste for beans for a long time to come, and it was only years later with children of her own and having to set a good example that she would touch the things. Who could blame anyone after picking four tons one summer? Her senior year in high school brought her a scholarship for the first year at Reed College in Portland, one of the country's outstanding liberal arts, undergraduate colleges. She had a position in the office of a national insurance adjustment corporation and demonstrated sufficient competence that the manager tried to dissuade her from accepting the Reed offer, but we all agreed, as did the office manager, that she should go to Reed; and she did.

To reach the bean fields she had to ride her bike across a very narrow bridge, sharing the space with the regular traffic. Good riding and good luck brought her through those summers, but each working day we worried about her crossing that dangerous bridge. Her mother said that her field pants looked like "Jacob's coat of many colors" by the time she no longer needed them. Patches had to come from what sources her mother could find, for new pants and goods for mending were in very short supply on store shelves.

For Gem it was an excellent experience in associated activity for a common purpose. She also went through some enculturation. One day she came home and while sitting with her mother in the kitchen as dinner was prepared—her mother always had food and drink ready for her as she came in tired, sat down on the short stepladder by the table, and enjoyed that blessed talk of mother and daughter—said, "I wish you would teach me American English."

"What happened, Gem?"

"We were hoeing corn this morning until the beans were ready, and when the hooter sounded at noon, I said, 'There's the hooter; let's eat' and the girls laughed and said, 'Come again, kid, that's not a hooter; that's a whistle.' I wish you would teach me the right words, not yours."

I came in about that time, and the embarrassed mother appealed to me.

"Sheeleigh, I have always heard the word 'hooter' in England. Isn't it used here? I don't want to embarrass Gem."

"The girls are right. We always use the word 'whistle' for the same thing the English call 'hooter.' It's just a bit of evidence that British English and American English are different things."

In September Gem registered at Reed College and the Cressman family became aware of a great gap in our little group.

Cecilia was a partner in our planning for the years ahead when we would have married graduate students and, shortly, young faculty members with small children. She had a remarkable capacity to help these young people adapt to their new and often difficult situation with the housing problems and many others, not the least of which, but often pushed out of consciousness, was combat memories. We would try to close the gap between academia and family life as we had done in the days before the war. She tried to anticipate their needs, not wait for them to develop. I remember coming home late one sunny afternoon in the spring to find the living room blessed with large clumps of beautiful sprays of pink and white apple blossoms. Cecilia, so proudly, showed them all to me.

"Where did these lovely things come from?" I asked.

"Ethel (not her real name) brought them and when she handed them to me I said how lovely they were, but 'Why did you bring them to me?' "

"I was working in the garden and I looked up and saw the blossoms and they made me think of you, and so I stopped work and cut them and here they are. I knew you would like them."

"Oh, Sheeleigh, these young people are so kind!"

My major postwar research problem grew out of the fact that many subsidiary or tangential problems of an interesting nature appear but are laid aside in the demand to get on with the main one. So it was with my Northern Great Basin program. One problem among many dominated my thinking and became so important in itself that in one form or another it directed my future research. The basic problem was: what had happened to the population of the Northern Great Basin as a result of the long, 2,000 years—longer than the period in which Western civilization has developed—of aridity and higher temperature. This worldwide post-Pleistocene period of warm temperature and lessened precipitation, called both the Hypsithermal and Altithermal, varied in its length and intensity in response to local conditions of terrain and permanent water supplies, such as glaciers, rivers, and major aquifers. The same conditions in a localized way applied in the Northern Great Basin. My experiences in 1934 with Spaulding at Big Spring and South Corral and then at Silver Lake—a part of the Fort Rock Basin with a reported depth of six feet of water in 1886, but only dust, sagebrush, and tumbleweed in 1938 when we first worked there—and many others kept me, with my interest in the lives of the people whose artifacts we were recovering, continually focusing my interest and stimulated me to the decision to devote my effort to finding answers.

Speculatively, it was unlikely, given the various topographic and meteorological conditions in the Northern Great Basin, that complete depopulation occurred. In thinking of this problem I had to remember the basic fact that humans depended entirely on the native fauna and flora for food. Since these were equally influenced by climatic changes, the options for the human population were limited. At any rate, there must have been a tremendous refugee problem. Migration of small groups toward some actual or hoped-for haven where conditions might be better seemed to be a promising lead. Some bits of evidence, Pacific shells, indicated at least indirect trade with the coast, and there was evidence of hunting parties having crossed the Cascade Mountains to bring back stories of that land, green and rich with water. The Columbia River was known and visited. If there was this migration from the Northern Great Basin, the probabilities were that it would be toward the Pacific, using the river systems as the routes of movement and support. No significant archaeological research had been done on the Oregon coast or the Columbia River, but some efforts at historical reconstruction by linguistic analysis had suggested relationships among the coastal enclaves as well as with the postulated early Great Basin language. Available evidence established the Great Basin as the prior place of occupation. Two rivers, the Klamath and the Columbia, transect the Cascade and the Coast ranges, and other rivers, short but rich in food resources, flow from the west side of the Cascades to the Columbia, and those rising in the Coast Range flow directly into the ocean.

Careful and thoughtful examination of all the evidence convinced me of the importance and validity of my project, and I formulated a hypothesis in the form of a question: what was the relation of the culture of the interior to that of the Oregon coast? In one form or another this problem dominated my research after World War II with the exception of two seasons when I returned to Fort Rock to round out my active field research in 1969. It was an exciting and challenging program for our postwar world.

The vision of departmental growth seen by Homer Barnett and me was one of orderly, planned expansion based strictly on demonstrated need for us to carry out our function in the total university educational scheme. Because the plan was carefully thought out and efficiently implemented, when accepted, we gained excellent administrative support. Our plan would result in the authority to grant the Ph.D. degree in 1952, granting nine Ph.D. degrees by 1963, the year of my retirement; bringing in research grants from 1952 to 1962–63 of approximately $500,000; a staff, which would increase from two in 1945 to eleven for 1963; and graduate students carrying out research projects in the United States, Africa, Micronesia, and Southeast Asia.

In addition to my own research after the war, I was interested in Homer's program. I knew well his interest in culture change and his developed interest in the Pacific area, so I raised with him the possibility, if he were interested, in a field program to study change in some area of the formerly Japanese-held islands that would now be under our jurisdiction. He was interested, and together we drew up a project to be submitted by the department, according to the regular procedure, to the Office of Naval Research. Homer told me how he had occasion one morning in the course of his work at the Smithsonian to call on the officer in charge at the O.N.R., and after finishing the matter he had come to discuss, the officer, who had a paper on his desk, asked Homer if he were the Dr. Barnett mentioned in this research application. Homer replied that he was. The officer then told him that they were inclined to fund the grant, but that in some minds it would conflict with a larger project, the Coordinated Investigation in Micronesian Anthropology, being promoted by a consortium of universities, and suggested perhaps the best solution would be to bring the University of Oregon into that cooperating group. A small contribution, $500, would be required. If the idea was agreeable to Homer, he should get the information about the grant, and if it were made, the University of Oregon would be included with the others and Homer would be the appointee.

Homer got in touch with me immediately, and I presented our case to the administration. President Newburn, after but little discussion, making it clear that he thought it was good not only for Dr. Barnett but also for the University of Oregon, said that he would make the grant. What a change from the Erb administration when, in 1940, I had to find $50 to buy a critical piece of equipment for our Lower Klamath Lake project, the last of our lake basin research programs and for which the equipment was absolutely necessary! I had

$200, but needed $50 more. He wrote me a letter suggesting various substitute ways of securing the instrument, all of which I had tried or rejected, and said, "If you can't get it, you will just have to get along without it."

I didn't "get along without it." With the approval of a private donor who had made some money available I was able to shift $50 of that money and get into the field and complete our long program of lake bed research.

It was truly a "fresh wind" blowing across the campus.

Homer returned to the department for the 1946–47 academic year and laid plans for a year's research on Palau Island in the company of a graduate student whose expenses were also funded. Homer was launched on the research program that would occupy the rest of his academic service.

The start of my own research program in 1946, six years after our last field expedition, was a kind of a trial run covering the John Day River from Dayville to Fossil, a small incorporated village several miles from the John Day River, but providing easy access. The area covered had always been a means of aboriginal travel from the Great Basin to the Columbia River, and since the route was provided with promising geological features, it was a likely place to find evidence of use by Early Man had such use occurred. We searched diligently but unsuccessfully for evidence of Pleistocene deposits. But we did excavate a cave and cremation sites, the latter above Fossil. I considered this an experimental step toward the major study I had outlined. Our results provided evidence of extension farther north of our cave culture found around the dry lakes, and the cremation sites carried evidence of Columbia River culture manifestations farther south than previously thought.[43] Actually this field season, short, with about five or six men, including W. D. for ten days, was more a therapeutic than scientific activity for the returned veterans who composed most of my party.

My research plan required excavation of a site or area in the Northern Great Basin with a continuity of occupation since the earliest period of use. Because of evidence that the Klamath Lake area had changed little during the post-Pleistocene with its constant water supply, that seemed the most promising place to try to find our continuity. Further, we could use the old tried and true method of excavating by starting with villages now abandoned but occupied at the time of white contact. We could thus work back in time and from a known culture, and if we could get overlapping sites in time, we could carry our record back in a continuous development. On the coast, the other end of the spectrum, we had to locate sites and hope to find some with evidence of long occupation. This meant a survey of the coast.

I went to my old friend, the American Philosophical Society, and was given a grant sufficient, with some university money added, to put a man and vehicle on the survey in 1947. My former student now now at Stanford, Joel Berreman, had made a survey from the California-Oregon border to Cape Blanco, and graciously gave his survey report to us, which reduced markedly the cost both in time and money for our survey. We would try at the coast eventually to locate sites showing promise of considerable depth and occupation for comparison with the culture column we hoped to construct from our Klamath area occupation. Then would come the study of the rivers for evidence of migration.[44] Our time schedule for this program was open-ended; certainly a long period would be required.

We started in 1947 a completely new practice of enrolling both men and women students in my field parties because we had as a result of early marriage among returning veterans married women students anxious to join our digs, and with a married woman as a member of our team, we would have a chaperon to satisfy all the university's dean of women's requirements. Cecilia's urging back in the thirties to take women was now fulfilled. And they were in every way just as good workers as the men. It was a great improvement for our department to have this freedom.

Two developments in the space of a few years had a profound influence on our program: first was the initiation and development under the Smithsonian Institution of the River Basin Surveys, designed to produce a complete survey of archaeological resources of all river basins in the United States that might be affected by the development of the extensive hydroelectric and flood control programs of the State and Federal governments. The director's office for this project covering the Pacific Northwest was set up on the University of Oregon campus under Dr. Philip Drucker in a vacant, temporary, wartime building. It was understood with President Newburn that for administrative purposes the office would approach the university through the usual channel of the department. Phil and I were old friends and the relation was extremely satisfactory. In 1949 when the basin survey work in this area tapered off, I shared the building with the then occupants while I and my assistants processed and wrote up the Klamath results.

The hydroelectric program of the Federal government moved ahead rapidly; work on the dam at The Dalles was scheduled. Since the Columbia was one of the rivers with the most promise of providing convincing evidence of any interior-coastal relations, it loomed extremely large in our program. As a matter of fact, the second year of our work on the coast closed with a short period of excavation at The Dalles. Since the Federal program under the Corps of Engineers was a carefully scheduled arrangement, we knew exactly how long a time we would have available to work in the reservoir area. But this would be after our Klamath excavations were completed.

The most important development not only for us but also for archaeology in this period, 1949, was the development by Dr. Willard F. Libby of the University of Chicago of the radiocarbon method of dating organic remains. Now we would have a means of ascribing a specific chronological date to an organic specimen in a site. Data could now be ordered chronologically in a calendrical system for the first time. While working on our Klamath dig I was asked by W. D. and other geologists to get a sample of charcoal from the volcano's ejecta of the eruption that formed the crater for Crater Lake to send to Dr. Libby for dating. If this event could be dated it would be a matter of the greatest importance in Pacific Northwest prehistory, for it would give a reference date, a horizon marker, wherever found.

I had asked Dr. Allison to come to my Klamath site for consultation — it will be recalled that he worked with us under Dr. Merriam's arrangement on the Fort Rock-Summer Lake project in the thirties. He agreed to accompany me to a place under the guidance of the chief naturalist of Crater Lake National Park to a site where the glowing pumice had buried a forest. The charcoal from the trees was exposed now at a highway cut just outside the park boundary. Although we had left our camp in lovely weather, at the summit of the Cascades it had been raining and was still misting. I had no idea how much charcoal might be needed for the determination, nor had my colleagues. I had brought two large empty beer cases and a number of newspapers. It was my duty to climb the exposed road cut, get chunks of charcoal, and throw them down to the newspapers at the base, where Ira gathered them in a pile. I was pretty agile then and, with the help of my pick, had no difficulty in locating portions of the standing trees, for each place where a piece of tree was close to the surface was marked by a slightly roughened surface. We took our two boxes back to camp, where I in bathing trunks sat in the sunshine cleaning the material and retaining enough fine, solid pieces to fill one beer case. When I finished the job I looked like a chimney sweep, but the Sprague River was right in front of our tents.

Sometime later when Dr. Libby kindly took the time on one of my Chicago stops between trains to show me his small lab and explain its working, he called my attention to a familiar beer case with a lot of fine chunks of charcoal still in it. How was I, at the time of collecting, to know that only a relatively few grams were needed? But Dr. Libby gave Dr. Crane at the University of Michigan some of the beautiful stuff to use to calibrate his instruments in the laboratory he was in the process of setting up.

Dr. Libby's report on our collection of charcoal gave a date from four runs averaging 6,453 ± 250 radiocarbon years ago for the eruption. Howel Williams had been very close in his estimated data. So, although we were working in the shadow of Crater Lake National Park, our conclusions about the chronology of occupation of the Great Basin were supported.

During the period of our excavations on the Klamath project, two events unrelated to each other but of considerable significance in my career stand out. A complete but very gratifying surprise came while in camp during the 1947 season, the start of our Klamath work, in the form of a telegram saying that the Executive Committee of the Pacific Division of the American Association for the Advancement of Science wished to nominate me, and if I accepted, elect me to the presidency of the division for the year 1948–49. My wired reply said that I would be honored to be elected to the post. I served at the meetings in Vancouver, British Columbia, in June 1949.

The second and scientifically vastly more important event was a phone call from a complete stranger in Eugene, who had been referred to me by Bill Tugman of *The Register-Guard*, and the man had been referred to Bill by Phil Brogan, my friend on the staff of *The Bend Bulletin*—my network of informants coming to my aid. My caller wanted to bring me some specimens he had collected from Fort Rock Cave a few days earlier. Phil and Bill thought they might be very important and referred him to me. I invited him to bring them to the office that afternoon. He had announced that he was a labor union official who had been in Lakeview on business, but stopped on his return drive, a very long and potentially boring one at times, at Fort Rock Cave to see if he might be able to dig up anything. He was a bit of a pothunter and always carried a small shovel with him in his car on these drives.

When he arrived he unfolded the wrapped-up newspaper and, of all things, there was a large piece of a Fort Rock sandal, dry and not treated with any preservative. I told him how we could not use any of our sandals for dating because they had all been treated with preservative. If he were willing to let me have that piece of sandal to send to Dr. Libby for dating—he would not get it back since it would be burned—it would be a most gracious and important contribution. He willingly let me have the sandal fragment. It was this piece of cast-off sandal, which the finder had thought not worth much, that provided the carbon-14 age for the Fort Rock sandals, 9053 ± 350, then the oldest, directly dated artifact in North American prehistory!

Dr. Libby had firmly established my scientific reputation, and those sandals from Fort Rock Cave became internationally famous. I never received any congratulations from the Smithsonian staff of bitter 1940 memories. Shortly after the dates were published, I was at meetings someplace and Kroeber had presided, causing him to linger briefly at his desk. I went up to him to give him my good news, but Kroeber, always the civilized person and gentleman, looked up to see me and beat me to the draw.

"Well, Cressman, radiocarbon dating has substantiated practically everything you claimed. Congratulations."

Our Klamath field party in 1949, our closing year except for a small group on some clean-up work in 1951, numbered about twenty-four men and women. It was a big project and we did a lot of work, and good work too. These students were all working without wages and paying their university registration fees and a mess fee.

At the close of our 1949 field season, I had an appalling amount of data to analyze and write up. After discussing the matter with Cecilia, I decided to apply for a renewal of my Guggenheim Foundation fellowship basically to continue the same problem of interrelation of areal cultures studied in 1940–41, but this time buttressed by Dr. Libby's supporting information. If I could be free of academic duties for a year, I could make excellent progress in my analysis. What a wonderful experience it was that Saturday afternoon working in my office to receive an airmail special delivery letter from the foundation announcing the granting of my application! I immediately applied to the university for and received sabbatical leave at half pay in 1949–50 to continue my study.

As I got into my work I knew I had to go to Mexico and see at first hand the monumental remains of the Indian civilization destroyed by the Spaniards to get a real feeling of cultural perspective in my current work. I made an application to the Wenner-Gren Foundation for a grant of $3,000 for a three-month period of study with Cecilia in Mexico. My application was approved.

Right after the New Year, 1950, Cecilia and I started our drive to Mexico City. Letters of introduction from the Guggenheim Foundation, the Wenner-Gren Foundation, and a couple of the old Carnegie Institution hands who had spent years working with their Mexican colleagues on excavation, restoration, and description of the ancient monuments opened every possible door for us. Our first experience of being caught in bullfight traffic convinced both of us of the necessity of hiring a licensed driver-guide. We did and survived and went everywhere without worries. In those three months, we went to, climbed over, into, and around more monuments than one could dream of. Cards to the local guardian of each monument from Dr. De la Borbolla, the director of the Museo Nacional, brought us special attention.

Only one place eluded us, Tikal. To get there we would have to enter Guatemala. Cecilia was traveling on a British passport, and the Guatemalans, for some reason, liked to make life difficult for such unwise people. I was advised by Dr. De la Borbolla to forget Tikal and stay in northern Yucatan and study Uxmal with its old Maya architecture, and Chichen Itza, which was close by and which showed the effect of Toltec influence on the Maya. This we did.

We visited museums, studied the location of monuments in the landscape, each monument as a whole and in detail, all the while lugging a 4 x 5 view camera and tripod and a small 35-mm. Bolsey for colored slides. Michoacan on the west, Oaxaca with Monte Alban and Mitla on the south, and Tula on the north marked the perimeter of our travels. In all our journey we had no problem until reentry into

Nightly brain session after dinner at The Dalles excavation, 1953. From right: Dave Cole, Lloyd Collins, Art Middleton (back to camera), Tom Newman, Don Thompson, and I.

our country at Laredo, where I was afraid I had lost Cecilia when she failed to return from the immigration office. I finally went to find her and discovered that some stupid bureaucrat read on her travel plan when she received her visa for Mexico that she planned to enter Guatemala, and she had not done that. He kept insisting she should have gone to Guatemala to reenter the United States. I thought the stupid ass was going to refuse her reentry in spite of all my protestations. Finally he relented, and I said, "Let's get out of here." And we did, into Laredo.

After three months I could see meaningful relations all the way from our hunting, fishing, and gathering cultures of the Northern Great Basin to the High Cultures of Mexico; I had an empathy now, not a textbook picture.

While our research in Klamath prehistory was in progress, Dr. Theodore Stern, who had replaced Robert Spenser as our linguistic specialist, carried out ethnological studies with a small group of students as a part of the university's Summer Session. I was able to secure his help frequently in making queries of his informants about old Klamath lifeways and artifacts. I closed out our Klamath fieldwork with the modest project of the 1951 season. My publication on Klamath prehistory[45] appeared in 1956 after the focus of our program

Carrying gear for which I was responsible to tent, The Dalles, 1953.

Completed excavation at the Roadcut Site, The Dalles, 1953. Surface of old U.S. 30 visible at top.

had moved to The Dalles area on the Columbia River. The schedule of dam construction followed by the Corps of Engineers made it necessary to close out our coast work after two seasons, 1952 and 1953, and move to The Dalles for preliminary work in 1952.

The Dalles was a great fishing area that attracted many Indians to gather that resource, and preliminary studies of the camp remains, middens, indicated the area had been in use for a long time. The project occupied us from 1952 through 1957, and we were able to construct a significant, continuous cultural record with recorded dates for about 11,000 years. The occupation had a longer span than that, but work conditions did not permit us to do more. The development recorded by our work holds generally for the Columbia Plateau, although there are local variations. We now had a cultural continuum better documented than that from the Klamath area, for this one was based strictly on radiocarbon determinations.

An important spin-off from our coast research and The Dalles was the initiation of research in southwest Alaska under Don Dumond, a doctoral candidate. It came about in this way. I had discussed with George Y. Harry of the Bureau of Commercial Fisheries of the U.S. Fish and Wildlife Service the significance of the lack of salmon bones in our earliest levels at The Dalles, raising the question of spawning, ecology, possible relation to cold, glacial melt water, etc. We had discussed the temporal significance of the appearance of various strata of molluscan and crustacean remains in the middens about our house pits. Harry thought that archaeology might help him get a history of the salmon runs from Bristol Bay before statistical records were kept. He thought he might be able to raise enough money for a summer testing by a couple of men if I could come up with a capable person. I saw an opportunity for Don for his thesis research, and in 1960 he went and subsequently developed the significant program of study and revision of the prehistory of southwest Alaska. His book, *The Eskimos and Aleuts*,[46] is inscribed for me with these kind words: "To The Chief who began it." Thank you, Don. His program continues after all the years.

As I became more deeply involved with my research at The Dalles and the demands of my teaching, I became convinced that it was important for me to see at first hand the late prehistoric sites in England and earlier ones in France, if possible. Cultural material from our The Dalles dig was so like that recovered from certain English sites and even on the Continent that it raised questions in my mind about the causes of the apparent similarities. Not that they were related; but why these striking similarities? A period of field and museum study in England along with consultations with English archaeologists might help; I was sure it would be beneficial. I could get Spring Term leave at full salary and then spend the summer at my own expense in the study. Cecilia and I made our plans to go.

Cecilia had not returned to her England following our marriage, and so much had happened that she had some anxiety about how she would be received and what she would find. This time, instead of the *Empress of France*, we flew the polar route on an overnight flight from Seattle to London, where we were met by a favorite cousin, Margaret Anderson, who drove us to tea at her apartment, then to our hotel for the night. That night Margaret phoned her widowed and crippled father, Colonel Knox, living near Salisbury in the heart of much of the archaeological history we were interested in, who invited us to come and stay with him and to make plans for our work. We were off to a good start.

Our trip was especially memorable for Cecilia, who was able to meet the few surviving relatives and some old friends, one in particular, Mabel Forbes, now Lady Whitson, who had advised Cecilia when the family moved from Edinburgh to London to try to get a job with the Fabian Research Committee, which she did. Lady Whitson was now in a retirement-nursing home, and the several days Cecilia spent with her were happy but rather heartbreaking, for each knew this was the last time.

As I moved through my study I began to feel the same sense of continuity of development with our Euro-American culture I had felt in Mexico for the Indian culture I was studying. Here was culture development, change, adaptation, and the necessity to meet problems with their challenges. I began to have a sense of wholeness, a completeness in my sense of culture history, something I had never quite felt before.

Toward the end of our stay we went north to see that farthest frontier of Rome, Hadrian's Wall. I had studied Latin for nine years; I had studied Roman history again in 1925–26. In England I had seen Roman roads that cut through Bronze Age burial barrows as they ran straight across country forming the communication system for efficient administration. Now, we stood at this wall, manned for almost three hundred years across the breadth of England to keep out the hostile natives from the north. Broken through occasionally by attacking tribes from those purple forested hills to the north, it was always recaptured and repaired, until A.D. 410 when the barbarian tribes of continental Europe swirled over the empire like a flood, capturing Rome, and this the last outpost of the empire was abandoned and the flood surged through the ruin. Cecilia and I stood together at the northern gate in the wall that day in 1954, talking and trying to understand something of the significance we were participating in—she, as a descendant of the attackers harrying the Romans from those forested hills to the north, a sense of continuity deep within her; I, with my background mostly derived from the New World, yet with much study of hers. Cecilia, as in Mexico, had been my partner in all the field and most museum study in which I had engaged. We discussed and shared; she, with her deep knowledge of British history and culture, helped me place my own observations in perspective. We stood close together; she, holding my upper arm tight between her two palms as I said, "I now am seeing all my knowledge of European history beginning to fall into place, bit by bit, to give me, as in Mexico, a feeling of empathy I never had before, an understanding of

Imperium Romanum, Imperial Rome, and I see the roots of your culture and its flowering in you.''

Looking up at me with a smile, she acknowledged, as she so often did, my affirmation with these lines of poetry in her soft northern speech:

> Day breaks on England down the Kentish hills,
>> Singing in the silence of the meadow-footing rills,
> Day of my dreams, O day!
>> I saw them march from Dover long ago,
>> With a silver cross before them, singing low,
> Monks of Rome from their home where the blue seas break
>> in foam,
>> Augustine with his feet of snow.
>> (James Elroy Flecker, *The Dying Patriot*)

A warm embrace, a last look toward those distant hills, and we turned to walk hand in hand in silence to our waiting car.

While Cecilia was in Edinburgh I went to Cambridge University to study in the Haddon Museum the Star Carr collection, excavated and reported on by Grahame Clark of Cambridge, with which I wanted to compare my early material from The Dalles. Geoffrey Bushnell, the curator of the museum and an authority on American prehistory, was especially generous with his help. Eric Thompson, the renowned Maya authority with whom I had a close acquaintance in the states, had returned to England after his retirement to live a few miles from the university. But oddly enough, he called his new home "Harvard." He and Mrs. Thompson were most gracious—Eric, now deceased, became Sir Eric a decent interval before his death. J. Grahame D. Clark, lecturer in archaeology at Cambridge and Fellow of Peterhouse, offered me the opportunity to attend a class in which a student was reporting on a dig—I thought how like home it all was. Mrs. Clark had asked him to bring me to tea, regretting that she would not have the opportunity to meet Cecilia because of her absence in Edinburgh. I was then the guest of Professor Clark with the Fellows of Peterhouse. I was provided with an academic gown for the occasion, since the gown was the regular dress, and seated on the left of the presiding Fellow. My hosts were careful to involve me in conversation. One, a historian, had been to Oregon and was a friend of Gordon Wright, who had shown his English guest some of the beauties of the Oregon coast. Conversation was easy. After dinner we all retired to the appropriate room and table, where the port and sherry were passed, but in opposite directions. Traditions! Sitting at the High Table in my gown with the students at their table in the Commons one step below recalled the similar practice at the seminary where, in my last year, I, too, as a Fellow sat in my gown at the High Table. The seminary practice had been adopted from the English university custom.

After the port and/or sherry, my host took me to see the wonderful new space he had just acquired for a research, laboratory, writing area, a huge room with very high ceilings in a very ancient building. He had just begun to move his papers in. I thought, "The problems of space know no national boundaries." My practical mind thought, but in silence, that he would need a lot of woolens to work in that room with but a single fireplace for heat. He then drove me to my lodgings, The Boar's Head, and this really memorable visit came to a close.

As a Fellow of the Royal Anthropological Institute I was warmly welcomed in London by the staff, who made every possible attempt to help me with contacts, the use of the institute's library, and other matters that might emerge. I was asked to deliver a lecture in their series in London at the customary hour of four o'clock to make it available to persons in London who would not be able to go home and then return for an evening lecture. Others outside of London could come in for the lecture and afterward return to their homes for dinner and time with their families. I had brought along a collection of 35-mm. slides of my fieldwork for just such an occasion should it arise, so I was prepared, unlike my Washington experience. I spoke to what was considered a "very good audience" and saw some of my Cambridge friends who had come for the occasion. My lecture was well received, with some good questions in the discussion period. Cecilia told me with reassuring kindness that she thought it was the best lecture she ever heard me give.

Cecilia and I, for after the lecture, were invited to join "The Diners," a small group of socially agreeable souls who always took the lecturer to an after-lecture dinner to add food and talk to the intellectual experience. The president of The Diners that year was Lord

Raglan, a person well known in British anthropology, especially the field of folklore. Apparently no one had thought to reserve a place, for there was some discussion on the subject of place, and then it was agreed that an Italian restaurant, close by in Soho, would be able to provide us space. "Apparently" was accurate, for when we arrived there was a bit more discussion. We finally went up a flight of stairs to an adequate but quite bare room, where we were eventually served by a very experienced, middle-age Italian waitress, who obviously had worked long with groups such as she had now drawn. The menu was varied and the orders were, too, which she supposedly wrote on a pad she carried in her apron pocket. It was a good party with much conversation, but I was glad to see our orders appearing. This waitress had solved the variation problem in her own way: everybody had the same, veal cutlet. There was a moment of surprised conversation about our orders, but the waitress replied something in Italian, quite unintelligible to me, but enough intelligible to the others that with good humor we all ate veal cutlet. The general opinion was that this was what one might expect from this restaurant. But what a happy ending to a thoroughly satisfactory day!

This period in England was one of the highlights in my professional career, so much more rewarding than we had dreamed of before we left Eugene. I suppose the main reason it meant so much in my professional life was that I was ready for it. It enriched my resource potential for research and especially for teaching; I could now breathe life into my lectures from experience of what I had seen instead of having to rely on only book knowledge. My classical studies, my year in Europe in 1925–26, my own research in prehistoric cultures capped by our three months in Mexico with the High Cultures, and now this sojourn with the late prehistoric peoples of Britain—we avoided France because of the uncertain civil condition there—rounded out my professional life with a wealth of experience, knowledge, and understanding to enrich my teaching, research, and writing. But the years to use it would be so few! How marvelous it would be to have had this preparation as a young teacher! The irony of it is that reality required the expending of years to achieve this preparation.

Cecilia had found England changed, so warm, so glad to see us, eager to help, so different from the stiff English manner she had known at the time of our marriage twenty-five years earlier.

My mother died while we were in England, but the cablegram announcing her death was delayed a week in delivery because of incorrect filing at the American Express. With her passing went the last of her generation of relatives. We sons were now the grandparent generation. It would take time at home to adjust to the fact that there was no longer an older, respected one in my parental generation to turn to in love and respect.

Our trip came to an end with Margaret Anderson, who had met us on arrival at Heathrow, taking us there to board our overnight Pan-Am direct flight to Idylwild Airport (now John F. Kennedy) in New York. Arriving there the next morning we were met by our daughter (now living in New Jersey) and her husband, Jim, who was cradling a small, blanket-wrapped bundle carefully against his shoulder.

"What's there?" we asked. Gem, her whole face shining with eagerness, gently lifted a corner of the blanket to show us their firstborn, then about six weeks old, Richard Michael. The grandparents even after a night on the plane could not help but see what a superior grandson they had brought to welcome us home. I thought it was rather symbolic: we oldsters coming from the Old World back to the New to be welcomed by two generations of young who belonged to that New.

Our autumn return to the campus from our English study-tour brought me back into the swirling activity of the heavy enrollment and associated activity of the post-World War II campus. In addition to my own research, there were questions of space for offices, classes, staff and requests for my services in nonacademic activities to which I should respond, all of which was confused, not existing in neat categories with special time assigned to each one. They were like the mixture or confusion of autumn leaves in a wild woodlot in a heavy wind storm. Yet each had to be handled on its own terms. With the help of an excellent staff, I managed to keep some order and develop the program of the department.

Our work at The Dalles was finally completed with my report to the National Park Service, but my monograph was not published until 1960.[47] In the meantime hydroelectric projects were being planned and started on the Rogue River under the National Park Service, on the Klamath River by the California-Oregon Power Company, and on the Deschutes by Portland General Electric. I had to do preliminary consultation and planning for these projects and get each one under way and follow it through. Immediately after the closing out of The Dalles work we contracted for a huge project in the John Day Dam Reservoir of the Columbia above slack water of The Dalles dam. This included both banks of the Columbia and extended to the McNary dam, where the first river basin project had been carried out, a distance of about seventy miles. I obviously could not personally excavate these sites, which in some cases were being excavated simultaneously, but I had to set up the contracts, visit the sites for inspection of work in progress, and in general exercise a distant control over it. The logistics in this work were all provided for in the preparation of the contract. This work was the result of congressional action which required that all construction areas under the administration of the Federal government had to be surveyed for archaeological and scientific resources; the cost of any proposed project would be a part of the contract. At the close of the project a report had to be filed, which meant all the material had to be at least grossly analyzed. Our daughter had married in 1948, and Cecilia and I had the pleasure of going together for the first time to these inspections. She always tried to take some kind of fresh fruit or other delectables of the kind the young like but are not often found on field camp menus. Some of these projects were completed before I retired, but others, such as the John Day, continued after my retirement, but under other supervision.

The importance of this contract research was that it all fitted into my master plan for the study of the relation of the culture of the interior to that of the coast, but it came into being before we had been able to get very far with our coast program.

Don Dumond's work in southwest Alaska continued under National Science Foundation grants and other sources, with me as Principal Investigator until my retirement. I went each summer to visit his work and participate for a short period. Dumond used the results of his first year's research as his dissertation. Tom Newman completed the work we had started on the coast at the Netarts sandspit in 1954 while Cecilia and I were in England and used that for his dissertation, the first Ph.D. degree given by the department, in 1955.

My fieldwork would stop with my retirement, but be resumed in 1966.

I extend congratulations to Thomas Newman, first recipient of the doctoral degree in anthropology from the University of Oregon, 1959.

Homer Barnett returned for a year after his absence on Palau with the Coordinated Investigation in Micronesian Anthropology project, then went on extended leave as staff anthropologist to the Trust Territory of the Pacific, and the last six of his eighteen months he was consultant to the high commissioner. In 1956–57 he was a senior professor fellow of the National Science Foundation, studying in New York. As our staff increased in size and members went on research grants, such as Dr. Barnett did, I could make replacements for one term from the unused half of the grantee's salary. I used this method to bring visiting professors for a term or a whole year, whichever the available money made possible. For example, Dr. Stern went to Burma on a Fulbright Award and subsequently to Thailand funded by research grants; and later, Dr. Vernon R. Dorjahn joined the staff and carried out studies in Sierra Leone, Africa. These men always were accompanied by one or more students or later supported independent work by students in their particular fields. I tried to get replacements who were distinguished authorities in the field of the staff member on leave so that area of study would be available to students. This procedure of bringing outsiders, even from abroad, helped to break down the isolation we felt, but for which we had to try to compensate. These visitors took back with them favorable impressions of the university and the high quality of our students. My friendship with some of these men continues.

Dr. Barnett became much sought after by other institutions, but was happy here and not at all eager to leave, even though our salaries were below those being offered by some of the institutions wanting to hire him. I was desperate to keep him, for he was really my teammate and his leaving would have been disastrous for both the department and, I am afraid, my state of mind. After discussing the matter with Cecilia, I said that with the budgets the way they were at Oregon and Homer with a family now and needing a better salary, I would be perfectly willing to forego my differential as head of the department and he could have that and any increase too if that were necessary to hold him. Cecilia agreed with me and said that we could do if it were necessary. I went to Dean Johnson and put my case before him, with no one but the three of us knowing our plan, and he was to keep it secret. Dean Johnson thanked Cecilia and me and said that he did not think it would be necessary, but he appreciated our offer. He found a way to keep Barnett's and my salaries in conformance with the budget.

In this period I was involved more and more in nonacademic activities as well as those on the campus. I had become reasonably well known and was called upon both within the state and nationally for service of one kind or another. One organization I am proud of, since I was responsible for starting it: the Pacific Northwest Anthropological Conference, which had its first organizational meeting of faculty and graduate students, a total of about ten or twelve, at Reed College in 1947. I chaired the meeting. When I retired, the attendance at the annual conference was between two and three hundred. Anthropology had grown!

One time-consuming but exceedingly satisfying campus duty was service for three years on the committee appointed to organize and lay out plans for an Honors College. In these meetings there was much discussion of educational philosophy with a stimulating exchange of ideas, though I must say that not all the ideas were equally stimulating. The Honors College was established and the Department of Anthropology participated in the program.

In 1948–49, as mentioned, I was president of the Pacific Division of the American Association for the Advancement of Science. 1951 found me president of the Western States Branch of the American Anthropological Association. Governor Douglas McKay's Advisory Committee on Indian Affairs called me to membership at the Salem meetings. This committee produced serendipitously a result utterly unanticipated but of great benefit to Oregon. Although there were many meetings with what seemed little progress, I think the fact that the Indians could talk without restraint was a very effective safety valve; the Bureau of Indian Affairs had only an observer, *not* a participant, present. The program of proposed termination of reservations was in progress, and at least two of the reservations were in Oregon.

One day the governor, obviously annoyed with the talking that seemed to go nowhere, said, "Just what do you Indians want anyhow?"

"We want to be treated like white people," came the reply quick as a flash. "We want to be able to buy liquor in the state stores and take it back to our homes and drink it like you white men do; we don't want to have to drink it all down before we enter the reservation to get pulled in by the agency police or get drunk and arrested outside. And we want to intermarry like you whites do."

"Liquor on the reservations is a Federal matter and we can do nothing about that, but the Federal government has a program which will probably correct that situation. But surely, you can marry whites and anybody you want to now."

I joined my voice to the Indians' in protest; they couldn't and I specified the law.

"Is that true, Van?" he asked quite incredulously. (Van Winkle was his attorney general, who always sat in an advisory position on the governor's right.)

Van shook his head in approval.

"Well, that will have to be changed; we'll change it in the next legislature."

The governor was as good as his word, but he ran into a buzz saw when the bill was introduced and referred only to Indians and whites; the law forbade intermarriage of a white to anyone with one-quarter or more nonwhite blood. There were many orientals and blacks who wanted to be included in the proposed corrective legislation, as they certainly should be. The governor had a fine floor manager, who in character was the same kind of person, and he saw the changed plan through the legislature permitting full racial equality in marriage to become the law in the State of Oregon.

I served two years on the Advisory Panel for Anthropology and Related Sciences of the newly formed National Science Foundation. Here I became a full skeptic of the reliability of panels "of one's peers." I argued quite vehemently against an application from a large university supported by a fellow departmental member of the applicant. It was obviously faulted from the basic assumptions on. Finally, Harry Alpert, the chairman, asked for a vote. On my right was a good friend of mine from a great eastern university, who explained his vote, "I think theoretically Luther is right, but I think we should give this man some money." Harry asked me if I would vote against it, and I said I would abstain. He got his money. Another applicant, whose project I argued against, and it had but lukewarm support from the rest of the panel, received a grant because Harry said that he was a "good guy" and ought to have some money. I abstained again when asked for my vote. All the while I thought we were dealing with basic science.

It was out of those two years of service that I suggested Harry's name for the new dean of the graduate school at Oregon, where he was appointed, and raised the level of the Graduate School significantly.

I also served three years, the last after my retirement, on the graduate fellowship evaluation committee of the N.S.F.

President Newburn complimented me by asking me to represent, along with my friend Ralph Huestis of the Biology Department, the university at the centennial celebration at the University of Chicago of the publication of Darwin's *Origin of Species*. As an added inducement he gave each of us the option of taking an extra day at the university's expense to contact any desirable source in our fields within some reasonable distance. I chose to go to Cleveland to visit the new Cleveland Health Museum and enrich that aspect of my experience. The director graciously gave me a full day of his time and knowledge. I could now add this to the list of museums in this country and abroad that I had visited in my field of study.

Following President Newburn, President Wilson gave me recognition by asking me to prepare a statement of "background information" for his commission under a foundation grant to study and prepare a report on the "Rights and Liberties of the American Indian." He had to have the report by a specific date. I promised, with the help of two very competent women graduate students, to have it for him. I worked out a schedule with the University of Oregon Press for printing and we went to work. I delivered the first copy to President Wilson in his office the morning of the day promised in a combination rain- and snowstorm. The commission, to which the report had been distributed before its first meeting, conveyed to me and my student assistants by a letter from its chairman, President Wilson, great appreciation for this extremely helpful contribution to its work.

These experiences although time-consuming were gratifying because they indicated the regard in which I was held by the administration, not in doing or asking favors for myself or the department, but for the larger function of the university. Quite frankly, it meant that because of their confidence, when I did make some proposal or file some request for my department or the museum, they had confidence in the validity and integrity of my proposal.

It had always been a basic value of our department that the students were our reason for being there as teachers. Teaching should not be a job, but a vocation. All research and communication through publication was for the purpose of improving our quality as teachers. With these values I brought our teaching program constantly under scrutiny. I had served when I first came to the university on the Committee for the Improvement of Teaching, and had carried out, with the cooperation of a statistician from the School of Education, various experiments in different kinds of teaching. I had also published a number of short papers. So my interest, as our staff increased in size and the student enrollment in numbers, was not a new facet of behavior.

When we began to offer the Ph.D. degree, we made some fundamental changes to separate the undergraduate program in emphasis from the graduate, the nonprofessional from the professional. We limited the number of hours in anthropology the department would accept at the undergraduate level in order to direct the student to a wider area of study, for an education, really, in humanities, science, languages, and mathematics. The core of the anthropology courses would adequately prepare the student if he or she chose the field as a profession. Too many students came with an unpatterned, long list of unrelated courses that had interested them as undergraduates, but their basic education was lacking; they only had credits. We provided courses at the senior level that would permit graduate credit for the superior student. We set up two introductory courses, one at the freshman level called General Anthropology, which was my course, and one at the sophomore level called Introduction to Cultural Anthropology and taught by Dr. Barnett. Both of these courses satisfied general university lower division requirements, but only one could be used. I taught my course until I retired, and Barnett kept his almost as long.

To improve the opportunities for discussion in our two lower division courses, since we now had a sufficient number of graduate students as teaching assistants or fellows, we reorganized the courses into two hours of lecture and one of discussion. The discussion groups were to be limited to twenty students and conducted by a T.A. or a T.F. The discussion would basically be related to the lecture subject of the week, but not necessarily limited to it. In the process, the T.A.'s and T.F.'s would get experience as teachers. I also used them in my class to help build the objective, multiple-choice exams, necessitated by the schedule imposed by the registrar's office for grade filing. I had each of us bring a set of proposed questions to a meeting, and we would then go over them for clarity, expected answers, and other matters relative to making them good questions, because each one had to have a clear, single answer. This exercise, which I went through with my T.A.'s each term, was a salutary experience for all of us.

Before proposing the introduction of a lecture-discussion program, we experimented on a voluntary basis for a year, with students taking the discussion hours as an extra activity and then rendering their opinion on the advisability of including the discussion groups as part of each course. The response of the volunteers was very positive. I then went to the dean with this supporting data for our proposal and had it adopted. In 1962 we had twenty-four discussion groups for my general course and eleven in the sophomore course on cultural anthropology. We were, I think, the first department in the College of Liberal Arts to adopt this method of instruction.

I loved that freshman course of mine. No one had to take it, but anyone might. I had basically a freshman enrollment, youngsters who were often scared, from all kinds of backgrounds, sophisticated urban to very isolated rural areas. I knew the widely varied environments of Oregon and so empathized with these youngsters. By 1945 I had been through a fairly rich series of experiences, and they were recent and meaningful in shaping my personality. Most of these kids would not, thank goodness, be interested in becoming professional anthropologists, but every one of them would have to live in a society and culture, as did human beings everywhere, often to meet the same kinds of problems even if in different settings. It was my purpose in this class to make the year's experience a meaningful practice in helping them in day-to-day life. Basically, I suppose in more sophisticated terms that, on a universal stage, is what anthropology is about. I tried to help them develop instruments of understanding and methods of response to the daily matters of life that their culture and their responses caused them to face. My function as I told them at the beginning was not to teach them what to think but HOW TO THINK; they then had to make the decisions to which their thinking might lead. Resisting the importunities of publishing house agents, I refused to write a textbook because, as I said, "If I do, I shall have a vested interest in what is in that book and want it to sell. I find ways every year to change this course in some small way to improve it, and having my own text would tend to prevent my doing that. I want to prepare the teaching material year by year and keep the course always free." This course was the most difficult to teach in all my experience, but it was also the most real fun. A graduate course, with the breadth of background and preparation it represented, was easy compared with this one. All my students, however, had one thing in common: their young lives before them.

I gave more time to preparing for this course than any other; I considered it that important. Even though I taught it year after year, it was never quite the same. I remember so vividly a lecture in the spring of 1962, the year before I retired. I had been going through a rather difficult period in my own life, and I felt keenly my responsibility to my students that morning. Our subject that morning was "religion," one which could be loaded with all kinds of booby traps, expected and hidden. Out of my own experience, I wanted to help them appreciate the significance of religion—not its denominationalism, but its meaning in a person's life as a human being everywhere and at all times. When the class was seated and waiting for me to take over, I surprised them by saying, "Put away your notebooks and pens and pencils, all note-taking materials; you won't need them. Even though we are not going to leave this room, we are going for a walk together, a walk through a landscape, and the name of it is LIFE, yours, mine, every man's, every woman's. We are going to look at the landscape as we walk together and try to see and understand many of the strange and not so strange objects, formations, scenery that we shall experience. Come, now, with me." For me, it was one of the most difficult lectures I ever gave. At the close there was an unaccustomed quiet as the students picked up their papers and pencils and in silence walked out. I was exhausted and stood back of the long demonstration table, waiting for all of the class to leave the room. Then I noticed a young man, neatly dressed, really striding down the aisle on my right; he obviously had a purpose. I thought, "Oh my God, what did I say while trying to be so careful?" I looked down at him as he pulled up, trying to give him a warm smile.

"What is it, son?"

"I just wanted to tell you, sir, that I am a fourth-year man and that is the most significant lecture I have heard in all four years."

My "Thank you" to him was heartfelt. What a compliment to me, but what a criticism of his educational experience.

I made it a practice at the end of the year to read a paper in which I tried to tie together into a meaningful relationship what I felt was the meaning of our year's study together. I called it "Hail and Farewell." I had both class sections together at night for that session, between four and five hundred students in a large lecture room. The room was usually well filled—I assumed by all the hopeful ones who thought all the salient points missed by their class absences might be revealed that night and be useful in the rapidly approaching final examination. It was only about three years ago that three women, all from my general class (two were mothers of teenage sons and the other was unmarried and in United Nations work), asked me to have lunch with them. We were talking about the class, and one of them asked if I knew why that big room was nearly always full when I read my paper. I told them what I thought.

"That's partly true, but you used to have a lot of students who had never taken your course but had heard of your paper, and they invited themselves to hear it."

I shook my head in disbelief.

"Have you got any copies of that paper?" Mabel asked.

"No. I was often asked for a copy, but I always replied that I considered it a kind of love letter, love experience with my class, one I did not want to cheapen by having it scattered around. I think enough time has passed now that I can share it; and if you want a copy, I'll supply the original if one of you will Xerox it."

"Fair enough. I'll come for it and see you get it back."

And Mabel did just that.

I read that paper, with a special preface, to my class at the last meeting before my retirement, and the room was full. I was given a standing ovation and applause, and I unashamedly wept as I accepted their expression of respect and affection.

I had come back to Paris in the spring of 1925 knowing that I had to give up the priesthood and be a teacher. That knowledge was well founded.

During the last year or two of my service there was, in addition to the routine affairs of an active, growing department and museum, the necessity of providing for my successor and additional appointments to carry on our program effectively. Negotiations were successfully carried out, with Dr. Albert C. Spaulding to become head of the department and David Aberlee to join the staff as a full professor. This would bring our staff to eleven.

I was asked in 1962 to accept the nomination for president of the Society of American Archaeology. I had previously been nominated twice for president of the American Anthropological Association. When the results of the election were read at the S.A.A. meetings in Tucson in 1962, the result was the same as it had been twice for the A.A.A. I didn't get enough votes. I had a western constituency and never was interested in or made any attempt to engage in politics. After the election, when I saw how distressing the economic condition of the S.A.A. was and the work that would be needed, I was glad that I had lost.

In 1962 Beaver Books of Portland, Oregon, published my *The Sandal and the Cave: The Indians of Oregon*, a small, nonprofessional yet authoritative book for senior high school and freshman college levels. Beaver Books consisted of Dorothy O. Johansen and Constance Bordwell. Connie was professor of history at Reed College and Dorothy was on the staff of the English department at the University of Oregon. It was through this connection that Cecilia and I had the good fortune to have Connie Bordwell join our family circle. Connie was my editor on that project. *The Sandal and the Cave* went through two printings. Then in 1981 there was a third printing by the Oregon State University Press, since Beaver Books now belonged to history. This book was my first venture into the field of nontechnical writing to interpret scholarly research, and I have always been grateful for the experience.

The university assured me that I would have office and laboratory space to continue my work as long as I desired after retirement. There was also the offer of a part-time teaching position to make use of me and to add to the extremely modest Social Security income I should have. The faculty of the department and museum gave Cecilia and me a reception on Sunday afternoon April 21. At an appropriate moment Dr. Barnett announced that as a retirement gift they were establishing the Cressman Emergency Student Loan Fund instead of some customary object usually given, because they thought I would appreciate this gift more than anything else. The departmental staff and former students had collected the funds. I should point out Cecilia connived with my colleagues in this matter. Graduate students, even young faculty members, often arrived with fellowships, but they could not get an advance to pay their fees until they had registered. Since they were often financially without funds until they could get an advance on their scholarship, they could not register because they lacked the money and so were caught. We faculty members often helped, but now there would be a fund from which a student could borrow without a lot of red tape and get on with his registration. (The generous action in setting up this loan fund indicates a deep understanding by my friends of the special relation Cecilia and I always enjoyed with our students. At Cecilia's death fourteen years later, I asked that all donations be made as gifts to the Cressman Student Emergency Loan Fund. And when I join Cecilia, I shall be grateful for the same kind of recognition.) The faculty had also voted to increase the amount of the Cressman Prize Essay award. Many rewarding letters of affection and respect for my work were gathered to be presented at the reception, memorabilia that I highly treasure. Our guests that afternoon at my request were not only from the ranks of faculty and administration but I also remembered my friends in the Business Office and the Physical Plant, with whom I had established friendly relations and who always helped me get things done.

A letter to Cecilia dated May 31, 1963, from a former graduate student, with his Ph.D. degree from the University of Arizona, helps keep this event in proper perspective. The letter follows:

Dear Cecilia:

This turning point cannot go by without me extending my congratulations to you. I, as does Janet, feel that you share the rewards of your husband. I know on several occasions that your support was felt and appreciated by graduate students during the more stressful academic crises. This is common knowledge among several old graduate students. Also it is common knowledge among these same students that you spent many lonely weeks so that Luther could do research. You share with him, as a partner in his scientific breakthroughs resulting from the long field periods.

Your encouragement and devotion to Luther and his work over these many years are an integral part of his brilliant career.

With love and affection,
(signed) Loyd R. Collins

At the alumni luncheon, June 8, 1963, during the commencement festivities, I and several colleagues were given awards for "distinguished academic service." I cherish the citation with my award as among the nicest things that happened to me in a long career. It follows:

University of Oregon MEDAL for distinguished academic service is awarded to LUTHER SHEELEIGH CRESSMAN.

Founder and Head of the Department of Anthropology, founder and Curator of the Oregon State Museum of Anthropology, Director of the Museum of Natural History, and Chairman of the Condon Lecture Series, Luther S. Cressman has for more than thirty years devoted himself

Checking artifacts at the University of Oregon Museum of Natural History.

unsparingly to the fuller realization of the University's educational objectives and purposes. As teacher and as administrator he has unremittingly insisted upon the principle of intellectual freedom and supported the recognition of individual rights, whether they be those of students, employees, colleagues, fellow Americans, or fellow human beings. The University is indebted to him for his long and loyal service, and for his leadership of the Department of Anthropology which has brought to it international renown.

(signed)

Arthur S. Flemming, President

University of Oregon,

June 8, 1963

My last official act, appropriately enough, was with Cecilia at twelve o'clock noon, June 22, 1963, outside Fort Rock Cave, where I gave the dedication address for the National Park Service naming Fort Rock Cave a National Historic Landmark.

June 30, 1963, at five o'clock in the afternoon, I took a screwdriver, removed my name from the office door, locked it, and with a large lump in my throat walked alone from the building to my car and drove home to be welcomed by Cecilia.

We planned to go east for a year to get away from the department with a new chairman, and not be in the wings for anyone who might wish to cry about the changes coming about, and to get acquainted with our small grandchildren, whom we had seen so infrequently. It would also provide a much-needed period of rest for both Cecilia and me, when we could lay plans with some freedom for the years ahead. After some summer work and with our house rented, we loaded our Ford again and turned toward the east, this time New Jersey. It was a strange feeling for both of us after the years at Oregon. We didn't know what the future would hold, but we knew we could meet it. After a leisurely drive through much country new to us, we arrived at Gillette, New Jersey, shortly to occupy a small, comfortable house on Cold Hill Road. There we would pick up our new lifeway, not life, but lifeway.

In the lovely autumn months in New Jersey, Cecilia and I could begin to think about our future. But before settling into that, we took the opportunity to relax from all we had been through by seeing parts of that historic country in its autumn beauty. I wanted particularly to go to Gettysburg and study the battlefield where the tide of the Confederacy broke in bloody defeat. Two world wars later and many smaller ones, but producing the same equally dead men, women and children, had intervened between then and now; we walked almost in despair over the battlefield. I told Cecilia about the old harness maker, my Dad's patient, covering our beat-up baseballs with real horsehide covers and complaining about the Minié ball from the Battle of Gettysburg still in his body, making his rheumatism worse when a storm approached. The battlefield became something more real than fortifications, monuments, and famous names.

As the weather roughened I began to think more and more about something to do at home that would carry on from what I had done. I began to feel, I'm afraid, like the warhorse in Job:

Hast thou given the horse strength? . . .
He saith among the trumpets, Ha, ha; and he smelleth the battle afar off, the thunder of the captains, and the shouting.

(Job 39:24-25)

To join in the battle I made application to the National Science Foundation for a grant to continue my study of the relation in the Northwest of the interior culture to that of the coast. Late in the spring I was informed that my application had been approved to start work in September 1964. We could plan the rest of our leave prudently with this information. We would return to Oregon by going first to the annual S.A.A. meetings at the University of North Carolina, where I would chair a session. I wished to see all I could of the Mound Builder earthworks in the southeast, so we would go to Georgia, then on to Moundville, Alabama, with its Mound State Monument. We would then go to Tucson and schedule our trip to bring us back to Eugene the day our home would be vacant in June.

I was learning both history and prehistory on this trip. My experience in the South previously had been while in transit, and I had never been in the Old South, the southeastern states of the Confederacy. It shouldn't have, but it did come as rather a shock to see on the campus of the University of North Carolina statues of soldiers in the

Confederate uniform. All the monument markers were to the "Rebels," as I had been taught to call them in my northern schools. The contemporary atmosphere of the North Carolina campus life was that history was history, past, and we are in the present. The Etowah Mounds in Georgia gave me my first real glimpse of the platform mounds on which probably stood temples or dwellings of very powerful chiefs. Then on to Moundville near Tuscaloosa, proud of having been the capital of the Confederacy. Mound State Monument and its director, Dr. Jarnette, added greatly to our knowledge. We stayed two nights in Tuscaloosa because of the superior accommodations. At dinner in the small dining room of the restaurant attached to the equally small but good motel, we sat next to a group of three generations. A little girl about the age of our small granddaughter in New Jersey, whom we were beginning to miss very much, reminded us of our Pat, and she wanted to flirt a little with the two nice neighbors. When the group rose to leave, a very neatly dressed member of the party, whom we assumed to be the grandfather, stopped and asked who we were. I told him, and that we were on our way home now after Mound State Monument and that we had flirted a little with his granddaughter because she reminded us of ours whom we had just left. He pulled a card from his pocket and, handing it to me, said, "I am the judge here and if any of my boys [police] see your Oregon license plate they might try to give you a rough time. They don't like Northerners who are causing trouble. Just show them this card and say I told you that they were not to bother you but help you along. Nice seein' you both. Have a good trip."

I thanked him for his help and wished him the best of luck and good night.

I said to Cecilia when alone, "Let's get out of this place the first thing in the morning and put miles behind us." She offered no objection. Arriving safely at Tucson, we spent some ten days exploring the desert, museums, and meeting with colleagues. Then through the great national parks, Zion and Bryce, and up along the east scarp of the Sierras after crossing the Great Basin. Here I saw more of the great, arid area I had studied farther north.

I started my N.S.F. project by going, now with Cecilia, to the University of British Columbia in Vancouver and to the museum to study collections there, then south to Seattle and the University of Washington, where we repeated the performance. There was also some discussion in a kind of seminar. We then moved south, eventually to San Diego, where we continued our study program. In the San Diego area, we went especially to see sites claimed to be Pleistocene in time. The courtesy extended to us in all these places was so gratifying.

With all the material I now had available I decided I would have to ask the N.S.F. to permit a change in the objective of my research because there was insufficient information in the intervening area to provide an adequate assessment of the interior-coast relation. I proposed that I should write a synthesis of Far West prehistory as a background; with that before us, the interior-coast problem became a manageable part of it. The N.S.F. was agreeable to my request, so I reorganized the objective of my research along with the needed changes in approach. The results of this research were published in 1977 under the title, *Prehistory of the Far West: Homes of Vanished Peoples*,[48] to a very warm reception. My only regret, and it was acute, was that Cecilia, who had helped so much, did not live by a space of two months long enough to hold it in her hands.

While I was engaged in the prehistory study, I thought that the availability of radiocarbon dating would make it profitable to return to the Fort Rock area and push that study further. The N.S.F. provided a one-year grant, and in a short period we located a series of closely situated caves with pumice, from Mt. Mazama on examination, which promised to provide an excellent opportunity for a detailed study of the human and ecological prehistory of the area. In Fort Rock Cave in 1966, after two weeks of very difficult excavation, I secured from the top of the gravel and below where we found the sandals a small, but adequate sample of bits of charcoal, which I sent with another sample to a laboratory for dating. I was shocked by the news that the important sample from the top of the gravel had been lost in the unpacking room. All we could do was to try to go back the next year and recoup our loss.

Another application to the N.S.F. was successful and I sent a party under the field direction of Stephen Bedwell, a doctoral candidate working under my direction. Steve had been my field manager the previous summer and was an experienced and thoroughly competent archaeologist who could be trusted at all times. His work, completed and accepted for his dissertation in 1969,[49] was in my opinion one of the outstanding pieces of research in Great Basin prehistory. It established a beginning date of 13,200 radiocarbon years ago for the earliest occupation of Fort Rock Cave, which was on the waterworn gravel. In addition, it provided a meticulously documented record of faunal, floral, climatic, and cultural change through that long period until 3,000 years ago. Collectors had destroyed the deposits from 3,000 years ago to the time the cave was abandoned. All chronology, with one exception, was determined from charcoal samples. The exception was the use of shells to date the most recent terrace in the basin. That date from carefully checked methodology fits into the pattern of the charcoal-derived series.

Steve went to a position at the University of Wisconsin at Oshkosh, where after two successful years, while trying out a boat and motor to be used by his student in summer fieldwork, he drowned in Lake Winnebago, unobserved. The drifting boat was found and Steve's body some fifteen days later far down the lake. I lost a warm and generous friend and anthropology, a promising young contributor.

The University of Oregon Press was in the process of printing a much-abbreviated edition of his thesis, so as a service to an old friend I took over the work of seeing the manuscript through publication. This book is largely undocumented and, unfortunately, has been used in seminars and classes, giving rise to the statement that his work lacks substantiation. If students and their teachers would do what they should, go to the original, they would find documentation to the utmost detail. I have seen what I call "sniping" but no documented, real proof of error in Steve's thesis.

While I worked on my prehistory I was called on for a number of consultations both in the field and on campuses of various western universities. Some of these resulted in publications in periodicals, others not.[50] I had also been giving part-time instruction in graduate student supervision and graduate lectures while finishing the prehistory.

On March 8, 1968, I received from the University of Oregon the "Award for Distinguished Service."

The secretary of the Department of Anthropology delivered to me in a staff meeting one afternoon in 1971, a telegram announcing that the Trustees of the Pennsylvania State University had voted to give me a Distinguished Alumnus Award at the 1971 commencement.

This news was not only an award but also a reward. Cecilia and I planned to be there in person with our young family for my honor. It was duly given.

During these years, without my knowledge, the Oregon Public Broadcasting Service through producer Betty Patapoff, whom I had worked with from time to time, had under way a program devoted to my research in Oregon. Betty had a grant from the National Endowment for the Humanities to prepare a script. I was brought into this program before Cecilia's death, but it was not until June of 1977 that I went into the field for location shooting. The film was completed under the title, "A Quest for Vanished Peoples." This thirty-minute film was approved by the P.B.S. for national showing. Its appearance in various places brought me warm responses from students who had been a part of those years.

Then Margaret Mead's death brought me into the public broadcasting program for the *Odyssey* film and later for British Central O independent producers.

The Northwest Anthropological Conference held its Thirty-Second Annual Meeting in Eugene, March 22–24, 1979. Since I had started the conference thirty-two years earlier, the coordinator of the meetings, Phyllis Lancefield-Steeves, asked me to address the conference at the banquet Friday night on the subject of the founding of the conference. I told Phyllis I could do that in two minutes and sit down. Our conversation, which was pretty one-sided, for Phyllis was a very good listener and I was in a troubled state of mind, was inconclusive. Finally I said that she and other graduate students had been asking recently how I became the kind of archaeologist I am and offered to talk about that. She urged me to do it. I said, "Phyllis, I shall have to tell how I became the kind of person I am, for I like to think I'm an integrated whole, not a series of segments with one called 'archaeology.'"

"Please go ahead and do it," she said and I agreed.

I tried to outline my address, but I simply could not. So I sat down at my typewriter and started "I was born. . . ." It was not a stream of consciousness, it was a string of memories of my growth and maturation and development. I finished at noon of the day I was to speak, knowing that it was much too long, but I intended to cut it in the afternoon. I tried to after lunch, but was quite unsuccessful and thought, as is frequently done, I could flip over pages. There were a lot of people in the audience, between three and four hundred. After a page or two, I sensed that they were *listening* and I kept reading. There was no coughing or leaving the room. I finished, exhausted, and sat down by Phyllis, saying, "How long did I talk?"

"An hour and a half," she replied.

"Oh my God, no!" I said, but I was being given a standing ovation and prolonged applause. Many came to thank me and urge most strongly the publication of what I had read. I asked someone to drive me home, where I reflected on the night's experience.

In a few days I pulled myself together and, after some changes in the manuscript, I sent a typed portion as a feeler to the University of Utah Press, which had published my prehistory. I had been informed that queries had come to press staff members asking if I had written anything of a less professional nature than the prehistory. The press expressed interest and so with some other encouragement I started on my memoirs, *A Golden Journey*, in the summer of 1979, a long, exhausting but rewarding effort.

The long life I have been sharing has been marked by both successes and failures as is Everyman's. Time and space make their insistent demands to which I have to yield with this brief confession: the failure I regret most keenly is that of the movements I saw so promisingly under way at my retirement, interdepartmental and interdisciplinary cooperation in space, purpose, and achievement. But, however faltering my faith in the future might be, I believe we have to face it. As evidence of this faith, on February 24, 1978, with my daughter Gem's concurrence, I deeded this property, my home at 2064 Potter Street, as a memorial to Cecilia, to the University of Oregon Foundation, retaining a life tenancy, the property to be sold on my death, and the annual income from the invested proceeds to be used above and beyond the annual budget appropriation to buy books for the library in the fields of anthropology and certain specified fields in the humanities. I felt that science did not share the impecunious condition of these fields. Each volume purchased will carry a bookplate, with a design including this line from Edna Saint Vincent Millay's poem, *The Pioneer*:

Take up the song, Forget the epitaph.

And now, as the circle nears its full closure, I must bring alive more fully the contribution of Cecilia to my life. Although she appears here and there in the story of my Journey, that is not the way it really was. There could have been none of this life story after 1927 without her. So I close my Journey with a love poem in prose to Cecilia. Lewis Mumford wrote me on September 24, 1980:

> "Your memoir on Cecilia's life . . . has moved Sophia and me to our very depths, . . . you have portrayed with marvelous sureness the wonderful quality of her whole personality. . . . It *is* a love poem.

And now to close the circle, I turn to my love poem, *Elegie*.

Elegie

(after Donne)

Sometimes I feel thy cheek against my face
Close-pressing, soft as is the South's first breath
That all the subtle earth-things summoneth
To spring in woodland and in meadow space.

Yea sometimes in a bustling man-filled place
Meseemeth some-wise thy hair wandereth
Across mine eyes, as mist that halloweth
The air awhile and giveth all things grace.

Or on still evenings when the rain falls close
There comes a tremor in the drops, and fast
My pulses run, knowing thy thought hath passed
That beareth thee as doth the wind a rose.

(Ezra Pound, *Camaraderie*)

I am sure, Cecilia, you remember that golden day of our early years together, and of the years we had fifty, when I, Sheeleigh, came home from my office obviously well satisfied with life, met you just outside the house, and we embraced and exchanged kisses.

Looking at me, those brown eyes alight with fun and happiness, you said, "You *are* my big, buffly-headed tomcat and you are walking today with your tail very high."

"If I'm your tomcat, then you are my puss, puss, pussy cat."

And that was like a christening – name-giving, for soon we were calling each other "Tom, Tom, Tommy Cat" and "Puss, Puss, Pussy Cat." These became our intimate names, rather secret within the family, and the small one became the Kitten. And these familiar names we used till we were together no more. I used to come home

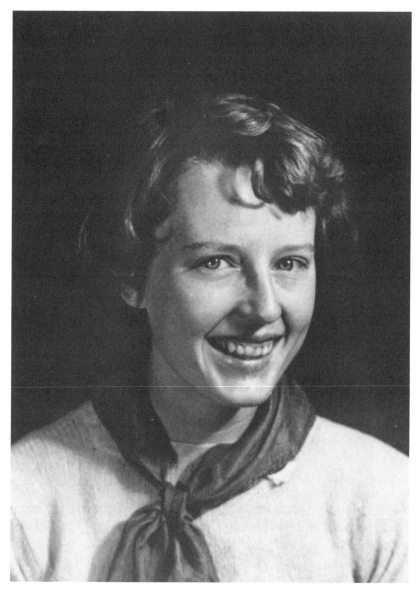

Gem (Mrs. James T. Nelson), about 1953. Photo by Jim Nelson.

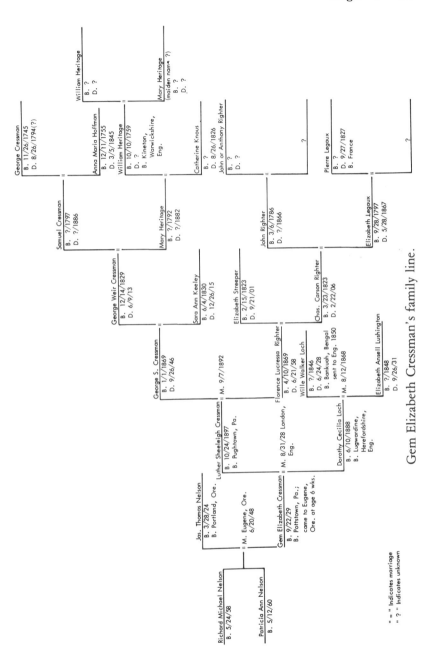

Gem Elizabeth Cressman's family line.

" = " indicates marriage
" ? " indicates unknown

from the office or elsewhere, enter the house, and not finding you at once, call, "Puss, Puss, Pussy Cat," and the answering "Tom, Tom, Tommy Cat" reply would come and I knew I was home. After you went, I used to come into the house and, not finding you, start to give the old call, only to realize its futility before I uttered any sound in that empty place. We gave a lot of poetry and play to our life!

You made this house a lived-in place, a home of warmth and love. Remember the time a new faculty member, used to period rooms, came into our living room, stopped—slightly surprised—and looked around.

"You have everything in this room, don't you?"

"Why yes, we live here."

Home you made a happy place as your friends and guests so well remember.

There was that first night in the apartment and we, model parents we hoped, agreed that when and if the small one should start to wail during the night outside her feeding schedule, we would be *strong* and not acknowledge her demand for attention—for her own good, of course. Yes, it happened: loud and persistent wails.

"Don't get up"—from the wide-awake parent to the other, also wide awake—"she just wants attention."

The continuing wails became almost abusive. We could stand it no longer, for we too needed sleep. So we both went to the crib and found her uncovered, almost wet enough to wring out, and so-o-o cold. Remorse and guilt overcame us. We ended that effort at discipline in a complete collapse of our intentions, and the small one came so comfortably and happily into bed with the guilt-stricken young parents. But we learned, didn't we!

Remember the Sunday morning when she was quietly playing on the bed, counting her toes or something important like that which infants spend a lot of time doing, and we were busy in the other room? There came that awful thump and then screams from that small bundle lying on the floor. We picked up the little victim and, happily, she seemed to quiet down; but since she had made her landing on her head, we thought it wise to call the experienced nurse who worked for the company with which we had her insured.

After hearing our account, she asked, "Did she cry after she fell?"

"She certainly did."

"Don't worry then, she is all right. If she didn't cry, then you should worry."

Later the nurse came and reassured us that our treasure was only shaken up. Those were the early days when, together, we forged our family into a very tight unit bound together by unselfish love.

At the end of our first year we were beginning to get our feet well on the ground, learning our way about, the location of "minefields" in the faculty, and such. We also moved from the little apartment to a house outside the town limits, a very nice house of a family going on a year's leave.

Remember, Puss Cat, how you were *so surprised*, when you phoned an order to the market or the drug store? After a call or two, the clerk responded, "Yes, Mrs. Cressman."

"How do they know who it is without my telling them?"

"They need to hear that soft, lovely voice of yours only once, dear, and you are marked, for it is unique in this town."

You brought more than your "clear northern voice" to the university; you brought a social sense, a sense of the amenities lacking in the community. How well I remember our second year when A.E. (George Russell) the Irish poet, economist, and public figure lectured here—a stop on a long, exhausting circuit. The head of my department, in charge, was apparently unaware of normal courtesies he should extend, so you had me ask him, just to be in the clear, if he had planned anything for A.E. At a rather puzzled, negative reply, I gave him your message: "We would like to have him as our guest then, for he must be awfully weary of those dreary hotel rooms; I knew him in England when I was with the Sociological Society."

So A.E. stayed with us, and you arranged a dinner for him at the hotel with *carefully chosen* guests, all of whom spoke freely to one another. After the successful dinner, A.E. and we talked late into the night. When I asked him to autograph a book of his poems that I had, he said, "I'll do this," and taking from his pocket several pens with different colors of ink, quickly sketched two charming views of his Irish landscape.

The next morning between breakfast and his departure for the train, we had time to walk up on the hill above our house where trees had been cut, sit on the stumps, and talk as the morning fog lifted and faded away, tendril-like, among tall fir trees under the sun's warmth. He was interested in the folklore of the Hopi Indians and curious about what seemed to be some parallels with the ancient literature of India. We returned to the house; and after his warm thanks to you, Puss Cat, for giving him such a happy respite in his long and tiring lecture tour, we left for his train. In our "illustrated" copy of his *Poems* I find his letter of thanks, dated December 31, 1930, from his New York address:

> Dear Cressman:
>
> . . . Thanks for that [a book of Indian texts I had sent him] and all your other kindnesses! . . . I have the pleasantest of memories of my stay with you and Mrs. Cressman. Please give her my kindest regards.
>
> Very sincerely yours,
>
> (signed) A.E.

What kind of memories would A.E. have carried with him of Oregon's university and its hospitality had you not, with your innate appreciation of the social fitness of behavior, invited him to be our guest and sped him on his journey with "the pleasantest of memories"!

That second year found us living "out on the hill" — as we always called it — outside the city limits, the thin population scattered, and beyond the delivery limits of the city's stores. It was a lovely place, except for the poison oak and the isolation. There was no bus service; and since you did not drive the car, when I was at the office or away, you were terribly isolated. You never complained, and we were happy there.

We somehow, I don't remember now, were told of a Mrs. Fisk, who lived close by, from whom we could get butter, milk and cream, eggs, chickens, and rabbits; and she delivered. That was a great help. But since the milk was not pasteurized, the pediatrician of course insisted that the milk, which was to be used in Gem's rather complicated formula, had to be boiled. You used to be so tired sometimes at night that you caught yourself just as you were falling asleep on your feet, stirring the formula. The milk was delivered late, and when everything else was done for the evening there was still that formula. And the small one grew rapidly less small.

I believe it was Mrs. Fisk who told us about a possible young girl to "baby-sit" some hours a day. The girl's mother, Mrs. Smith, came with her to see if Clatys was old enough and responsible enough to do the work. Mrs. Smith decided against it, but was willing to accept the opportunity herself—if it were satisfactory to us, as, of course, if was. So Mrs. Smith, soon to be called by her very young charge, "MiMi," because "Mrs. Smith" was a little too much for her limited speech ability, came into our lives. She became MiMi to all of us and, as Gem said many years later, her second Mummy. Mr. Smith became "Mr. Mi."

You always said, Puss Cat, how greatly MiMi helped you not only with Gem but also in learning the new ways of our country. Gem could not have had a better second Mummy. In addition to helping you with American ways, she was able to help Gem learn the ways expected of her here, as you wished. MiMi came to help us in Eugene the next August and continued to help our family until I went on sabbatical leave in August 1940. The warm friendship lasted through the years.

You followed the English custom, quite new here, of giving Gem her dinner and putting her to bed with her stories, then I came for the good-night ritual as the teller of tall tales or reader, often with a robustious ending, a roughhouse, and much laughter; then good night and the light out.

You and I then sat down quietly to our dinner, our first opportunity for grown-up talk of the day. These were golden moments of communication over the affairs of the day, perhaps news from England, or my scattered family, and husband-wife talk.

You know, Puss Cat, I think it's wonderful that we never engaged in bickering. We certainly had our disagreements; but they were for the most part defused easily, and even our more serious disagreements we worked out. We both had a strong feeling that words have meanings, and we used them deliberately to convey those meanings. Words used in anger cannot be called back, even with apology, although the hurt may be lessened, for the initial use of the word had had its intended impact. At any rate, whatever the reason, the actuality made for a smooth flowing of the course of our family life. And how wonderful it was!

Before we were married you used to copy poems to send me. In this way you introduced me to Yeats and others. One poem of A.E.'s you sent me carries a few lines which I think provide the best description, that I can think of, of your extraordinarily high standards of behavior, social participation, and responsibility:

No blazoned banner we unfold—
One charge alone we give to youth,
Against the sceptred myth
To hold the golden heresy of truth.

(A.E., "On Behalf of Some Irishmen Not
Followers of Tradition," Collected Poems)

"Against the sceptred myth To hold the golden heresy of truth"! What an ideal. You introduced me to that poem and so to the ideal's statement, and I truly think our lives were guided by it.

Your poems also served as a kind of mirror reflecting your personality to me. Through these poems I came to know you before our marriage to a certain extent: your sensitivity, your feeling for elegance, your keenness of perception whether of flowers, persons, motives, or in other words, of life. From the wistful desire for peace in Yeats's poem, The Lake Isle of Innisfree, the country's peace away from "the pavement gray," through the tragic The Countess Cathleen to the rollicking The Fiddler of Dooney, they all brought me messages, statements about your personality. I don't think you consciously intended that, but the fact that you chose them to send me reflected your values. Again, thank you, my dear.

Yes, Puss Cat, you brought to our marriage a value system, "Against the sceptred myth, To hold the golden heresy of truth," internalized, intrinsic to your very being. You never wore a "shoulder patch" or shouted a slogan to affirm your support of a movement, your support or opposition was personal and based on your own tested values.

You weighed a cause before deciding your position and your decision was respected. At one time the American Association of University Women invited you to join. You thanked them, but pointed out that you had no college degree, in fact, had never been to college. To their assurances that the requirement could be waived in your case because you were so much better educated than many members, you replied, "But the condition that I should be a college graduate would not be met; I am grateful for your courtesy, but I just do not meet the conditions for membership and, consequently, I have to decline."

You were elected treasurer of the Faculty Women's Club and were astonished to find that the "books would not quite balance." You were assured that the small difference was really of no significance; the club needed to know only the approximate balance, anyhow. I remember your homecoming that night, Puss Cat, and the tip of your tail was waving back and forth from side to side and the slits in your eyes were very narrow. "I kept the books for the Fabian Research Committee and they had to 'pass audit' by professionals every year, and here as treasurer, I am told they don't need to balance, just approximately. If I am to be treasurer and keep the accounts, the books are going to balance; or why keep a record?"

You worked for causes, such as the United Nations, but you worked within an appropriate organization because you believed in the end the organization had a view; this is quite a different kind of motivation from that which commits a person to a certain line of action because he or she belongs to a given group. The first kind of behavior is based upon commitment to a value, your kind of commitment; the second type, so widely characteristic of "joiners," does not carry a commitment as essential and, consequently, may be as short-lived as the interest of the organization in the subject.

Some years ago a number of civic-minded organizations in Eugene undertook the very laudable task of trying to change the customary housing patterns of the city by which the black population was, in practice, segregated into a forlorn district without adequate utilities, adjacent to a developing industrial section. The program was entirely laudable, for the housing conditions were disgusting for human beings. A group of very active participants worked hard on this program. Apparently the old hostility to having blacks enter a white neighborhood is still sanctioned by some of the once-active supporters of the elimination of housing segregation. Just recently one person, quite strongly involved in the earlier program, advised a neighbor not to sell or lease the house to a black: "Just put it in the hands of a realtor; they just don't tell blacks of the vacancy."

You'll remember another experience in the racial field. A women's organization also in Eugene joined the effort to ameliorate the racial antagonism here. The organization invited Bill Berry, the head of the National Association for the Advancement of Colored People in Portland, to lecture in Eugene. To do this, Bill had to stay overnight. The planners found themselves faced with the fact that neither of the two hotels would accept Bill as a guest without requiring him to submit to demeaning conditions, as Marian Anderson and others had done earlier. So the planning committee, all substantial citizens and not living in one- or two-room apartments, were at an impasse.

Then one had a bright idea: "Let's ask Mrs. Cressman; her husband teaches a course on race relations." So they called you and, of course, you said we had an available room and would be glad to have Mr. Berry. It always struck me a little odd that as far as that host group was concerned "there was no room at the inn." Bill we found to be a very charming guest, much more so than many white lecturers for whom there would have been "a vacancy at the inn." Whenever Bill came to Eugene after that night, he had a standing invitation to stay with us and he was happy to accept. We had many a good talk, too.

Puss Cat, remember that sunny autumn afternoon, the day before homecoming with its big football game, when you received a call from the university housing bureau saying that a party of three Negroes, the mother, sister, and fiancée of _____, the star halfback, or what have you, had been told that the apartment for guests in the new dormitory, Carson Hall, was available for them. But a mistake had been made, and would we possibly have room for them for the night?

You replied, "We would be glad to have them if two of them won't mind sharing a double bed, and the other may have a single bed."

"Thank you so much; they will get in touch with you."

Now it just happened the player, whose family had come to see him play his best in this big game, was essential to any hope of success for the Oregon team. You and I, Puss Cat, were very skeptical of the whole story, but obviously not in a position to do anything about it. The Athletic Department or the coach must have heard about "the deal," for the reservation of the apartment had been quite firm. If the player with his family and fiancée had to endure this indignity, he certainly would probably not be in a very good frame of mind for the game. So someone with "power" got busy, and it was not long until you had another call, thanking you but explaining that a big mistake had been made and that the guests did have a firm reservation after all.

In a few minutes you had a call from the player's mother, asking if she might call on us that evening to thank you for your courtesy. The three ladies came and we had a very pleasant visit; they were much more charming, and, yes, decent than the university official who first called you. I have "reconstructed" what happened at the university, but I am really quite sure that I am correct. The interesting thing, dear Puss Cat, is that your lack of racial prejudice, honesty, and commitment were recognized and honored.

There was also the time the dean of women tried to expel that girl, a major in my department and my advisee. She didn't expel easily and came to see me. It is a long story, but the act for which the dean tried to expel her merited discipline, but not expulsion. Further, the dean did not have authority to expel anyone; only the president could do that. She simply usurped his authority, and most of the girls were afraid to fight, even with a case. Not my advisee!

So I went to work on the case. The outcome was that the dean had to tell the girl she could return, that the expulsion was invalid. After my intervention, the disciplinary committee heard the case, as it was supposed to, and recommended reasonable discipline for the girl. This was a reasonable solution, at least so we thought. But not the dean. The case had become a kind of cause célèbre. A meeting was called by the dean of personnel at which this matter was supposed to be settled. The presiding officer, Dean Onthank, presented the apparent solution to the group. Then the dean of women played what she thought was her trump card: the girl had to live in approved housing (the dean did the approving), but no dormitory would have her — at least so said the dean — her sorority certainly wouldn't, and she, the dean, would not permit her in any off-campus housing; in fact she would not permit her even to stay in a hotel in Eugene that night, so the girl would have to leave Eugene before night.

Asking the chairman to excuse me for a moment or two, I called you, told you the situation, and asked if you would be willing to rent the girl our available room with the understanding that she obey the sanctions imposed on her by the disciplinary committee. I explained what the dean was trying to do. Your reply was an unhesitating "Yes." I returned to the meeting, took the floor, and said that I had just talked to Mrs. Cressman, who said that she would be glad to rent our available room to the girl with the understanding that she obey the sanctions. I did not think the dean would dare intimate that our home could not meet with her approval. We never asked her. The dean's efforts were circumvented. The girl came to live with us, kept her part of the bargain, and graduated; we found her a decent and pleasant tenant and friend, with whom we maintained contact for a good number of years. This affair and your constructive part in it started a project that eventually resulted in the reorganization and "spelling out" clearly in printed form the procedures of the disciplinary system for students at the university.

In the late thirties you urged me to take girls on our field parties, but the conditions at that time made it practically impossible to do so. When my students received Summer Session credits for fieldwork, they were considered enrolled students. A mixed party at that time, even if we could have afforded the extra logistical cost and provisions, would have been unthinkable without a chaperon. A married girl would have satisfied the requirements, but at that time married students, especially in the Department of Anthropology, were almost nonexistent. We started mixed field parties after the war in 1947 when the necessary chaperonage requirements were easily met; your strong support for girls going on our field parties helped make it the standard procedure after that. I wasn't just being stubborn and prejudiced before the war, dear. When we could have mixed parties, I started them at once and found the girls just as good workers as the boys, and often a big help in morale.

Your unstinting devotion to the university also found expression in the help you gave to the formation and development of the Museum of Natural History. For example, there was that collection of Oregon artifacts that the Lew Pattersons of Portland, an old Oregon family, had and which they were considering giving to the university. The Orin Staffords of the university—Professor Stafford was Professor of Chemistry—were the mutual friends who brought us together so the Pattersons could decide whether the Museum of Natural History was an appropriate place to house the collection.

The Pattersons invited us to lunch at their Portland home, with the Staffords, of course, to see whether they thought that I would be a reliable custodian who could be trusted on behalf of the university and to give us some opportunity to see and hear what the collection contained. Our "collecting" expedition was during the war and the final Roosevelt administration. Mr. Patterson was a graduate of the Stanford University Law School, a Republican in politics, rather affluent and conservative. He remembered as a boy of ten or twelve years of age driving around the Oregon country with his grandmother in a buckboard and team of horses to find Indians who still had their native materials and buying these to save them from perishing. The materials were, thus, authentic and valuable. Mrs. Patterson was a compatible partner to her husband. We discovered before lunch that our host had an almost virulent dislike for President Roosevelt and all he stood for. Mrs. P. agreed. Now, you and I, Puss Cat, who were quite of the opposite persuasion, politically and philosophically, tried to be very discreet, since apparently no basic moral values were involved in the discussion.

Lunch was served. It began with a very large, half grapefruit shell, each one filled with an opaque, sharp sauce, which concealed a lovely burden of delicious, little Olympic oysters. My heart sank, for I knew how you loathed raw oysters. I should have had no fear, my dear, for you ate them as though they were your favorite food. As our hostess cleared the cocktail dishes, you said, "How delicious the cocktail was."

As Mrs. Patterson went to the kitchen, I leaned close to you and hissed, "Liar." And at the first opportunity, I asked you; "My dear, however did you manage to swallow those delicious oysters?"

"I wasn't going to lose that collection for the university because of a few raw oysters; though each one required a special effort, for it threatened to go aground."

"Responsibilities accepted and duties well performed," I replied. With your help, Puss Cat, that collection came to the university. Thank you.

As I think back over our life together, Puss Cat, I hear repeatedly three words that describe the foundations on which we built: SHARING, COMMITMENT, LOVING. Basic was the fact that we were deeply, intensely, and unselfishly in love with each other. We had commitments to each other, to our work together, and to the "golden heresy of truth." And we loved to share our experiences, from the sighting of a lovely shell on the beach to the life and death of a close friend or a dear relative. After my retirement and escape from the clock's tyranny, we had so much more time to talk quietly, to read poetry to each other, just to talk, dear, and sometimes to be together in meaningful silence. These hours in their way were golden,

Cecilia at our picnic table, Devil's Lake, High Cascades, warning an inquisitive intruder that the coffee in her mug is hot. Seconds later he found that she was telling the truth, and he jumped back "swearing" rudely at her. Photo by L. S. Cressman.

too, as were our early ones, but the latter had a quality of richness, meaning, and precious time that we treasured, a property with which we could no longer be profligate. The years took on the patina of ancient ivory.

In those golden hours we talked after dinner over coffee, we talked driving long miles in "my eastern Oregon country" with its stark beauty. We talked as we lingered over our picnic lunch in the shade of a spruce tree by a sparkling stream in the High Cascades, or wherever we might be, about many subjects, for we both had seen many years of life and were of a mind to reflect. Further, those years were a time of change: cacophony replaced harmony, contention sub-stituted for participation, lawlessness challenged discipline, and our whole value system was in a state of turmoil. You and I in our long lives had been participants and observers of these changes since their first overt expression in 1914 by the assassin's bullet at Serajevo, and we had much, as thoughtful people, to talk about.

The changing position of women in this changing world was often a subject we explored. Together we wondered about the relation of the imperatives of nature in man and woman to both the old and the new expectations presaged for the future. Long before the Women's Liberation Movement, you and I had explored this subject. We believed in the equality of man and woman and their differences, which made each complementary to the other. I remembered a paint-ing, probably not great art, but significant in its symbolism, that I had seen in 1926 in a gallery in Munich. It was called *Die Quelle*, the Source, the Spring. A young woman, nude, her body carrying the first delicate curves of early pregnancy, holding a jar of water, stands on a masonry arch over a gushing spring. The symbolism was clear and persistent if one reflected. You remember how I held forth for the uniqueness of woman as the SOURCE of so much of whatever it is that makes up living. The contribution of the male to the making of a life is really so minimal and, who knows, in the not-distant future may even be displaced, on wish of the woman, by a needle in the hands of a surgeon pricking the ovum to activate its development pro-cesses. Ever since studying that painting, I have thought of Woman as the SOURCE, and after a half century of life with you, Cecilia, I find all my beliefs validated.

One night, long after my retirement, we lingered happily over coffee, our conversation skipping about in time and subjects. We settled fortuitously on the subject of that unrivaled period, those few spring days in 1926 together in your England.

Your eyes were bright and mischievous: "You wrote me a very nice and fervent letter on your return to Paris."

"I remember very well, but you should have seen the one I didn't send."

Eager and more mischievous, you said, "You wrote another? What did you do with it?" as though meaning "Do you still have it?"

"I tore it up and wrote the one you received."

The letter I sent you, dear Cecilia, was much more than a fervent and honest affirmation of my love when we thought that we should never see each other again; it was a song of gratitude to you for your gift that year, the Gift of Life, the full acceptance of its responsibilities, duties, and rewards. Thirty months after the night I wrote that letter, all the desires and hopes I in Paris sang so fervently to you in London came full cycle to fulfillment. And fifty years later, my dearest, my love and gratitude know no limit.

Among the many tributes to you after you kept your rendezvous was a letter from a student—you knew each other well—now advanced to grandmother status, saying you were one of the few GREAT LADIES she had known. May I call you a modern Renaissance woman, especially one who gave the lie to the First Canon of the Chivalric Courts of Love presided over by great ladies, Eleanor of Aquitaine and others, stating, "Love could not exist in marriage," for you were living proof that love could and did exist and flower in marriage, that marriage is the appropriate environment for love to reach its apogee. You had learned to look at all life, human life, yours and mine, as a part of the Great Stream of Being, following its appropriate course to the eventual merging with that Great Stream. You saw the whole human being as something greater than, more significant than the sum of its parts, but each of those parts you saw as complementary to others. You perceived no dualism, mind and body, body and soul; right and wrong, good and bad did not inhere in the body or its parts, those were moral attributes derived from social values, values themselves with no inherent relation to the objects to which they were often directed, as the history of morals so frequently demonstrates. You, dear Puss Cat, were extraordinarily free of these parochialisms.

Elegance was yours, good taste, discrimination; to be common, to be vulgar was utterly alien to your being. You provided a quality to life, an ambience, if you will, that has been unique in my experience. To have been for fifty years your comrade, husband, lover has given my life a richness it could never otherwise have attained.

Music you knew, loved, and played and continued to enjoy at concerts, as long as your body permitted. The riches of English literature were yours and its poetry your daily companion. You had a remarkable command of its riches and could quote easily and at length. Remember how, as we walked above the surf and watch the water's ebb and flow against the Pacific beaches, you would quote from Keats?

> The moving waters at their priestlike task
> Of pure ablution round earth's human shores, . . .
>
> *(The Last Sonnet)*

Or on an autumn drive:

> Season of mists and mellow fruitfulness!
> Close bosom-friend of the maturing sun;
> ·
> For summer has o'er-brimm'd their clammy cells.
>
> *(To Autumn)*

When I railed at the modern, crass commemoration of Christmas, which ignored the true message of the day, you looked at me in sympathy, but at the same time as much as to say, "Dear Tom Cat, we are not the first," and quoted from Milton's *On the Morning of Christ's Nativity*:

> The Shepherds on the Lawn,
> Or ere the point of dawn,
>   Sate simply chatting in a rustick row;
> Full little thought they than
> That the mighty Pan
>   Was kindly com to live with them below;
> Perhaps their loves, or els their sheep,
> Was all that did their silly thoughts so busie keep.

The tedium of repetitive dishwashing you reduced, certainly, by reading and memorizing from little books of Shakespeare's plays carefully placed in the window above the sink. You used to come to bed sometimes *so tired*, never complaining how tired you were, but lying down and after a sigh, repeating from Alice Meynell's *Renouncement*:

> But when sleep comes to close each difficult day,
>   When night gives pause to the long watch I keep,
> And all my bonds I needs must loose apart,
> Must doff my will as raiment laid away, —
>   With the first dream that comes with the first sleep
> I run, I run, I am gathered to thy heart.

In poems you typed out and sent me over the early years, you conveyed to me thoughts on the wide-ranging nature of love: "We make the Golden Journey to Samarkand,'' the characterization you gave to the act itself, and then love's almost limitless range from the wondrous symbolism of divinity coming to humanity, the concept of incarnation, to the tenderness of the moth's kiss. Yeats tells beautifully the first in excerpts from *Leda and the Swan*:

> A sudden blow: the great wings beating still
> Above the staggering girl, . . .
> How can those terrified vague fingers push
> The feathered glory from her loosening thighs? . . .
> A shudder in the loins engenders there
> The broken wall, the burning roof and tower
> And Agamemnon dead. . . .
> So mastered by the brute blood of the air,
> Did she put on his knowledge with his power
> Before the indifferent beak could let her drop?

And then from Robert Browning's *In a Gondola*:

> The moth's kiss, first!
> Kiss me as if you made me believe
> You were not sure, this eve,
> How my face, your flower, had pursed
> Its petals up; so, here and there
> You brush it, till I grow aware
> Who wants me, and wide ope I burst.

Christmas Eve, December 24, 1976. You remember, Puss Cat, for some three years how you had been having circulatory problems expressing themselves in attacks of dizziness, fortunately of short duration. It was a case of anoxia, insufficient oxygen reaching the brain, but the prognosis was for the condition to worsen. There was, unfortunately, no treatment, but you accepted the situation as a normal course in the stream of life. Then while we were with Gem in the autumn of 1976, you had a very frightening attack in which you collapsed, quite suddenly, and remained unconscious for a short period. You recovered after a day's rest and joined the normal family activities. This attack was, at least to me, a strong, flashing red light of warning. Not only days, but hours, became more precious.

Christmas Day, 1976, we were to be the guests of our friends, the Sterns. Their two children and daughter-in-law were staying with them over the holidays, and we looked forward to a very happy

Christmas party. You and I were having dinner at home this Christmas Eve, and it was a rather gay affair. I had bought a mince pie especially for the occasion. Our talk was about happy things—the party next day, Christmases past, friends and what they would be doing on the morrow—and we remembered that it was already tomorrow in your England.

We had finished the entrée. I was clearing the table for dessert, and while doing this, I had brought in our magnificent pie. You were standing to cut and serve it. Because your hand and the point of the knife did not always agree on the exact target, I said I would help you find the center. So I did and I took the remaining dishes to the kitchen, leaving you standing and serving the pie. Then I heard the most awful crash and dashed in to you lying unconscious on the floor, the dessert plate and a piece of pie on a chair. What that crash was to signal!

After an hour and a half I finally reached the "on-call" doctor; but by then you were showing signs of recovering consciousness on the davenport, where I had succeeded in lifting you, and your pulse and breathing were strong and steady. The doctor saw no necessity to come. He thought with your vital signs what they were, your recovery would follow your normal pattern, but he would come if I wanted him to do so. I replied that, given the situation, I would wait. He was sure you had not suffered a stroke. Your recovery did follow the expected pattern, and I was able to help a quite conscious Puss Cat to bed.

The next day, Christmas Day, I had the doctor, still the "on-call," come to the house. He said that he thought you would be able to be up on the davenport the next day, but there wasn't anything, really, he could do. I could bring you to the hospital, and they could run some tests on you there if I wanted that, but he didn't think they would show anything we didn't already know. I said that I saw no point in it. Monday, you felt like getting up and spent the day mostly on the davenport. A few friends dropped in to see you. Perhaps you stayed up longer than was wise, but you were so happy up and so reluctant to go back to bed. Then you finally went to bed with my help. You left that living room for the last time, after forty-five years of meaningful and happy life centering on it.

One month from Christmas Day you physically left our house for the last journey.

Cecilia, dressed to go out for a family dinner with Jim and Gem Nelson, 1975. Photo by L. S. Cressman.

Discussing designs on prehistoric Oregon basketry excavated in 1938 by my field party, as a part of the Oregon P.B.S. documentary film on my work in Eastern Oregon, ''A Search for Vanished People.''

You were so wonderful as a patient, all through that last month as the ties to life became weaker and weaker. You voiced but one complaint and that so true to your character: "Why can't one be permitted to die with dignity!" The doctor assigned a very competent nurse and an aid to help with your care. What a help they were! You could take less and less food and became weaker and more heart-breakingly frail.

Periods of irrationality occurred, usually at night. The "reality" you then perceived and responded to was always a confusion of memories, real and imagined, of events or situations experienced in your earlier years.

There was the time, and this was a bad one, when you thought your parents were expecting us "upstairs for tea" (in the Harcourt Terrace house). I was keeping them waiting, and *we couldn't keep your parents waiting*! This belief even took us out to the living room and you insisted that we should telephone them because it was discourteous to keep them waiting. Eventually, emotionally and physically drained, I got you back to bed. Then there was the night you insisted that Cameron House (on Loch Lomond), where you had spent so many happy summers in your early years, was on fire.

Another night I was reading in the living room just before coming to bed, and you called to me, "Put out that light, you fool, the Germans are on the beaches." The expression, "you fool," you would never ordinarily have used to me even had you felt I deserved it. Fortunately, I remembered a story of your own experience in World War I when you were caught in an air raid on your way home from work and were impelled, as all others, to run. The steady constable standing out in the street called to you, "Take cover, you fool, take cover." There it was! I had learned that irrationality could not be countered by assertions of reality; to you, my dear, what you thought you saw was as real as what I saw.

There was but one light moment in all this. One night you wanted something, but your speech was slurred and I had some difficulty in understanding you. Finally I understood that you wanted your hot-water bottle refilled. That was done, and you took it and cuddled it to you with a sigh of pleasure. Some time later I again woke from a very uneasy sleep to hear you ask for something and I understood the word "hot."

"Do you want the hot-water bottle refilled?"

"No. I want a hot cup of tea."

You really disliked tea, almost loathed it. Surprised and thinking I still had not heard correctly, I asked again if you wanted the hot-water bottle filled.

"No, don't be stupid [the first time you had ever said that to me], I want a hot cup of tea!"

"I'll get it for you in just a minute."

As I went to the kitchen, I wondered if we had any tea, since some time back, with your approval, I had thrown out a lot of very old tea given by friends who thought, because you came from England, you must be a tea drinker. I was in luck. There on the top shelf I found a package of bagged tea. Since I had put the water on to boil, I quickly had your cup of hot tea on a tray coming to you.

I had you sit up, and steadying you with an arm, I helped you with the tray. You took a sip, and your face brightened with sheer pleasure, "Boy, that is good!" And you drank that whole cup of hot tea as though it was the only thing you had ever wanted. I asked if you would have another cup, but you wanted to lie down and go back to sleep. After giving me a warm smile, you did just that for the rest of the night. I took the tray to the kitchen, shaking my head and wondering.

A few days later I was sitting beside you on the edge of the bed trying to persuade you to have something to eat, but you would just smile and shake your head.

In an effort to give a bit of a light touch to the situation, I asked, "How about a hot cup of tea?"

"A what?"

"A hot cup of tea. You had one two nights ago and thought it was wonderful."

"I did? Ugh, I must have been crazy!"

"No, my dear, it was just the essential Briton in you coming out."

Later one afternoon I sat on the side of your bed, holding and caressing your hand. You lay peacefully, looking up at me, and then surprised me by saying, "Dear Daddy, you are so kind to me."

"If I am kind, dear Puss Cat, I am very happy, for you deserve all I can give you."

Your eyes were happy, and then you dozed off again. This same experience, failure of identification, occurred a day or two later. This time I tried to appeal to you rationally: "But I am not your Daddy, dear Cecilia."

Your eyes were puzzled, almost apprehensive, as you asked, "Who are you then!?"

"I am your husband, your Sheeleigh, your Tom Cat, lover, friend, and comrade."

Your eyes still puzzled and anxious, looked up at me almost appealingly, then mercifully closed as sleep again called you. The realization that none of my cue words could elicit a meaningful response was acute pain, a scalpel drawn across living flesh. Memory assuaged the pain as I recalled how you had adored your Daddy—you had never called me Daddy—and had told me many times how he had been "so kind" to you during that long, bedridden winter.

Then came that afternoon, the first of the last four days, when we had those blessed ten minutes of the truth. I held you, so frail, in a sitting position. Your mind was brilliantly clear, as were your eyes. You wanted to talk, and we both knew it was the last with all that that meant. No nonsense, no falsehoods, no dreams. I urged you to stay with me; there could be no life without you, for you had given me the wonderful life we shared.

You said, "You have important things to do, to say and write; you must do them and you can." Then, looking at me with that complete honesty I knew so well, you said, "I have loved you since the first day I saw you, and if there is anything after this, I am sure we shall be together. I am going very fast now." Through my tears, I eased you down to the pillow. Then, "The wind is in my hair and I must go," and so you said to me your last au revoir.

That night, as I came to bed, you said, "There is something I must tell you. Dr. Ross [our physician of many years back] told me to tell you that he thought you were in danger; there are men outside he thinks may try to harm you."

"I think it's safe, dear; all doors are locked and the windows, too, and the outside lights are on."

You were very insistent. "Dr. Ross was worried; he thought you were in danger and that I should tell you."

So I walked out to the living room and, after a minute or two, returned to the bedroom as you watched me from your pillow. "Everything is safe now, dear heart, I have put an armed guard at each door and window, too; it's quite safe."

You smiled in relief and went to sleep. Your last thoughts, even though irrational, had been for my safety.

Three nights later, January 25 in the early morning about 1:30, I went a second time from my drowsing on the davenport to see how you were, for I knew from the first visit that the end was very near. I found your incomparable spirit had gone. I kissed your forehead, pulled up the sheet to cover your terribly cold face, and walked back alone to my davenport. With morning, I called the morticians. They came and, after giving me a moment alone with you, carried you out of this house of ours; and just as I had helped you come into it that August afternoon in 1931, I stood on the steps outside and saluted your going. Our partnership was not over, only agonizingly reorganized, dear one.

> Love is most nearly itself
> When here and now cease to matter.
> (T. S. Eliot, "East Coker," *Four Quartets*)

And now, dear Puss Cat, I must tell you that I have really agonized over the propriety of doing what I am going to do now. But the circumstances of my finding your letter, never posted, leads me to believe that I have your permission to use it for the purpose I have in mind. I have been attempting to convey, terribly haltingly, I am afraid, something of the wonder you are, as I had the good fortune to know. This letter in your own words shows the depth and beauty of your character infinitely better than anything I have been able to say, even with Lewis Mumford's perceptive and articulate help.

I was going through the painful task of sorting your papers and found a bundle of letters we had written each other over the years. I knew you had sorted your letters earlier, discarding some and keeping others, but I did not know which ones. I found a letter I had written you September 9, 1927, on our return from Uckfield: "Perhaps I cannot be with you at breakfast in the flesh, but I shall be in spirit and may this note make the spirit more real. . . ." I remember taking the letter out to post so it would be with you at breakfast. The cancellation reads: Sept 10 12:45 A.M. 1927.

When I took my letter from its envelope, to my utter surprise, there was another with it and I saw at once your handwriting. Your letter was folded like mine to fit the same envelope together. On the envelope you had written "D.C.C. [D.C.C. was Dorothy Cecilia

Cressman] Keep." So I think you meant the two letters to be for whoever should chance to find them in the task I was carrying through. And so, my dear, I feel free to share with others this beautiful expression of your love, which never wavered.

> 46, Harcourt Terrace
> London, S.W. 10
> September, 1927.

Sheeleigh darling,

This is hail & farewell or farewell & hail, as you will. I have wanted you so desperately since the first Sunday when you kissed me that I have hardly known how to bear it—sometimes at night here, sometimes when I have been in your arms, I dared not let you touch me in case my last restraints should break. I wonder how often you knew it! I love you, darling, as I sometimes dreamed & feared, but never believed I should love anyone. When I first met you—all the time till you wrote to me from Paris I think, & sometimes afterwards, you were like the child of my body that I loved, whose head was on my breast, so often. Now the child is mixed with the man, & nearly lost in him, though not always or completely. Dear, I want you wholly & without reserve.

Our lives are so twisted that you must go now. Remember that I shall always welcome you, a year hence, or more, whether you come in friendship or in love. Only, darling, if you come in *love* do not fail me by coming for anything less than utter necessity. Do not come for pity or to spare me pain, but only because you must. My passion I can turn otherwise, not ignobly, nor need it be wasted, even if it does not find its natural release. Anything else than passion from you would smash me as nothing else could for my life long. I wish still that your life should be fulfilled by the love of a woman of your own age, not instead of mine, but beyond it.

Darling I shall not write like this again. Letters in my casual hands are often misaddressed & I can run no risks of that sort. Don't misunderstand my letters after this one.

Please destroy this completely. Your memory is good enough to know what I have written, & to have it with you when life most hurts you.

I can never thank you enough for your gentleness, for your understanding, & *for your passion*. Without it my life must have been maimed. As it is, whatever happens I have the memory of the hours we have spent together, & of the feeling of your hands & lips fulfilling my dreams.

I am not afraid for you, Sheeleigh. The spirituality in the boy I knew 18 months ago was a thing I then knew nothing could break. The man has not failed the boy, nor will he do so.

Sometime when you were here in the Spring last year I cut my hair shorter, & for some unknown, sentimental reason kept a curl. Here is the hair of the dog who has bitten you, & herself to boot, as a safeguard against dangers.

I love you, Sheeleigh darling.

Dorothy Loch

My dearest one, fifty years after you wrote this letter you spoke your last words to me: "I have loved you since the first day I saw you!" I am glad you didn't post your letter for this treasure has come to me after all these years at a time when I needed it most. Your whole life has been a manifestation of the love so beautifully expressed. And I came to you as you wished out of the "utter necessity" of my love

Death did not end your love, dear heart, nor mine; it was an agonizing experience. Your love, so essential in my life as archaeologist, teacher, every part of it, is still my daily comrade; nor has it been limited to my waking hours. Milton, blind, wrote what to me is a poem of tragic deprivation, *On His Deceased Wife*.

> Methought I saw my late espoused Saint
> Brought to me like Alcestis from the grave,
> Whom Joves great Son to her glad Husband gave
> Rescu'd from death by force though pale and faint.
> Mine as whom washt from spot of child-bed taint,
> Purification in the old Law did save,
> And such, as yet once more I trust to have
> Full sight of her in Heaven without restraint
> Came vested all in white, pure as her mind:
> Her face was vail'd, yet to my fancied sight,
> Love, sweetness, goodness, in her person shin'd

So clear, as in no face with more delight
But O as to embrace me she enclin'd
I wak'd, she fled, and day brought back my night.

I, too, had a dream, a dream of you, so beautiful, so strength-
giving, carrying on that love expressed in your unposted letter and
your last words to me that I feel I must share it.

You kneeled, "all raiment laid away," lovely with happy
eyes, sitting slightly back as though on your heels;
your arms extended toward me and hands lowered and
slightly curved in, as though holding a large salver; and
you spoke to me softly but invitingly, "DRINK, DRINK,
DRINK."

Not taste, not sip but DRINK, DRINK, DRINK. So you return
even in a dream, dear one, as THE SOURCE, THE SOURCE that you
still are. Though you, like Milton's "espoused Saint," vanished with
my waking in response to your urging, DRINK, DRINK, DRINK,
unlike him—but then I did not have to return to blindness—I was
refreshed in spirit and the strength you gave me continues with me.
THE SOURCE!

A *bientôt,* Puss Cat, *a bientôt.*

Home is where one starts from. As we grow older
The world becomes stranger, the pattern more complicated
Of dead and living. Not the intense moment
Isolated, with no before and after,
But a lifetime burning in every moment
And not the lifetime of one man only
But of old stones that cannot be deciphered. . . .
Old men ought to be explorers
Here and there does not matter
We must be still and still moving
Into another intensity
For a further union, a deeper communion
Through the dark cold and the empty desolation, . . .
                  In my end is my beginning.

(T. S. Eliot, "East Coker," *Four Quartets*)

And in MY END, Cecilia, Puss Cat, is OUR
NEW BEGINNING AND TOGETHER!

Notes for In the Beginning

1. To verify the oral history relating to my home I requested the Chester County Historical Society in West Chester, Pennsylvania, to search the archival property records. The search showed that, William Penn

> "by deed of Esoffment dated 4-10-1686 conveyed to Major Robert Thompson a tract of 10,000 A. [acres] in Pennsylvania. . . ,'' including the land under consideration. The original grant was not made to the Pugh family.
>
> The archives researcher's report states: "The [land on which our home was built] was at some time possessed by the Pugh family . . . It is possible that the Pughs lived on the land long before the actual purchase 1783. Jonathan Pugh is listed as a taxable in Coventry in 1778."

The building date, at least the year of the start of construction is firm. In cleaning up the debris following the disastrous 1917 fire, we found the cornerstone with the date of 1774, the starting year according to custom, cut into it. That was our first evidence of the date of the house.

2. My youngest brother, Fred, during his second year, 1931, in the University of Pennsylvania Medical School, asked one of his professors, Dr. James W. McConnell, associated professor of neurology in the Graduate School of Medicine, to come out home to see Dad, who had developed certain alarming symptoms, to diagnose his illness. A special poignancy attaches to this meeting: Dr. McConnell and Dad had been classmates at the Medical School, and he had been Dad's best man at his wedding, thirty-nine years earlier.

Dr. McConnell of course came to see his old friend. After a few minutes of conversation and observation he said, "George, you have Parkinson's disease. Do you know what that means?"

"Yes," said Dad, showing no sign of emotion.

"You are going to need help, probably a lot of it."

"I'll be all right, Jim; I have Florie and she is as strong as an oak."

And so she was all through those next fifteen difficult years.

3. Dad's obituary in the *Daily Local News*, West Chester, Pennsylvania, September 27, 1946, emphasized many of the characteristics I have mentioned.

> Dr. Cressman Dies At Home At Pughtown.
> Veteran Physician Was Well Known in Northern End of County.
>
> ----
>
> SURVIVED BY SIX SONS.
> Dr. George S. Cressman, veteran medical practitioner and long-time resident of Chester County, died last night at his home in Pughtown, about 10 o'clock, at the age of 77. He had been in failing health for the past several years.

Born at Lafayette Hill, Montgomery County, on January 1, 1869, Dr. Cressman was a son of the late George W. and Sarah K. Cressman. In 1890, when he was 21, he graduated from the University of Pennsylvania Medical School, Philadelphia, and shortly thereafter took up the practice of his profession in Chester County.

Dr. Cressman belonged to the beloved and now rapidly vanishing clan of American country doctors whose experience in the treatment of domestic ills extended backward into the era of the horse and buggy, the unpaved rural road and the kerosene lamp. He was a family physician in the truest sense of the word, versatile in general practice, kindly, wise and understanding in his dealings with the farm folk with whom he elected to spend his career.

In his work, he covered much of Chester County, traveling the highways between Pottstown and West Chester, and between Elverson and Phoenixville, a familiar and loved figure to hundreds of families for whom he had faithfully responded to routine and emergency calls.

Dr. Cressman was active in the community life of his neighborhood and identified himself with numerous rural groups and enterprises, was a member of the Pickering Masonic Lodge at Byers, and a member of St. Matthews Lutheran Church, Anselma, where his wife, Florence, was the organist for many years.

He was also a member of the Chester County Medical Society, and a few years ago was guest of honor at a dinner given by the Society to mark the anniversary of half a century spent in medical practice.

Dr. Cressman is survived by his wife, Florence Righter Cressman, and six sons. . . .

There are eleven grandchildren and two great-grandchildren.

4. Manuscript in my possession.
5. Short biographical notes on author's brothers:
Cressman, George R(ighter). B. Aug. 8, 1893. B.A. Pennsylvania State College, 1915. High school teaching, military service, return to teaching, educational administration. Ph.D. University of Pennsylvania. Retired 1956, head, Department of Education, West Chester State University; had reputation of being a superb teacher. Taught four more years as professor of education at Villanova University. Author of books and Digest of School Laws, Pennsylvania, etc. Retired, living with wife Martha at the Country House, Wilmington, Delaware.
Cressman, Charles S(treeper). B. Nov. 3, 1895; d. July 10, 1973. B.A. Pennsylvania State College, 1916. Employment at General Electric Company, Schenectady, N.Y. Interrupted by military service in the United States and Europe 1918–19, followed by return to previous employment.

Joined Bethlehem Steel Corporation Jan. 1, 1925. Retired Feb. 1, 1961. Chief engineer, Bethlehem Mines Corporation. (Information on employment kindly furnished by William R. McQuillen, Supervisor of Personnel and Office Administration. Natural Resources Group, Bethlehem Steel Corporation, Bethlehem, Pa., June 3, 1982.)

Cressman, A(lbert) Wallace. B. Sept. 6, 1900. Worked after graduation from high school until his eighteenth birthday, when he enlisted in the U.S. Marine Corps. A few days after the armistice was signed, instead of going to France as replacements, was sent to Santo Domingo. I registered him for entry into Penn State, and he was discharged after being returned to the States. B.A. Pennsylvania State College, 1923. Employed in Bureau of Entomology, U.S. Department of Agriculture. Retired 1962, G.S. 14 Civil Service rating as Investigation Leader for Citrus Insect Investigation, now living in retirement in Baton Rouge, La., with wife Louise.

Cressman, Morris H(abliston). B. June 6, 1904; d. Oct. 19, 1971. B.A. Pennsylvania State College, 1925. Structural engineer. He was the engineer on several important buildings, and at the time of his retirement in June 1969 was the assistant to the assistant to the vice-president for research and development, United States Steel Company.

Cressman, Frederic E(belhare). B. Aug. 5, 1906; d. Aug. 16, 1983. B.A. University of Pennsylvania, 1928, in history and French. Entered medical school after a year of premedical study and received the M.D. degree in 1933. Interned at Chester County Hospital, followed by entrance into the U.S. Regular Army, Medical Corps, as a first lieutenant. Following intervening tours of duty, while on duty at the Gorgas Hospital in the Canal Zone, he was ordered in 1942 to return to the States to organize and train the 62nd General Hospital. As a lieutenant-colonel, he took the 62nd to service in the United Kingdom, Salisbury Plain, from where he was ordered to return on Dec. 1944 to the Fitzsimmons Hospital in Denver because of a pulmonary infection. After a year's futile treatment following by surgery he was discharged Jan. 31, 1946, for 100 percent physical disability with the rank of lieutenant-colonel. He later took special training in ophthalmology and carried on a private practice for several years until complete retirement. He was a diplomate: American Board of Ophthalmology; a Fellow of the American Academy of Ophthalmology, and a Fellow of the International College of Surgeons.

6. The moral conventions of the time did not permit any kind of recreational play, for example, playing catch with a baseball on Sunday, although taking a walk to look for flowers in spring was accepted.

7. The 1914 freshman class consisted of 629 new students and 40 others. My class graduated in 1918, seven weeks ahead of the regularly scheduled date—this was the second wartime commencement. All vacations and final examination periods had been dropped to enable as many students as possible to graduate before being called to military duty. Of my class of 669, only 245 remained to graduate; 382 had withdrawn for military duty and 42 are unaccounted for. In June, I, the student commander, took the first

R.O.T.C. unit to the infantry officers' training camp at Plattsburg Barracks, New York, to complete our training for commissions. In 1981, sixty-seven years after I entered Penn State, the freshman class numbered 4,645 — 1,270 more than the whole student body of my time. I am indebted to my long-ago student at Oregon, now professor emeritus of sociology at Penn State, Dr. Paul B. Foreman, for these statistics.

8. Dr. Harris was a victim of the influenza pandemic in 1918. I, at the time, was in the Field Artillery Officers' Training School learning to kill and destroy and, fortunately, never had to do either.

9. George, Charlie, and I had been confirmed some years earlier in the Barren Hill Lutheran Church, where the young Florence Righter and George S. Cressman had been married and whose ashes now rest in the adjacent cemetery.

10. I never wrote verse as stated by Margaret. The compliment is undeserved.

11. Margaret Mead, *Blackberry Winter: My Earlier Years* (New York: William Morrow & Co., Inc., 1972), 83–84.

12. This excerpt is from the General Theological Seminary catalog, 1976–78, page 5.

13. At the present it is responding to the social demands of the 1960s and 1970s for restructuring both internally and in its relation to the vital city; it is in the city but not of it.

14. "A Comparative Study of the Adult Education Program of Corporations and Labor Unions." Published in part as "The Curriculum of the Corporation School" in 1924 in *The Journal of Social Forces.*

15. Margaret is quite wrong in saying we had my brother's car for our honeymoon (*Blackberry Winter*, 116). We had his Buick Roadster for a week's vacation before Margaret went to Samoa in 1925.

16. Mead, *Blackberry Winter*, 116.

17. Compare William J. McGill (retiring president of Columbia University), "A Ghost in the Library and a Shout in the Street," *Columbia* (Winter 1979): 8–15.

18. Franklin H. Giddings, *Studies in the Theory of Human Society* (New York: Macmillan Co., 1922), vi.

19. A. L. Kroeber et al., *Franz Boas, 1858-1942*, American Anthropological Association, Memoir no. 61 (Menasha, Wisconsin, 1943), 23.

20. Ibid., 27.

21. Ibid., 13.

22. Ibid., 11.

23. Ibid., 12.

24. Ibid., 15.

25. Ibid., 27.

26. Ibid., 30.

27. Ibid., 28.

28. Ibid., 24 (order of paragraphs reversed).

29. Franz Boas et al., *General Anthropology* (Boston: D. C. Heath and Co., 1938), 4.

30. Mead, *Blackberry Winter*, 119.

31. Luther S. Cressman, *The Social Composition of the Rural Population of the United States* (New York: George H. Doran Co., 1925).

32. Mead, *Blackberry Winter*, 132. This error was corrected in subsequent printings of the book.

33. Ibid., 147.

34. It had long been common scientific knowledge that there never had been an "Aryan race" or language, and that there was no relation between race and language. Even so, the presence of this scientific knowledge did not prevent Hitler, a generation later, from using this myth to justify his war to subjugate Europe to his "master race," the Aryan heirs, and to eliminate "inferior breeds" in the Holocaust.

35. Luther S. Cressman, "Ritual, the Conserver," *American Journal of Sociology* 35 (January 1930): 564–72.

36. Henry W. Nevinson, *Essays in Freedom*, 16, as quoted in Harold J. Laski, *A Grammar of Politics* (New Haven: Yale University Press, 1925).

37. Mead, *Blackberry Winter*, 123.

38. Frank Jewett Mather, Jr., *A History of Italian Painting* (London: Stanley Paul & Co., Ltd., 1923), 5. Mather was a professor of art and archaeology at Princeton University.

39. My itinerary was as follows:
Amsterdam in the Netherlands.
Cologne, Germany, for cathedral.
Weimar, for Goethe's home and memorabilia.
Jena, reason forgotten.
Berlin, for museums, architecture, city's ethos.
Dresden, for museums.
Nuremberg, for Dürer's home, museum, architecture (fifteenth century).
Munich, for museums, both art and archaeological (Greek), ethos. To visit and "catch up with" Carl Goedel, who as a small boy came with his family from Philadelphia as my family's first summer boarders when I was not yet five years old. Our families had kept in contact in spite of wars and revolutions. Carl, a musician, had common interests with me and in addition was fluent in five or six languages, one of which was English.
Heidelberg, to see that famed university.
Zimmern unter Dhaun, a small village near Kreuznach, to spend a week with the widowed mother of Carl Goedel and her daughter Elizabeth, about my age. Tragedy, natural and political, had reduced Dr. Goedel from a position of prominence as pastor of a Berlin church to this village, where he died. I heard from Carl after World War II, then in Rome that his mother had died and Elizabeth had died in childbirth. Carl's letters from Rome just stopped.

Strasbourg, again to visit the Mekeels and go to Colmar to see Grünewald paintings. Then to return to Paris to go to Italy. I wanted to be in Rome for Easter observances.

Paris, to pick up quarterly installment of fellowship due at Bankers Trust on Monday, the week before Easter, but it didn't arrive. I could not buy the ticket for the Italian trip until the installment came, for I was flat broke. The funds arrived Tuesday, so I bought a round-trip ticket, left Paris Wednesday night, second class, to arrive in Rome Friday morning.

Rome, for practically everything from Greco-Roman to Easter Mass at St. Peter's. There was also the opportunity to observe the rising power of Mussolini.

Naples, for museums and to visit Pompeii to see the remains of that city covered by mud and ash from an eruption of Mt. Vesuvius, to see Vesuvius closely, to visit Paestum to see Greek temples.

Orvieto and Assisi, for paintings at Orvieto and to see something of Assisi, the birthplace of St. Francis, and the Basilica and Giotto's frescoes.

Sienna, for paintings and Renaissance public-building architecture.

Florence, the aesthetic climax.

Direct return to Paris for reflection and "regrouping."

40. Danegeld: "A tax levied in England from the 10th to the 12th century to finance protection against Danish invasion." (*The American Heritage Dictionary of the English Language*, 1969).

In other words, Danegeld was a tribute exacted from the English by the marauding Danes as the price for not expanding their raids on the countryside. By extension the expression has come to apply to various methods of gaining protection; but read instead of "protection": promotion, professional advancement, security, and the "geld" or tribute money as fawning loyalty, uncritical or even dishonest support of superiors or organizations. We have various colloquialisms to express rather coarsely the honest man's contempt for the person who lives by paying his Danegeld, no more to be cleared of the taint than Lady Macbeth of the stains of Duncan's blood.

41. Mather, *History of Italian Painting*, 276.

42. Dana Carleton Munro, *A History of the Middle Ages* (New York: D. Appleton and Company, 1902), 38.

43. Mead, *Blackberry Winter*, 162.

44. Margaret Mead, *Coming of Age in Samoa: A Psychological Study of Primitive Youth for Western Civilization* (New York, William Morrow, 1928).

45. For example, this letter dated September 21, 1982, from Sidney Ratner, Professor Emeritus of History, Rutgers University:

> Dear Luther,
>   I thought you would like to have this brief statement of my recollection of your teaching in 1925:
>   "In the spring of 1925, as a freshman at the College of the City of New York, I took a required course in American Government. After a few weeks, my instructor became ill, and his place

was taken by Luther Cressman. He soon created a warm rapport with the class. He made the class assignments on various problems interesting and significant by lucidly explaining the nature of the problems and by giving vivid statements on the real life-situations and social conditions that created these problems. He treated each student as a responsible individual with a mind of his own, and often got students to work out their own approach and solution to a problem, by use of the Socratic method. I still have a vivid recollection of having studied with him.''

I was pleasant having a chance to talk with you last night. Best wishes on your revision of your autobiography. Louise joins me in warm regards.

Cordially yours,
(signed) Sidney Ratner

46. Luther S. Cressman, "New York's Bludgeon Law," *American Review of Reviews* 77 (January 1928): 77–80.

47. Luther S. Cressman, "Goblins and Death Cells," *The Survey* 59 (March 15, 1928): 741–43.

48. Mead, *Blackberry Winter*, 164.

49. Excerpts from the "final judgment rendered in the proceedings for divorce instituted before the Court or Original Jurisdiction in civil matters of this district by Mrs. *MARGARET MEAD CRESSMAN* vs. *MR. LUTHER S. CRESSMAN*, Hermosillo, Sonora, Mexico, July 31, 1928:

> "By writ dated 16th day of June this year the said lady appeared before this court instituting an action for divorce against Mr. Luther S. Cressman, submitting:
> "'. . . That Mr. Cressman, without any justified cause, abandoned the conjugal domicile on August 19, 1927, and that since that day both husband and wife had been de facto separated with interruption of the marital relation:
> "'. . . In the answer it is stated that the facts submitted in the complaint are true and that if Mr. Cressman abandoned the conjugal domicile this was due to the fact that the characters of both husband and wife were incompatible. . . .'"

When I was invited to submit my biography for inclusion in *Who's Who in America*, 1938 edition, I omitted mention of our divorce for two reasons: it was not relevant to my professional qualifications; and in New York, where we were domiciled at the time of the divorce, the only accepted grounds for divorce was adultery, and I thought it wiser not to mention it since that did not apply in our case. Margaret has written that since we had not had a child or produced a book that I ignored the matter as not being significant. That is her interpretation alone, for we never discussed the matter, nor do I join her in equating the two achievements.

50. Mead, *Blackberry Winter*, 102.
51. Ibid., 163–65.
52. Some few months later, when in Doylestown near Buckingham with my daughter, I asked her to drive me the few miles to Buckingham to photograph the headstone now marking Margaret's grave. Fred and Barbara Roll later borrowed the negative for Fred to make a studio print that now hangs in the community house of "Margaret's Village," Peri, Manus.
53. When the following letter, which was originally submitted to *The New York Times*, did not appear, I submitted it with its present title to *Columbia*, the magazine of Columbia University (July 1983, Letters, 9ff). Subsequently, May 3, 1983, it appeared with a slight, but I thought significant, editorial change. The *Times* editor changed my copy, "celebrity, and having been made that by the media," to read, "She became a celebrity and . . ." The *Times* syndicated the letter to all its North American clients.

A Marguerite for Margaret

I was Margaret Mead's husband from 1923 to 1928, after a six-year engagement, a period leading up to and covering her Samoan field trip. The ancient code of comradeship, a relationship Margaret and I enjoyed until her death, compels me to make this statement. In the current academic media brouhaha about Margaret's first field trip to American Samoa, from 1925 to 1926, no recognition has been given to facts that are of the greatest importance in understanding her experience and appreciating its significance.

Margaret's work, errors and all, like that of all of us has to be evaluated in terms of the value system and what was happening to it at the time the work was in progress. No one, at least in what I have read, has made the least effort to do that; perhaps no one could. Those postwar years, the fabled twenties, provided those of us at Columbia opportunities to be a part of a process of change in our society and intellectual life that can never be repeated. Margaret and I were central to such a group at Columbia and responded to the challenges of the period.

Margaret's mother passed on to her the ideal of women's rights and in the difficult process of persuading her father to let her go to college she learned who the "enemy" was. Our long engagement gave me the opportunity to observe her devotion to the ideals of equality of the sexes (not similarity) and that women could do anything men could and as well. The idea would become almost an obsession with her.

She chose the challenge of the field of anthropology and what it demanded of its professionals to validate her belief in women's capabilities and, therefore, their proper demand for equality of opportunity, recognition, and reward.

To say that Franz Boas [professor of anthropology at Columbia from 1899 to 1936] sent Margaret to Samoa to gather information to support his idea of the greater importance of nurture over nature is utter nonsense. He had a much more pressing problem on his hands. He had this brilliant, emotional, driving young woman student, whose abilities he recognized and admired, insisting that he support her desire to do her first field work out-side of North America, just as he would do for a man. For a young, lone woman to do this was something new and it created many problems. Counterpressure on Boas to refuse her proposal came from Edward Sapir, a Canadian anthropologist who was a frequent visitor at Columbia, and others who cited her frailty as a woman as a drawback. This infuriated her.

One thing was certain, she could go no place for field work without Boas's approval. He knew his obligation to support his troublesome young student and to provide her an opportunity consonant with her training that would let her demonstrate her ability to perform as she promised. He was fully sensitive to the trauma he would inflict on the girl if he frustrated her deeply rooted ambition. He suggested to Margaret that she go to American Samoa and learn what the adolescent experience was like there.

Boas wisely chose this problem for its vitality in the public consciousness, the interest it held for Margaret, and as one in which her youth would be to her advantage. Finally, American Samoa was a safe place for an unescorted young woman, a consideration important to Boas both as a person and insti-tutional sponsor. He was investing with great deliberation in the promise of the professional future of his brilliant young student. Some doubting Thomases differed with Boas on his decision, but none shared his depth of understanding and appreciation of the young Margaret.

If Margaret, in going to Samoa, wanted to prove some preconceived idea, it certainly was not the nature of adolescence in a Samoan village population—that she would try to learn—but that a woman, Margaret Mead, could be a professional anthropological field worker as well as any man of comparable preparation. That she proved, but apparently not to all men's satisfaction then or now, for when—after ten years was it?—Derek Freeman, the hunter, shouted, "TALLY HO!" men and hounds dashed from the halls of academe to join the chase; but I am sure the quarry is still free. How fragile the thin veneer of tolerance over the ancient biases!

All social science, but especially anthropology, owes Margaret Mead a tremendous debt. At twenty-three years of age she did what no woman in anthropology had done. She went on a poverty-level fellowship compared to the generous stipends now given. She violated the canons of the Establish-ment by writing a report that was interesting, readable, and relevant to the lives of people in our society. She popularized anthropology. The depart-ments in which some of her critics, both friendly and hostile, now teach owe their existence to Margaret's popularization of the subject matter. If what she wrote in *Coming of Age in Samoa* tended to produce an outburst of demand for greater sexual freedom among our young people, it did that because it was a lance puncturing the old pustule of hypocrisy. She became a celebrity, and having been made that by the media she cleverly turned it to her own use to support her programs.

Over a half-century ago, this twenty-three-year-old girl who had never before been out of the country, went to an isolated island under financial conditions a contemporary graduate student would probably reject as demeaning, and there made her first field study. She had the firm conviction that she could establish and hold her place in the profession with men. Her record proves she was right and in the doing she became a pioneer in the women's movement. We all are indebted to her in some degree. Colleagues as scholars will correct her errors, the perspective of time establish her scientific work, and we, her professional associates, will gain stature both personally and professionally, if we rightly honor the remarkable young girl and the woman Margaret became.

L. S. Cressman
Emeritus Professor of Anthropology
University of Oregon, Eugene, Ore.

Notes for Gestation's Interlude

1. All historical references are drawn from Gordon Loch, *The Family of Loch* (privately printed by T. and A. Constable, Ltd., Edinburgh: University Press, 1934).

2. "My grandfather [George Loch] died comparatively young and he sold the Estate before his death. . . . Mr. Fraser tells me that the sale to Mr. Ramsay of Barnton was nearly broken off from my Grandfather bargaining to receive £ 800 for the Quarry at Craigleith—from which subsequently a great part of the New Town of Edinburgh was built and in which in consequence yielded an annual profit of several thousand!" (Loch, *Family of Loch*, 1939–40).

"The land included a piece, sold separately for £ 800, on which was afterward discovered the stone obtained from the Craigleith Quarry. The stone was used widely in the building of the new town of Edinburgh and the London Docks, and brought in very large sums" (ibid., 236, n1).

3. See *The Pirate Coast* by Sir Charles Belgrave (London: G. Bell and Sons, Ltd., 1966) for a description of Francis Erskin Loch's service in the Persian Gulf against the pirates and for other interesting insights into the life of the British serving in the Honourable East India Company during the years 1818–20.

4. Captain Telfer was an artilleryman, but his lady love would agree to marry him only if he would refuse to leave Britain for active service, which he would have to do sooner or later. Since he preferred Venus to Mars, he resigned his commission, married, and the name became Telfer-Smollett. The double name also had something to do, I believe, with the transfer of the Cameron property at the death of the owner.

Notes for Journey's End

1. Eugene's architecture, except for public buildings, reflected the forest resource basis of Eugene's economy. All but a few houses of the

wealthy were of frame construction and one story in height. Exceptions were red brick or plaster and frame. Public buildings and the university used red brick masonry. After World War II the university constructed the science complex utilizing the new technology, building with steel and concrete and some asbestos (to be removed later at great expense).

The track of an abandoned tram system occasionally showed forlornly through the blacktop or concrete on a few streets that connected the university area to the downtown district. It had been cheaper to cover the abandoned tracks than remove them. Many streets had boardwalks instead of concrete walks for pedestrians. In our dry summers the long grass grew between the boards and was a constant source of annoyance to ladies with their long skirts that always seemed to sweep up hungry fleas.

New arrivals between late spring and early fall, as we were, were always puzzled by the large racks of slab wood, four feet wide and varying in length on the parking strip in front of many houses. Wood was the main fuel for furnace and fireplace and slab wood was the cheapest source. Old-growth body fir was also used, as was sawdust. These large racks of slab wood were there for seasoning during the dry summer. Before the autumn rains started, mobile sawing units reduced these huge racks to stove length to be thrown into the basement of the householder by high school or university students to earn some extra money.

We used in our furnace old-growth body fir until near the end of World War II, when we had to use slab. We used ten to twelve cords per year, and had the wood split and cut to sixteen-inch wedges with heavy bark delivered to our basement door for $4.50 per cord. Occasionally we dared to buy a half cord of oak delivered for $7.00 The price quoted to me by Rexius Fuel in Eugene, February 11, 1985, for "seasoned fir," the nearest equivalent to old growth, was $99 per cord and for oak $119 per cord!

2. July 27, 1928, University of Minnesota:

> I very much appreciate your letter telling me about you—for I am much interested in you and your future. I very much understand your move [to Ellensburg, Washington], and I have a feeling it was a very wise thing to do, and that it will be good for you. It is very worthwhile to get away from the many unpleasant associations that are connected with New York. You'll like the west. There's sunshine—lots of it—and fine, fresh breezes that blow away the mustiness, the staleness that gets accumulated in N.Y. There's a healthy optimism out there. The people are real people, too, who set human values above success. So this is all good luck and good wishes. You must meet my friends the Coffins in Yakima, Wash. I almost wish I were going out.
>
> Yours sincerely,
> (signed) Will F. Ogburn

3. Dr. Gregory Bateson, a product of the western European intellectual tradition, some twenty years later shared our opinion:

> Bateson found the West Coast "a good place to gestate ideas. If you have a new idea in the East, they'll shoot it down, but if you have an idea in California and nourish it and let it get some feathers on it, then you can take it to the East and see if it can stand up." (Jane Howard, *Margaret Mead, A Life* [New York: Simon and Schuster, 1984], 266.)

What Bateson said was true of California was equally true of the other Pacific coast states, a fact I discovered soon after my arrival. Does Gregory's metaphor of shooting a bird on the wing change at the end to shooting a standing bird, something no true hunter would do?

4. Luther S. Cressman, "Aboriginal Burials in Southwestern Oregon," *American Anthropologist* 35 (January–March 1933): 116–30.

5. Sources of research money for individuals before the National Science Foundation's establishment were very limited and grants were small. One source was the National Research Council. The procedure for application was simple beyond words compared to the bureaucratic nightmare of today. Some years after my application to the N.R.C. when Robert Lowie, professor of anthropology at the University of California at Berkeley, and I were reminiscing, he told me about my 1932 application to the N.R.C.

Anthropology and psychology comprised a division, administered as a unit, by the council. The chairmanship alternated between representatives of the two fields. A psychologist, whose name I have forgotten, served as chairman, with Robert sharing the responsibilities. The day they had to make their decisions on applications found them at a table with a good-sized pile of applications. The chairman picked up one, gave it a quick glance, and said, "Lowie, here's an anthropologist at the University of Oregon who wants $400 to do some digging at a place called Gold Hill, Oregon. Do you know anything about him?"

"I think, from all I know, he is a very responsible person and will make good use of the money."

"Good, we'll give him the money."

6. Luther S. Cressman, *Contributions to the Archaeology of Oregon: Final Report on the Gold Hill Burial Site*, University of Oregon Studies in Oregon, v. 1, bulletin 1 (Eugene: University of Oregon Press, 1933).

7. The letter, dated September 21, 1982, began, "Dear Luther," and was signed, "Sidney Ratner." He is professor emeritus of history, Rutgers University. The letter concerned a statement he had made about my teaching in 1925.

8. Luther S. Cressman, "Some Effects of Thyroid Disorder in Women," *Human Biology* 3 (December 1931): 529.

9. Ibid., 546.

10. Luther S. Cressman and Edna Spenker, "Notes on Some Quantitative Evidence of the Effect of Thyroid Disorder upon the Birth-rate," *Human Biology* 4 (September 1933): 516–19.

Edna joined in another article not referred to in this text: Luther S. Cressman and Edna Spenker, "Federal Regulation of Child Labor in Oregon," *The Commonwealth Review* 14 (January 1932): 154–57.

Her Master of Arts thesis, carried out under my direction, "Fifty Years of Population Growth in Oregon," became a valuable source book of information that planners used in the building of the Bonneville Dam, the first unit in the series of publicly funded hydroelectric dams on the Columbia River. Since then it has been often borrowed from the university library, and Keith Richard, the university archivist, told me on February 27, 1985, that it is still being used, but now in a microfilm form to preserve the original.

My knowledge of her subsequent career is fragmentary, pieced together from sporadic notes, an occasional letter, and spotty information gleaned from mutual friends from time to time. After graduation she worked on the staff of Senator W. E. Borah from Idaho for some time, married a geologist whose home was in Salt Lake City but who often served assignments with the U.S. Geological Survey in Washington, D.C., where she became an active congressional lobbyist for the League of Women Voters. A card from Tokyo or some other distant source would bring a memory and bit of news. In spite of nearly dying in the process, she had borne and helped raise to adulthood two or three sons.

Or last contact with her occurred in the early period of Cecilia's declining health. She was in Salt Lake City and wrote us from there that she wished to write an article for publication on "Our Favorite Professor," the private name that a group of girls apparently had for me. She wanted to come to Eugene and have Cecilia and me come to her hotel room, where we could record for her our reminiscences and hers of those early days at Oregon. I had to write that Cecilia felt, regretfully, that she was too frail to be able to undergo the demands such a recording would require, and we had to decline. My letter was not returned or acknowledged.

You, too, Edna, were also too frail, I am afraid.

11. Luther S. Cressman and Bess Templeton, "A Job Analysis of the Work of the Dean of Girls in High Schools in the Pacific Coast States, *The Commonwealth Review* 13 (January 1932): 323–40.

12. Bess wrote in the same letter: "I met Marx, who was in Law School, in the Fall of 1933. He was finishing his Law Degree and I was completing my Master's Program in Education. I resigned in June 1935 and was married that August at home in Portland, Ore.

"Even though it was the end of my professional career, it was the beginning of an active life in volunteer activities."

Bess returned to the Oregon campus in June 1981 for the fiftieth anniversary of her graduating class and endowed the Bess Templeton Cristman Award, "To be granted to the junior woman who best exemplifies the outstanding qualities of Leadership, Scholarship, and Service to others." The amount is equal to in-state tuition. It was a delightful pleasure and surprise to have Bess and her husband, Marx Q. Cristman, call on me and return to the house where Cecilia and I had enjoyed her friendship so long ago.

13. Letter from Thomas P. Bowden, secretary pro tem to David L. Sills, to me, July 10, 1985, in the absence of Dr. David L. Sills, executive associate, Social Science Research Council. I had written Dr. Sills on July 3, 1985, to confirm attendance information I had in my files.

14. Loye Miller, *Journal of First Trip of University of California to John Day Beds of Eastern Oregon*, University of Oregon, Museum of Natural History, bulletin no. 19 (Eugene, 1972).

15. Miles S. Potter, *Oregon's Golden Years* (Caldwell, Idaho: Caxton Press, 1977), 6.

16. Luther S. Cressman, *Archaeological Survey of the Guano Valley Region in Southeastern Oregon* (in collaboration with R. H. Back, J. V. Berreman, H. S. Stafford, Fred Hoffstead, Carl Reynolds), University of Oregon Monographs, Studies in Anthropology no. 11 (Eugene, 1936), 42, 45.

17. Florence M. Hawley, review of *Archaeological Survey of the Guano Valley Region in Southeastern Oregon*, by L. S. Cressman, *American Anthropologist*, n.s., 39 (1937): 332–34.

18. For photographs of Big Spring, see Cressman, *Survey of the Guano Valley Region*, 41, pl. 12D.

19. See ibid., 34, pl. 10.

20. See ibid., 14, pl. 4B.

21. Major Roscius H. Back, Howard S. Stafford, Fred W. Voget, and Lloyd Ruff.

22. The "association" was the unequivocal evidence that the knives had been deposited where found by the worker and examined by us before the deposition of the pumice from the eruption of Mt. Mazama.

23. Old Joe was a relic of time and culture now passed. I have seen many cowboys — buckaroos, as they were frequently called (the word is the American corruption of the Spanish word, *vaqueros*, introduced into the North American Southwest by the *conquistadores* — but the reality bore little relation to the romanticized figure of Hollywood. On the big ranches, the old buckaroos, usually unmarried, gradually lived out their last years on the ranch they had served so long as retainers of a sort, doing what chores they could, or, as in Old Joe's case, settling among friends who would look after them. Their family connections usually belonged to a distant past.

I remember vividly Old Tom, the first one of this type I met, while on a short family vacation on the western edge of the ranch country our first summer in Oregon. Old Tom spent much of his time sitting in a comfortable chair on the porch of the lodge where the cottage guests might assemble for dinner. We stopped to speak to him one evening and, thinking I might strike up an interesting bit of conversation, I made some admiring remarks about horses. I started "a bit of conversation" all right, but not what I had anticipated.

"Don't talk about horses to me," he replied, and continued, "I rode the outer range for twenty years, and if I never see a horse again it will still be too soon."

24. The removal from the University of Oregon of upper division and graduate work in science left remnant portions of collections in geology and biology in a very infelicitous position to put it mildly. The University of Oregon administration apparently expected the curatorial duties to be performed as a labor of love in addition to teaching and research services. The herbarium was in a somewhat more favorable position in the Botany Department budget as I remember it. The funds available in 1935 for curatorial services were: geology–none; botany–$100; zoology–$50.

My success with the Oregon State Museum of Anthropology and President Boyer's sympathetic understanding of the function of museums in a university suggested that with a little aggressive work something equally beneficial could be achieved for these neglected collections, both because of their intrinsic value and then because good resources in these fields were essential to a high standard of work in my own area of interest.

I discussed informally and individually with the men responsible for the collections a proposal for the formation of a Museum of Natural History with a director responsible to the president, to be composed of the various collections as autonomous museums. The others responded warmly to the idea, and because I had been responsible for the proposal, they suggested that I should be the director, a duty I was glad to accept since it gave me the opportunity to expand the whole museum field as should be done.

On July 3, 1936, the State Board of Higher Education accepted President Boyer's motion establishing a Museum of Natural History at the University of Oregon. The director of the museum, as specified in the administrative protocol activating the board's action, reported directly to the president's office and each "collection" became its own museum with an earmarked sum in the budget, expendable through the director's office but only on the recommendation of the particular curator.

25. It was announced in the 1937 catalog as "Anth. 448s Field work in Anthropology (G). Three to six hours."

26. We wanted to take back for the Museum of Natural History collections some good rattlesnake specimens. Most of those we killed were too badly damaged to be useful as study specimens. I tried to solve our problem by having one taken with our snake capture stick, then kept alive in a well-aired, empty gas can during the day while we worked in the cave. When back at camp I poured a good supply of chloroform into the can and fastened the lid tight, hoping that the chloroform would be lethal. I moved

the can after a reasonable interval to observe the result of my effort, but was greeted by a loud, angry rattle of warning. My experiment was a dismal failure. But we wanted an undamaged specimen.

I told Lloyd Ruff, my second-in-charge, that I was going to try something else. I got the medicine dropper and the chloroform and told the assembled crew of students that with their help I was going to squirt chloroform into the snake's mouth and over all openings in its ugly head. I told Lloyd that, when we were ready, he would remove the snake with the snake stick fastened close back of the head, making very sure the loop was tight, and then put the snake at a special spot on the ground and place one foot firmly on it to keep it from thrashing around. I would kneel in front of the snake with my eye dropper and chloroform and a lot of confidence in my assistant.

I asked if there were any questions and, hearing none, told Lloyd to bring the snake to where I was kneeling. I found my face awfully close to that ugly head of a very unwilling specimen-to-be. Filling the dropper, I put in practically into that repulsive mouth and emptied most of the contents there; the remainder I squirted over its head. I told Lloyd to hold everything until I got to my feet and then release the snake. My somewhat unorthodox method worked like a charm, for our specimen never moved again. After this demonstration the crew under Lloyd's direction could collect specimens in my absence. We took back to Eugene for the museum what a committed herpetologist would call some "fine specimens."

27. George Grant MacCurdy, ed., *Early Man* (Philadelphia: J. B. Lippincott Company, 1937), 8.

28. Ibid., 19, 22.

29. Luther S. Cressman, et al., *Archaeological Researches in the Northern Great Basin*, Carnegie Institution of Washington, Publication no. 538 (Washington, D.C., 1942), fig. 73d,e.

30. Ibid., 27–31, appendices A., D.; Luther S. Cressman, *Klamath Prehistory*, American Philosophical Society Transactions, n.s., v. 46, pt. 4 (Philadelphia, 1956), appendix C, 479.

31. Luther S. Cressman, "Western Prehistory in the Light of Carbon 14 Dating," *Southwestern Journal of Anthropology* 7 (1951): 29–313.

32. Luther S. Cressman, Howel Williams, Alex D. Krieger, *Early Man in Oregon: Archaeological Studies in the Northern Great Basin*, University of Oregon Monographs, Studies in Anthropology no. 3 (Eugene: University of Oregon Press, 1940), 76–77.

33. John C. Merriam, *Paleontological, Geological, and Historical Research*, Carnegie Institution of Washington Year Book no. 38 (Washington, D.C., 1939), 307.

34. Cressman, Williams, and Krieger, *Early Man in Oregon*, 14.

35. On our return home Cecilia commented that President Erb probably thought the dinner was a "cooked-up affair, for Dr. Merriam kept emphasizing through the whole dinner, how important your work was and

how necessary it was that you should have an assistant." Our dinner was simply a gesture of honor to a great man with no ulterior motive.

36. Luther S. Cressman, *Early Man and Culture in the Northern Great Basin of South Central Oregon*, Carnegie Institution of Washington Year Book no. 38 (Washington, D.C., 1939), 314–17. Note particularly Stock's information on page 316.

37. Lewellyn L. Loud and Mark R. Harrington, *Lovelock Cave*, University of California Publications in American Archaeology and Ethnology, v. 25, no. 1 (Berkeley, 1929).

38. *Essays in Historical Anthropology of North America*, Smithsonian Miscellaneous Collections 100 (Washington, D.C., 1940), 51–116, 445–502.

39. Cressman, et al., *Researches in the Northern Great Basin*.

40. See ibid., fig. 12, fig. 83 e, f.

41. Luther S. Cressman, "History of Evacuation Program" (Salem: Committee on Conservation of Cultural Resources, Oregon Defense Council, 1944), unpublished ms.; Luther S. Cressman, "World War II History Project Progress Report," *Oregon Historical Quarterly* 45 (September 1944): 235–52; Luther S. Cressman, "Oregon Archives Program," *Oregon Historical Quarterly* 46 (June 1945): 170–73.

42. The following is a list of the Condon Lectures through 1963:

The Ancient Volcanoes of Oregon. By Howel Williams, Chairman, Department of Geological Sciences, University of California.

Malaysia—Crossroads of the Orient. By Fay-Cooper Cole, Emeritus Chairman, Department of Anthropology, University of Chicago.

The Ancient Forests of Oregon. By Ralph W. Chaney, Professor of Paleontology, University of California.

The China That Is To Be. By Kenneth Scott Latourette, D. Willis James, Professor of Missions and Oriental History and Fellow of Berkeley College, Yale University.

The Pacific Island Peoples in the Postwar World. By Felix M. Keesing, Executive Head, Department of Sociology and Anthropology, Stanford University.

Pacific Coast Earthquakes. By Perry Byerly, Professor of Seismology, University of California.

The Near East and the Foundations for Civilization. By Robert J. Braidwood, Associate Professor of Old World Prehistory, The Oriental Institute, Chicago.

Evolution and Geography: An Essay on Historical Biogeography with Special Reference to Mammals. By George Gaylord Simpson, Curator of Fossil Mammals and Birds, The American Museum of Natural History; Professor of Vertebrate Paleontology, Columbia University.

The Life in the Sea. By Ralph Buchsbaum, Department of Biological Sciences, University of Pittsburgh.

The Constitution of Matter. By Robert Oppenheimer, Director of Institute for Advanced Study, Princeton.

The Physical and Chemical Basis of Inheritance. By George W. Beadle, Chairman, Division of Biology, California Institute of Technology, Pasadena.

The Ecology of Man. By Paul B. Sears, Chairman, Conservation Program, Yale University.

The Astronomical Universe. By Otto Struve, Chairman, Astronomical Department; Director, Leuschner Observatory, University of California.

The Foundation of Human Evolution. By Sir Wilfrid E. LeGros Clark, F.R.S., Director, Department of Human Anatomy, Oxford University.

Glaciers. By Robert P. Sharp, Chairman, Division of Geological Sciences, California Institute of Technology, Pasadena.

Chemical Evolution. By Melvin Calvin, Professor of Chemistry; Lawrence Radiation Laboratory, University of California, Berkeley.

The Impact of Modern Astronomy on the Problems and Origins of Life and the Cosmos. By Sir Bernard Lovell, O.B.E., F.R.S., Professor of Radio Astronomy and Director of the Experimental Station, Nuffield Radio Astronomy Laboratories, University of Manchester.

The Cultural Roots and Social Fruits of Science. By René Jules Dubos, Professor, Rockefeller Institute, New York City.

43. Luther S. Cressman, *Archaeological Research in the John Day Region of North Central Oregon*, American Philosophical Society Proceedings, v. 94 (Philadelphia, 1950), 369–90.

44. Luther S. Cressman, "Oregon Coast Prehistory: Problems and Progress," *Oregon Historical Quarterly* 54 (December 1953): 291–300.

45. Luther S. Cressman, *Klamath Prehistory*, American Philosophical Society Transactions, n.s., v. 46, pt. 4 (Philadelphia, 1956).

46. Don E. Dumond, *The Eskimos and Aleuts* (London: Thomas and Hudson Ltd., 1977).

47. Luther S. Cressman, et al., *Cultural Sequences at The Dalles, Oregon: A Contribution to Pacific Northwest Prehistory*, American Philosophical Society Transactions, n.s., v. 50, pt. 10 (Philadelphia, 1960).

48. Luther S. Cressman, *Prehistory of the Far West: Homes of Vanished Peoples* (Salt Lake City: University of Utah Press, 1977).

49. Stephen F. Bedwell, "Prehistory and Environment of the Pluvial Fort Rock Lake Area of South Central Oregon," Ph.D. diss., University of Oregon, 1969.

50. Warren L. d'Azevedo et al., eds., *The Current Status of Anthropological Research in the Great Basin: 1964*, Desert Research Institute, Technical Report Series S-H, Social Sciences and Humanities Publications no. 1 (Reno, 1964), 275–93; Cynthia Irwin-Williams, ed., *Early Man in Western North America: Symposium of the Southwestern Archaeological Association, San Diego, 1968*, Eastern New Mexico Contributions in Anthropology, v. 1, no. 4 (Portales, New Mexico: Eastern New Mexico University, 1968), 78–87.

Index

DATE DUE

APR 3 '92			

HIGHSMITH   # 45220